TOKYO GHOUL:re 1

東 京 喰 種

SUI ISHIDA

re

TOKYO GHOUL:re ①

1: Bone   4

2: Reader to Leader   51

3: Bell   73

4: Remit to See, Limit to See   95

5: Resist   113

6: Reaction to a Reaction   131

7: Remind   151

8: Regent   171

9: Recreation   191

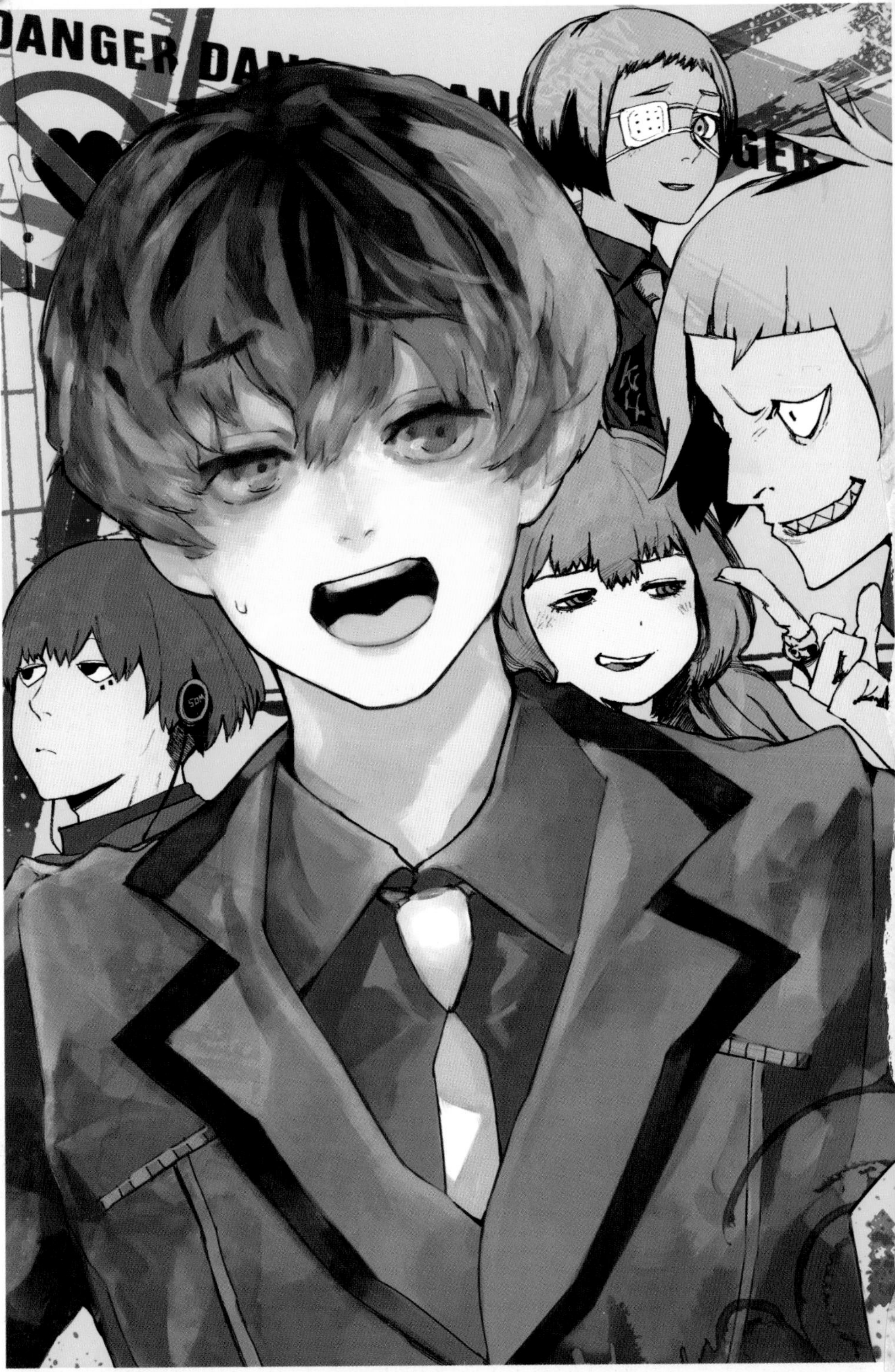
DANGER

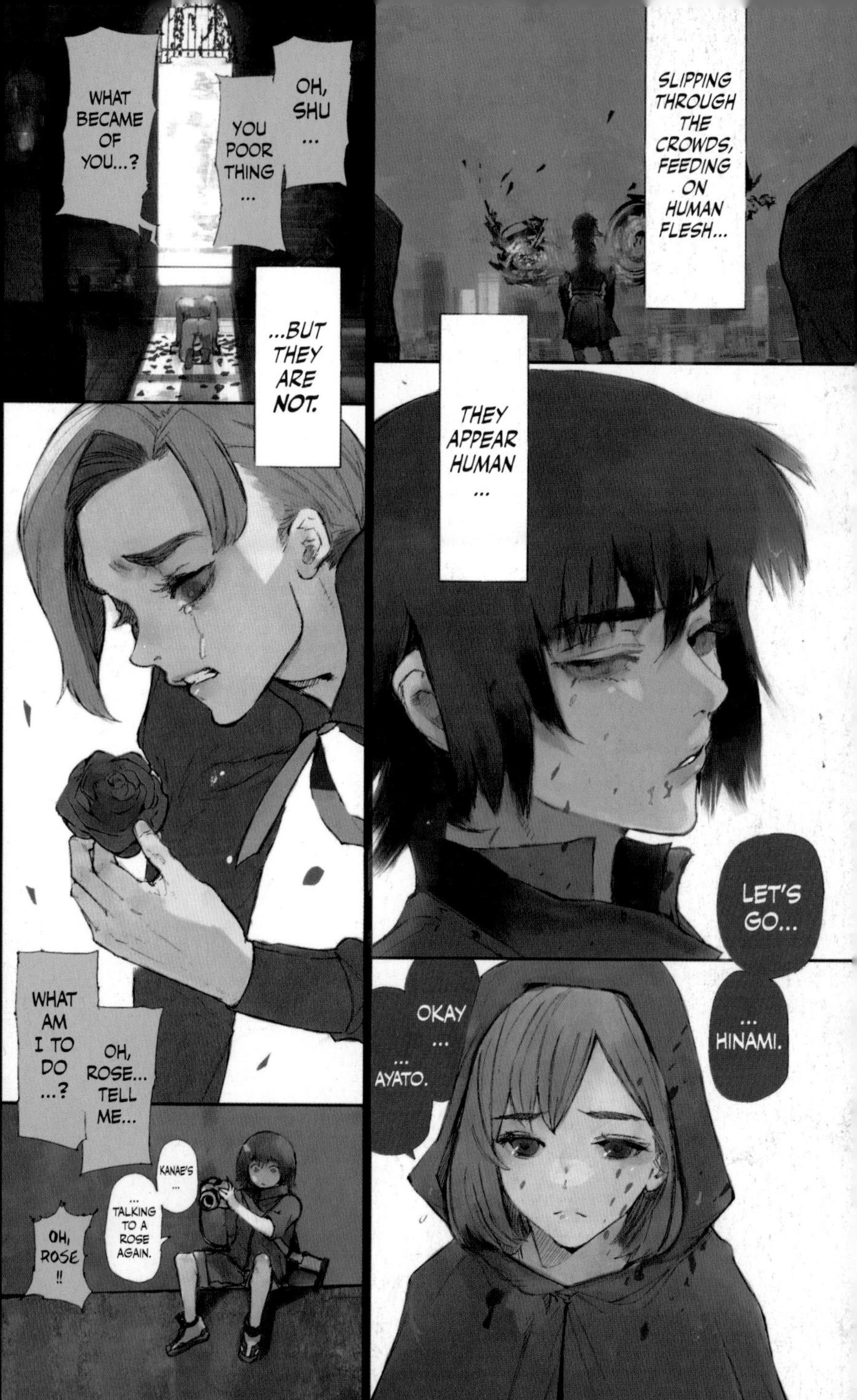
SLIPPING THROUGH THE CROWDS, FEEDING ON HUMAN FLESH...
OH, SHU...
YOU POOR THING...
WHAT BECAME OF YOU...?
THEY APPEAR HUMAN...
...BUT THEY ARE NOT.
LET'S GO...
...HINAMI.
OKAY... ...AYATO.
OH, ROSE... TELL ME...
WHAT AM I TO DO...?
KANAE'S...
...TALKING TO A ROSE AGAIN.
OH, ROSE!!

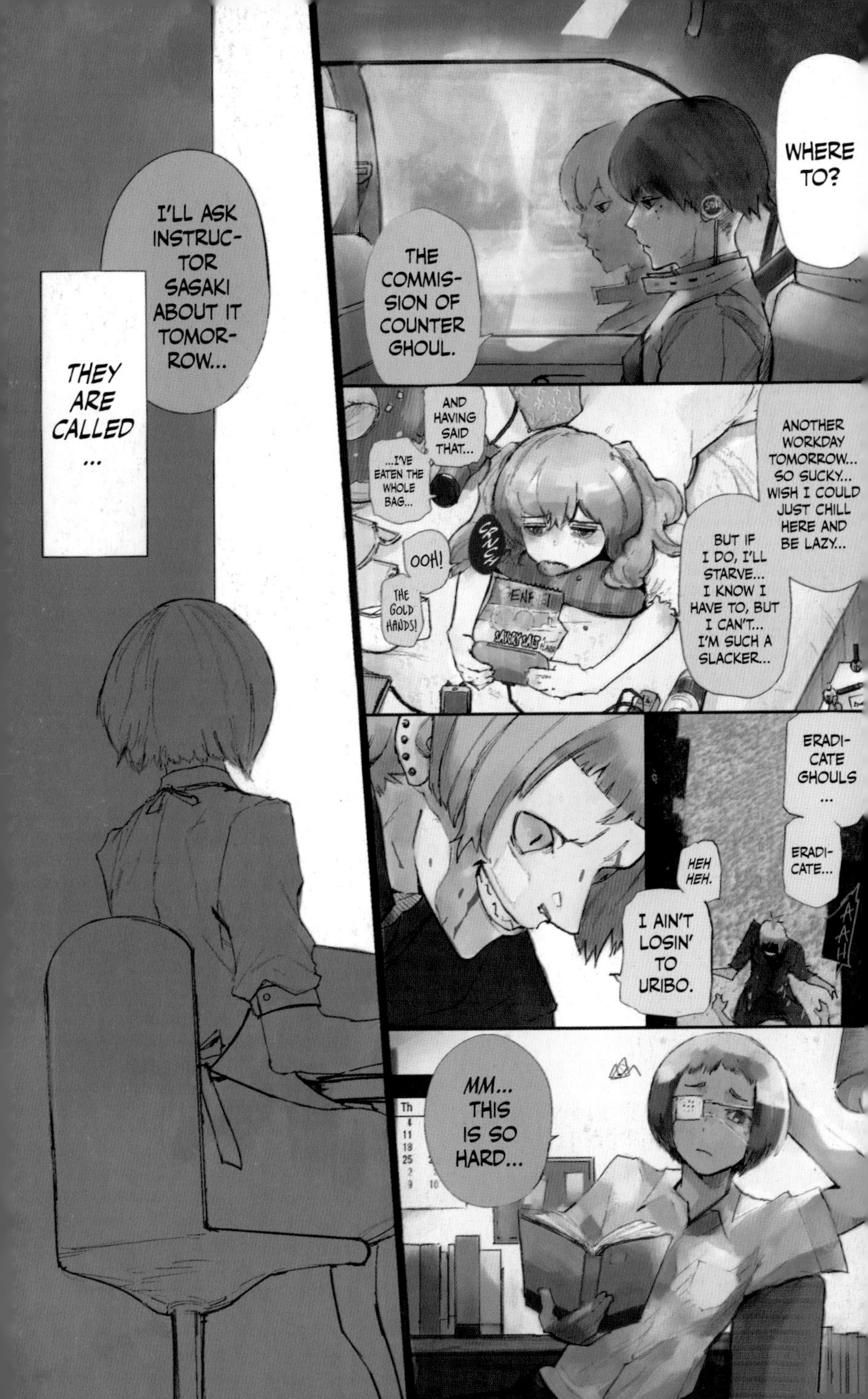
WHERE TO?
THE COMMISSION OF COUNTER GHOUL.
ANOTHER WORKDAY TOMORROW... SO SUCKY... WISH I COULD JUST CHILL HERE AND BE LAZY...
BUT IF I DO, I'LL STARVE... I KNOW I HAVE TO, BUT I CAN'T... I'M SUCH A SLACKER...
AND HAVING SAID THAT...
...I'VE EATEN THE WHOLE BAG...
CRNCH
OOH!
THE GOLD HANDS!
ERADICATE GHOULS...
ERADICATE...
AAH
HEH HEH.
I AIN'T LOSIN' TO URIBO.
MM... THIS IS SO HARD...
I'LL ASK INSTRUCTOR SASAKI ABOUT IT TOMORROW...
THEY ARE CALLED...

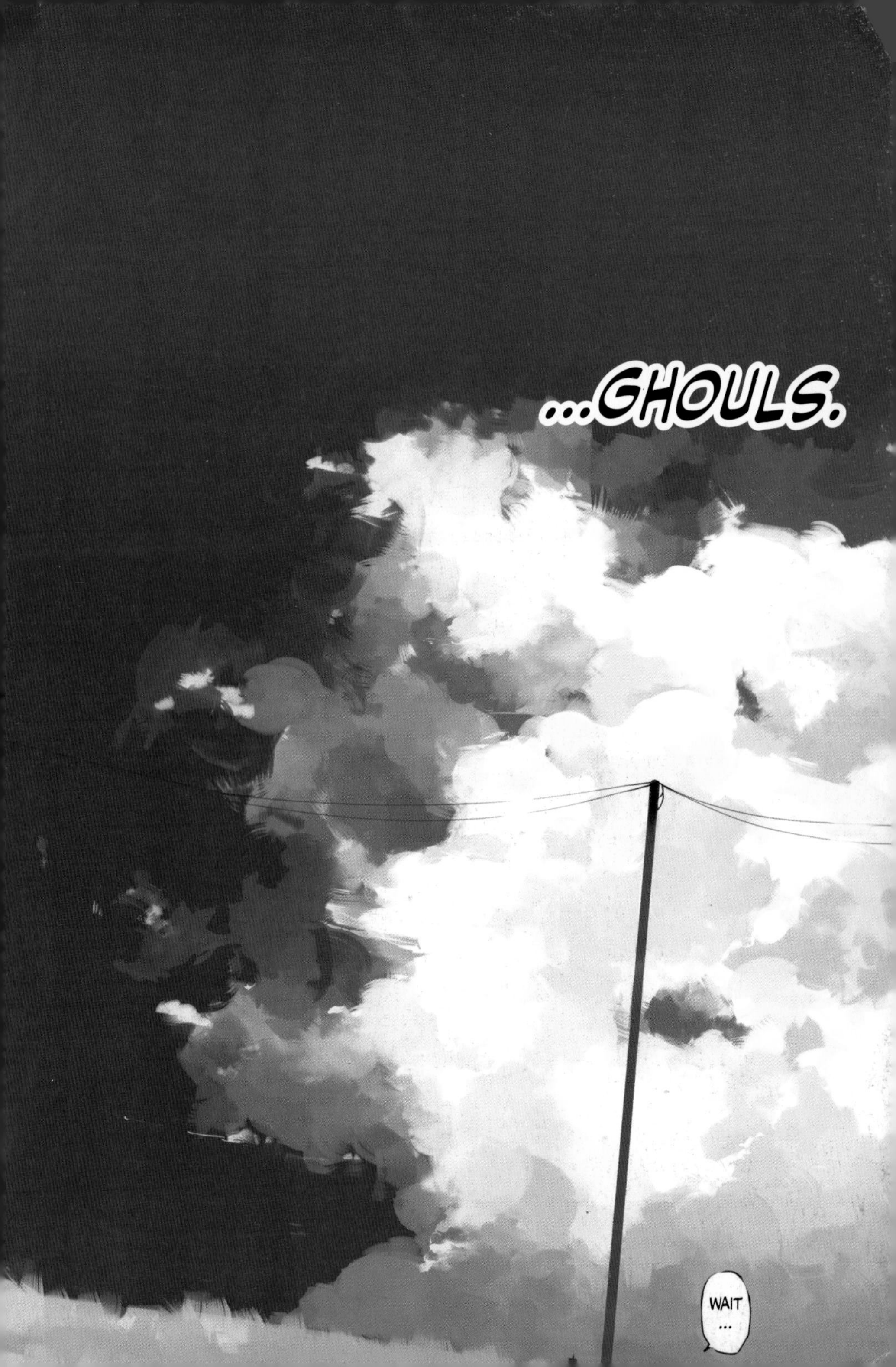
...GHOULS.
WAIT
...

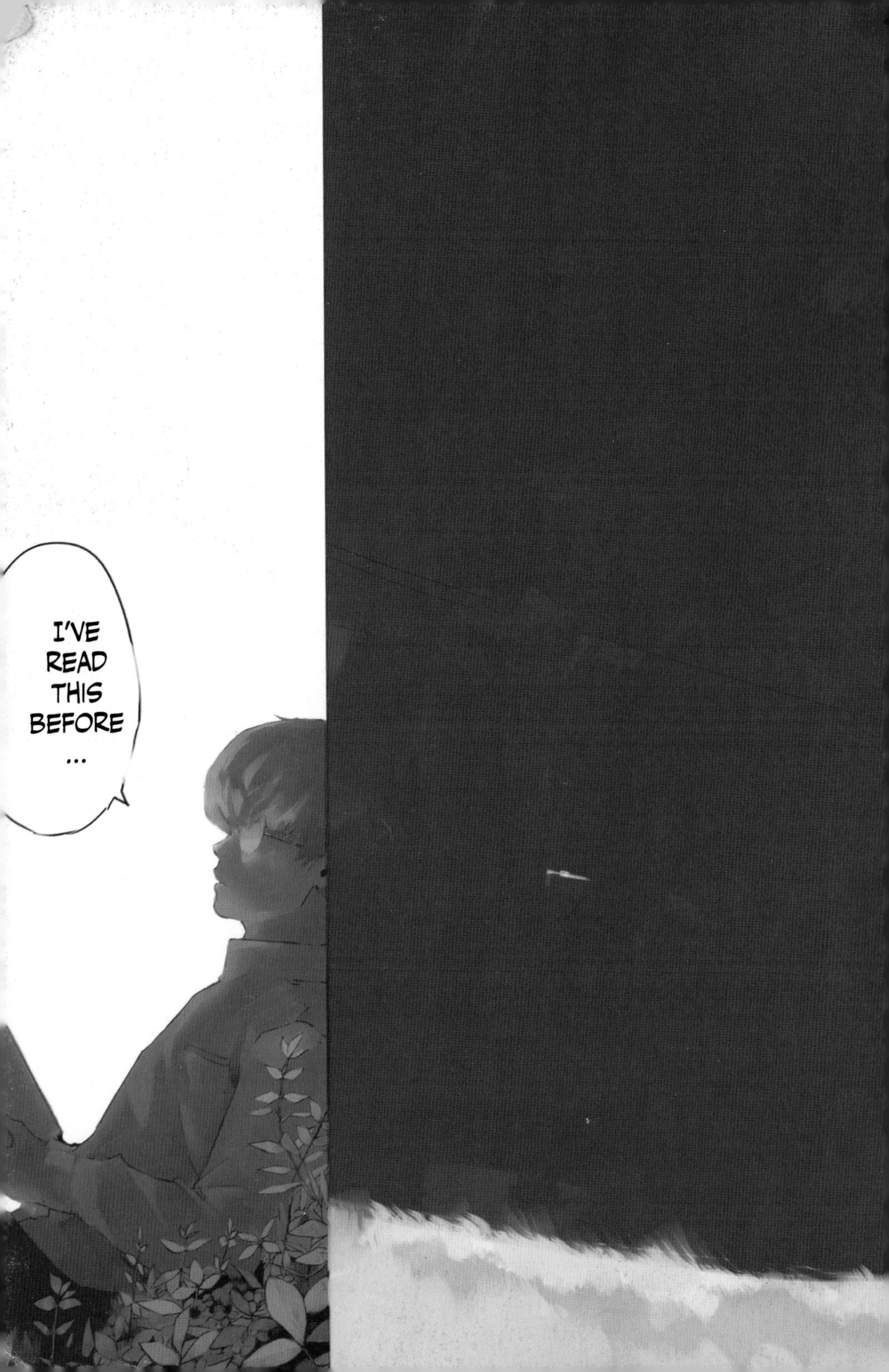
I'VE READ THIS BEFORE...

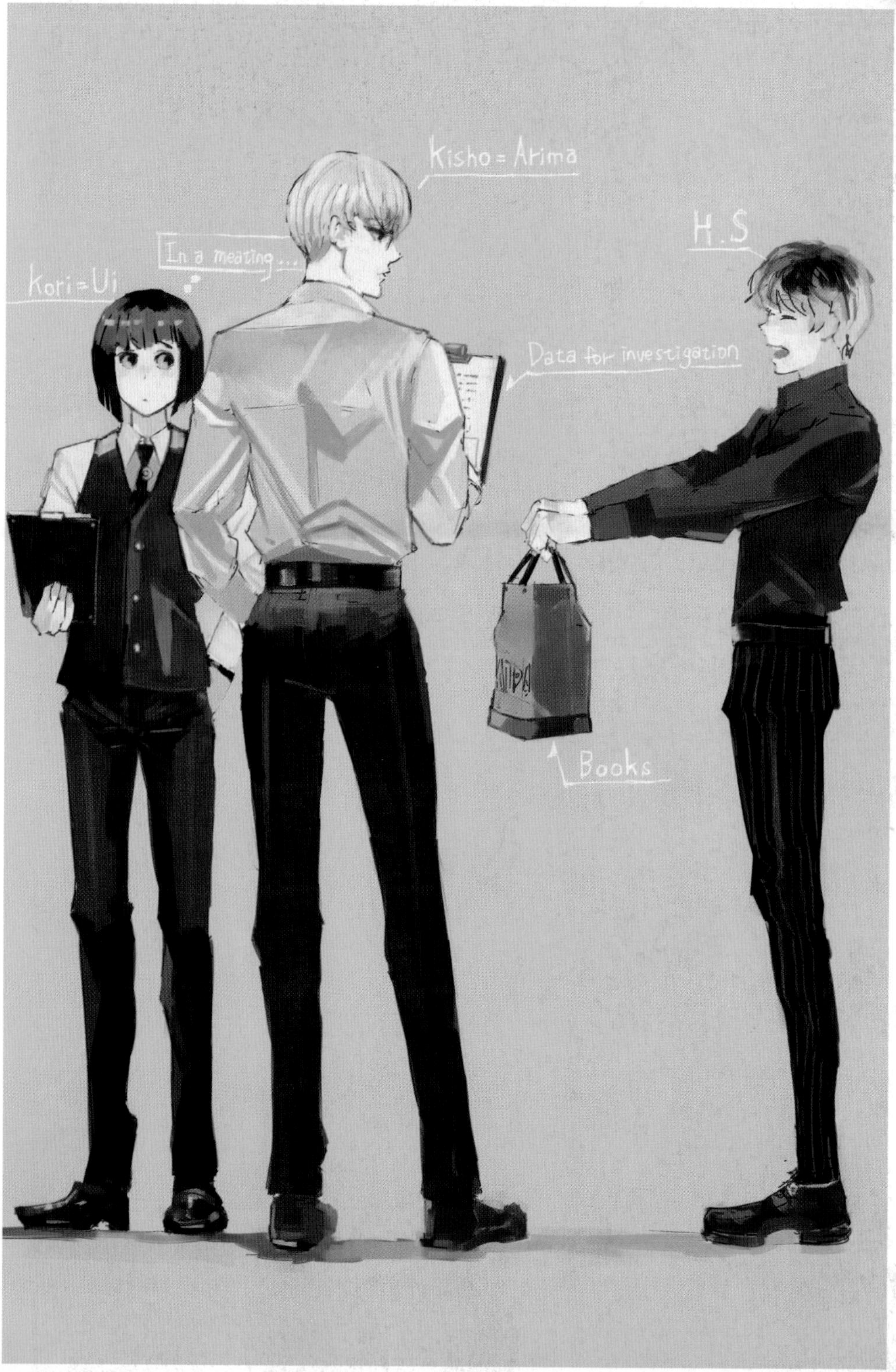

Kisho=Arima
H.S
In a meating...
Kori=Ui
Data for investigation
Books

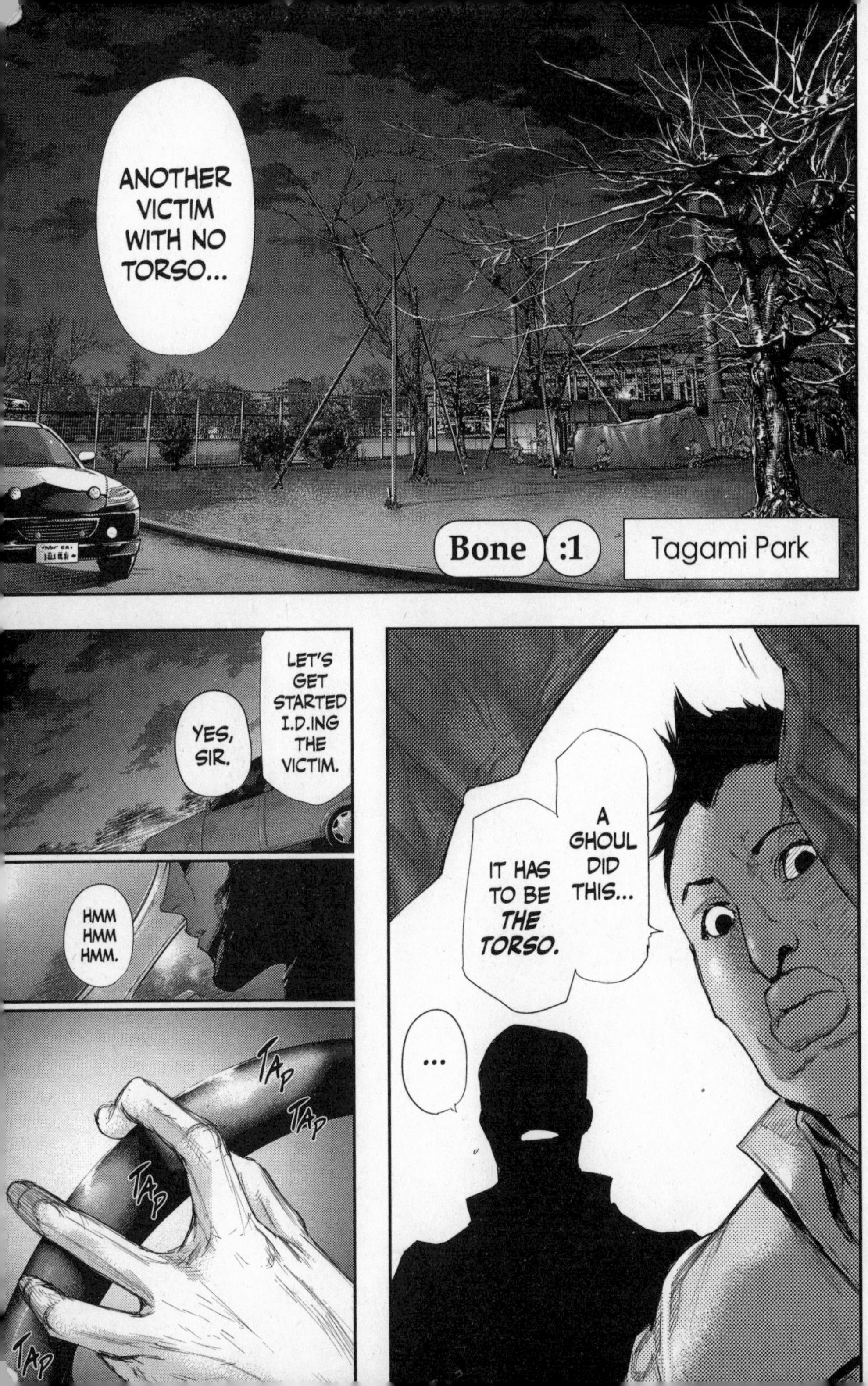
ANOTHER VICTIM WITH NO TORSO...
Bone :1
Tagami Park
A GHOUL DID THIS...
IT HAS TO BE THE TORSO.
...
LET'S GET STARTED I.D.ING THE VICTIM.
YES, SIR.
HMM HMM HMM.
TAP
TAP
TAP
TAP

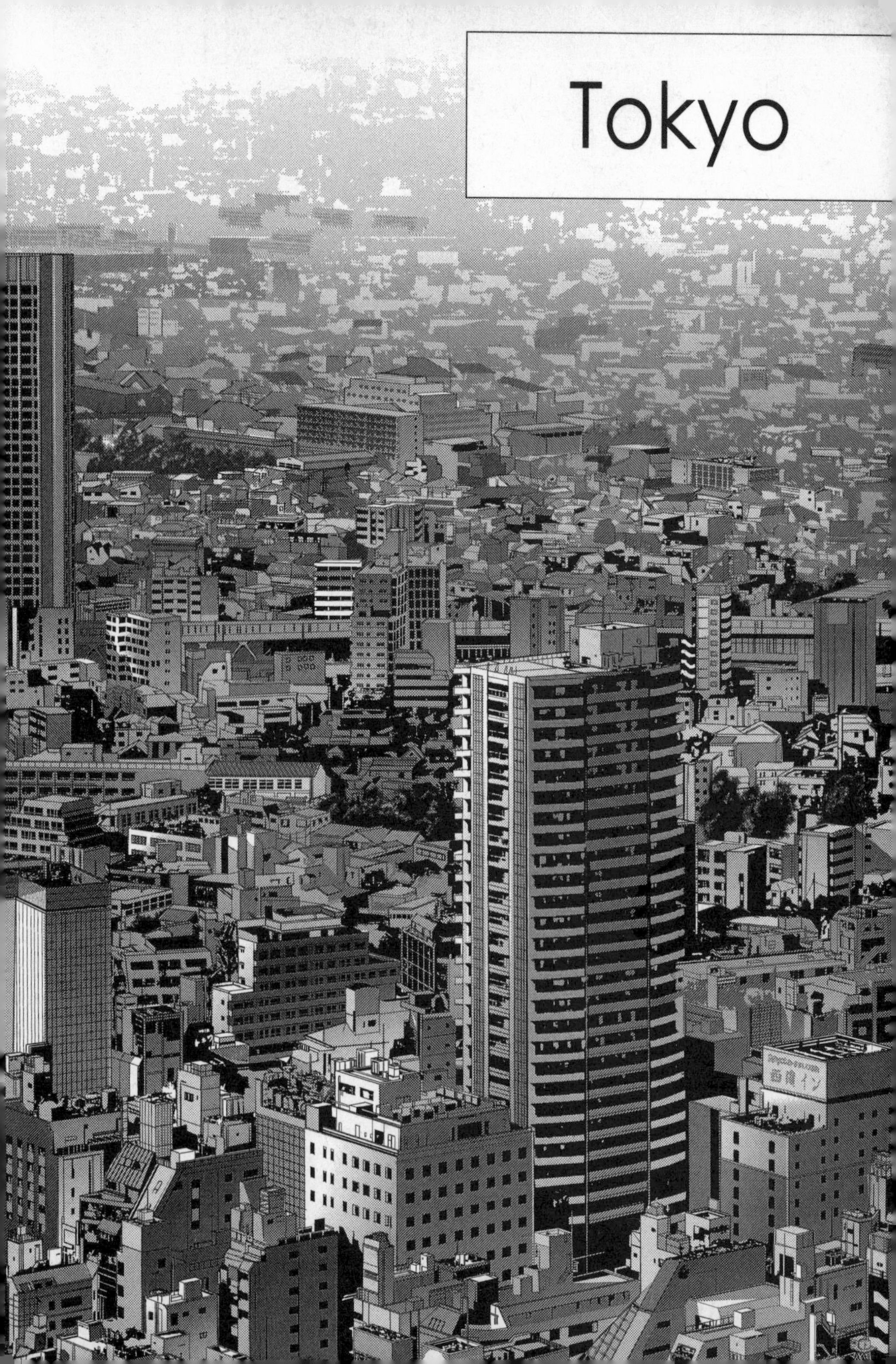
Tokyo

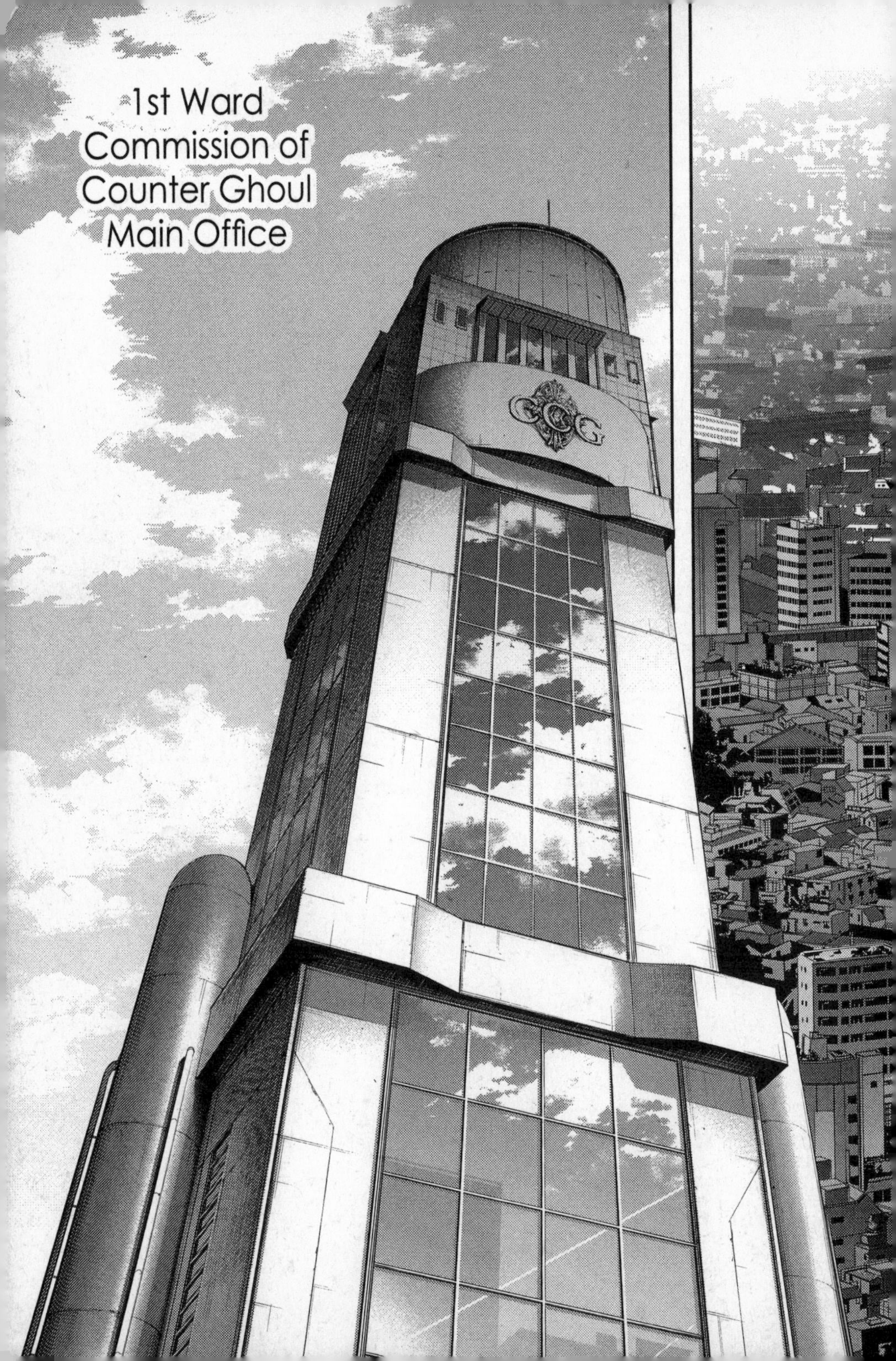
1st Ward
Commission of
Counter Ghoul
Main Office

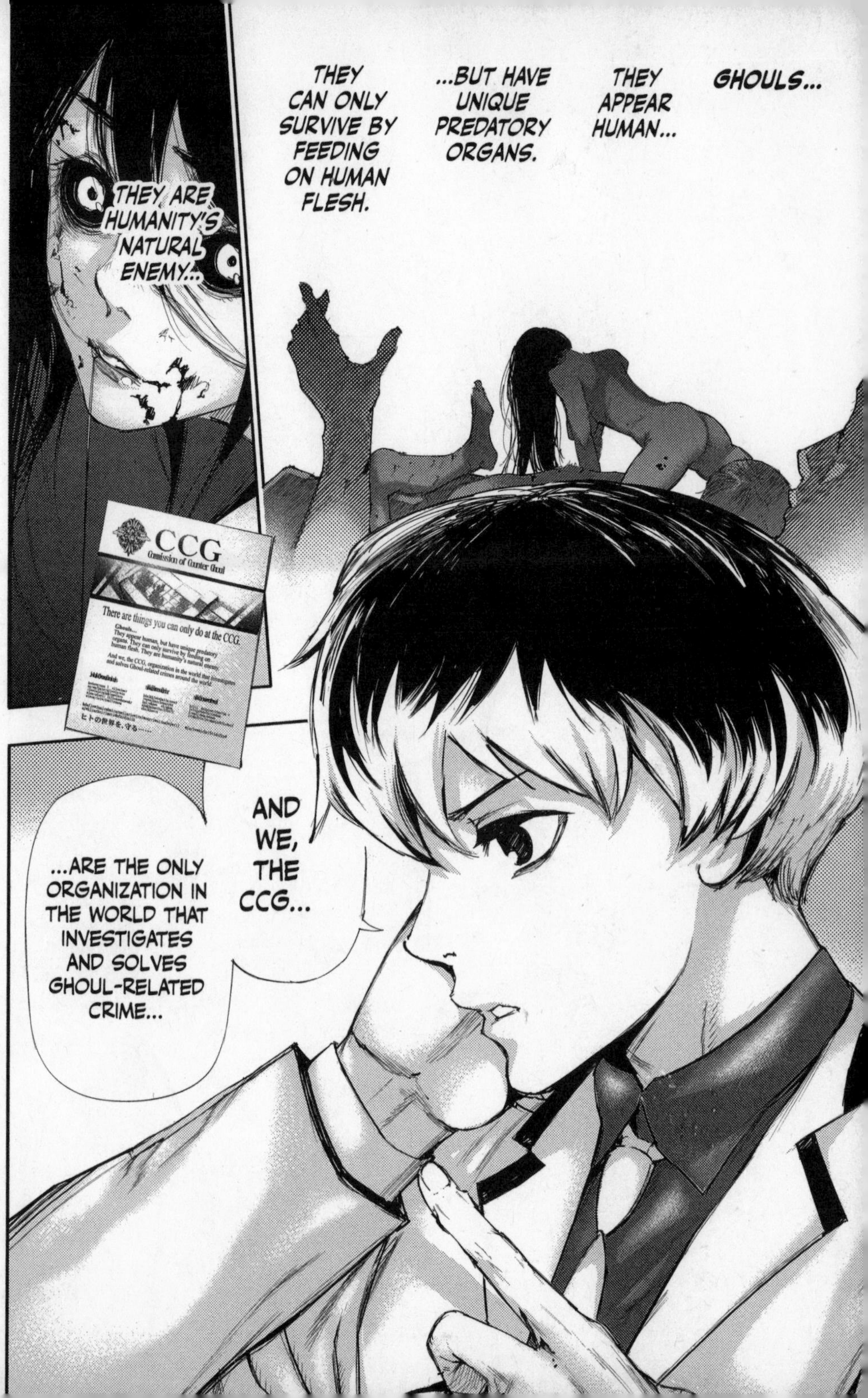
GHOULS...
THEY APPEAR HUMAN...
...BUT HAVE UNIQUE PREDATORY ORGANS.
THEY CAN ONLY SURVIVE BY FEEDING ON HUMAN FLESH.
THEY ARE HUMANITY'S NATURAL ENEMY...
CCG
Commission of Counter Ghoul
There are things you can only do at the CCG.
AND WE, THE CCG...
...ARE THE ONLY ORGANIZATION IN THE WORLD THAT INVESTIGATES AND SOLVES GHOUL-RELATED CRIME...

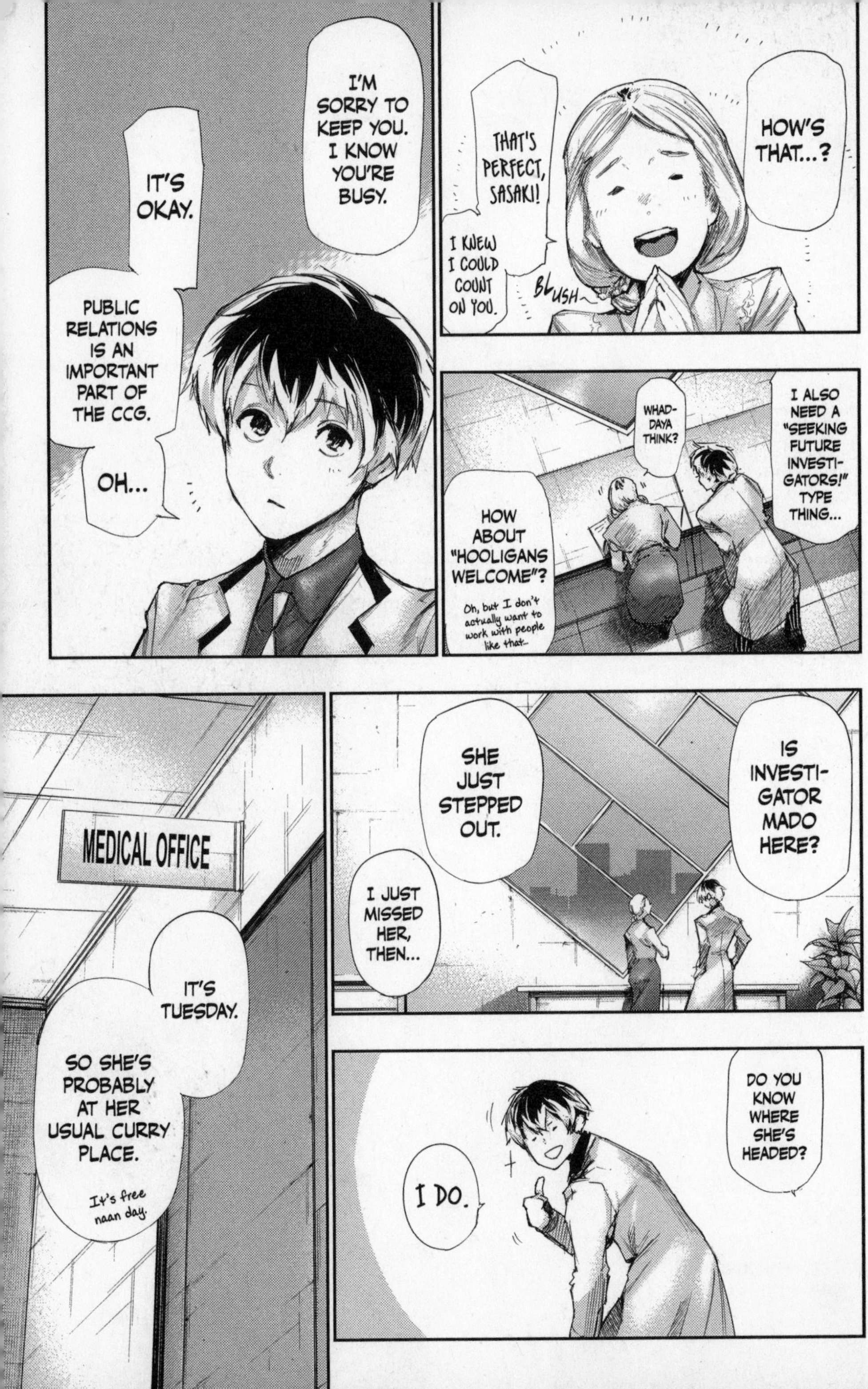
HOW'S THAT...?
THAT'S PERFECT, SASAKI!
I KNEW I COULD COUNT ON YOU.
BLUSH
I ALSO NEED A "SEEKING FUTURE INVESTIGATORS!" TYPE THING...
WHAD-DAYA THINK?
HOW ABOUT "HOOLIGANS WELCOME"?
Oh, but I don't actually want to work with people like that...
I'M SORRY TO KEEP YOU. I KNOW YOU'RE BUSY.
IT'S OKAY.
PUBLIC RELATIONS IS AN IMPORTANT PART OF THE CCG.
OH...
IS INVESTIGATOR MADO HERE?
SHE JUST STEPPED OUT.
I JUST MISSED HER, THEN...
DO YOU KNOW WHERE SHE'S HEADED?
I DO.
MEDICAL OFFICE
IT'S TUESDAY.
SO SHE'S PROBABLY AT HER USUAL CURRY PLACE.
It's free naan day.

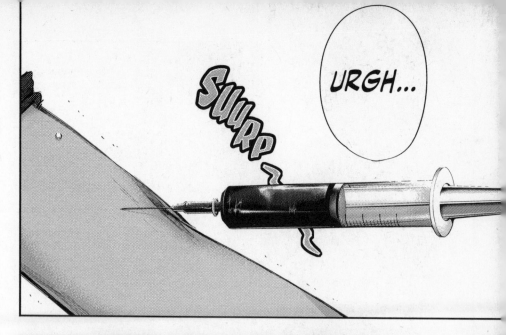

URGH...

SUURP

YOU ARE SUCH A WUSS...

... MUTSUKI.

WELL...

HOW'RE YOU GONNA BE AN INVESTIGATOR LIKE THAT?

UH...

I JUST CAN'T...

WHEN-EVER I SEE BLOOD, I...

UGH...

Toru Mutsuki (19)
Rank 3 Investigator
165 cm / 48 kg

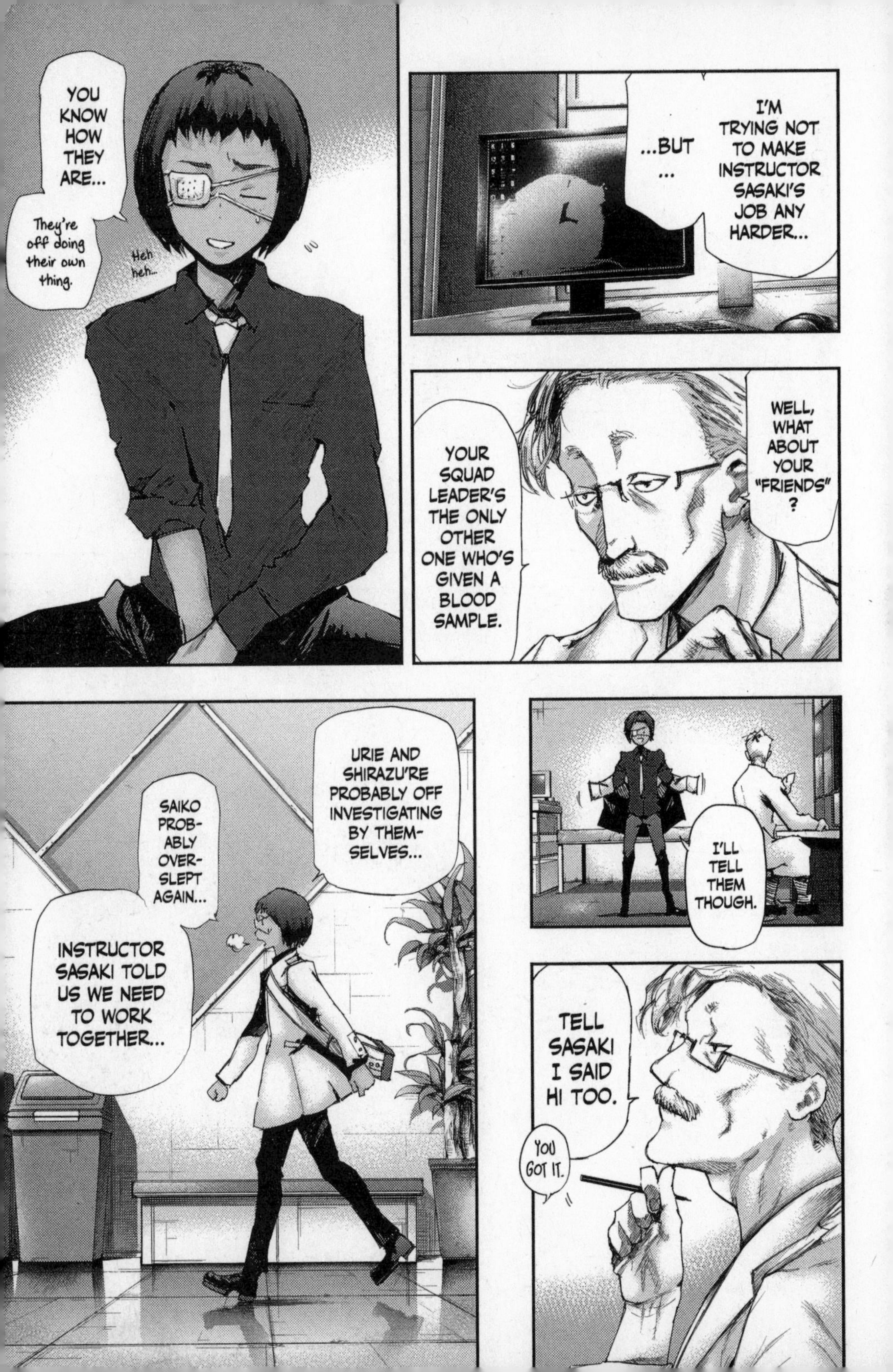
I'M TRYING NOT TO MAKE INSTRUCTOR SASAKI'S JOB ANY HARDER...
...BUT ...
WELL, WHAT ABOUT YOUR "FRIENDS"?
YOUR SQUAD LEADER'S THE ONLY OTHER ONE WHO'S GIVEN A BLOOD SAMPLE.
YOU KNOW HOW THEY ARE...
They're off doing their own thing.
Heh heh...
I'LL TELL THEM THOUGH.
TELL SASAKI I SAID HI TOO.
YOU GOT IT.
URIE AND SHIRAZU'RE PROBABLY OFF INVESTIGATING BY THEMSELVES...
SAIKO PROBABLY OVERSLEPT AGAIN...
INSTRUCTOR SASAKI TOLD US WE NEED TO WORK TOGETHER...

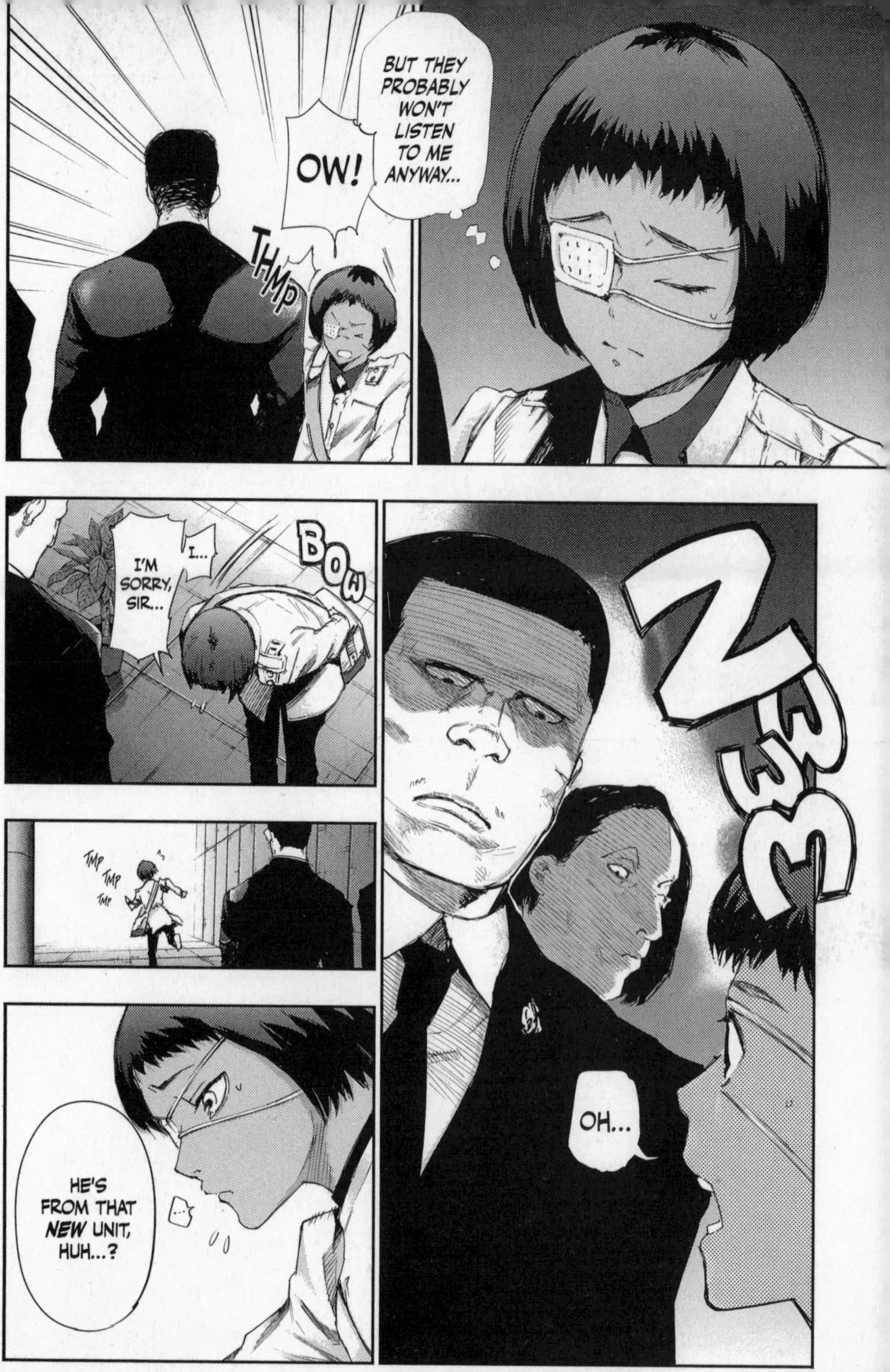
BUT THEY PROBABLY WON'T LISTEN TO ME ANYWAY...
THMP
OW!
OH...
BOW
I...
I'M SORRY, SIR...
TMP TMP TMP
...
HE'S FROM THAT *NEW* UNIT, HUH...?

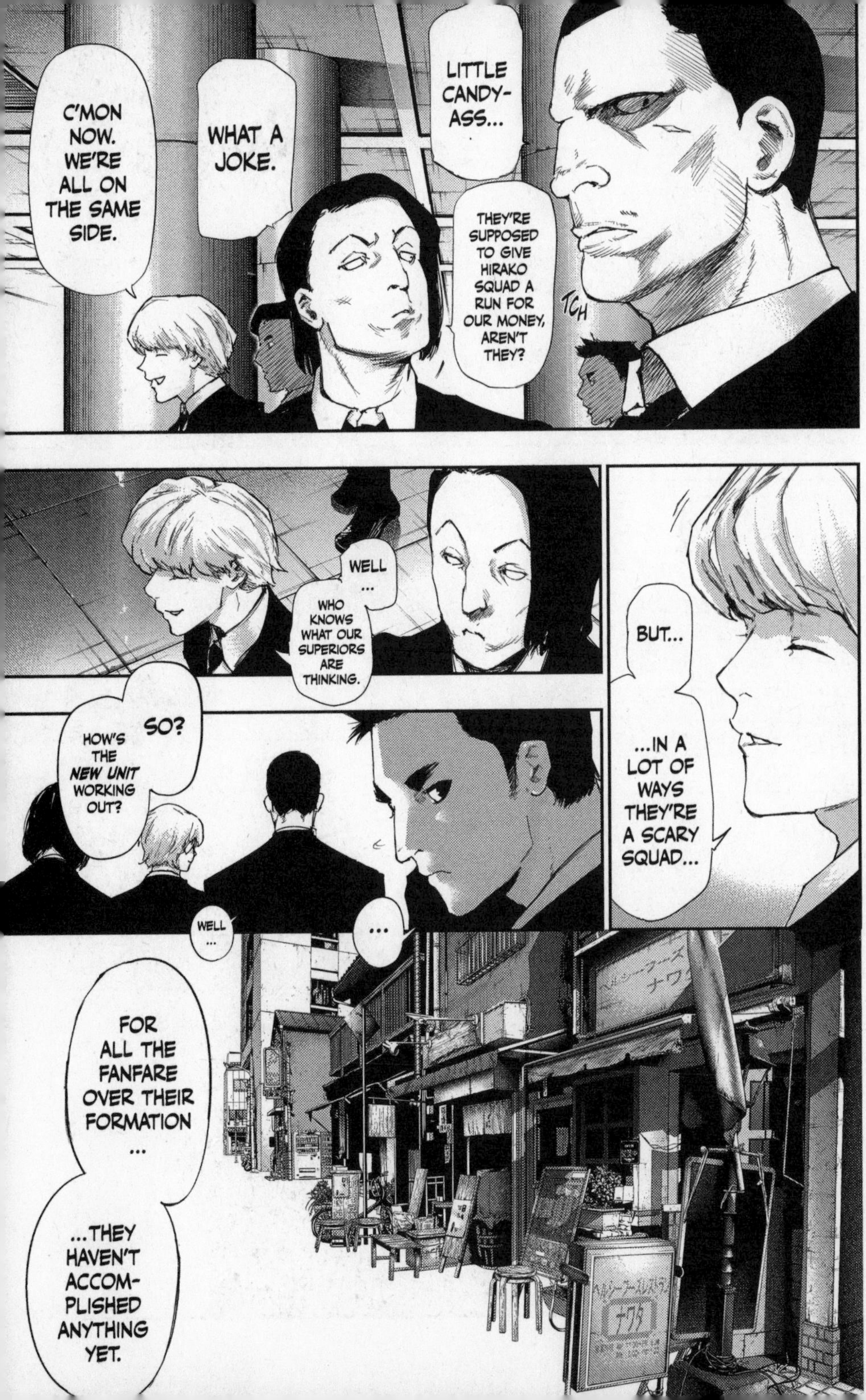
LITTLE CANDY-ASS...
TCH
THEY'RE SUPPOSED TO GIVE HIRAKO SQUAD A RUN FOR OUR MONEY, AREN'T THEY?
WHAT A JOKE.
C'MON NOW. WE'RE ALL ON THE SAME SIDE.
BUT...
...IN A LOT OF WAYS THEY'RE A SCARY SQUAD...
WELL ...
WHO KNOWS WHAT OUR SUPERIORS ARE THINKING.
SO?
HOW'S THE *NEW UNIT* WORKING OUT?
...
WELL ...
FOR ALL THE FANFARE OVER THEIR FORMATION ...
...THEY HAVEN'T ACCOMPLISHED ANYTHING YET.

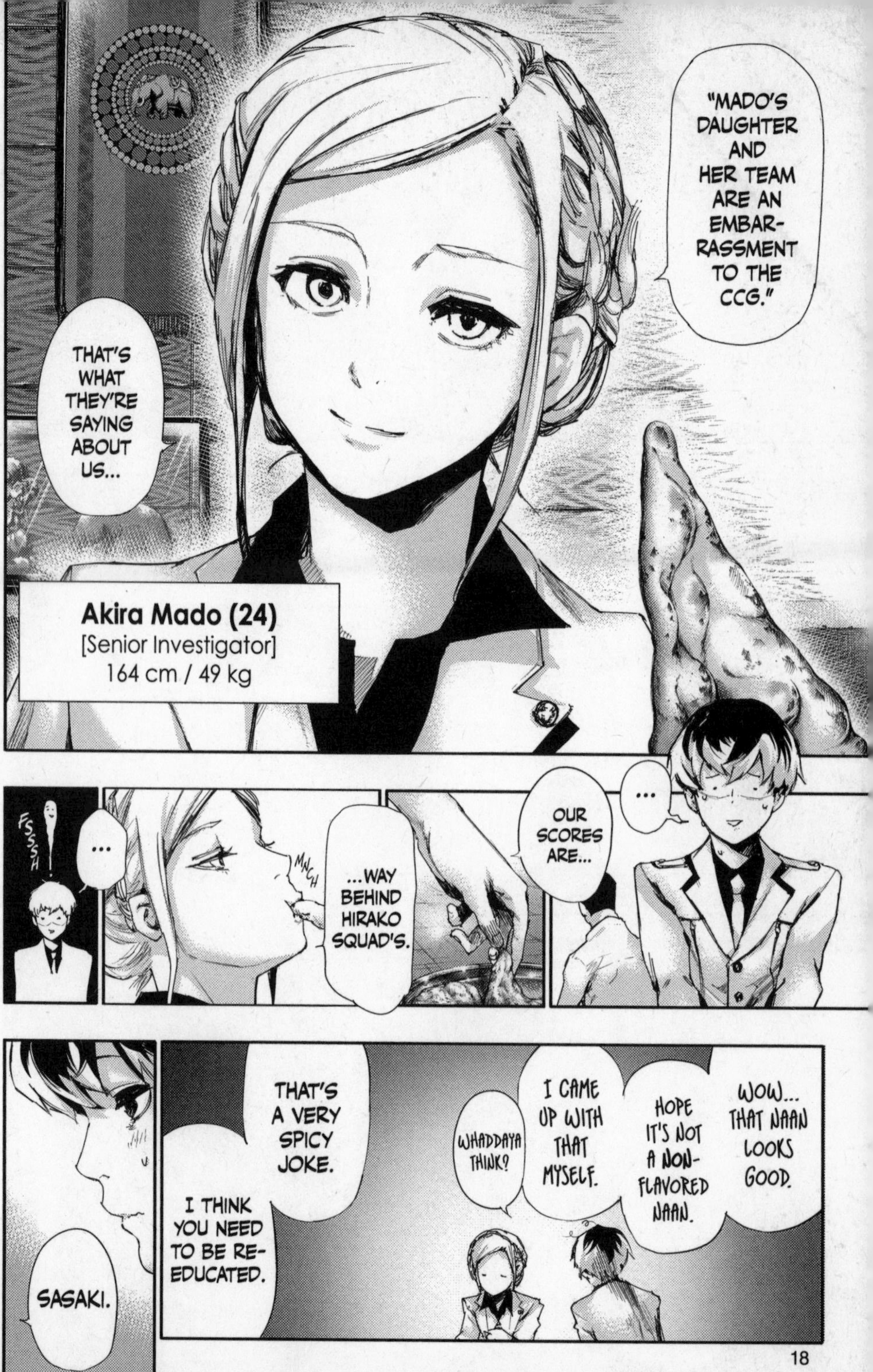
"MADO'S DAUGHTER AND HER TEAM ARE AN EMBARRASSMENT TO THE CCG."
THAT'S WHAT THEY'RE SAYING ABOUT US...
Akira Mado (24)
[Senior Investigator]
164 cm / 49 kg
...
OUR SCORES ARE...
...WAY BEHIND HIRAKO SQUAD'S.
MNCH
...
FSSSH
WOW... THAT NAAN LOOKS GOOD.
HOPE IT'S NOT A NON-FLAVORED NAAN.
I CAME UP WITH THAT MYSELF.
WHADDAYA THINK?
THAT'S A VERY SPICY JOKE.
I THINK YOU NEED TO BE RE-EDUCATED.
SASAKI.

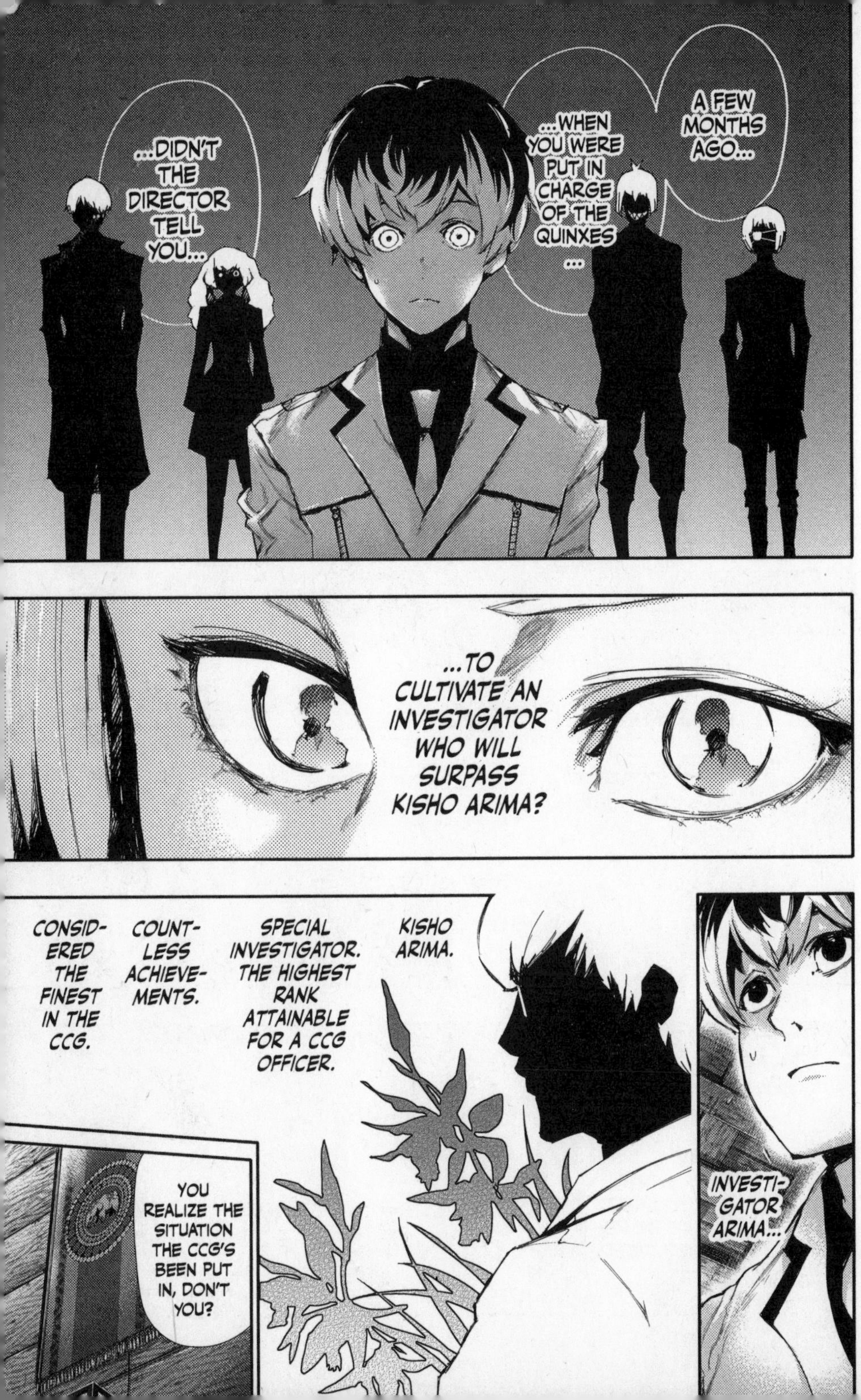
A FEW MONTHS AGO...
...WHEN YOU WERE PUT IN CHARGE OF THE QUINXES...
...DIDN'T THE DIRECTOR TELL YOU...
...TO CULTIVATE AN INVESTIGATOR WHO WILL SURPASS KISHO ARIMA?
INVESTI-GATOR ARIMA...
KISHO ARIMA.
SPECIAL INVESTIGATOR. THE HIGHEST RANK ATTAINABLE FOR A CCG OFFICER.
COUNT-LESS ACHIEVE-MENTS.
CONSID-ERED THE FINEST IN THE CCG.
YOU REALIZE THE SITUATION THE CCG'S BEEN PUT IN, DON'T YOU?

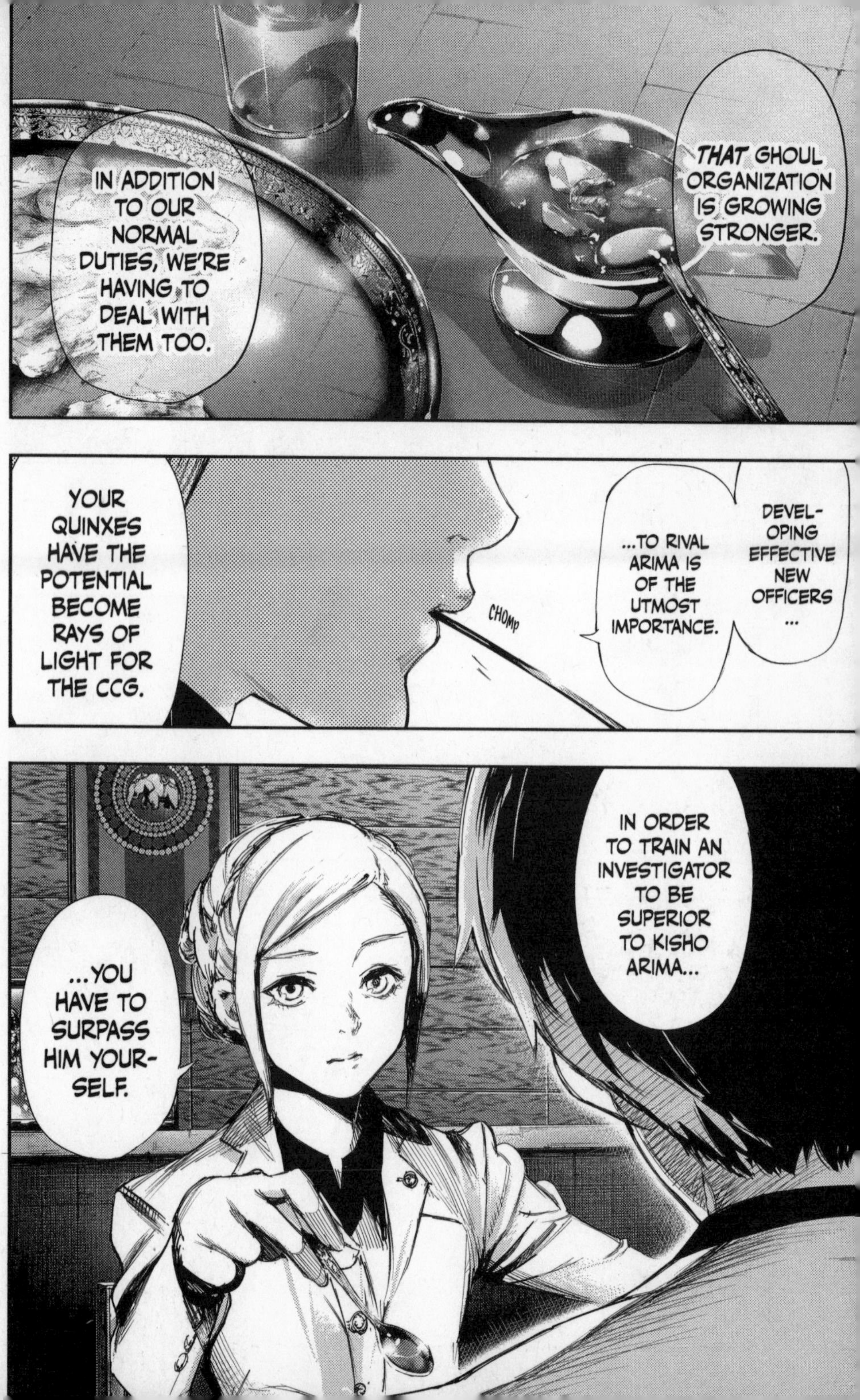
THAT GHOUL ORGANIZATION IS GROWING STRONGER.
IN ADDITION TO OUR NORMAL DUTIES, WE'RE HAVING TO DEAL WITH THEM TOO.
DEVEL-OPING EFFECTIVE NEW OFFICERS...
...TO RIVAL ARIMA IS OF THE UTMOST IMPORTANCE.
CHOMP
YOUR QUINXES HAVE THE POTENTIAL BECOME RAYS OF LIGHT FOR THE CCG.
IN ORDER TO TRAIN AN INVESTIGATOR TO BE SUPERIOR TO KISHO ARIMA...
...YOU HAVE TO SURPASS HIM YOUR-SELF.

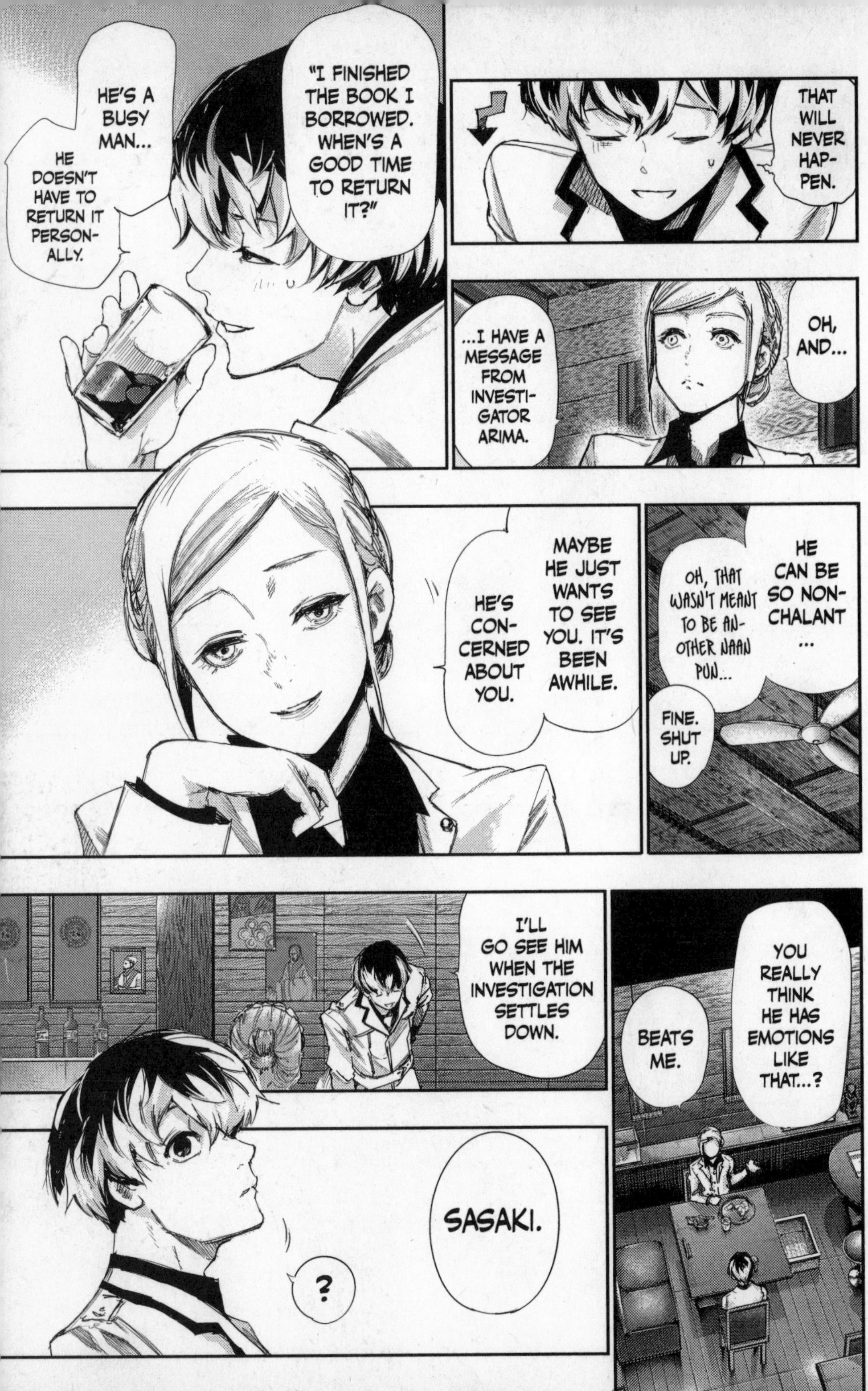
THAT WILL NEVER HAP-PEN.
OH, AND...
...I HAVE A MESSAGE FROM INVESTI-GATOR ARIMA.
"I FINISHED THE BOOK I BORROWED. WHEN'S A GOOD TIME TO RETURN IT?"
HE'S A BUSY MAN...
HE DOESN'T HAVE TO RETURN IT PERSON-ALLY.
HE CAN BE SO NON-CHALANT ...
OH, THAT WASN'T MEANT TO BE AN-OTHER NAAN PUN...
FINE. SHUT UP.
MAYBE HE JUST WANTS TO SEE YOU. IT'S BEEN AWHILE.
HE'S CON-CERNED ABOUT YOU.
YOU REALLY THINK HE HAS EMOTIONS LIKE THAT...?
BEATS ME.
I'LL GO SEE HIM WHEN THE INVESTIGATION SETTLES DOWN.
SASAKI.
?

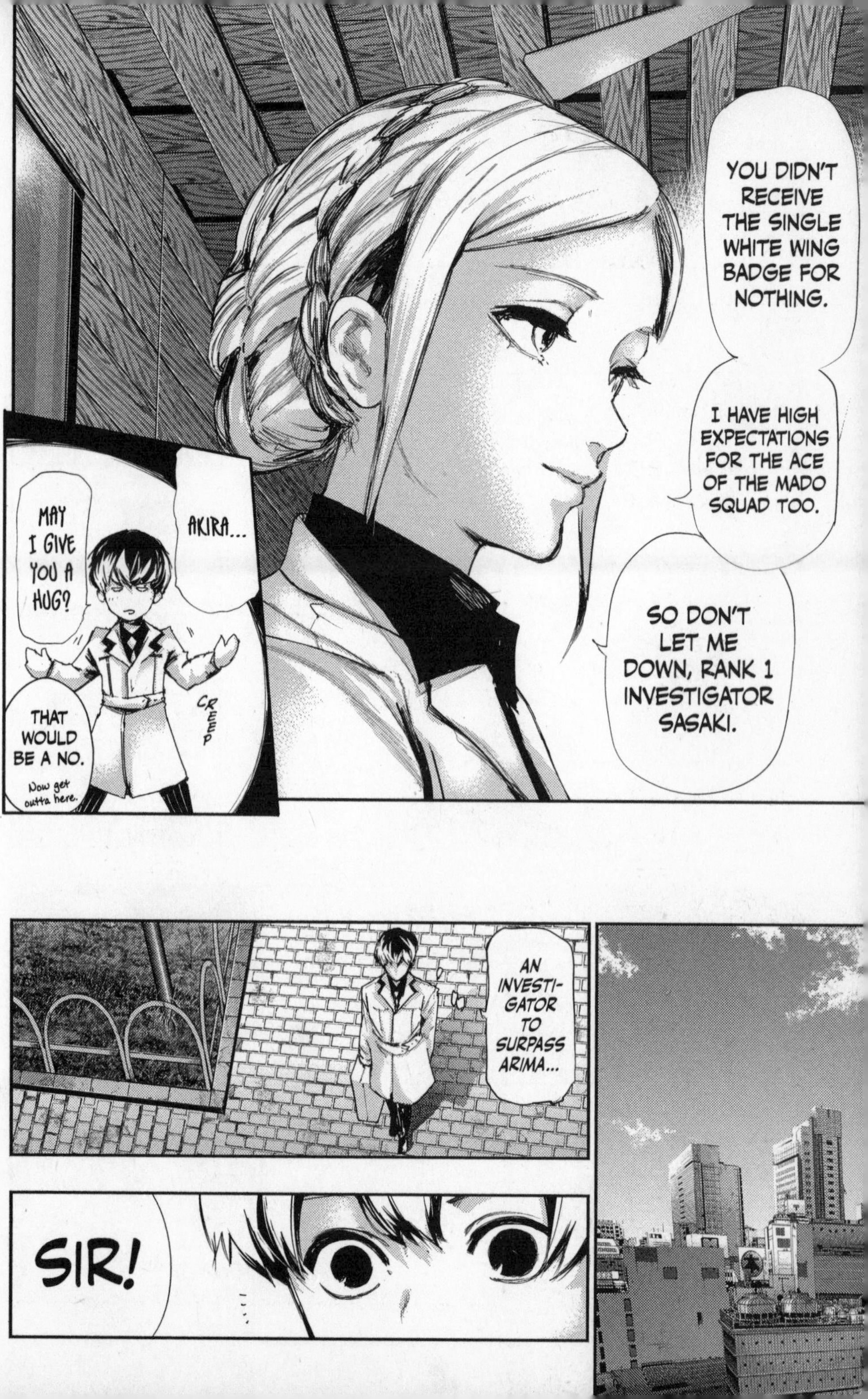
YOU DIDN'T RECEIVE THE SINGLE WHITE WING BADGE FOR NOTHING.
I HAVE HIGH EXPECTATIONS FOR THE ACE OF THE MADO SQUAD TOO.
SO DON'T LET ME DOWN, RANK 1 INVESTIGATOR SASAKI.
AKIRA...
MAY I GIVE YOU A HUG?
CREEP
THAT WOULD BE A NO.
Now get outta here.
AN INVESTI-GATOR TO SURPASS ARIMA...
SIR!
...

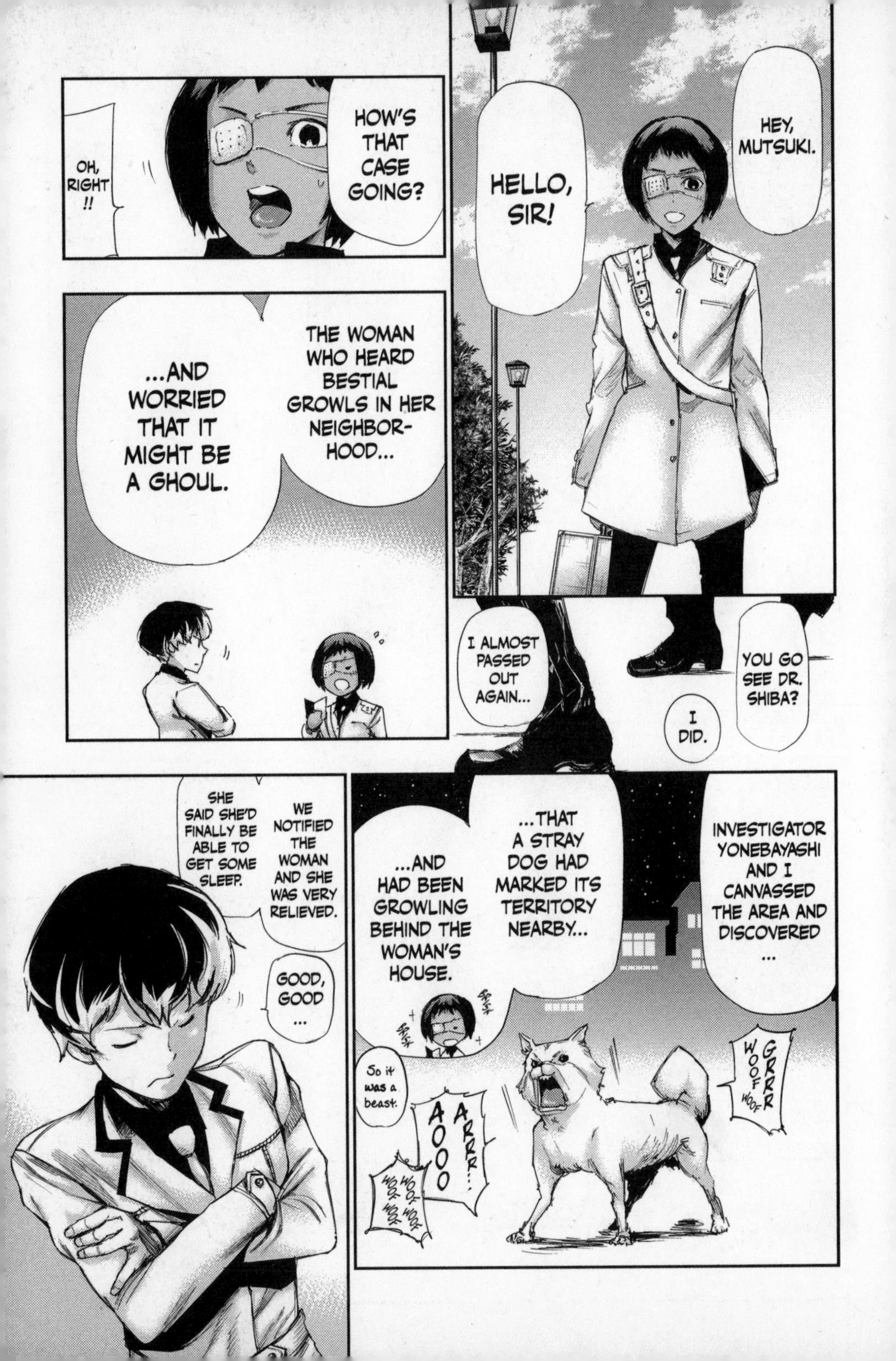
HEY, MUTSUKI.
HELLO, SIR!
YOU GO SEE DR. SHIBA?
I DID.
I ALMOST PASSED OUT AGAIN...
HOW'S THAT CASE GOING?
OH, RIGHT !!
THE WOMAN WHO HEARD BESTIAL GROWLS IN HER NEIGHBOR-HOOD...
...AND WORRIED THAT IT MIGHT BE A GHOUL.
INVESTIGATOR YONEBAYASHI AND I CANVASSED THE AREA AND DISCOVERED ...
...THAT A STRAY DOG HAD MARKED ITS TERRITORY NEARBY...
...AND HAD BEEN GROWLING BEHIND THE WOMAN'S HOUSE.
GRRR
WOOF WOOF
BRISK BRISK
AOOO
ARRR...
WOOF WOOF WOOF WOOF
So it was a beast.
WE NOTIFIED THE WOMAN AND SHE WAS VERY RELIEVED.
SHE SAID SHE'D FINALLY BE ABLE TO GET SOME SLEEP.
GOOD, GOOD ...

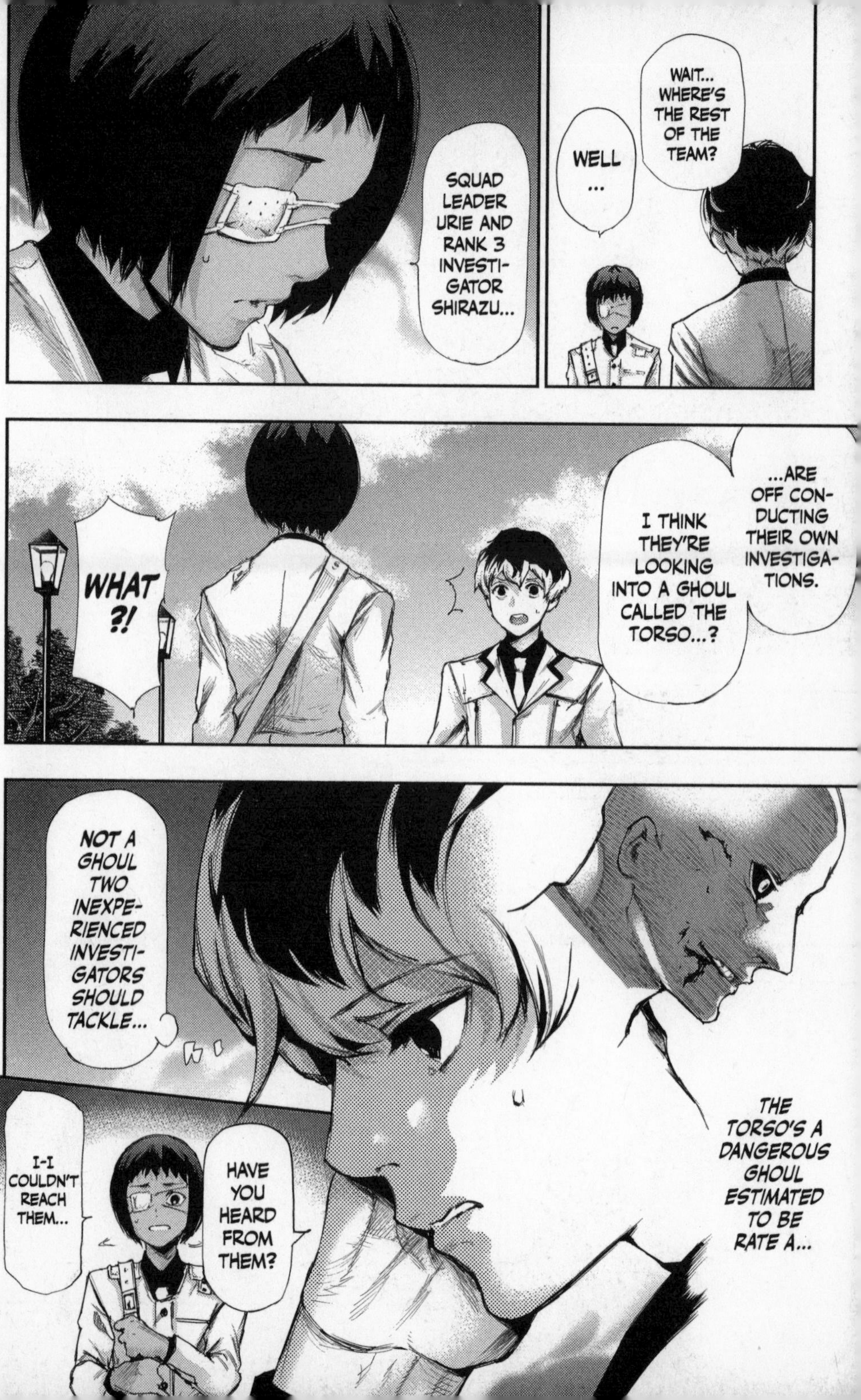
WAIT... WHERE'S THE REST OF THE TEAM?
WELL ...
SQUAD LEADER URIE AND RANK 3 INVESTIGATOR SHIRAZU...
...ARE OFF CONDUCTING THEIR OWN INVESTIGATIONS.
I THINK THEY'RE LOOKING INTO A GHOUL CALLED THE TORSO...?
WHAT ?!
THE TORSO'S A DANGEROUS GHOUL ESTIMATED TO BE RATE A...
NOT A GHOUL TWO INEXPERIENCED INVESTIGATORS SHOULD TACKLE...
HAVE YOU HEARD FROM THEM?
I-I COULDN'T REACH THEM...

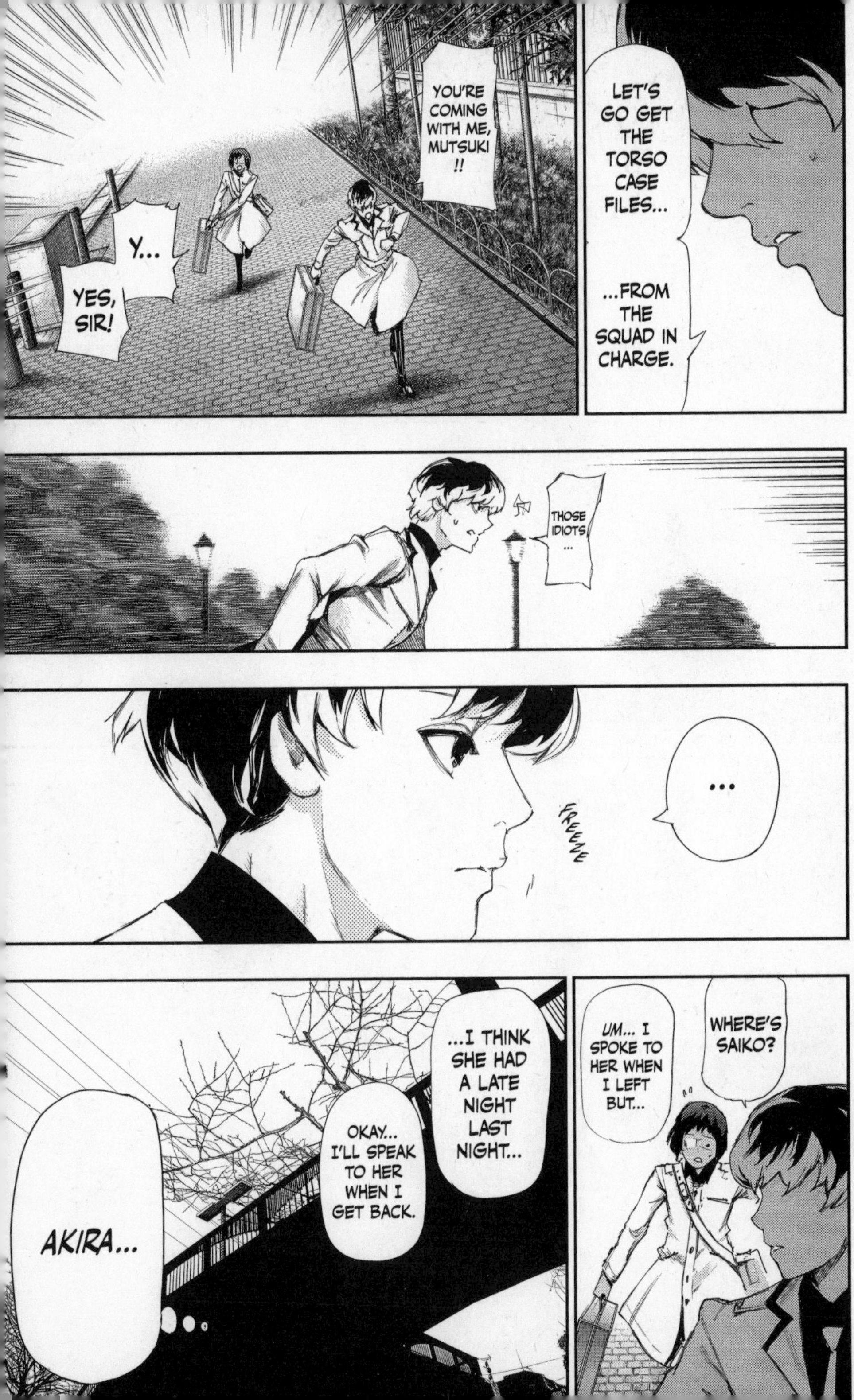
LET'S GO GET THE TORSO CASE FILES...
...FROM THE SQUAD IN CHARGE.
YOU'RE COMING WITH ME, MUTSUKI !!
Y...
YES, SIR!
THOSE IDIOTS ...
...
FREEZE
WHERE'S SAIKO?
UM... I SPOKE TO HER WHEN I LEFT BUT...
...I THINK SHE HAD A LATE NIGHT LAST NIGHT...
OKAY... I'LL SPEAK TO HER WHEN I GET BACK.
AKIRA...

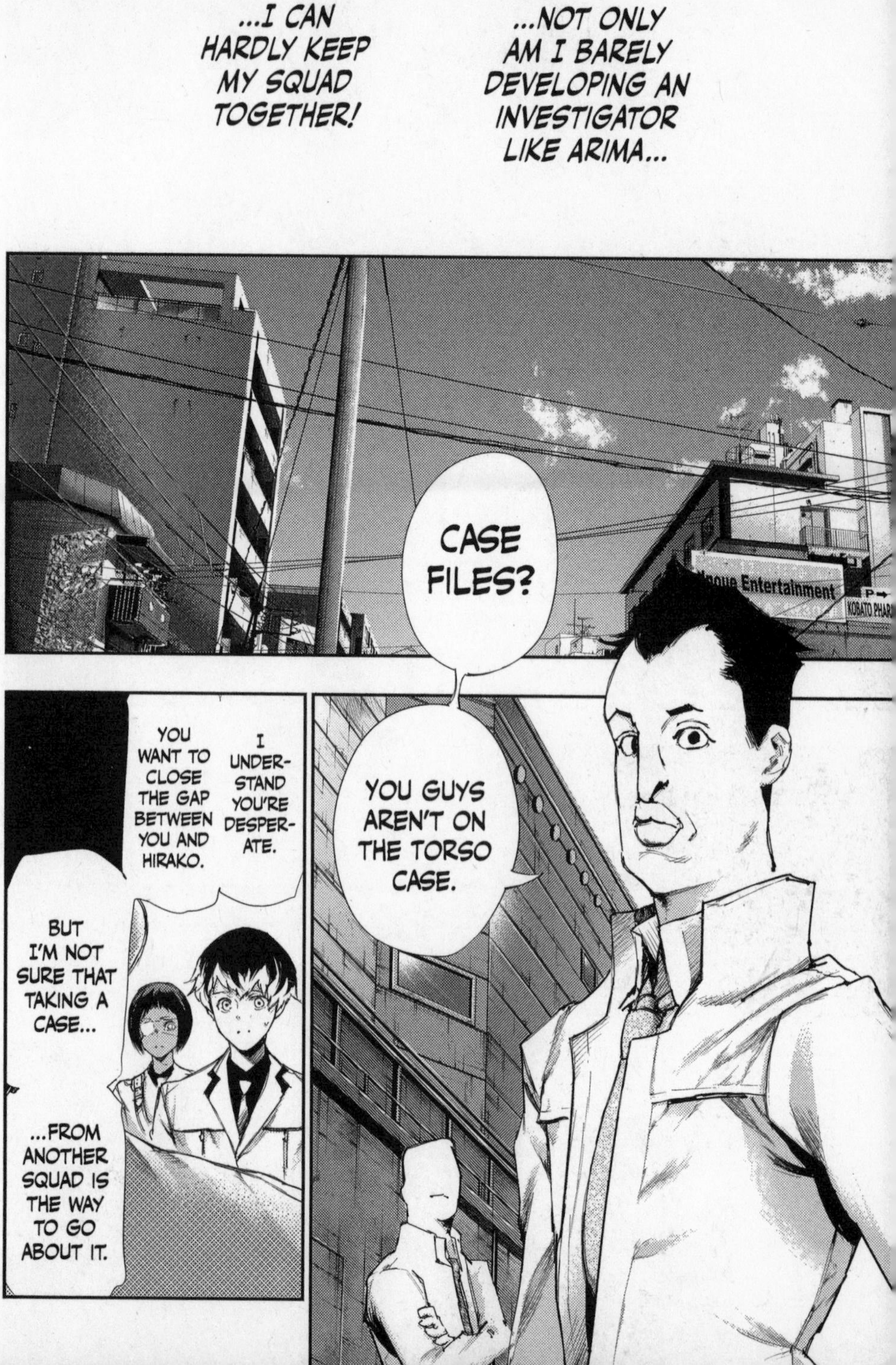
...NOT ONLY AM I BARELY DEVELOPING AN INVESTIGATOR LIKE ARIMA...
...I CAN HARDLY KEEP MY SQUAD TOGETHER!
CASE FILES?
YOU GUYS AREN'T ON THE TORSO CASE.
I UNDER-STAND YOU'RE DESPER-ATE.
YOU WANT TO CLOSE THE GAP BETWEEN YOU AND HIRAKO.
BUT I'M NOT SURE THAT TAKING A CASE...
...FROM ANOTHER SQUAD IS THE WAY TO GO ABOUT IT.

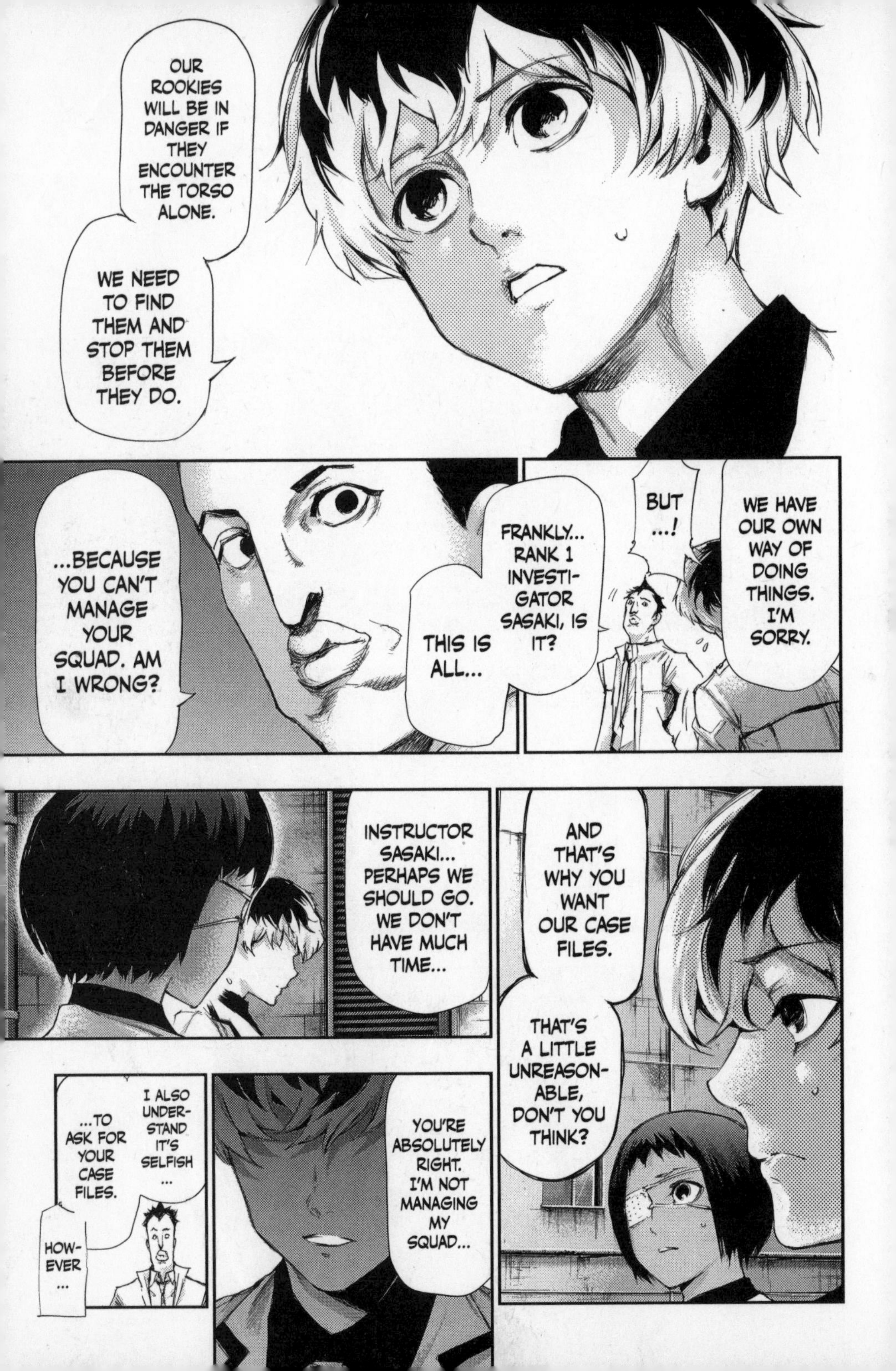
OUR ROOKIES WILL BE IN DANGER IF THEY ENCOUNTER THE TORSO ALONE.
WE NEED TO FIND THEM AND STOP THEM BEFORE THEY DO.
WE HAVE OUR OWN WAY OF DOING THINGS. I'M SORRY.
BUT ...!
FRANKLY... RANK 1 INVESTI-GATOR SASAKI, IS IT?
THIS IS ALL...
...BECAUSE YOU CAN'T MANAGE YOUR SQUAD. AM I WRONG?
AND THAT'S WHY YOU WANT OUR CASE FILES.
THAT'S A LITTLE UNREASON-ABLE, DON'T YOU THINK?
INSTRUCTOR SASAKI... PERHAPS WE SHOULD GO. WE DON'T HAVE MUCH TIME...
YOU'RE ABSOLUTELY RIGHT. I'M NOT MANAGING MY SQUAD...
I ALSO UNDER-STAND IT'S SELFISH ...
...TO ASK FOR YOUR CASE FILES.
HOW-EVER ...

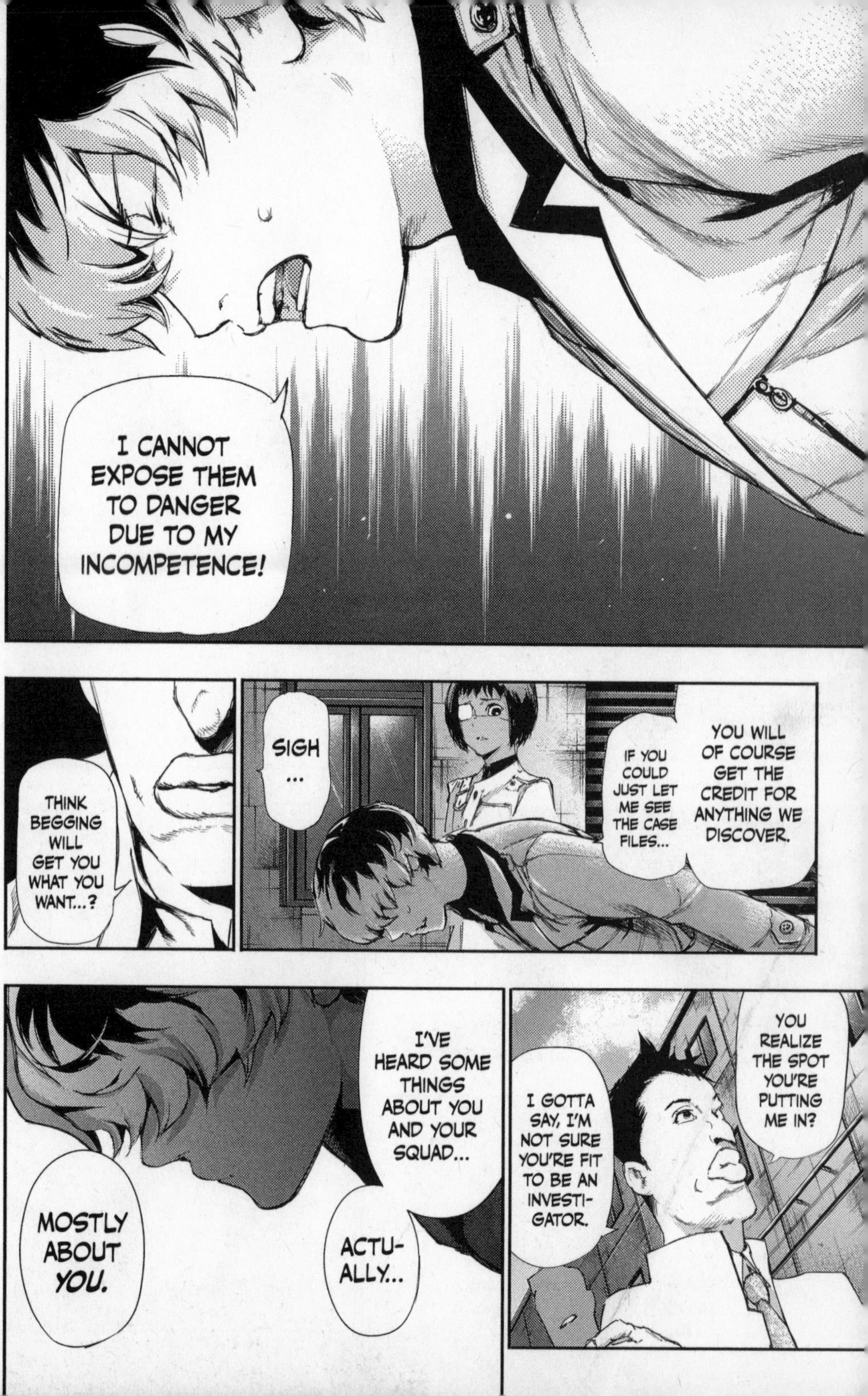
I CANNOT EXPOSE THEM TO DANGER DUE TO MY INCOMPETENCE!
YOU WILL OF COURSE GET THE CREDIT FOR ANYTHING WE DISCOVER.
IF YOU COULD JUST LET ME SEE THE CASE FILES...
SIGH ...
THINK BEGGING WILL GET YOU WHAT YOU WANT...?
YOU REALIZE THE SPOT YOU'RE PUTTING ME IN?
I GOTTA SAY, I'M NOT SURE YOU'RE FIT TO BE AN INVESTI-GATOR.
I'VE HEARD SOME THINGS ABOUT YOU AND YOUR SQUAD...
ACTU-ALLY...
MOSTLY ABOUT *YOU.*

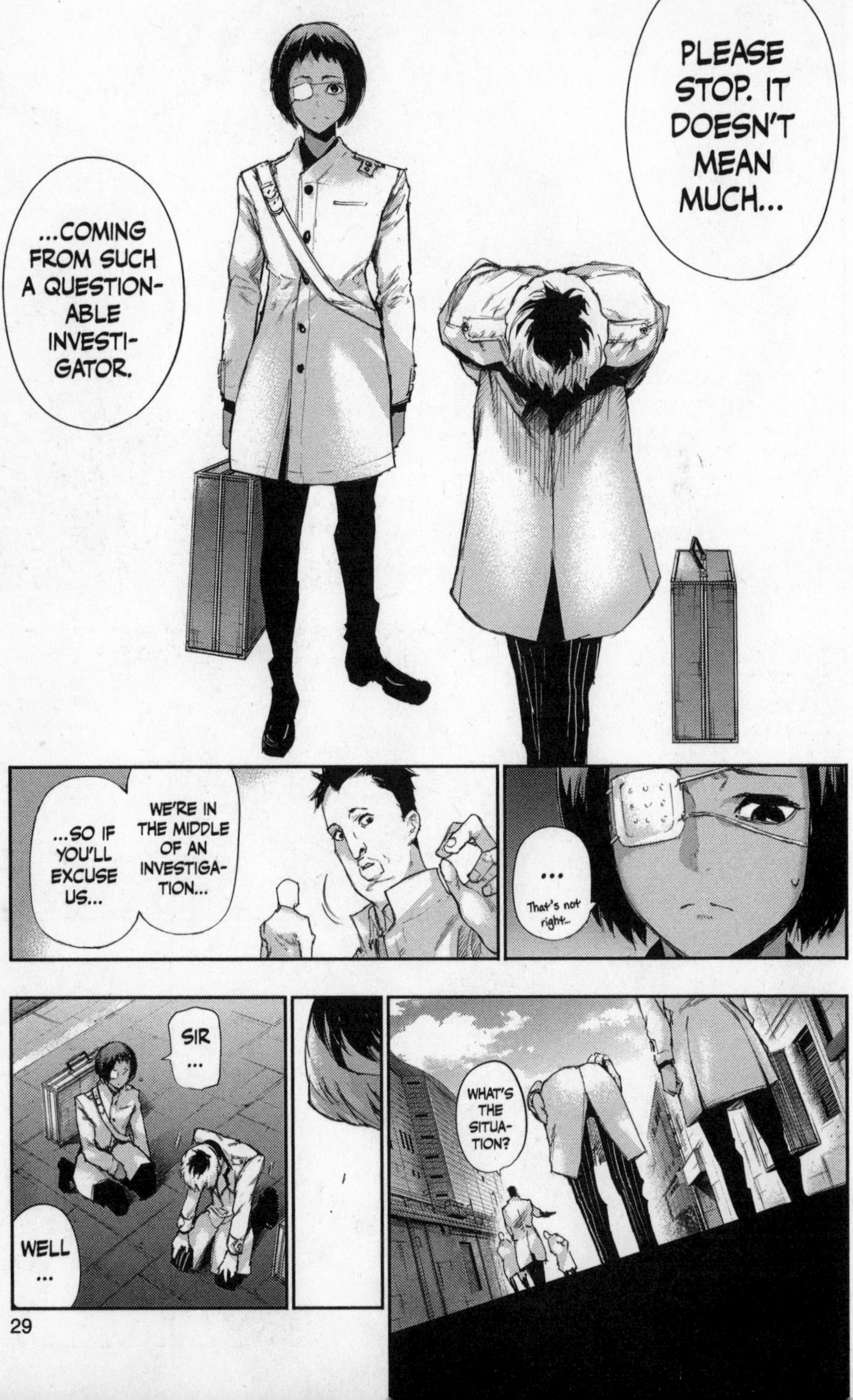
PLEASE STOP. IT DOESN'T MEAN MUCH...
...COMING FROM SUCH A QUESTIONABLE INVESTIGATOR.
...
That's not right...
WE'RE IN THE MIDDLE OF AN INVESTIGATION...
...SO IF YOU'LL EXCUSE US...
WHAT'S THE SITUATION?
SIR...
WELL...

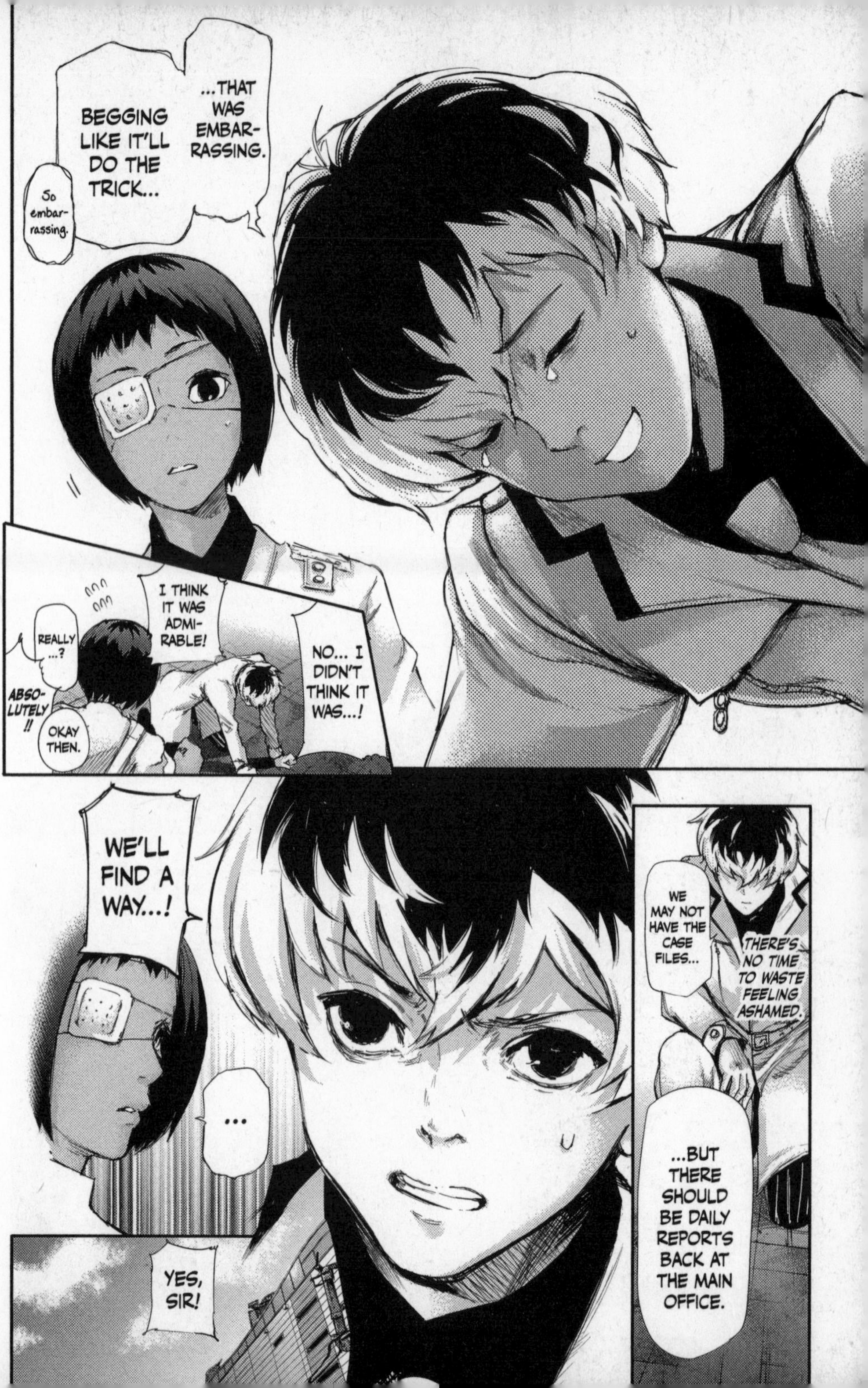
...THAT WAS EMBARRASSING.
BEGGING LIKE IT'LL DO THE TRICK...
So embarrassing.
I THINK IT WAS ADMIRABLE!
NO... I DIDN'T THINK IT WAS...!
REALLY ...?
ABSOLUTELY !!
OKAY THEN.
WE MAY NOT HAVE THE CASE FILES...
THERE'S NO TIME TO WASTE FEELING ASHAMED.
...BUT THERE SHOULD BE DAILY REPORTS BACK AT THE MAIN OFFICE.
WE'LL FIND A WAY...!
...
YES, SIR!

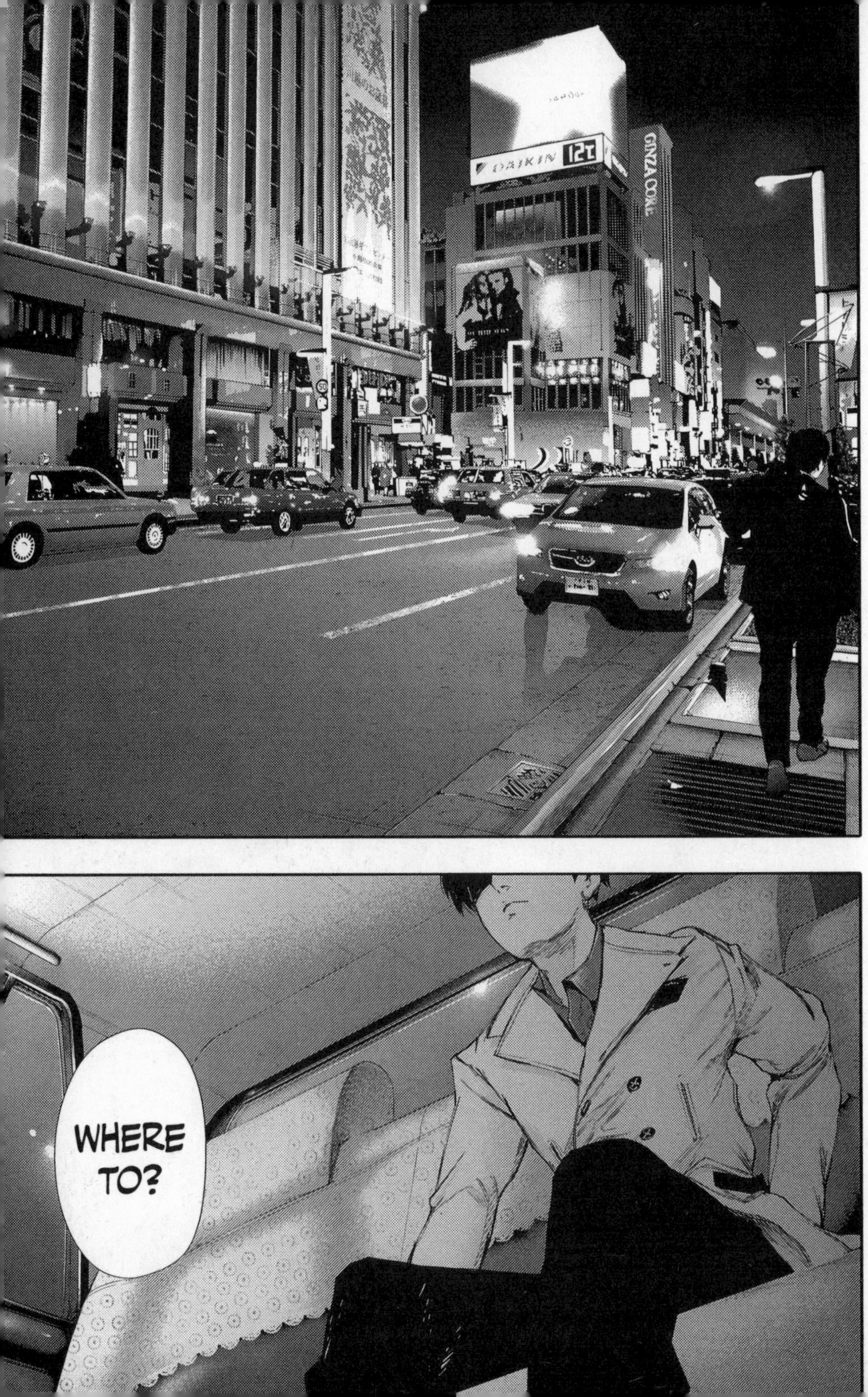
DAIKIN
GINZA CORE
WHERE TO?

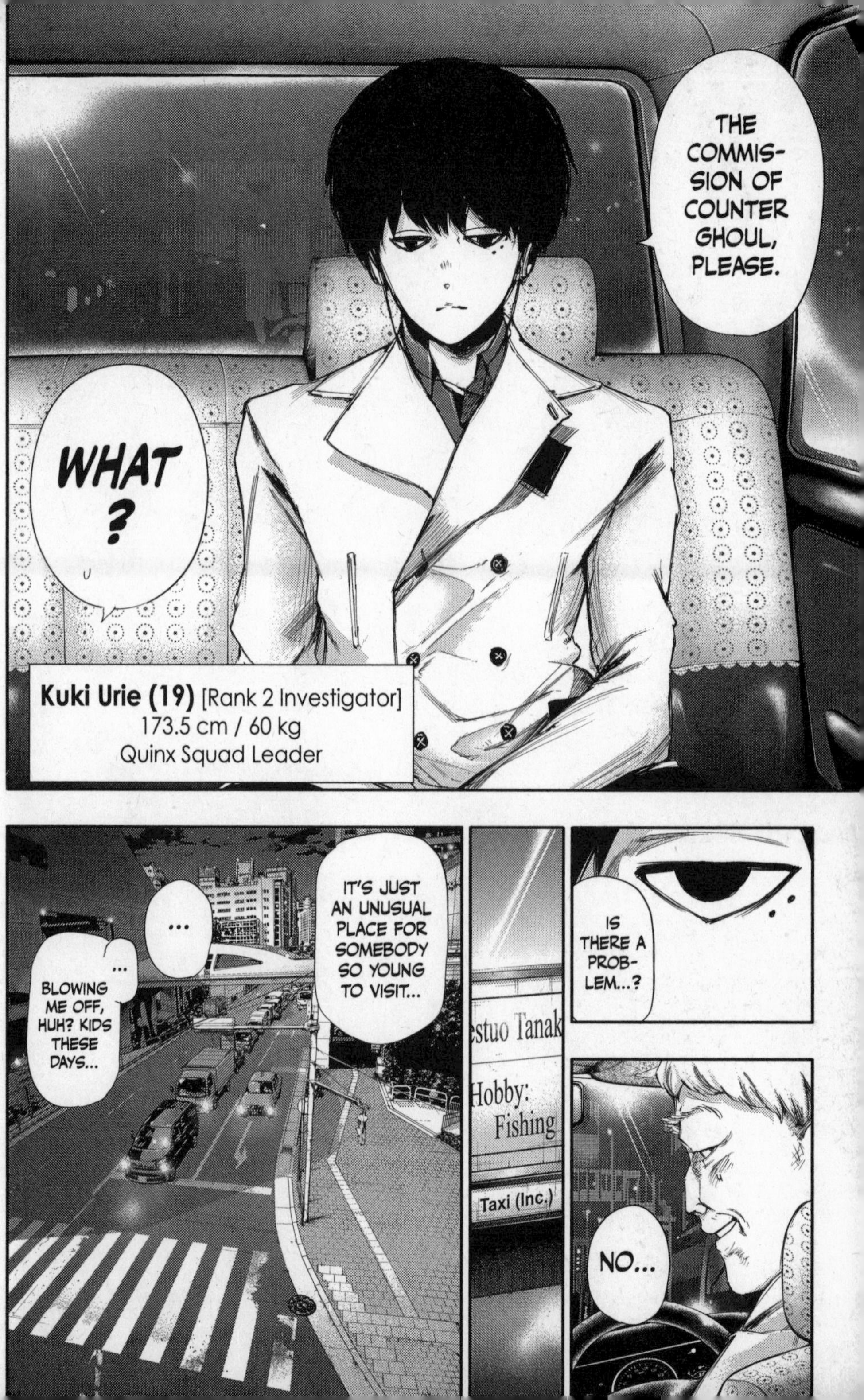
THE COMMISSION OF COUNTER GHOUL, PLEASE.
WHAT?
Kuki Urie (19) [Rank 2 Investigator]
173.5 cm / 60 kg
Quinx Squad Leader
IS THERE A PROBLEM...?
NO...
estuo Tanak
Hobby: Fishing
Taxi (Inc.)
IT'S JUST AN UNUSUAL PLACE FOR SOMEBODY SO YOUNG TO VISIT...
...
... BLOWING ME OFF, HUH? KIDS THESE DAYS...

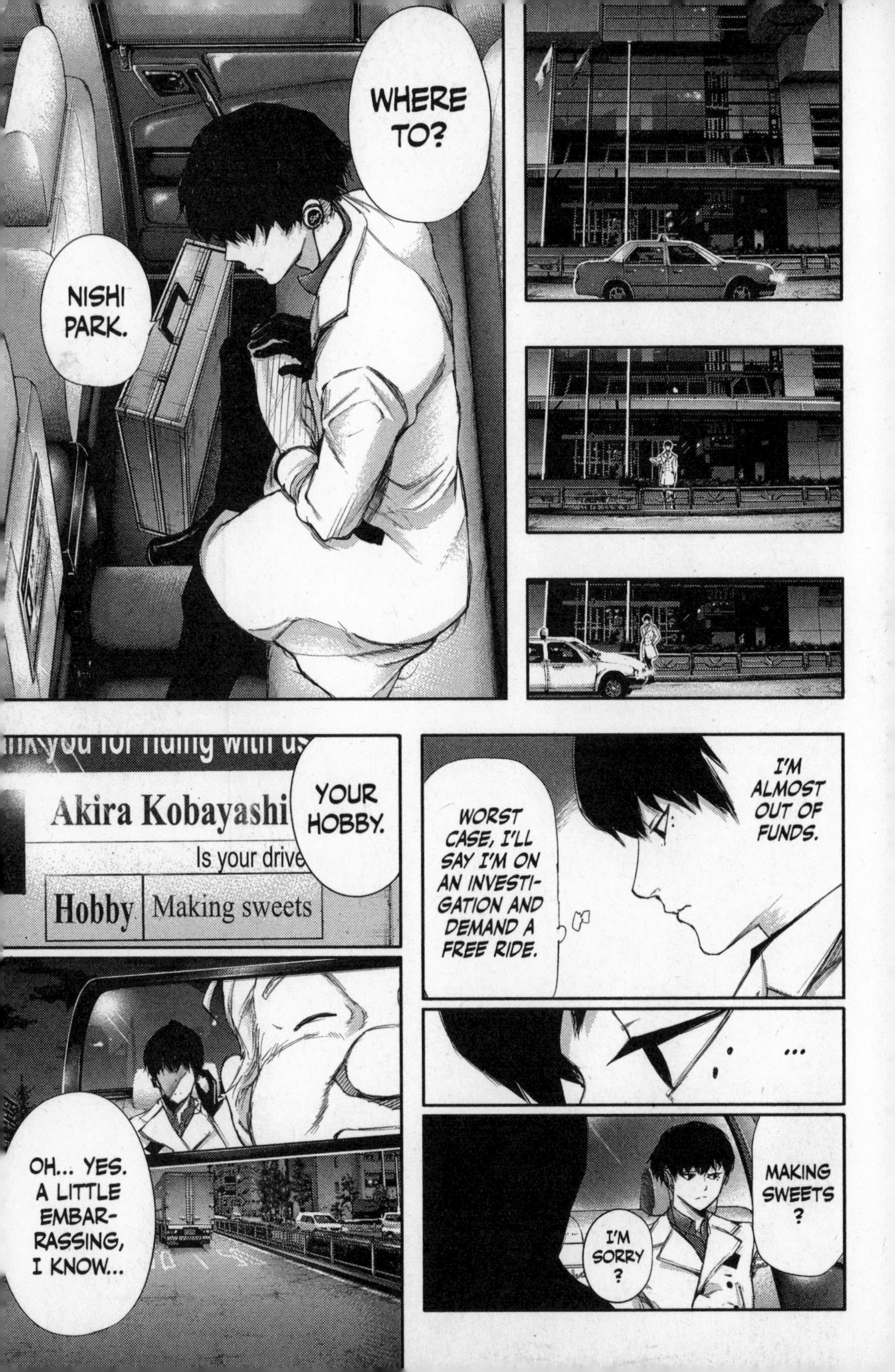
WHERE TO?
NISHI PARK.
I'M ALMOST OUT OF FUNDS.
WORST CASE, I'LL SAY I'M ON AN INVESTIGATION AND DEMAND A FREE RIDE.
Akira Kobayashi
Is your drive
Hobby
Making sweets
YOUR HOBBY.
...
MAKING SWEETS?
I'M SORRY?
OH... YES. A LITTLE EMBARRASSING, I KNOW...

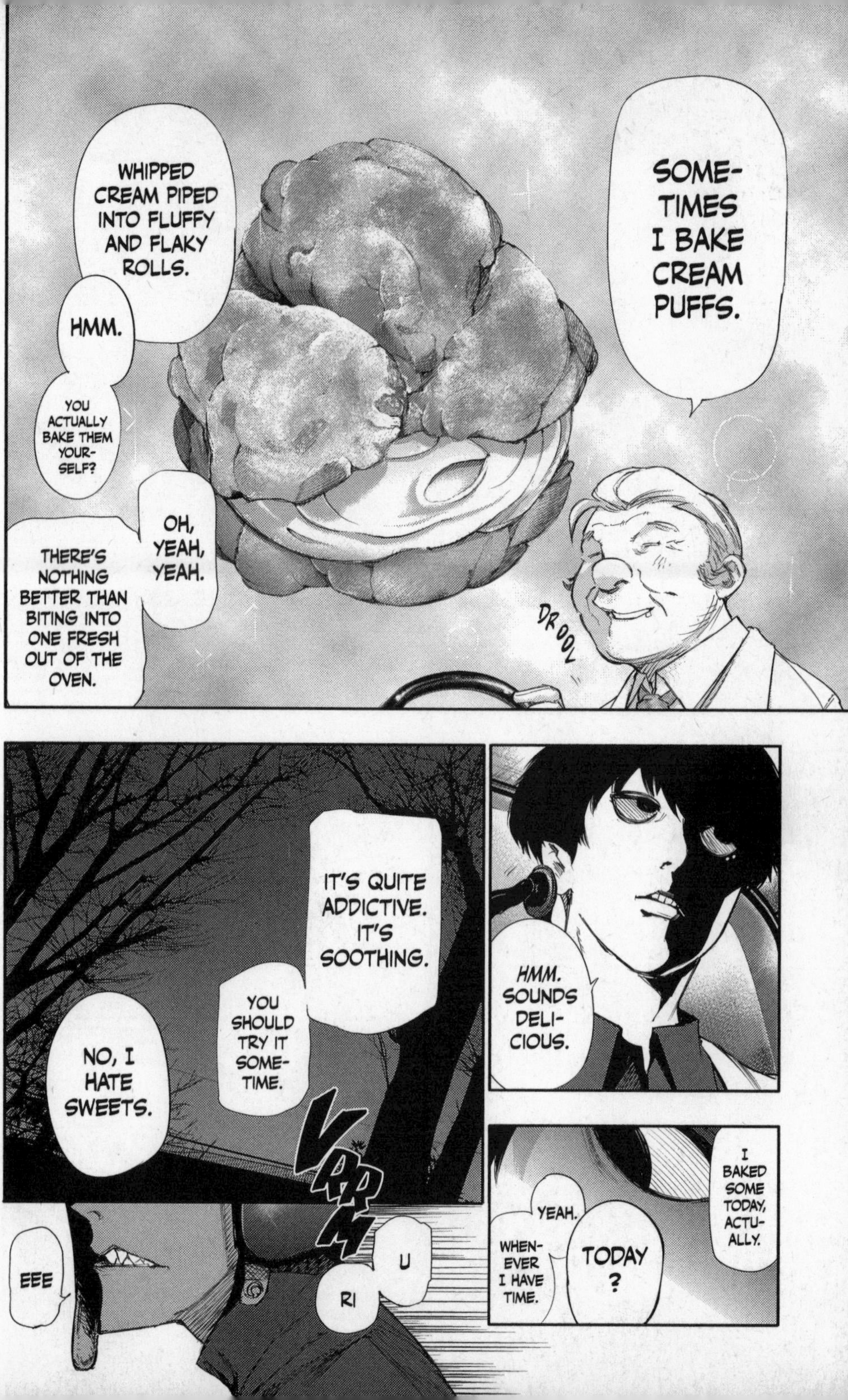
SOME-TIMES I BAKE CREAM PUFFS.
WHIPPED CREAM PIPED INTO FLUFFY AND FLAKY ROLLS.
HMM.
YOU ACTUALLY BAKE THEM YOUR-SELF?
OH, YEAH, YEAH.
THERE'S NOTHING BETTER THAN BITING INTO ONE FRESH OUT OF THE OVEN.
DROOL
HMM. SOUNDS DELI-CIOUS.
I BAKED SOME TODAY, ACTU-ALLY.
TODAY?
YEAH.
WHEN-EVER I HAVE TIME.
IT'S QUITE ADDICTIVE. IT'S SOOTHING.
YOU SHOULD TRY IT SOME-TIME.
NO, I HATE SWEETS.
VRRM
U
RI
EEE

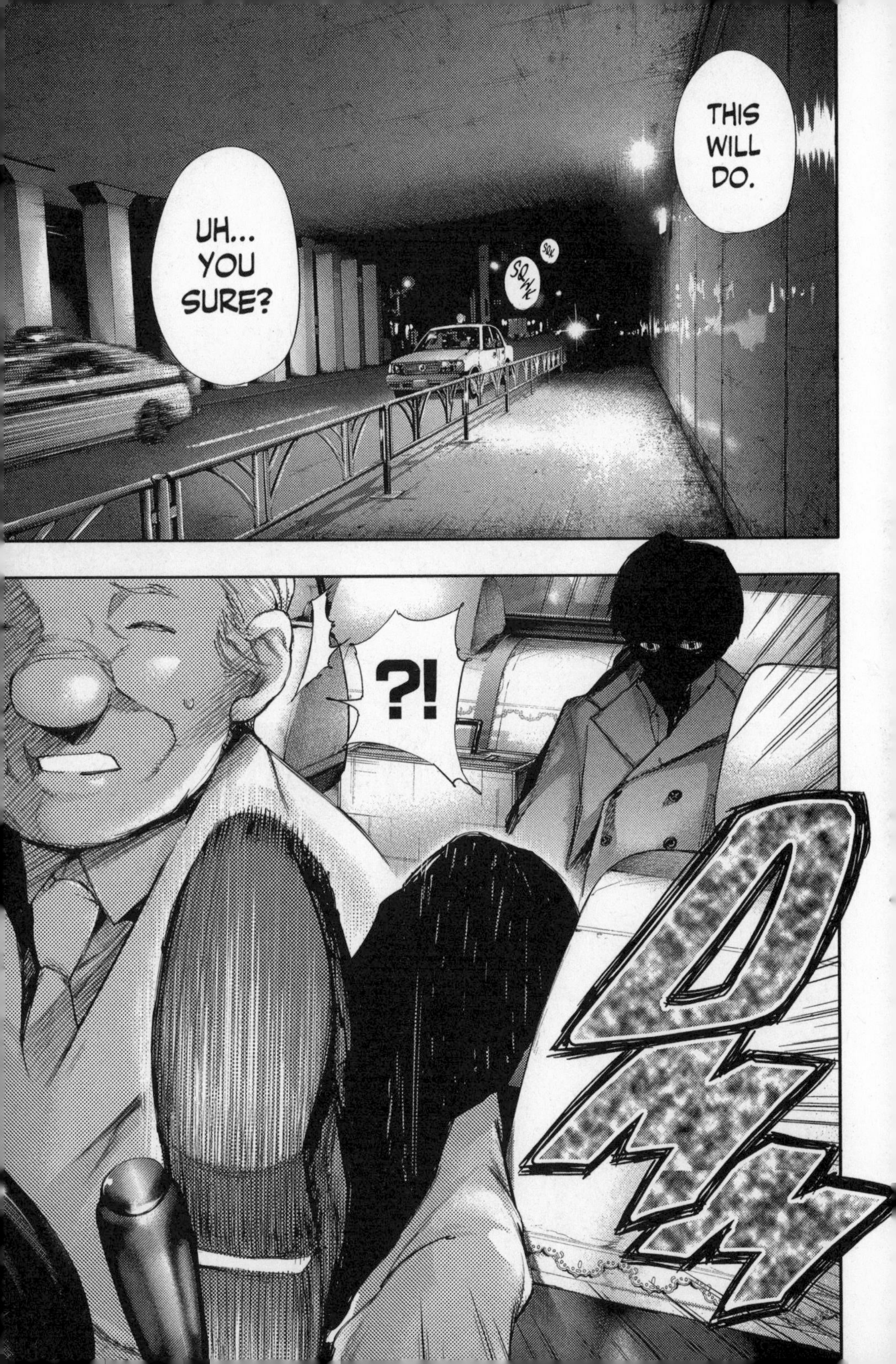
THIS WILL DO.
UH... YOU SURE?
SQK
SQWK
?!

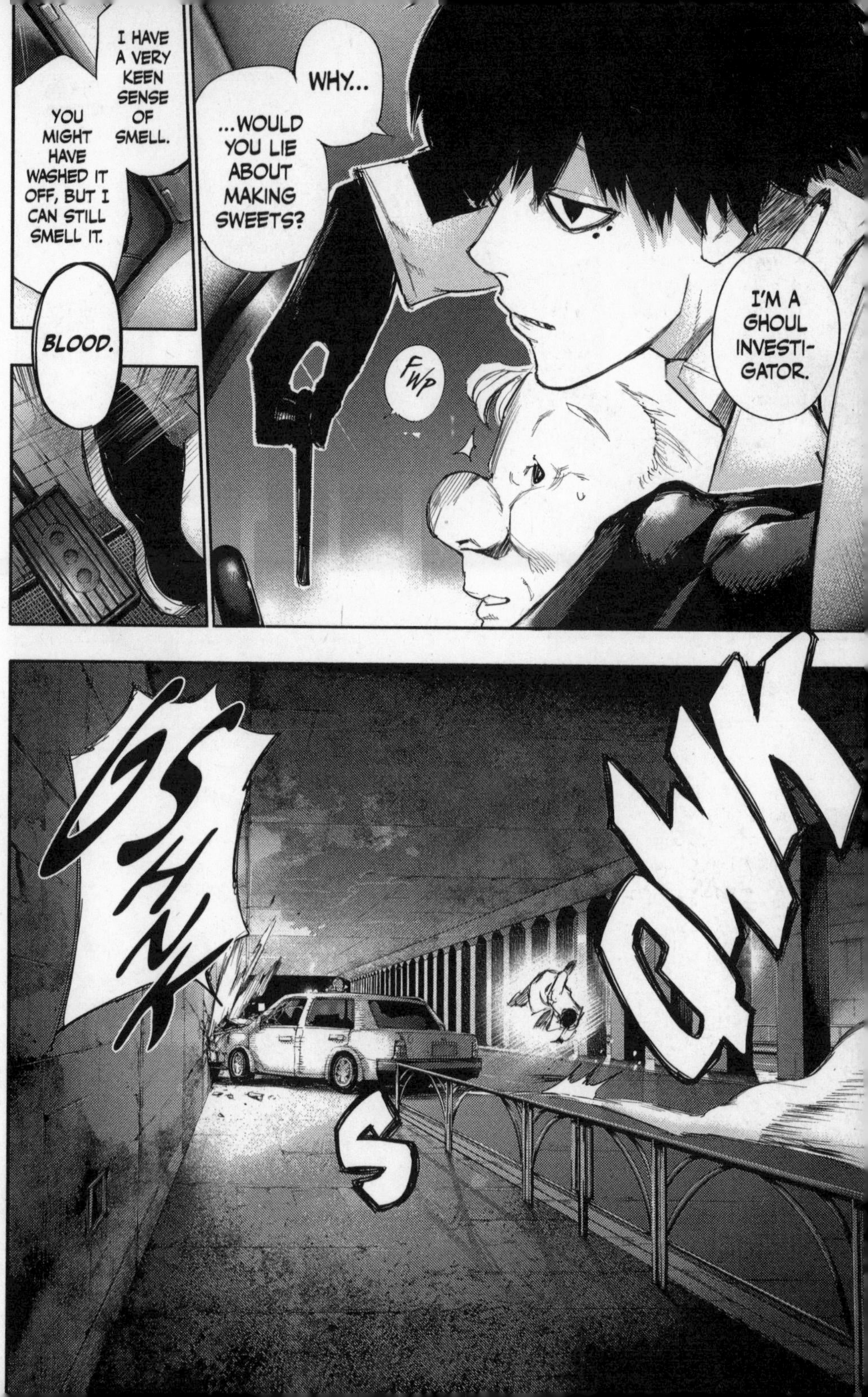
WHY...
...WOULD YOU LIE ABOUT MAKING SWEETS?
I'M A GHOUL INVESTIGATOR.
FWP
I HAVE A VERY KEEN SENSE OF SMELL.
YOU MIGHT HAVE WASHED IT OFF, BUT I CAN STILL SMELL IT.
BLOOD.
GWK
DSHNK
S

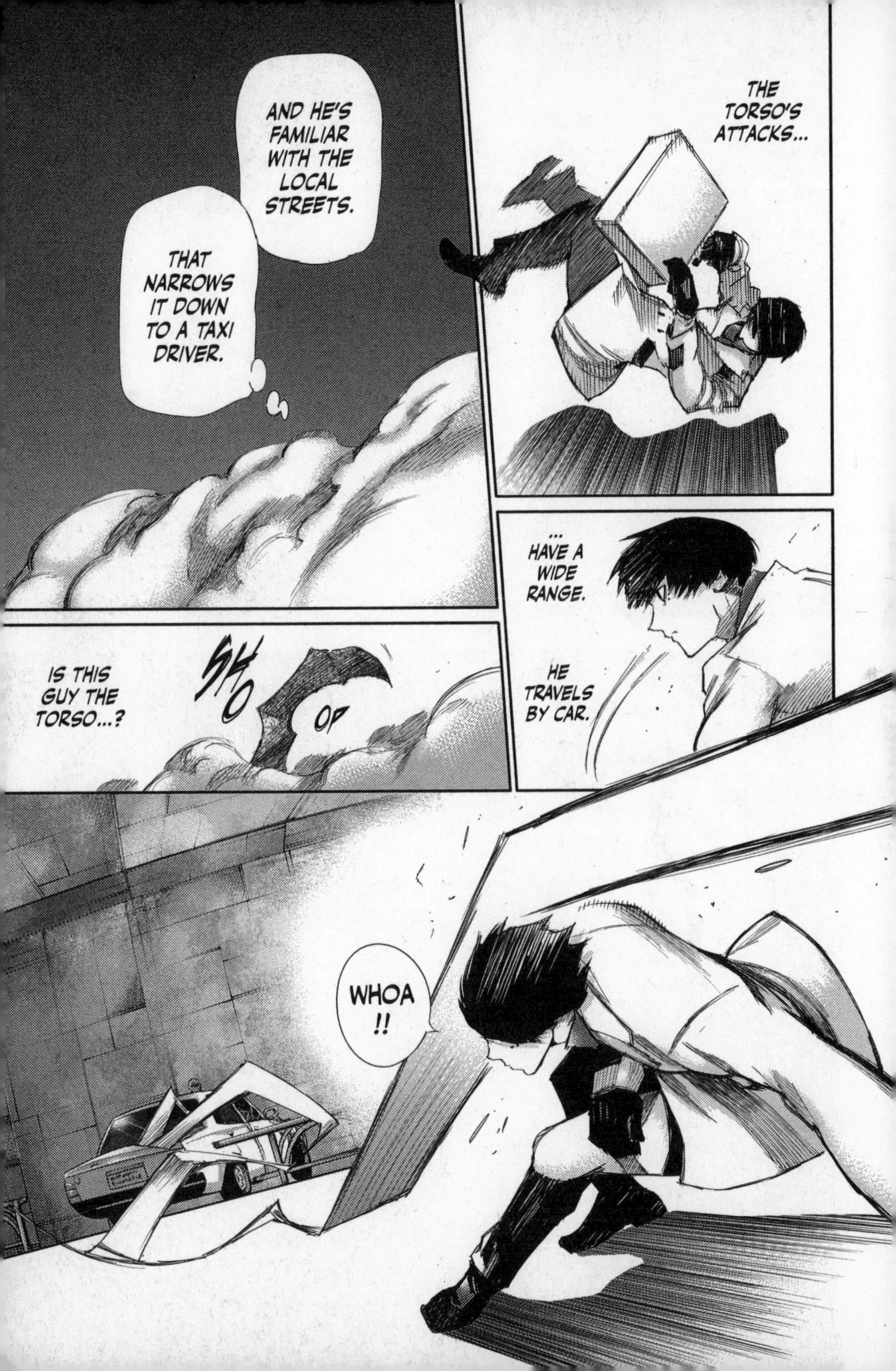
THE TORSO'S ATTACKS...
... HAVE A WIDE RANGE.
HE TRAVELS BY CAR.
AND HE'S FAMILIAR WITH THE LOCAL STREETS.
THAT NARROWS IT DOWN TO A TAXI DRIVER.
IS THIS GUY THE TORSO...?
SKOOP
WHOA !!

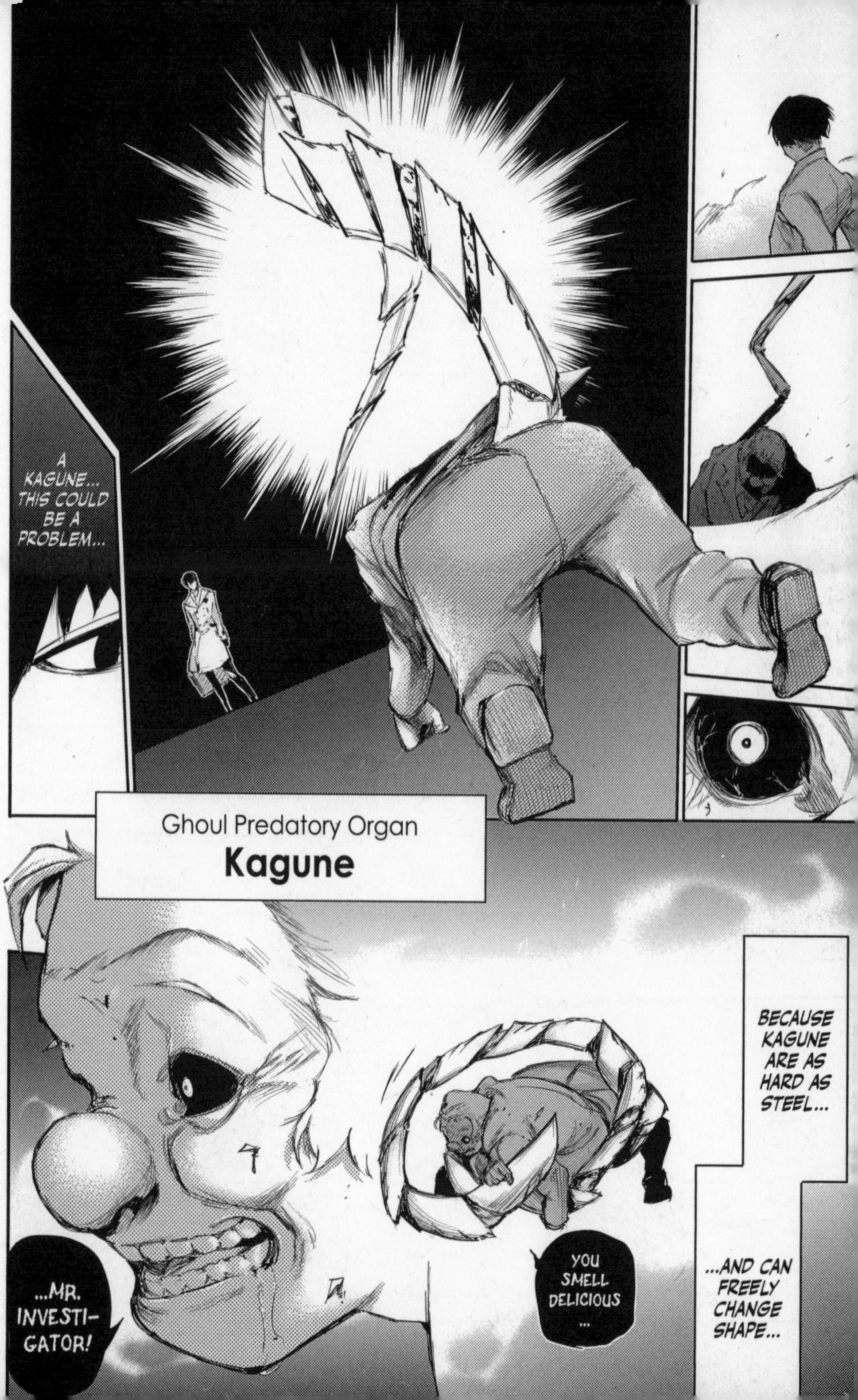
A KAGUNE... THIS COULD BE A PROBLEM...
Ghoul Predatory Organ
Kagune
BECAUSE KAGUNE ARE AS HARD AS STEEL...
...AND CAN FREELY CHANGE SHAPE...
YOU SMELL DELICIOUS ...
...MR. INVESTI-GATOR!

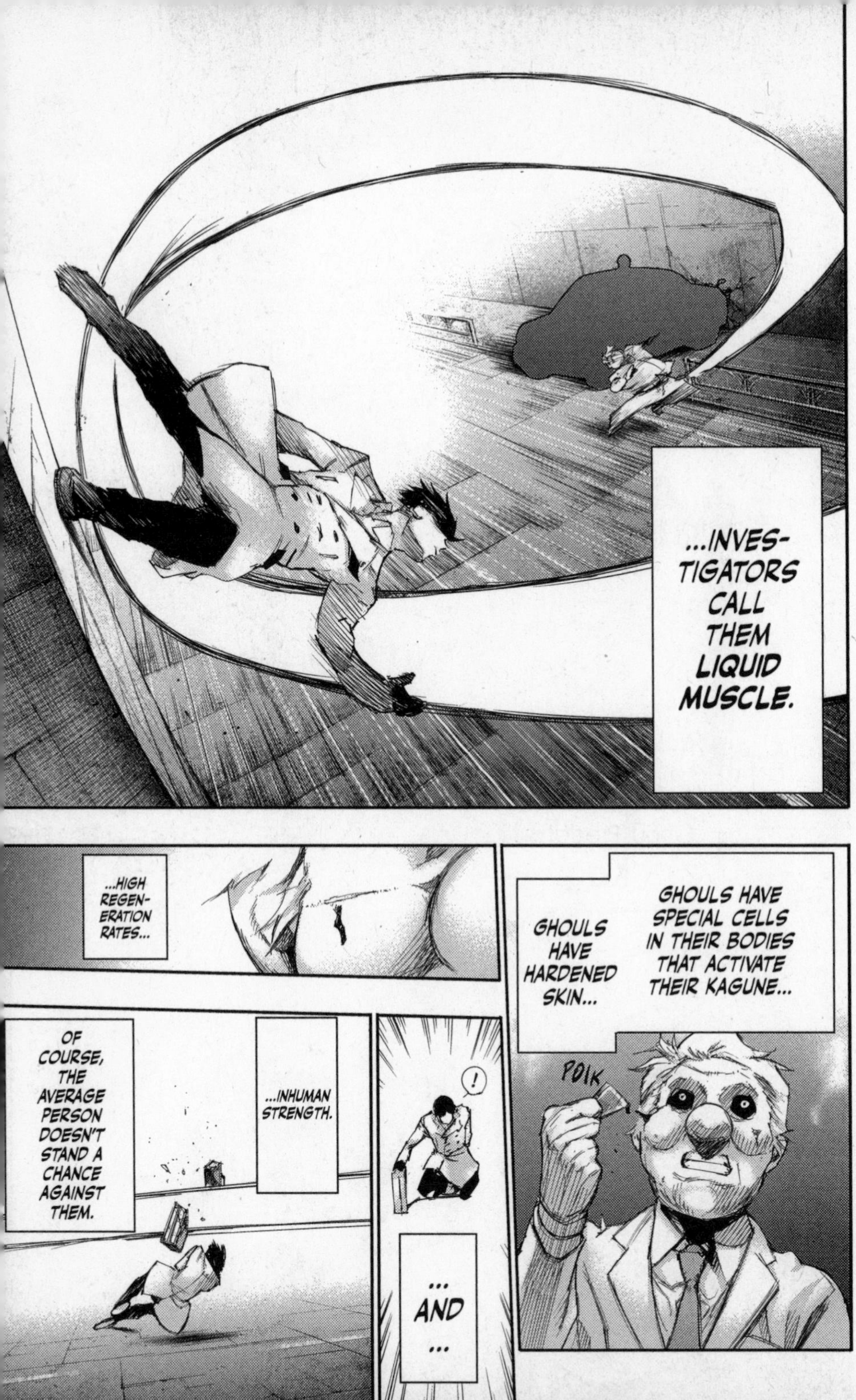
...INVES-TIGATORS CALL THEM LIQUID MUSCLE.
GHOULS HAVE SPECIAL CELLS IN THEIR BODIES THAT ACTIVATE THEIR KAGUNE...
GHOULS HAVE HARDENED SKIN...
POIK
...HIGH REGEN-ERATION RATES...
... AND ...
!
...INHUMAN STRENGTH.
OF COURSE, THE AVERAGE PERSON DOESN'T STAND A CHANCE AGAINST THEM.

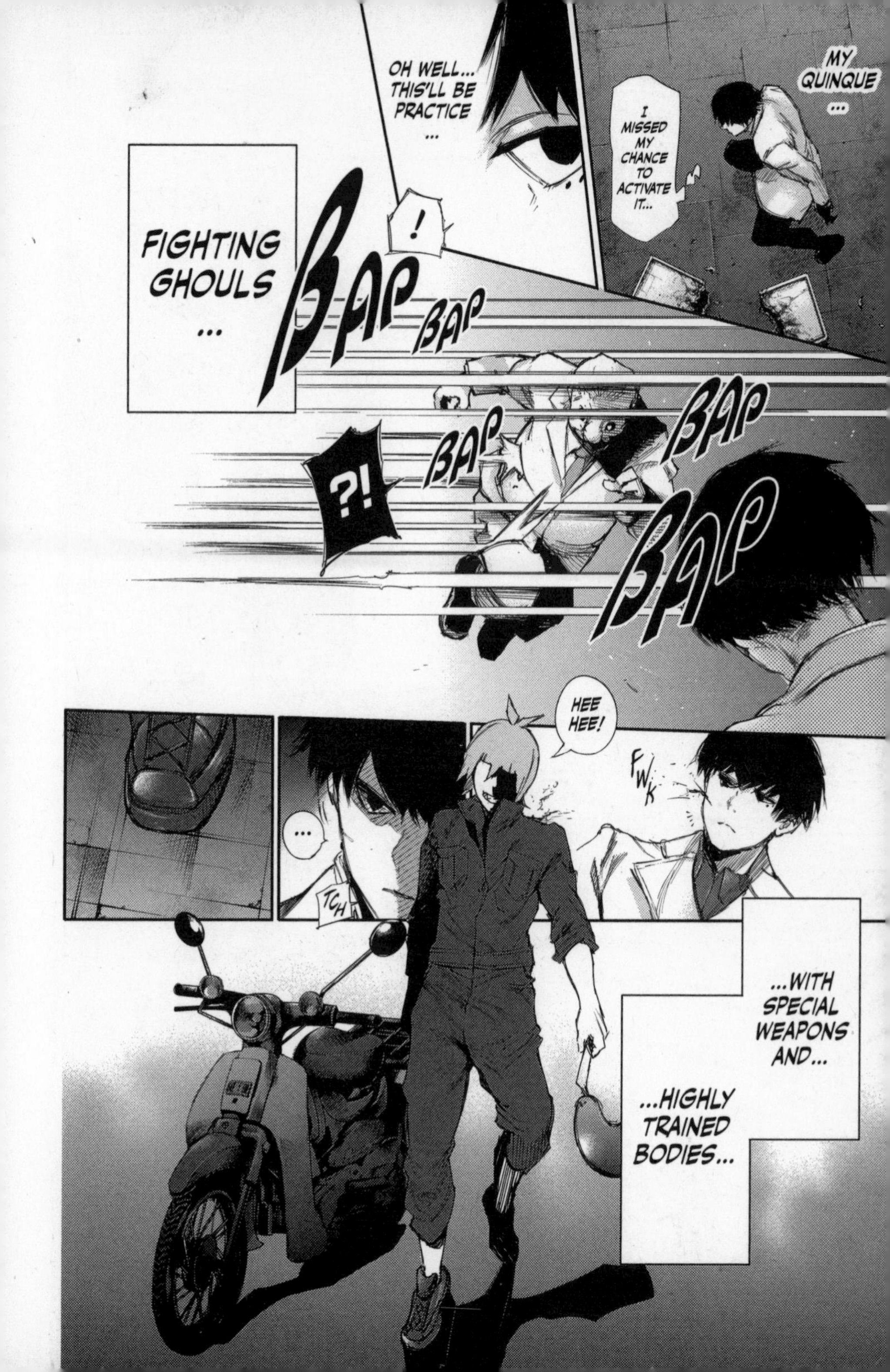
MY QUINQUE ...
I MISSED MY CHANCE TO ACTIVATE IT...
OH WELL... THIS'LL BE PRACTICE ...
!
FIGHTING GHOULS ...
BAP BAP
BAP
BAP
BAP
?!
HEE HEE!
FWK
...
TCH
...WITH SPECIAL WEAPONS AND...
...HIGHLY TRAINED BODIES...

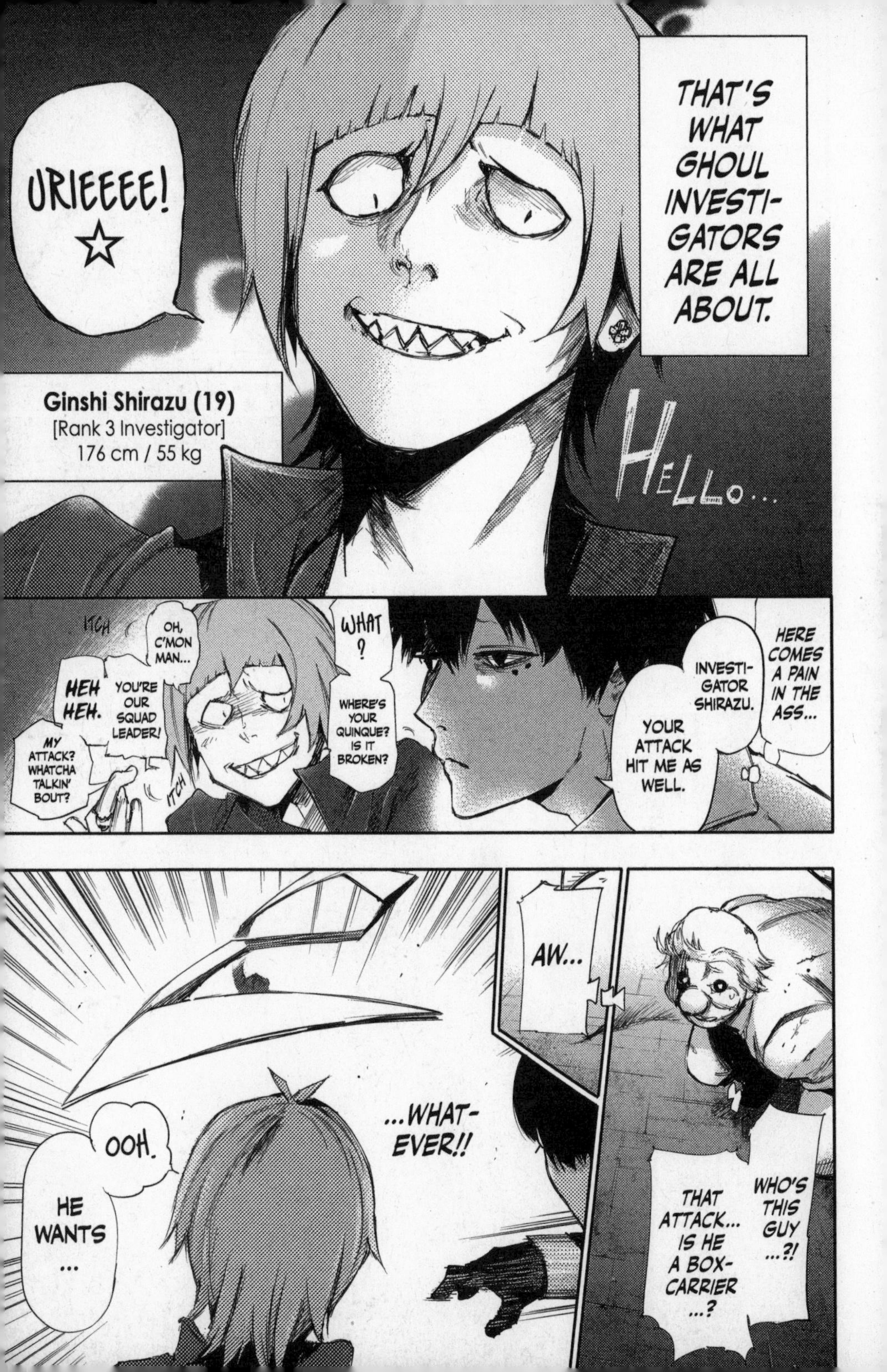
THAT'S WHAT GHOUL INVESTIGATORS ARE ALL ABOUT.
URIEEEE! ☆
HELLO...
Ginshi Shirazu (19)
[Rank 3 Investigator]
176 cm / 55 kg
HERE COMES A PAIN IN THE ASS...
INVESTIGATOR SHIRAZU.
YOUR ATTACK HIT ME AS WELL.
WHAT?
WHERE'S YOUR QUINQUE? IS IT BROKEN?
OH, C'MON MAN...
ITCH
YOU'RE OUR SQUAD LEADER!
HEH HEH.
MY ATTACK? WHATCHA TALKIN' BOUT?
ITCH
WHO'S THIS GUY ...?!
THAT ATTACK... IS HE A BOX-CARRIER ...?
AW...
...WHAT-EVER!!
OOH.
HE WANTS ...

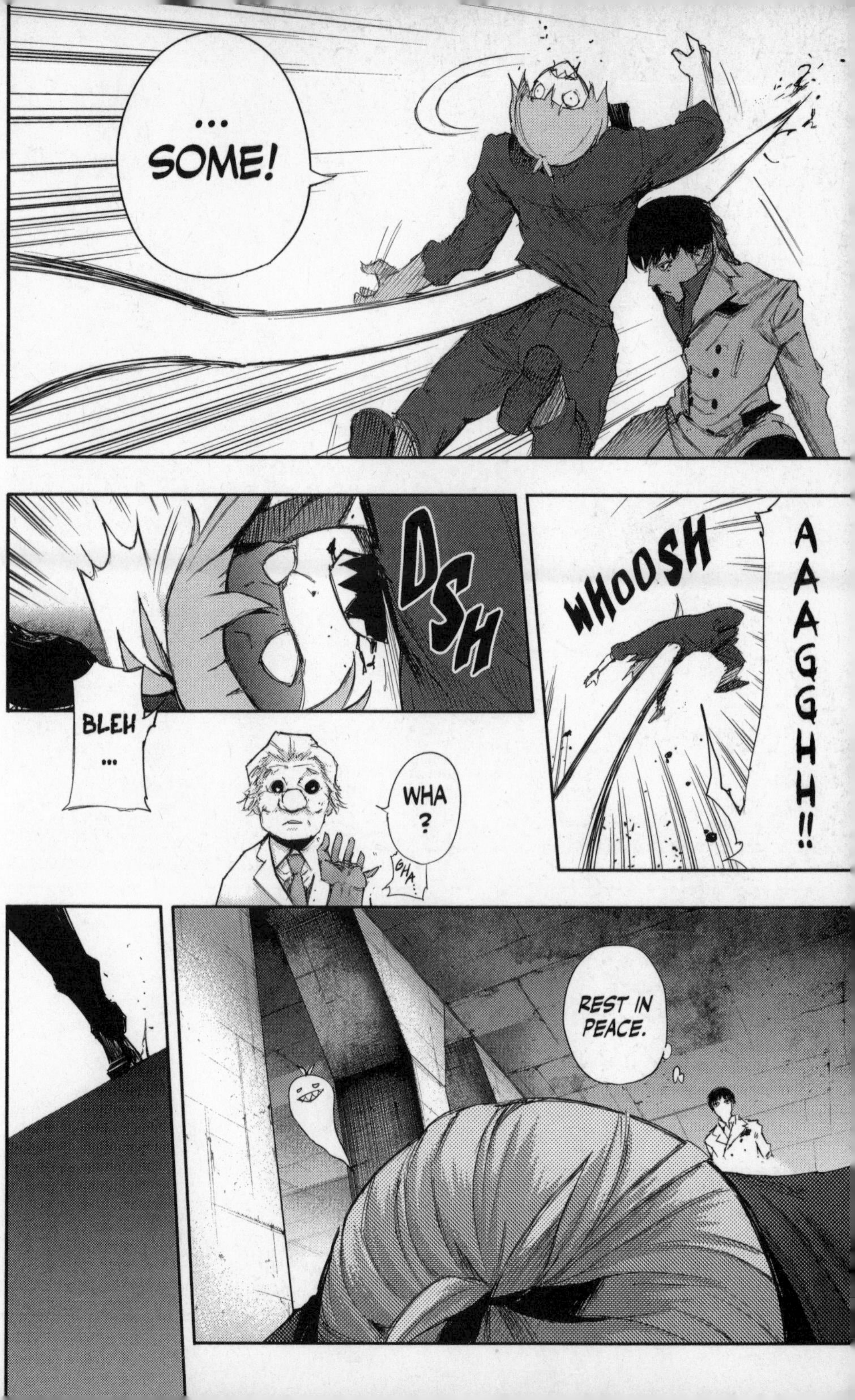

... SOME!
WHOOSH
AAAGGHH!!
DSH
BLEH ...
WHA ?
GHA...
REST IN PEACE.

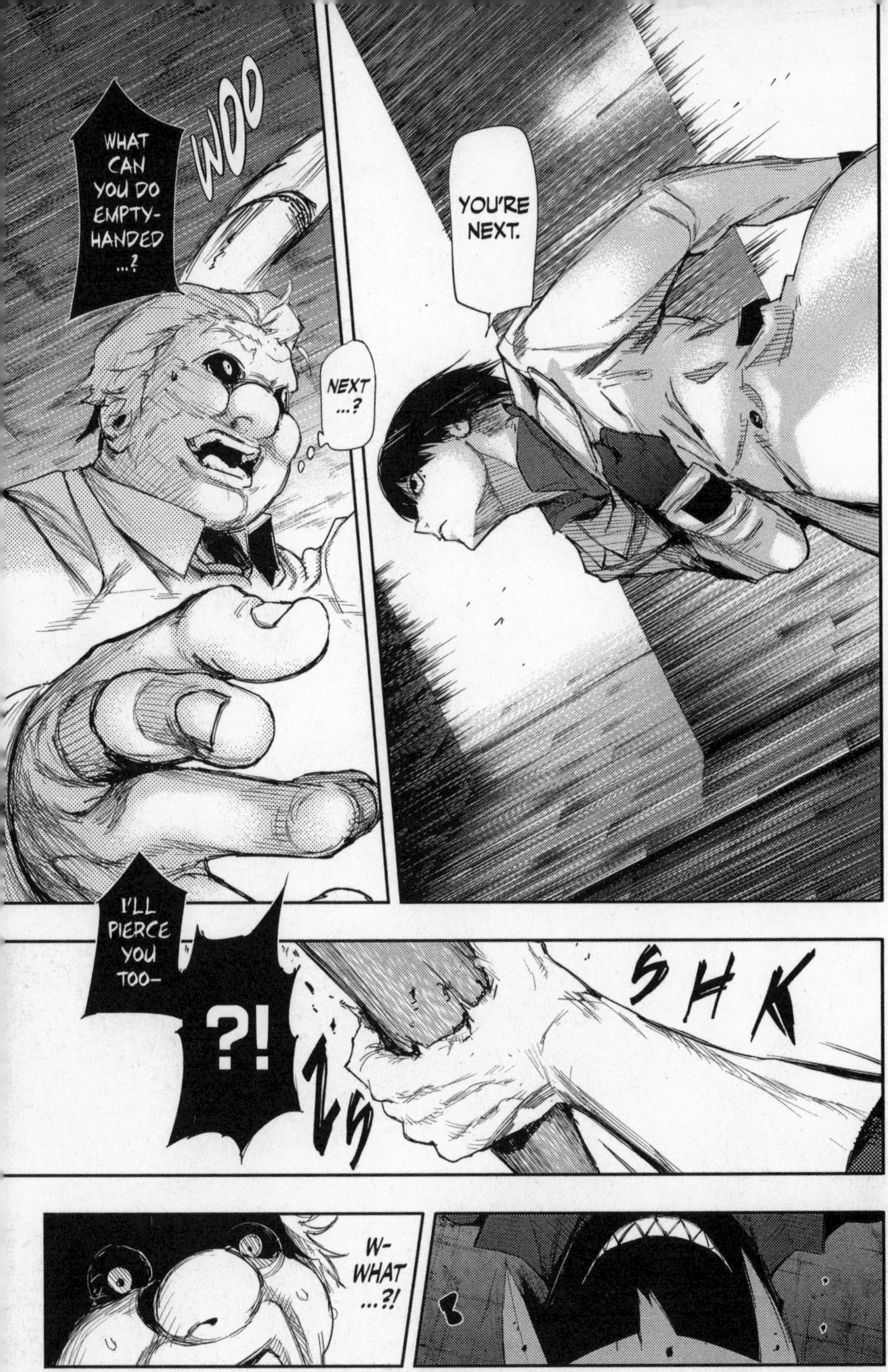
YOU'RE NEXT.
WHAT CAN YOU DO EMPTY-HANDED ...?
WOO
NEXT ...?
I'LL PIERCE YOU TOO-
SHK
?!
ZS
W-WHAT ...?!

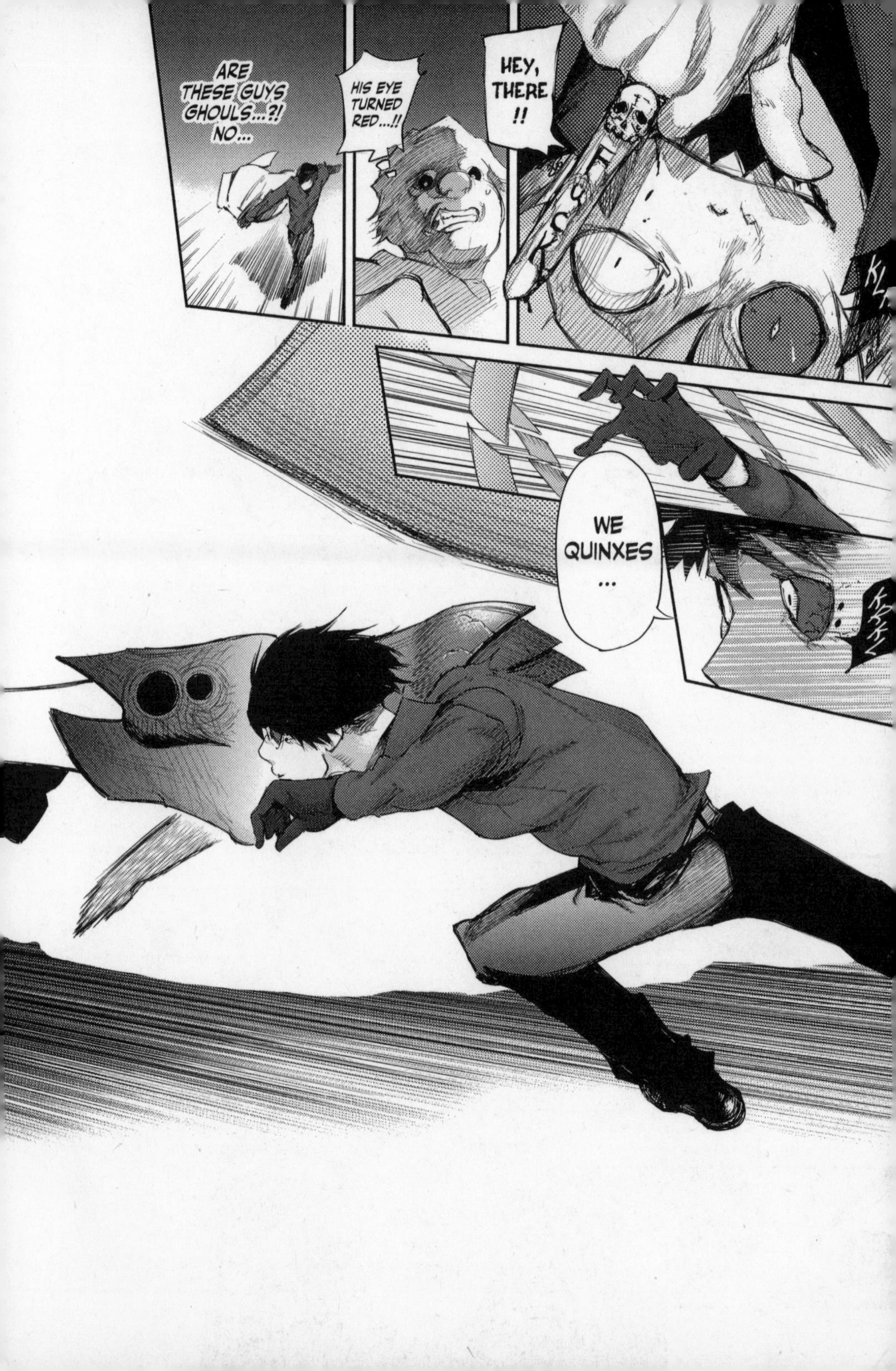
HEY, THERE !!
HIS EYE TURNED RED...!!
ARE THESE GUYS GHOULS...?! NO...
WE QUINXES ...

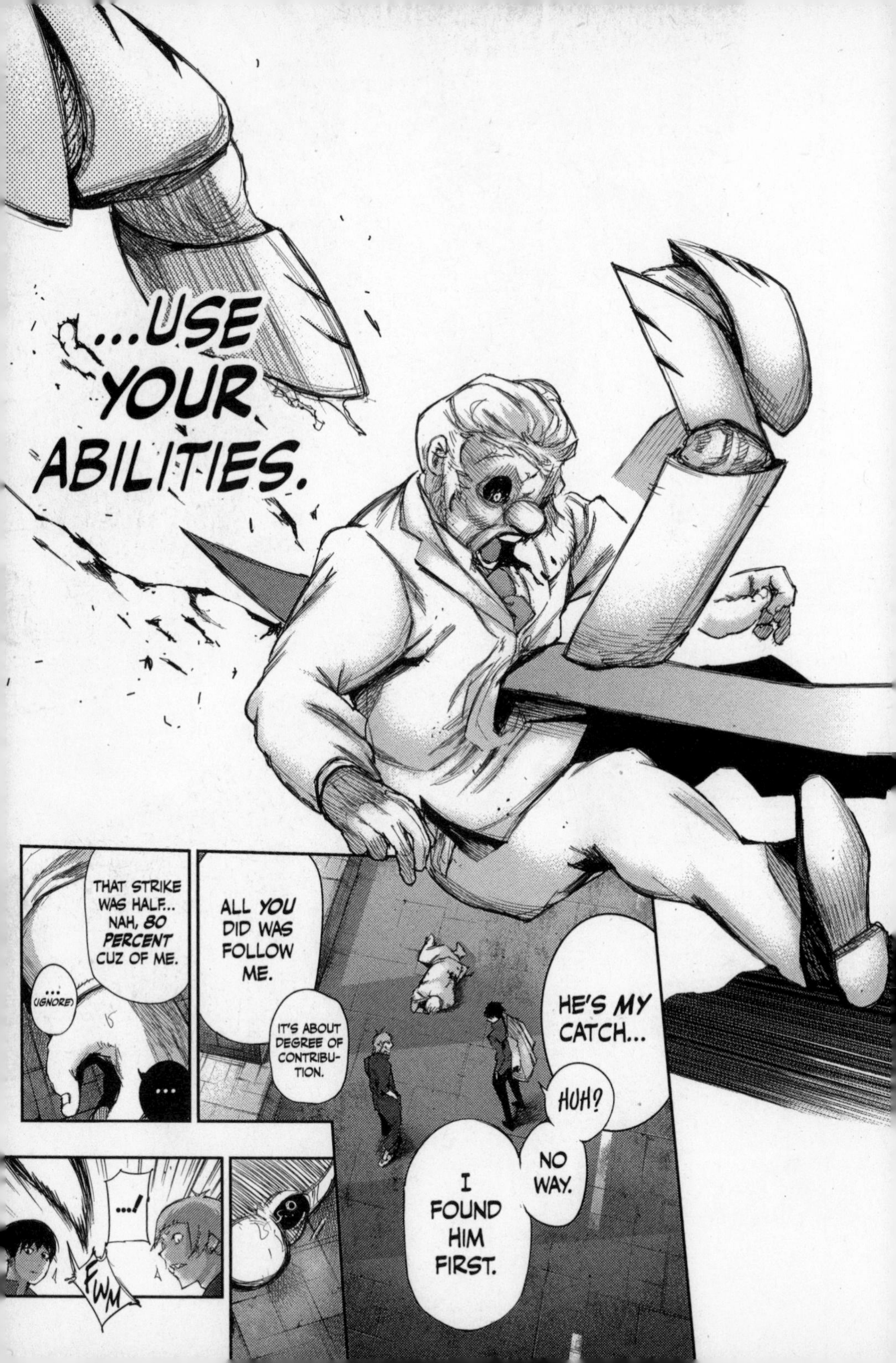
...USE YOUR ABILITIES.
HE'S MY CATCH...
HUH?
NO WAY.
I FOUND HIM FIRST.
ALL YOU DID WAS FOLLOW ME.
IT'S ABOUT DEGREE OF CONTRIBUTION.
THAT STRIKE WAS HALF... NAH, 80 PERCENT CUZ OF ME.
... (IGNORE)
...
...!
FWM

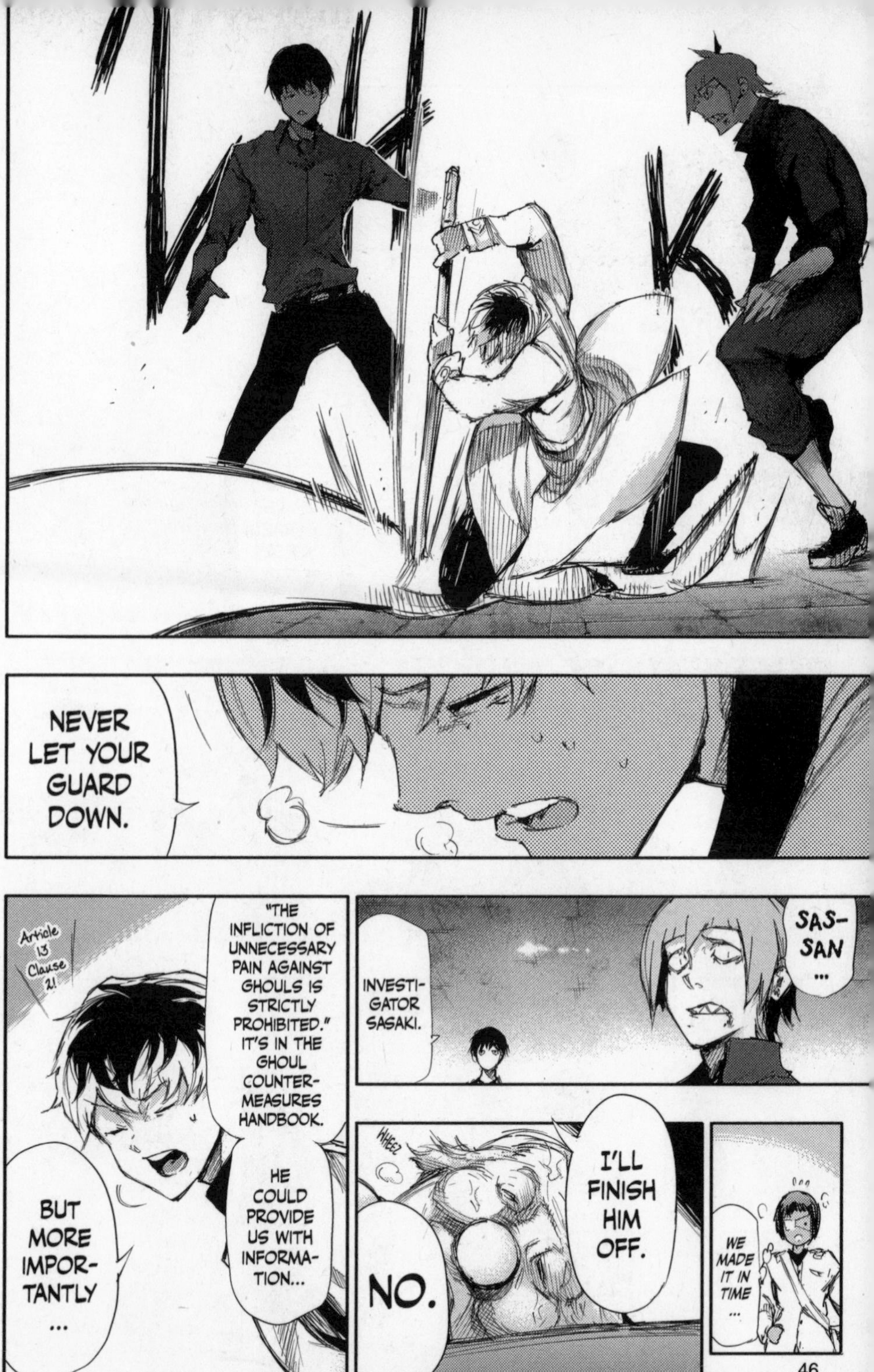
NEVER LET YOUR GUARD DOWN.
SAS-SAN...
INVESTIGATOR SASAKI.
WE MADE IT IN TIME...
WHEEZ
I'LL FINISH HIM OFF.
NO.
Article 13 Clause 21
"THE INFLICTION OF UNNECESSARY PAIN AGAINST GHOULS IS STRICTLY PROHIBITED." IT'S IN THE GHOUL COUNTERMEASURES HANDBOOK.
HE COULD PROVIDE US WITH INFORMATION...
BUT MORE IMPORTANTLY...

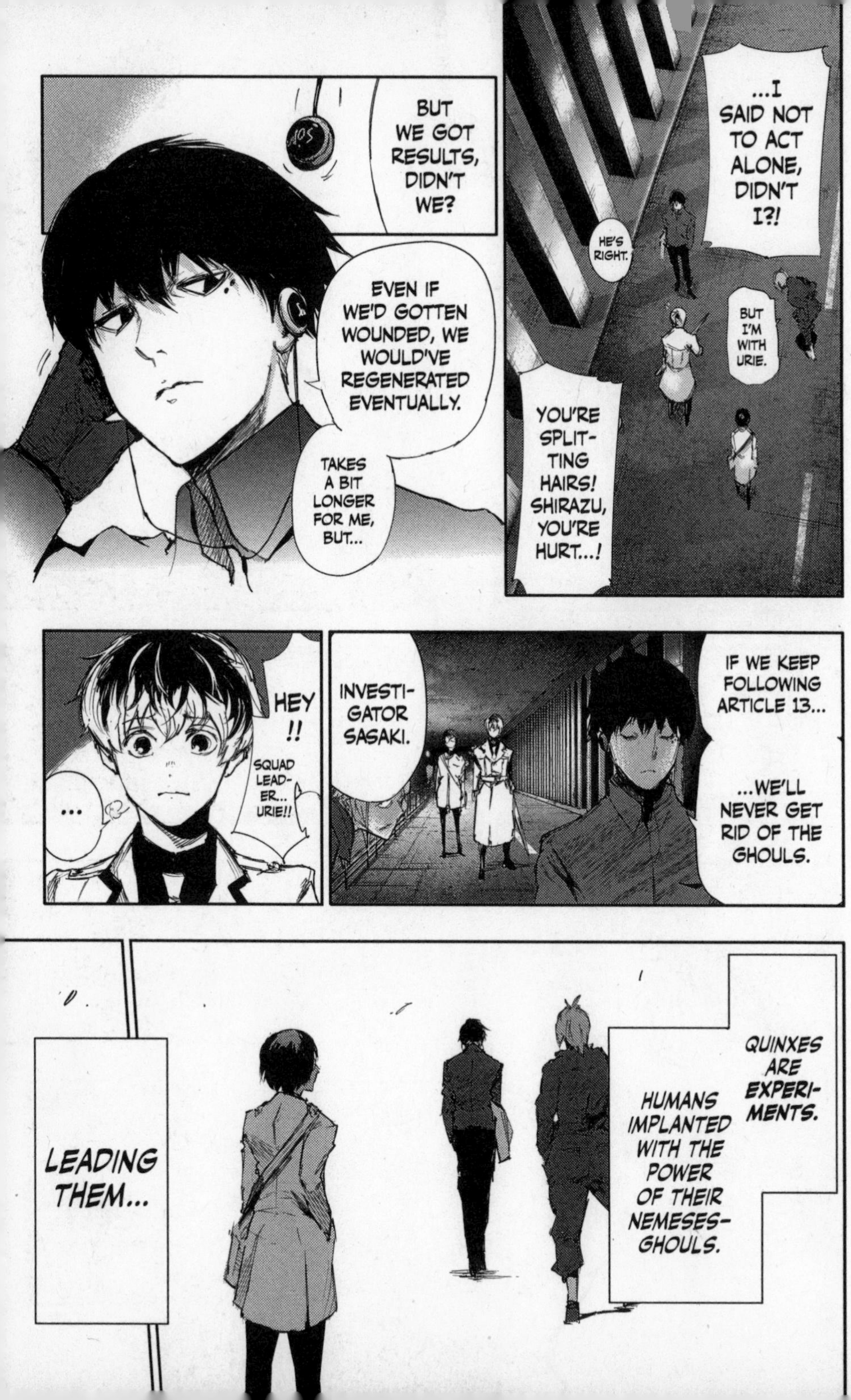
...I SAID NOT TO ACT ALONE, DIDN'T I?!
HE'S RIGHT.
BUT I'M WITH URIE.
YOU'RE SPLITTING HAIRS! SHIRAZU, YOU'RE HURT...!
BUT WE GOT RESULTS, DIDN'T WE?
EVEN IF WE'D GOTTEN WOUNDED, WE WOULD'VE REGENERATED EVENTUALLY.
TAKES A BIT LONGER FOR ME, BUT...
IF WE KEEP FOLLOWING ARTICLE 13...
...WE'LL NEVER GET RID OF THE GHOULS.
INVESTIGATOR SASAKI.
HEY!!
SQUAD LEADER... URIE!!
...
QUINXES ARE EXPERIMENTS.
HUMANS IMPLANTED WITH THE POWER OF THEIR NEMESES-GHOULS.
LEADING THEM...

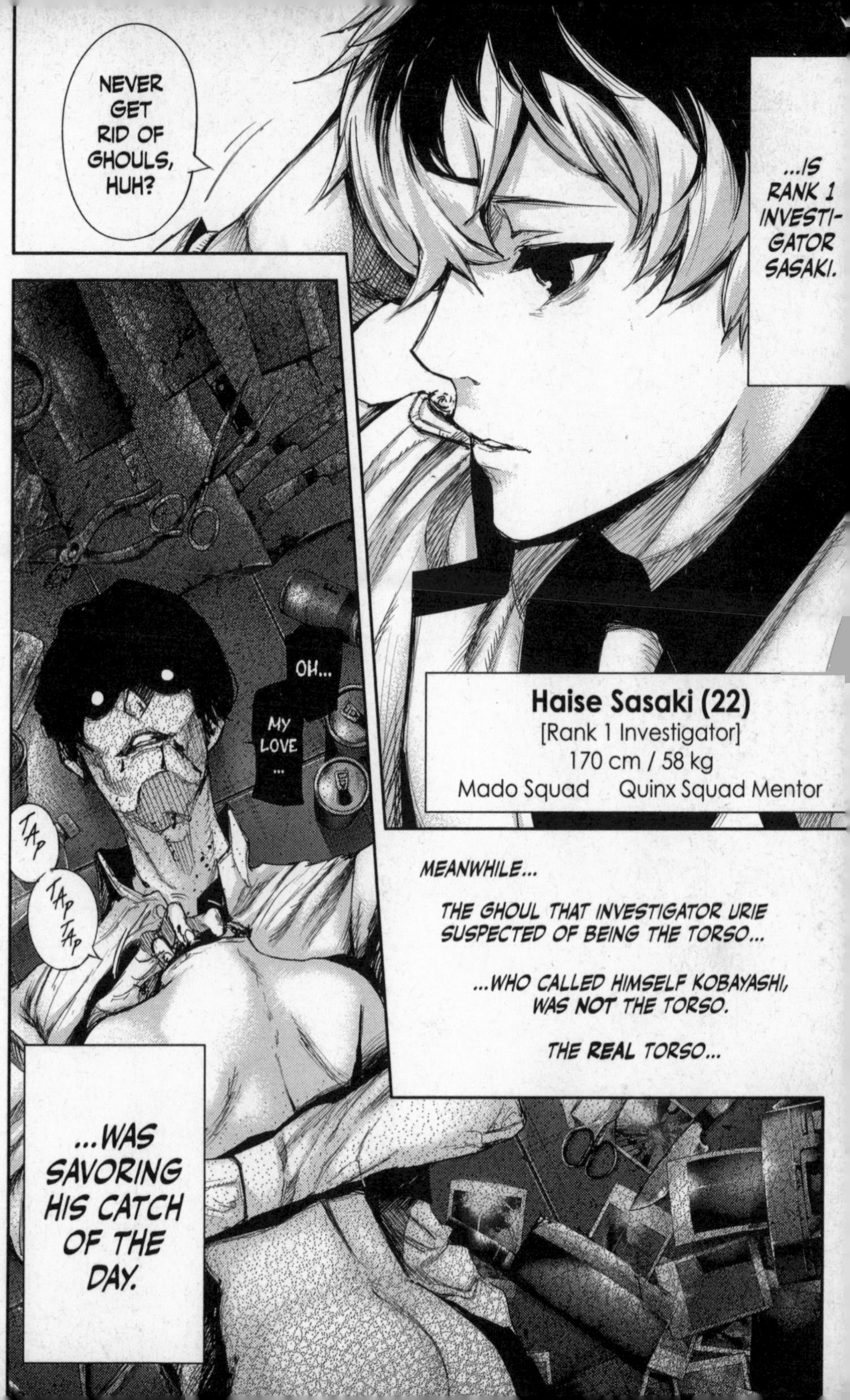
...IS RANK 1 INVESTIGATOR SASAKI.
NEVER GET RID OF GHOULS, HUH?
Haise Sasaki (22)
[Rank 1 Investigator]
170 cm / 58 kg
Mado Squad Quinx Squad Mentor
MEANWHILE...
THE GHOUL THAT INVESTIGATOR URIE SUSPECTED OF BEING THE TORSO...
...WHO CALLED HIMSELF KOBAYASHI, WAS NOT THE TORSO.
THE REAL TORSO...
OH...
MY LOVE...
TAP
TAP TAP TAP
...WAS SAVORING HIS CATCH OF THE DAY.

Quinx Squad Daily Report
Date: 9/3   Weather: ☼   Responding Investigator: Mutsuki
Incident: Ghoul Growls

Actions Taken: Investigated reports of "Ghoul-like growls" with Rank 3 Investigator Yonebayashi. Searched the premises and surrounds of the female caller's home over the course of three days. We heard the sounds on the third night. We arrived at the scene with our Quinques and found two dogs fighting.

Alternative actions: Perhaps the more appropriate response would have been to clear up the caller's misconception that Ghouls growl.

Notes: For health reasons, Investigator Yonebayashi only took part in the first day of the search.

Comments: Nice Surprise. I'm glad it wasn't a Ghoul. Danger can be lurking anywhere. Investigations like these are important for civilians' sense of security.

Quinx Squad Daily Report
Date: 9/5   Weather: Responding Investigator: Urie
Incident: Guerrilla Investigation

Actions Taken: I urged the squad members to conduct individual investigations the past few weeks. In order for us to perform at a higher level, it's important to discover Ghouls on our own and not just follow up on known suspects. I felt it was necessary for the squad to have the ability to conduct investigations from an individual perspective. I personally investigated Wards 5 through 7 and gained testimony pertaining to the Torso case, and shifted my investigation accordingly.

Alternative actions: We are still in the early stages of advancing squad abilities and I should have accompanied the investigators. As squad leader, I feel responsible.

Notes: Requesting a reimbursement of around $1,900 for investigation expenses. I will provide receipts.

Comments: I respect your eagerness, but Investigator Mado placed Investigator Sasaki in charge of guiding the squad's growth. Personally, I would like to see you bring the squad together. I'll see what I can do about your request for a reimbursement.

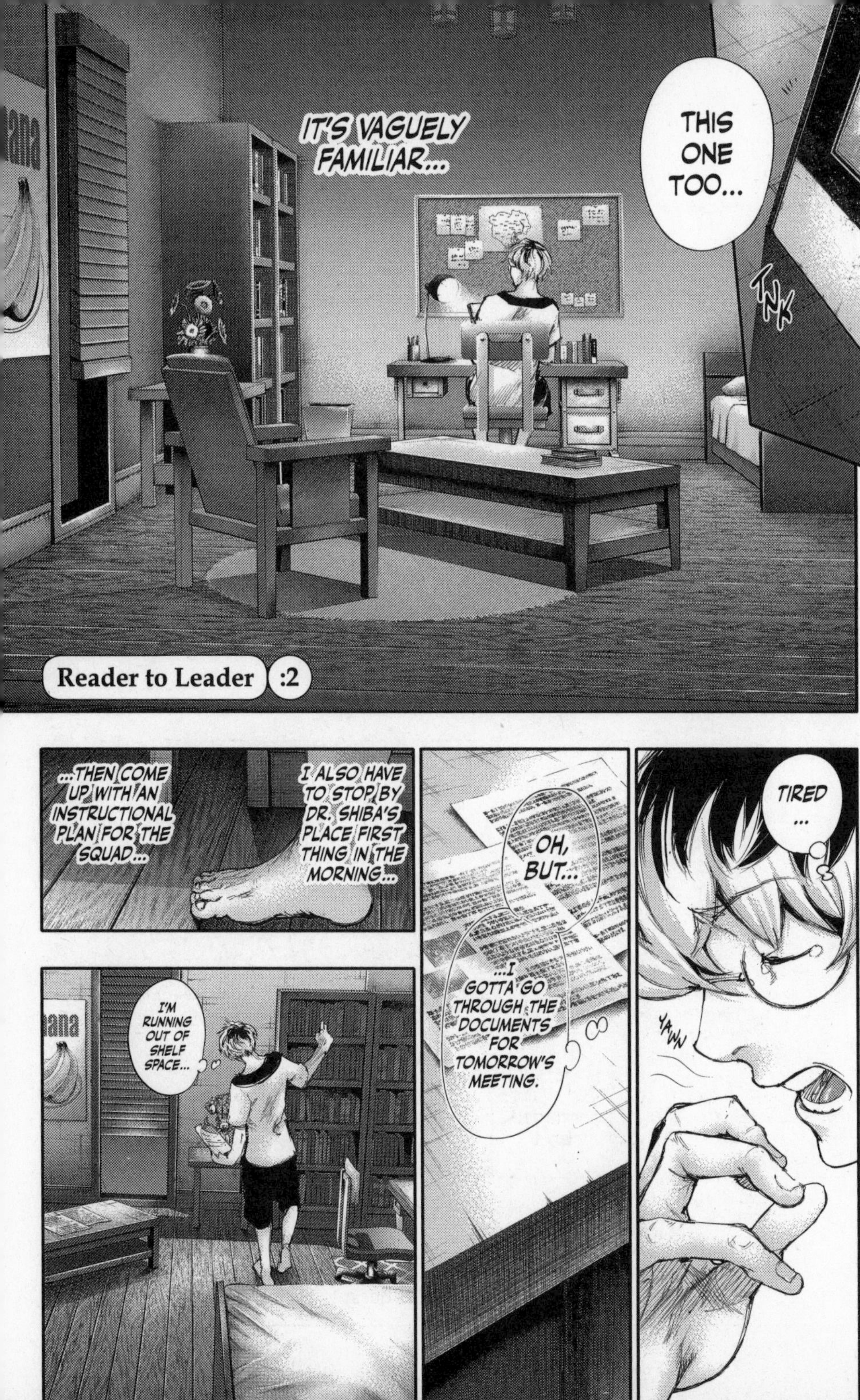
THIS ONE TOO...
TNK
IT'S VAGUELY FAMILIAR...
Reader to Leader :2
TIRED ...
YAWN
OH, BUT...
...I GOTTA GO THROUGH THE DOCUMENTS FOR TOMORROW'S MEETING.
I ALSO HAVE TO STOP BY DR. SHIBA'S PLACE FIRST THING IN THE MORNING...
...THEN COME UP WITH AN INSTRUCTIONAL PLAN FOR THE SQUAD...
I'M RUNNING OUT OF SHELF SPACE...

Reader to Leader :2

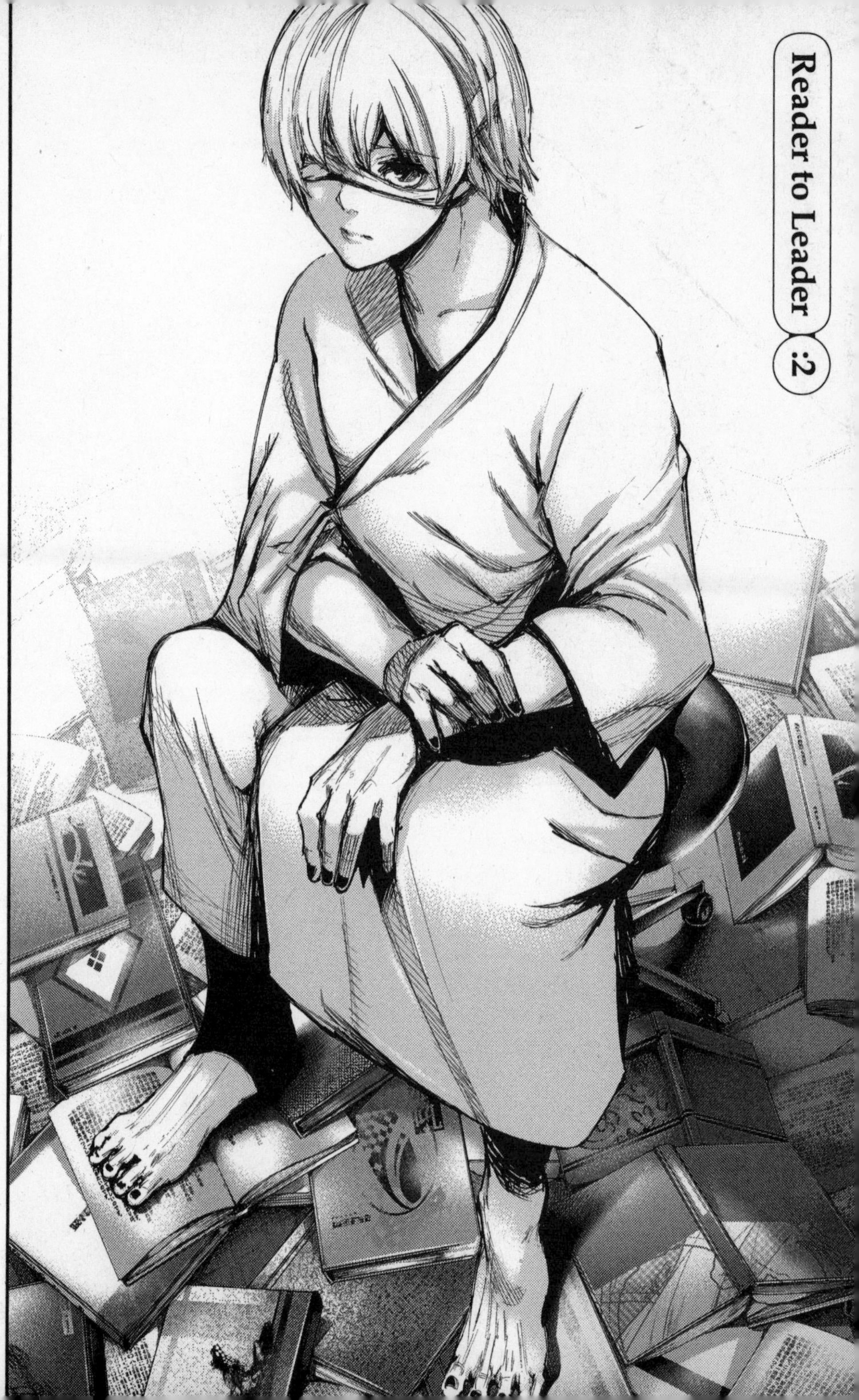

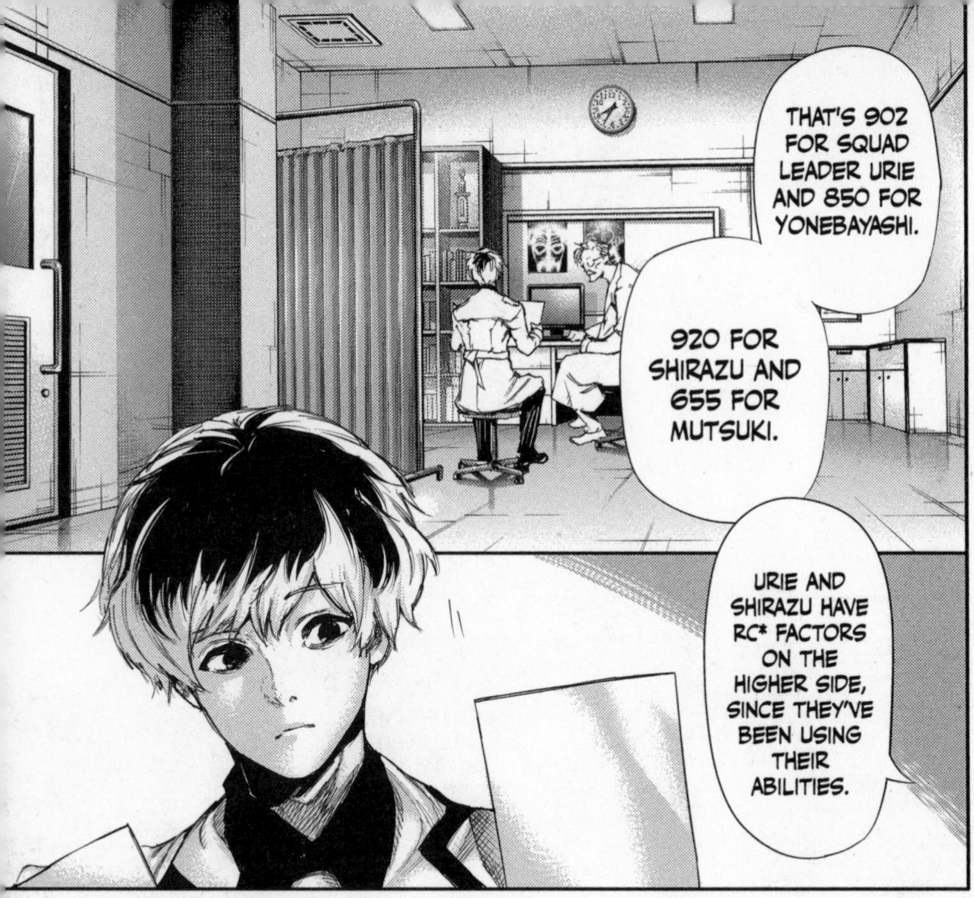
THAT'S 902 FOR SQUAD LEADER URIE AND 850 FOR YONEBAYASHI.
920 FOR SHIRAZU AND 655 FOR MUTSUKI.
URIE AND SHIRAZU HAVE RC* FACTORS ON THE HIGHER SIDE, SINCE THEY'VE BEEN USING THEIR ABILITIES.

*Red Child (RC) Cell

Cells found in abundance in Ghouls.
Believed to be involved in the formation of Kagune.
Named for their resemblance to a curled-up fetus.
Also present in small amounts in humans, with average levels falling between 200 and 500.

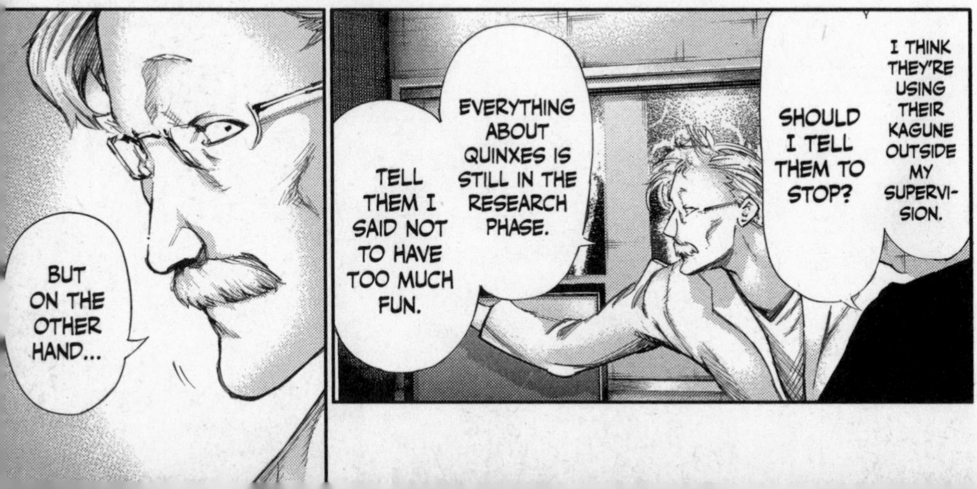
I THINK THEY'RE USING THEIR KAGUNE OUTSIDE MY SUPERVISION.
SHOULD I TELL THEM TO STOP?
EVERYTHING ABOUT QUINXES IS STILL IN THE RESEARCH PHASE.
TELL THEM I SAID NOT TO HAVE TOO MUCH FUN.
BUT ON THE OTHER HAND...

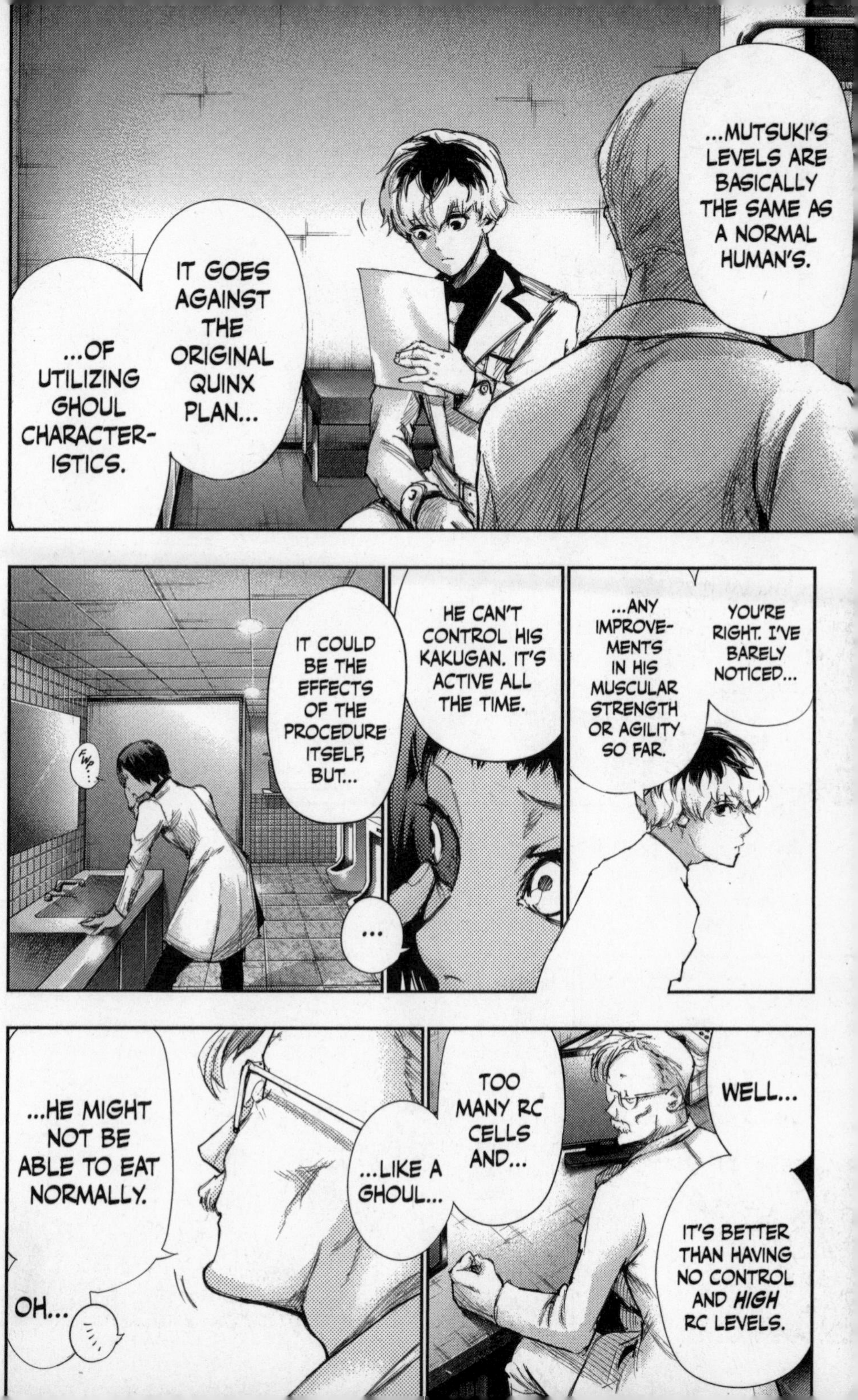
...MUTSUKI'S LEVELS ARE BASICALLY THE SAME AS A NORMAL HUMAN'S.
IT GOES AGAINST THE ORIGINAL QUINX PLAN...
...OF UTILIZING GHOUL CHARACTER-ISTICS.
YOU'RE RIGHT. I'VE BARELY NOTICED...
...ANY IMPROVE-MENTS IN HIS MUSCULAR STRENGTH OR AGILITY SO FAR.
HE CAN'T CONTROL HIS KAKUGAN. IT'S ACTIVE ALL THE TIME.
IT COULD BE THE EFFECTS OF THE PROCEDURE ITSELF, BUT...
...
FWP...
WELL...
IT'S BETTER THAN HAVING NO CONTROL AND *HIGH* RC LEVELS.
TOO MANY RC CELLS AND...
...LIKE A GHOUL...
...HE MIGHT NOT BE ABLE TO EAT NORMALLY.
OH...

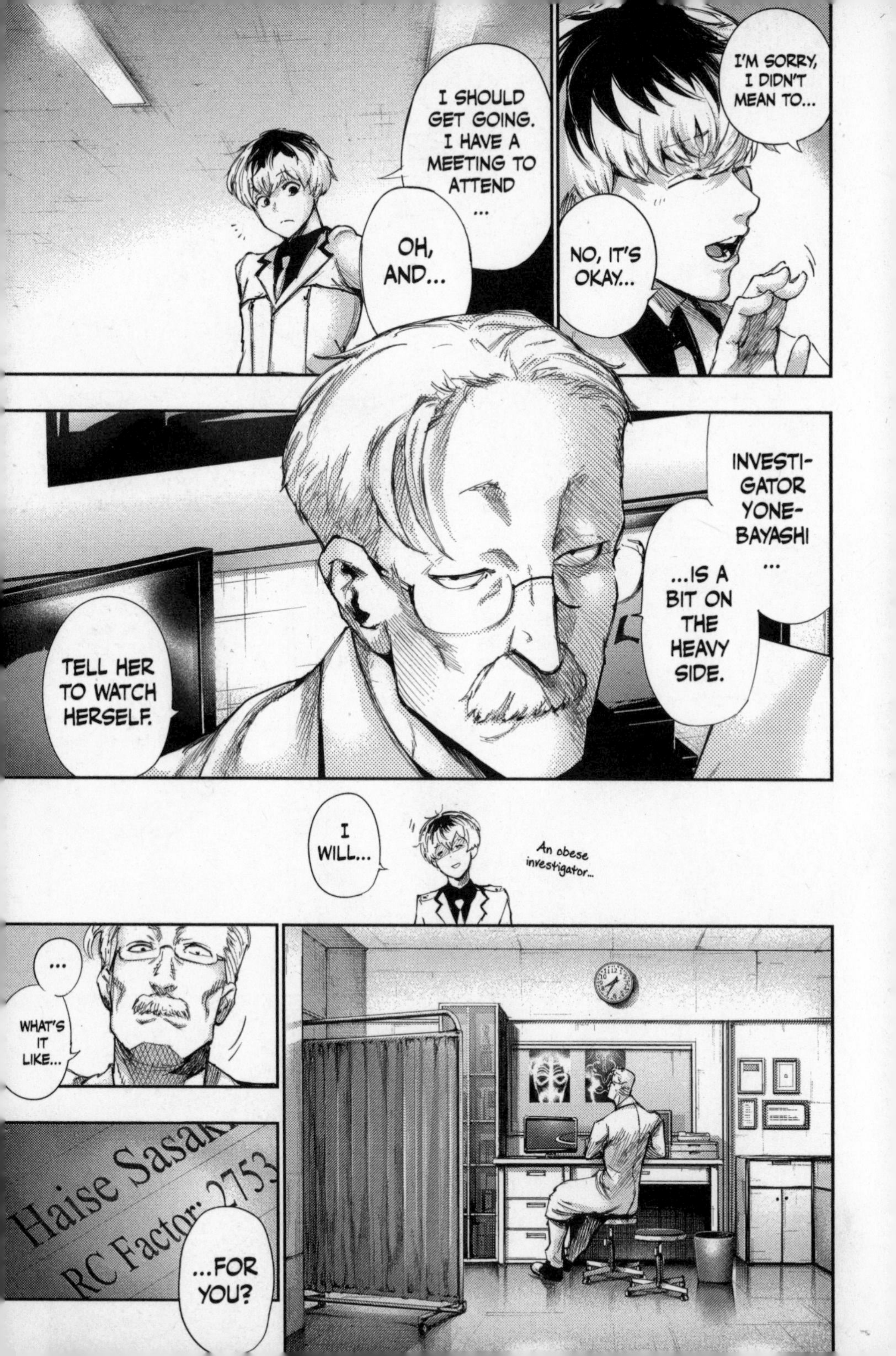
I'M SORRY, I DIDN'T MEAN TO...
NO, IT'S OKAY...
I SHOULD GET GOING. I HAVE A MEETING TO ATTEND ...
OH, AND...
INVESTI-GATOR YONE-BAYASHI ...
...IS A BIT ON THE HEAVY SIDE.
TELL HER TO WATCH HERSELF.
I WILL...
An obese investigator...
...
WHAT'S IT LIKE...
Haise Sasak
RC Factor: 2753
...FOR YOU?

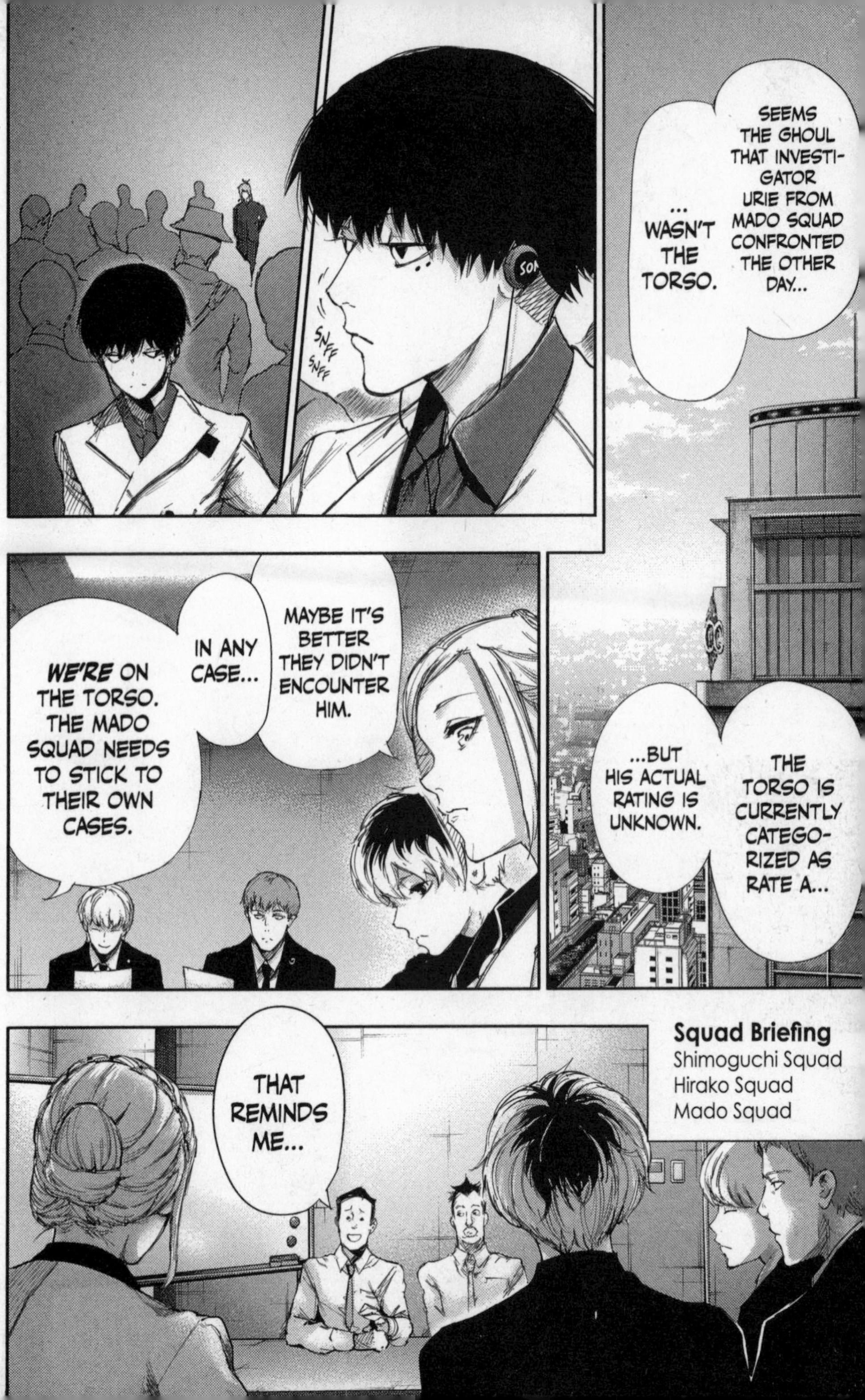
SEEMS THE GHOUL THAT INVESTIGATOR URIE FROM MADO SQUAD CONFRONTED THE OTHER DAY...
...WASN'T THE TORSO.
THE TORSO IS CURRENTLY CATEGORIZED AS RATE A...
...BUT HIS ACTUAL RATING IS UNKNOWN.
SNFF SNFF
MAYBE IT'S BETTER THEY DIDN'T ENCOUNTER HIM.
IN ANY CASE...
WE'RE ON THE TORSO. THE MADO SQUAD NEEDS TO STICK TO THEIR OWN CASES.
Squad Briefing
Shimoguchi Squad
Hirako Squad
Mado Squad
THAT REMINDS ME...

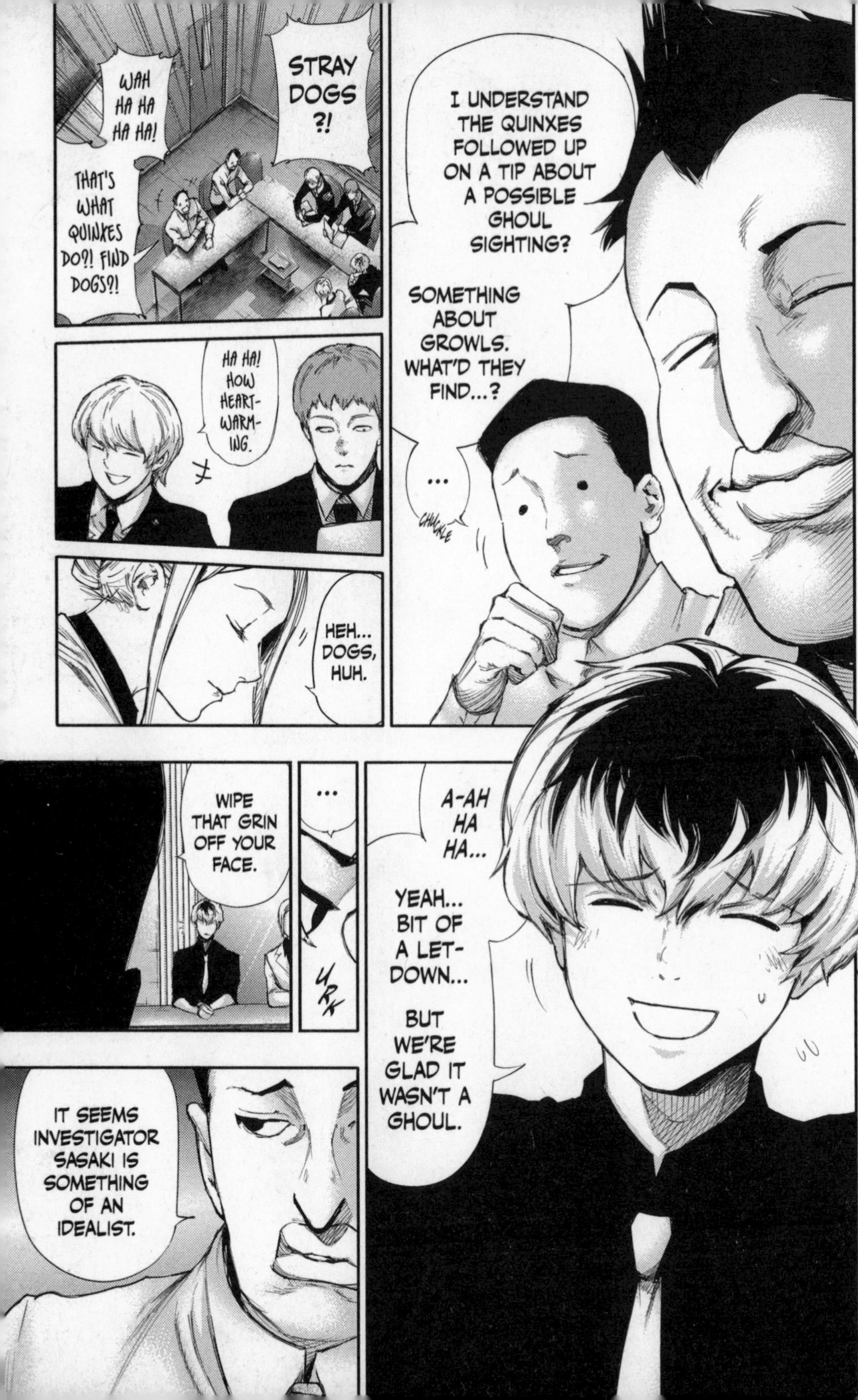
I UNDERSTAND THE QUINXES FOLLOWED UP ON A TIP ABOUT A POSSIBLE GHOUL SIGHTING?
SOMETHING ABOUT GROWLS. WHAT'D THEY FIND...?
...
CHUCKLE
STRAY DOGS ?!
WAH HA HA HA HA!
THAT'S WHAT QUINXES DO?! FIND DOGS?!
HA HA! HOW HEART-WARMING.
HEH... DOGS, HUH.
A-AH HA HA...
YEAH... BIT OF A LET-DOWN...
BUT WE'RE GLAD IT WASN'T A GHOUL.
...
URK
WIPE THAT GRIN OFF YOUR FACE.
IT SEEMS INVESTIGATOR SASAKI IS SOMETHING OF AN IDEALIST.

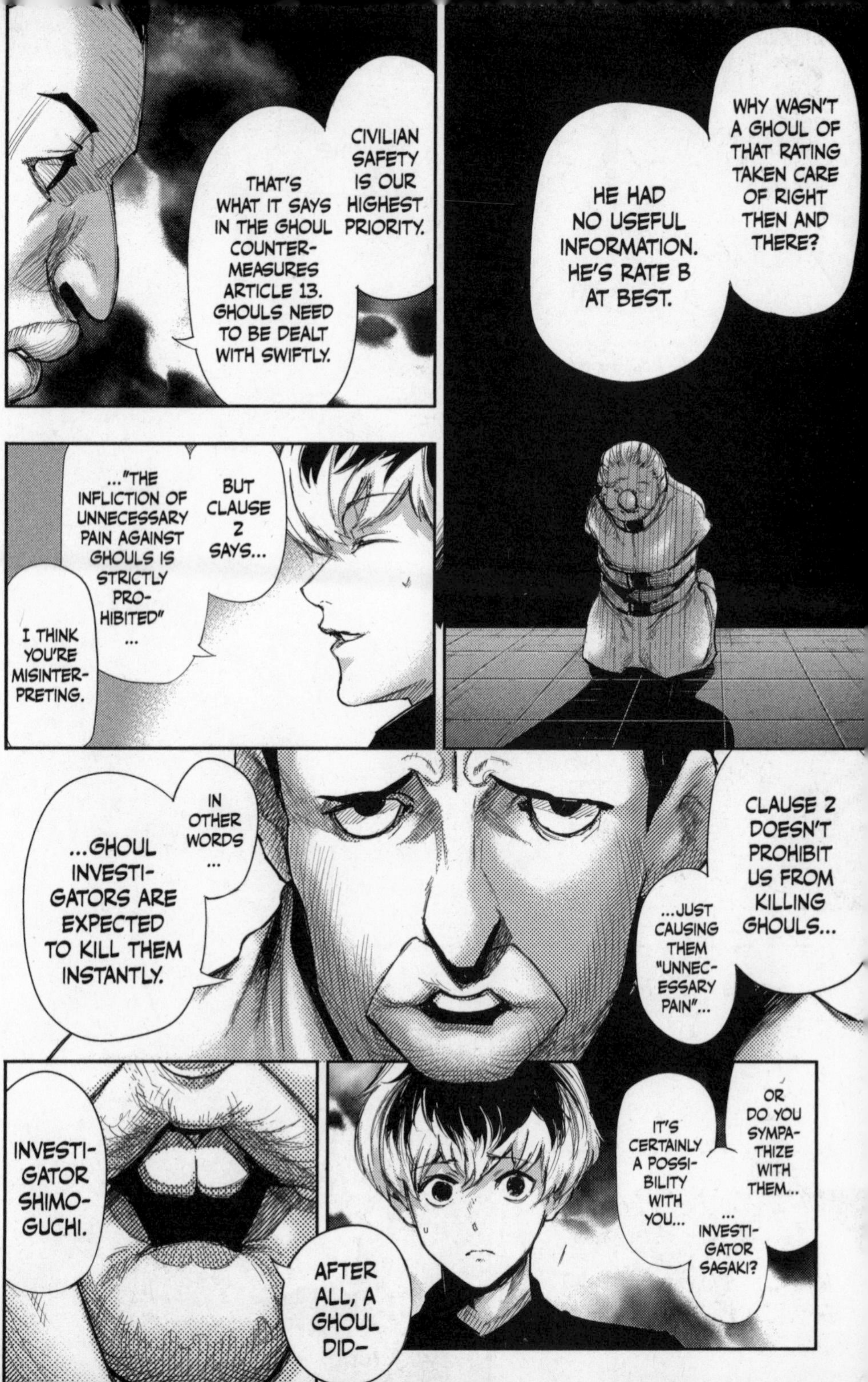
WHY WASN'T A GHOUL OF THAT RATING TAKEN CARE OF RIGHT THEN AND THERE?
HE HAD NO USEFUL INFORMATION. HE'S RATE B AT BEST.
CIVILIAN SAFETY IS OUR HIGHEST PRIORITY.
THAT'S WHAT IT SAYS IN THE GHOUL COUNTER-MEASURES ARTICLE 13. GHOULS NEED TO BE DEALT WITH SWIFTLY.
BUT CLAUSE 2 SAYS...
..."THE INFLICTION OF UNNECESSARY PAIN AGAINST GHOULS IS STRICTLY PRO-HIBITED" ...
I THINK YOU'RE MISINTER-PRETING.
CLAUSE 2 DOESN'T PROHIBIT US FROM KILLING GHOULS...
...JUST CAUSING THEM "UNNEC-ESSARY PAIN"...
IN OTHER WORDS ...
...GHOUL INVESTI-GATORS ARE EXPECTED TO KILL THEM INSTANTLY.
OR DO YOU SYMPA-THIZE WITH THEM...
... INVESTI-GATOR SASAKI?
IT'S CERTAINLY A POSSI-BILITY WITH YOU...
AFTER ALL, A GHOUL DID-
INVESTI-GATOR SHIMO-GUCHI.

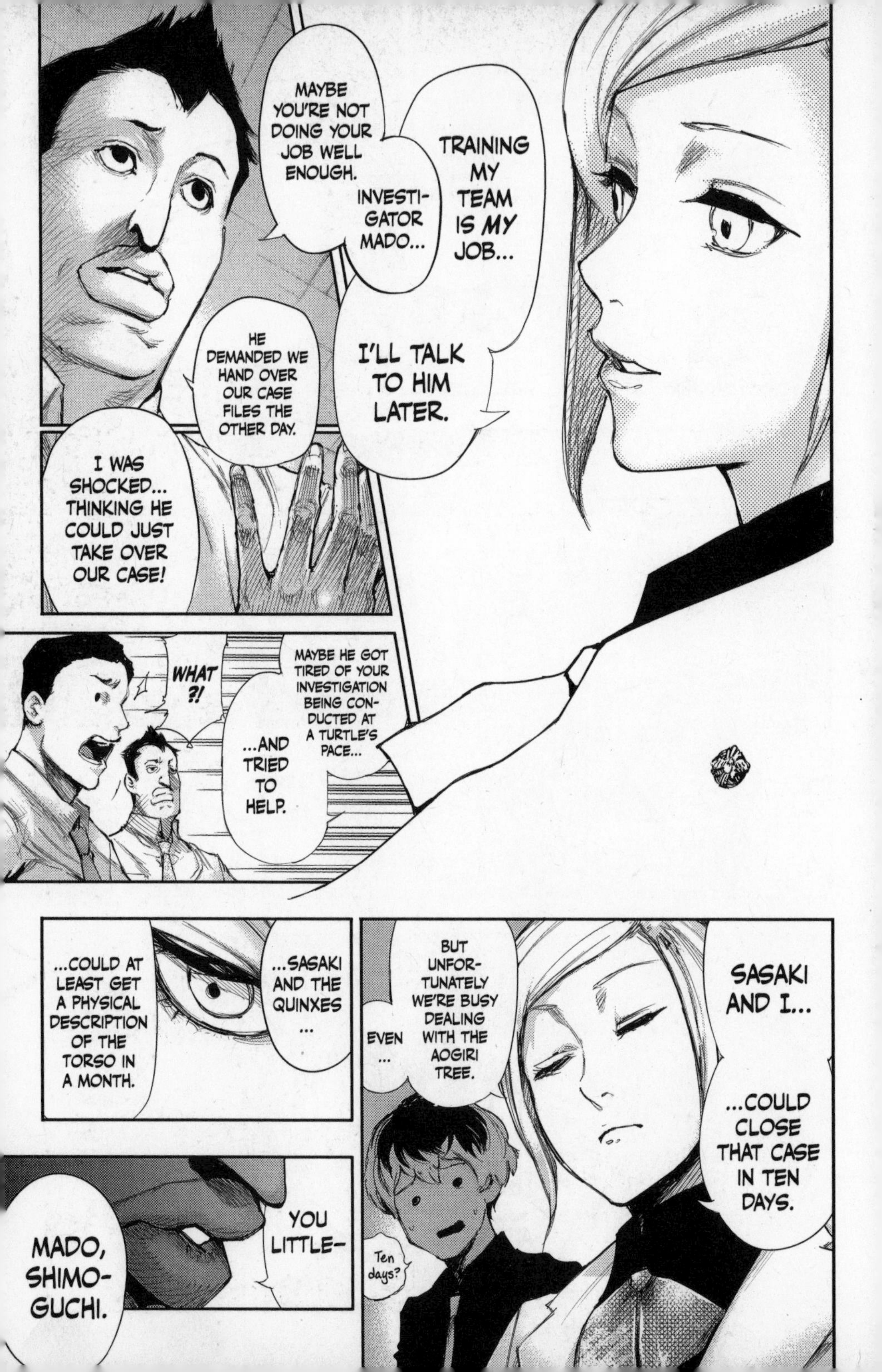
TRAINING MY TEAM IS MY JOB...
MAYBE YOU'RE NOT DOING YOUR JOB WELL ENOUGH.
INVESTI-GATOR MADO...
I'LL TALK TO HIM LATER.
HE DEMANDED WE HAND OVER OUR CASE FILES THE OTHER DAY.
I WAS SHOCKED... THINKING HE COULD JUST TAKE OVER OUR CASE!
MAYBE HE GOT TIRED OF YOUR INVESTIGATION BEING CON-DUCTED AT A TURTLE'S PACE...
...AND TRIED TO HELP.
WHAT?!
SASAKI AND I...
...COULD CLOSE THAT CASE IN TEN DAYS.
BUT UNFOR-TUNATELY WE'RE BUSY DEALING WITH THE AOGIRI TREE.
EVEN...
Ten days?
...SASAKI AND THE QUINXES...
...COULD AT LEAST GET A PHYSICAL DESCRIPTION OF THE TORSO IN A MONTH.
YOU LITTLE-
MADO, SHIMO-GUCHI.

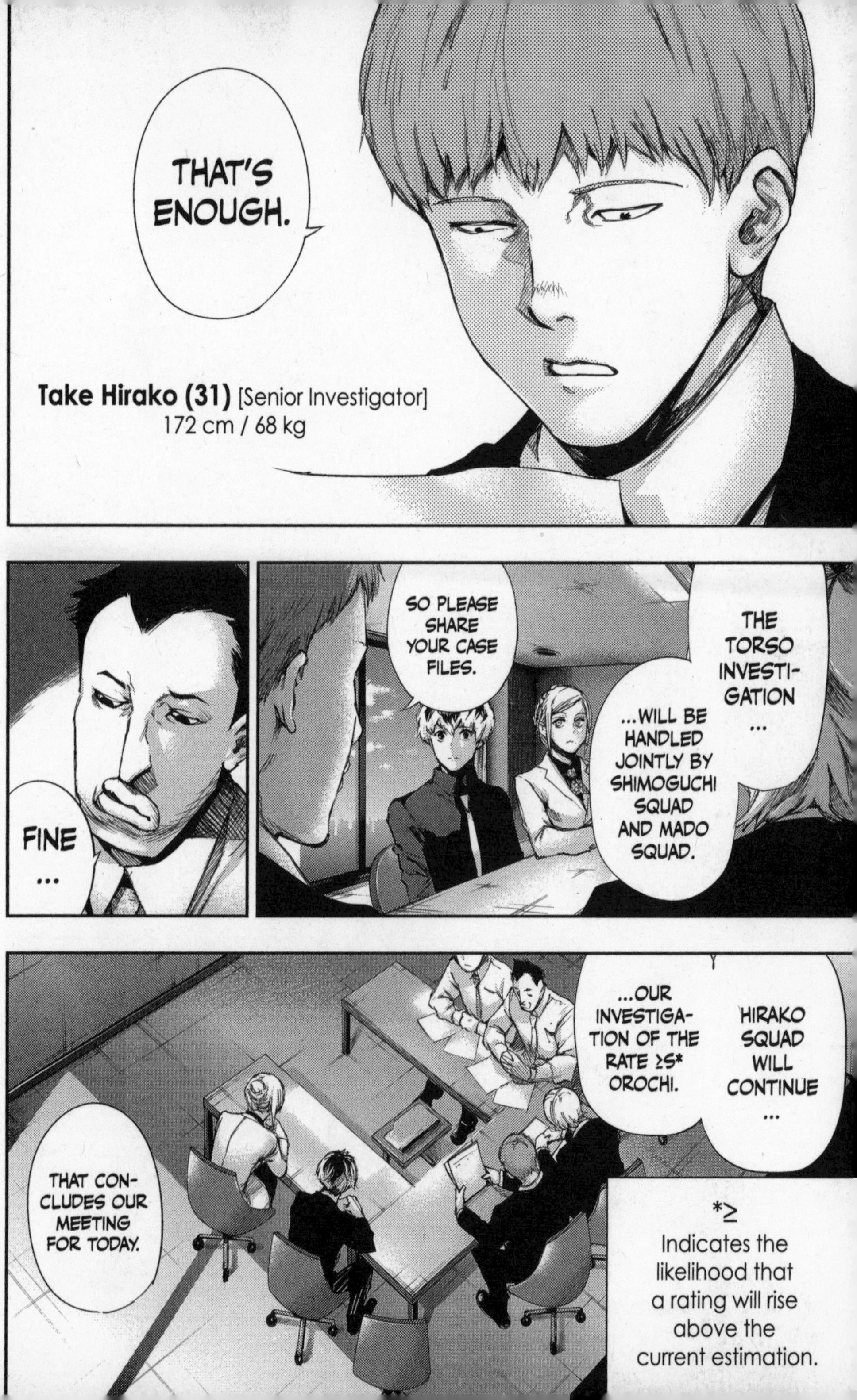
THAT'S ENOUGH.
Take Hirako (31) [Senior Investigator] 172 cm / 68 kg
THE TORSO INVESTIGATION...
...WILL BE HANDLED JOINTLY BY SHIMOGUCHI SQUAD AND MADO SQUAD.
SO PLEASE SHARE YOUR CASE FILES.
FINE...
HIRAKO SQUAD WILL CONTINUE...
...OUR INVESTIGATION OF THE RATE ≥S* OROCHI.
*≥ Indicates the likelihood that a rating will rise above the current estimation.
THAT CONCLUDES OUR MEETING FOR TODAY.

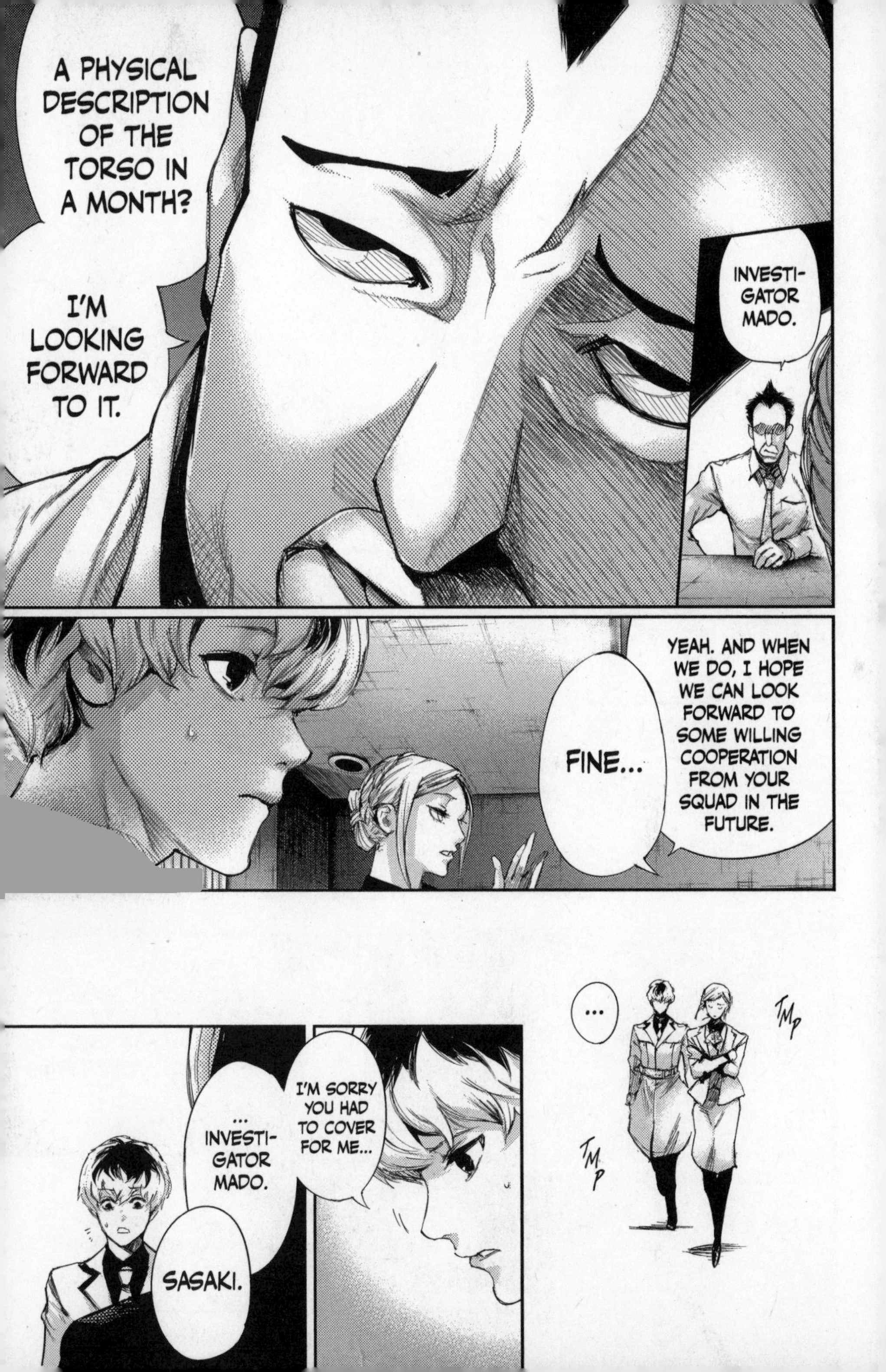
A PHYSICAL DESCRIPTION OF THE TORSO IN A MONTH?
I'M LOOKING FORWARD TO IT.
INVESTI-GATOR MADO.
YEAH. AND WHEN WE DO, I HOPE WE CAN LOOK FORWARD TO SOME WILLING COOPERATION FROM YOUR SQUAD IN THE FUTURE.
FINE...
TMP
...
TMP
I'M SORRY YOU HAD TO COVER FOR ME...
... INVESTI-GATOR MADO.
SASAKI.

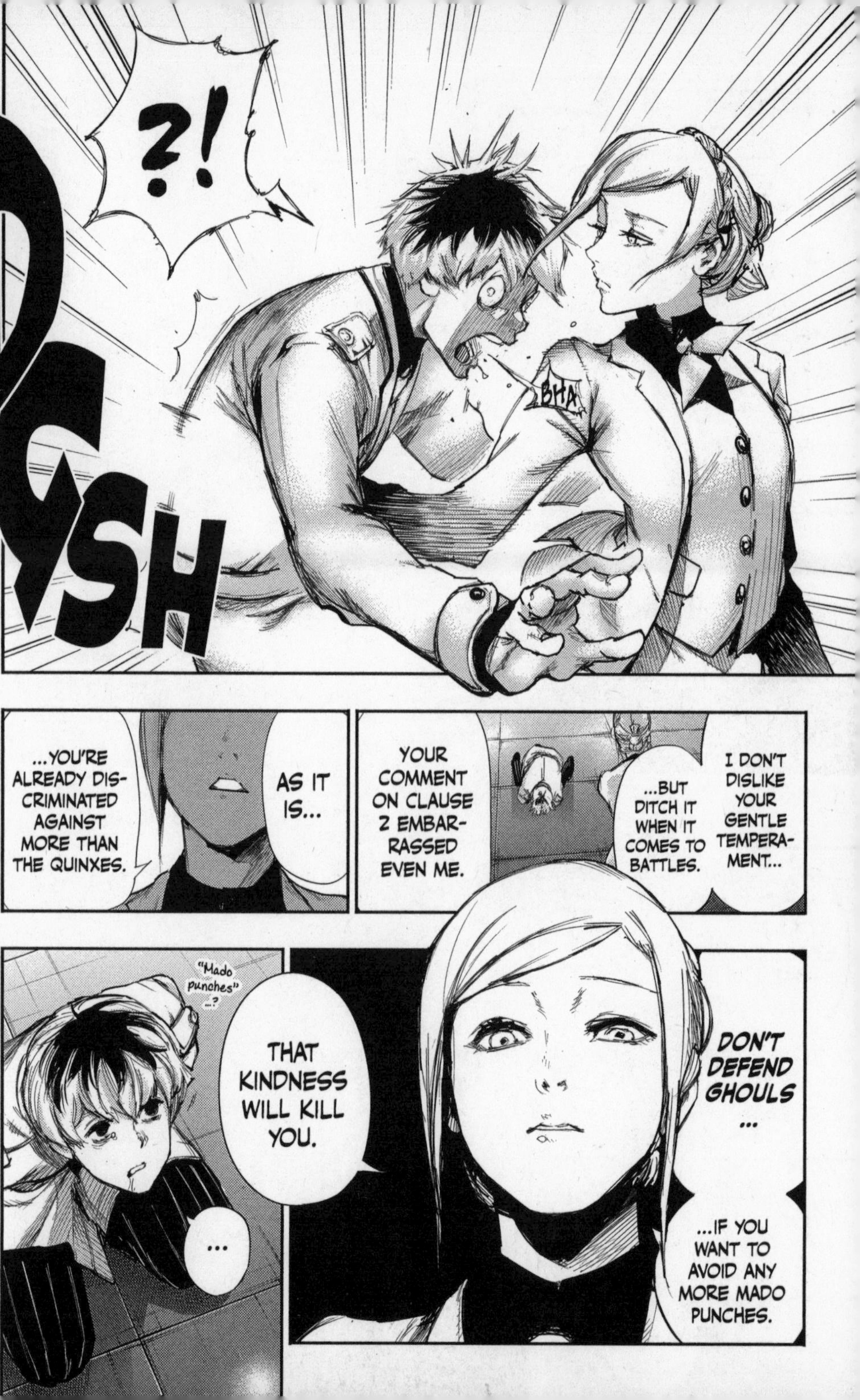
?!
BHA
DGSH
I DON'T DISLIKE YOUR GENTLE TEMPERAMENT...
...BUT DITCH IT WHEN IT COMES TO BATTLES.
YOUR COMMENT ON CLAUSE 2 EMBARRASSED EVEN ME.
AS IT IS...
...YOU'RE ALREADY DISCRIMINATED AGAINST MORE THAN THE QUINXES.
DON'T DEFEND GHOULS...
...IF YOU WANT TO AVOID ANY MORE MADO PUNCHES.
THAT KINDNESS WILL KILL YOU.
"Mado punches" ...?
...

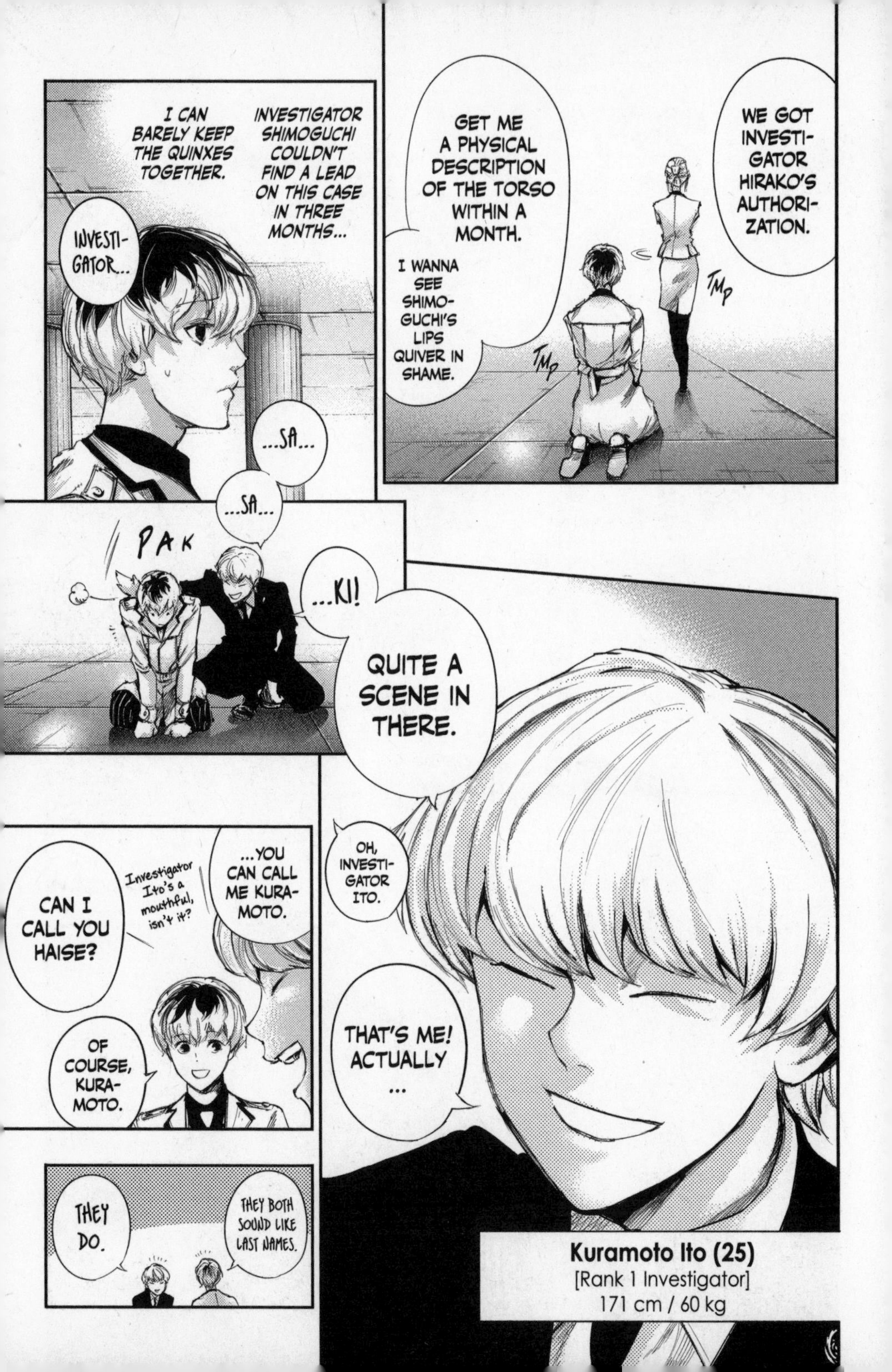
WE GOT INVESTI-GATOR HIRAKO'S AUTHORI-ZATION.
TMP
GET ME A PHYSICAL DESCRIPTION OF THE TORSO WITHIN A MONTH.
I WANNA SEE SHIMO-GUCHI'S LIPS QUIVER IN SHAME.
TMP
INVESTIGATOR SHIMOGUCHI COULDN'T FIND A LEAD ON THIS CASE IN THREE MONTHS...
I CAN BARELY KEEP THE QUINXES TOGETHER.
INVESTI-GATOR...
...SA...
...SA...
PAK
...KI!
QUITE A SCENE IN THERE.
OH, INVESTI-GATOR ITO.
THAT'S ME! ACTUALLY ...
Kuramoto Ito (25)
[Rank 1 Investigator]
171 cm / 60 kg
...YOU CAN CALL ME KURA-MOTO.
Investigator Ito's a mouthful, isn't it?
CAN I CALL YOU HAISE?
OF COURSE, KURA-MOTO.
THEY BOTH SOUND LIKE LAST NAMES.
THEY DO.

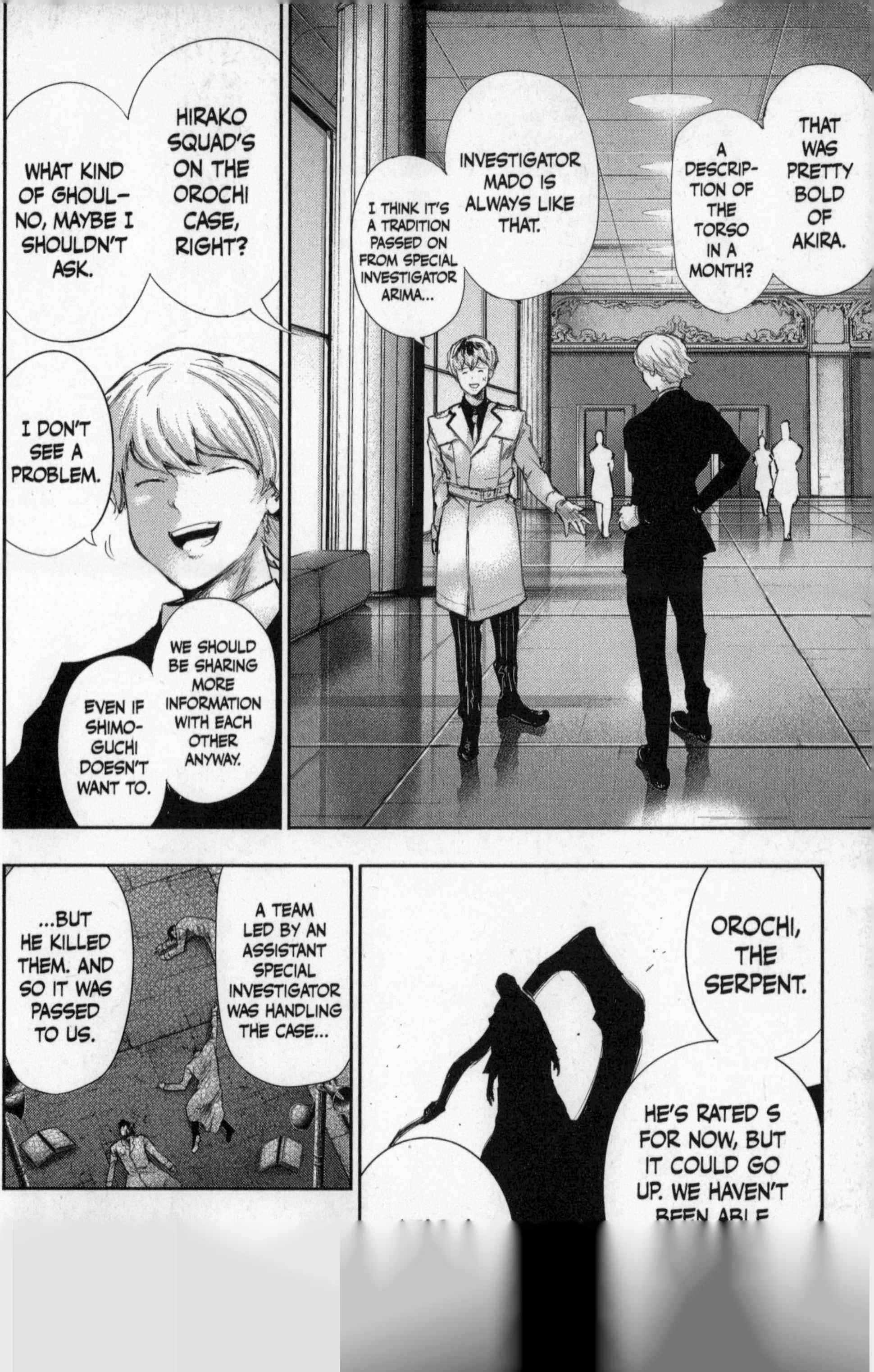
THAT WAS PRETTY BOLD OF AKIRA.
A DESCRIPTION OF THE TORSO IN A MONTH?
INVESTIGATOR MADO IS ALWAYS LIKE THAT.
I THINK IT'S A TRADITION PASSED ON FROM SPECIAL INVESTIGATOR ARIMA...
HIRAKO SQUAD'S ON THE OROCHI CASE, RIGHT?
WHAT KIND OF GHOUL— NO, MAYBE I SHOULDN'T ASK.
I DON'T SEE A PROBLEM.
WE SHOULD BE SHARING MORE INFORMATION WITH EACH OTHER ANYWAY.
EVEN IF SHIMOGUCHI DOESN'T WANT TO.
OROCHI, THE SERPENT.
HE'S RATED S FOR NOW, BUT IT COULD GO UP. WE HAVEN'T
A TEAM LED BY AN ASSISTANT SPECIAL INVESTIGATOR WAS HANDLING THE CASE...
...BUT HE KILLED THEM. AND SO IT WAS PASSED TO US.

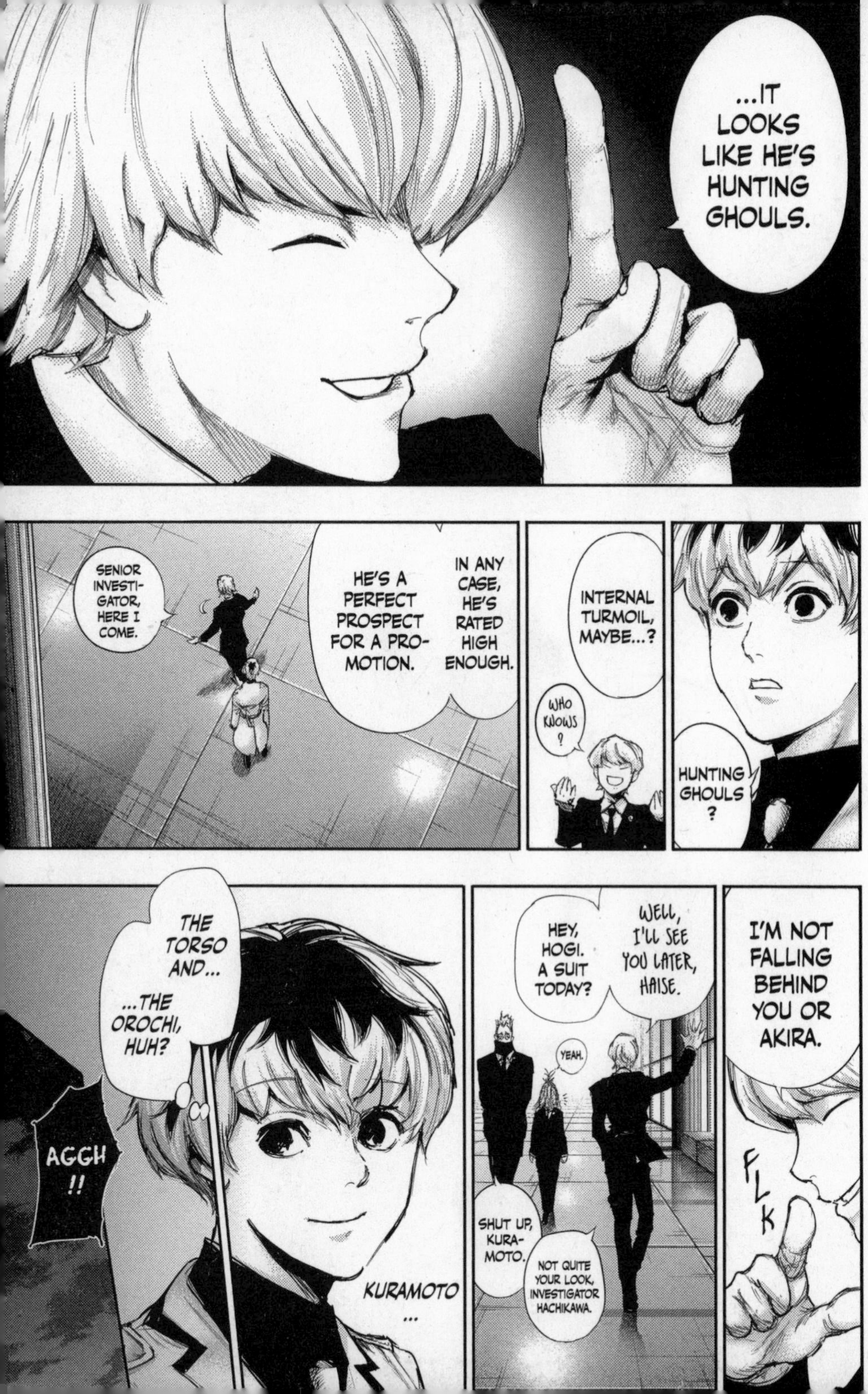
...IT LOOKS LIKE HE'S HUNTING GHOULS.
HUNTING GHOULS?
INTERNAL TURMOIL, MAYBE...?
WHO KNOWS?
IN ANY CASE, HE'S RATED HIGH ENOUGH.
HE'S A PERFECT PROSPECT FOR A PRO-MOTION.
SENIOR INVESTI-GATOR, HERE I COME.
I'M NOT FALLING BEHIND YOU OR AKIRA.
FLK
WELL, I'LL SEE YOU LATER, HAISE.
HEY, HOGI. A SUIT TODAY?
YEAH.
NOT QUITE YOUR LOOK, INVESTIGATOR HACHIKAWA.
SHUT UP, KURA-MOTO.
THE TORSO AND...
...THE OROCHI, HUH?
AGGH!!
KURAMOTO...

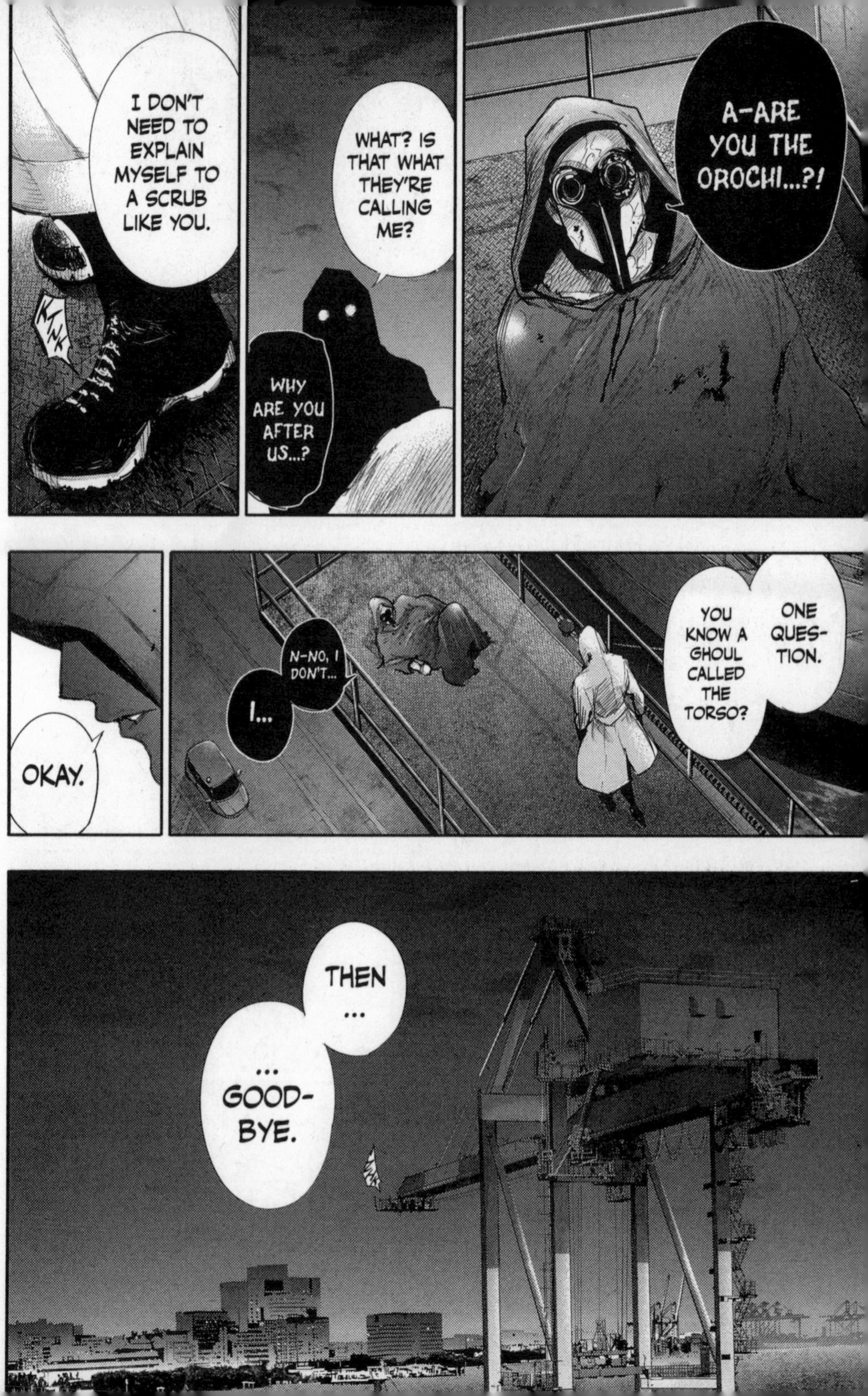
A-ARE YOU THE OROCHI...?!
WHAT? IS THAT WHAT THEY'RE CALLING ME?
WHY ARE YOU AFTER US...?
I DON'T NEED TO EXPLAIN MYSELF TO A SCRUB LIKE YOU.
ONE QUES-TION.
YOU KNOW A GHOUL CALLED THE TORSO?
N-NO, I DON'T...
I...
OKAY.
THEN...
...GOOD-BYE.

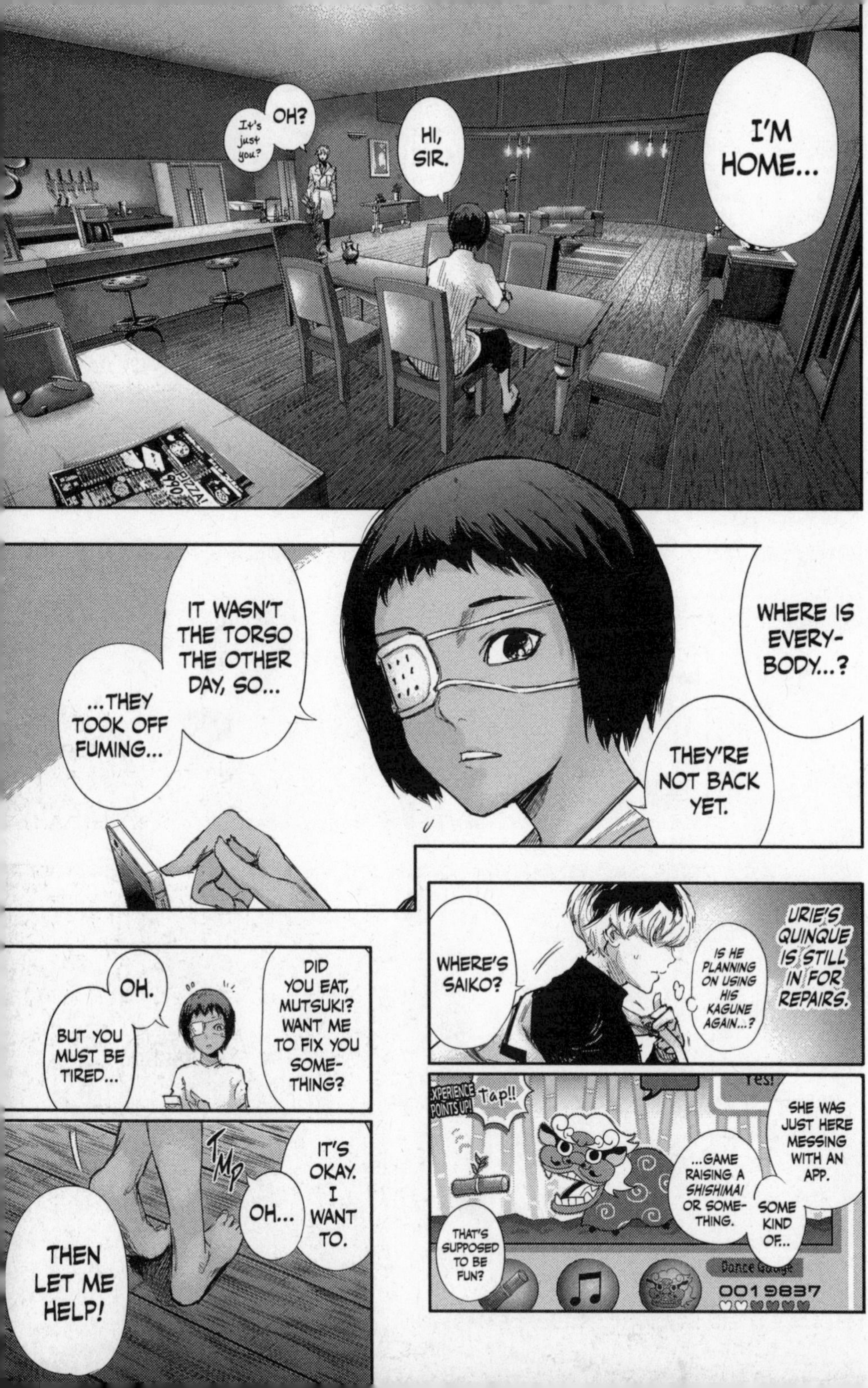
I'M HOME...
HI, SIR.
OH?
It's just you?
PIZZA! 990
WHERE IS EVERY-BODY...?
THEY'RE NOT BACK YET.
IT WASN'T THE TORSO THE OTHER DAY, SO...
...THEY TOOK OFF FUMING...
URIE'S QUINQUE IS STILL IN FOR REPAIRS.
IS HE PLANNING ON USING HIS KAGUNE AGAIN...?
WHERE'S SAIKO?
Yes!
SHE WAS JUST HERE MESSING WITH AN APP.
SOME KIND OF...
...GAME RAISING A SHISHIMAI OR SOME-THING.
Tap!!
EXPERIENCE POINTS UP!
THAT'S SUPPOSED TO BE FUN?
Dance Gauge
0019837
DID YOU EAT, MUTSUKI? WANT ME TO FIX YOU SOMETHING?
OH.
BUT YOU MUST BE TIRED...
IT'S OKAY. I WANT TO.
TMP
OH...
THEN LET ME HELP!

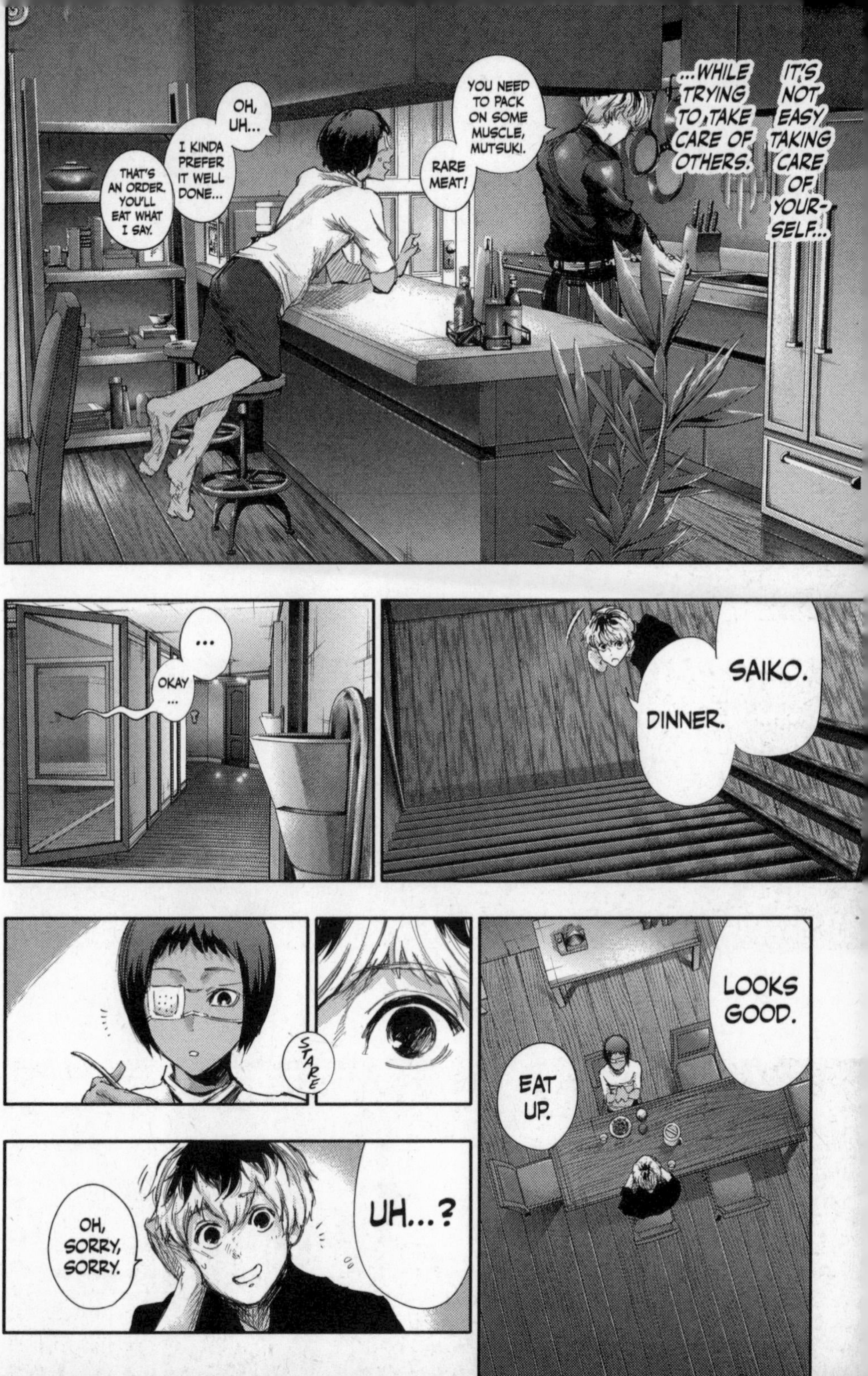
IT'S NOT EASY TAKING CARE OF YOURSELF...
...WHILE TRYING TO TAKE CARE OF OTHERS.
YOU NEED TO PACK ON SOME MUSCLE, MUTSUKI.
RARE MEAT!
OH, UH...
I KINDA PREFER IT WELL DONE...
THAT'S AN ORDER. YOU'LL EAT WHAT I SAY.
SAIKO.
DINNER.
...
OKAY...
LOOKS GOOD.
EAT UP.
STARE
UH...?
OH, SORRY, SORRY.

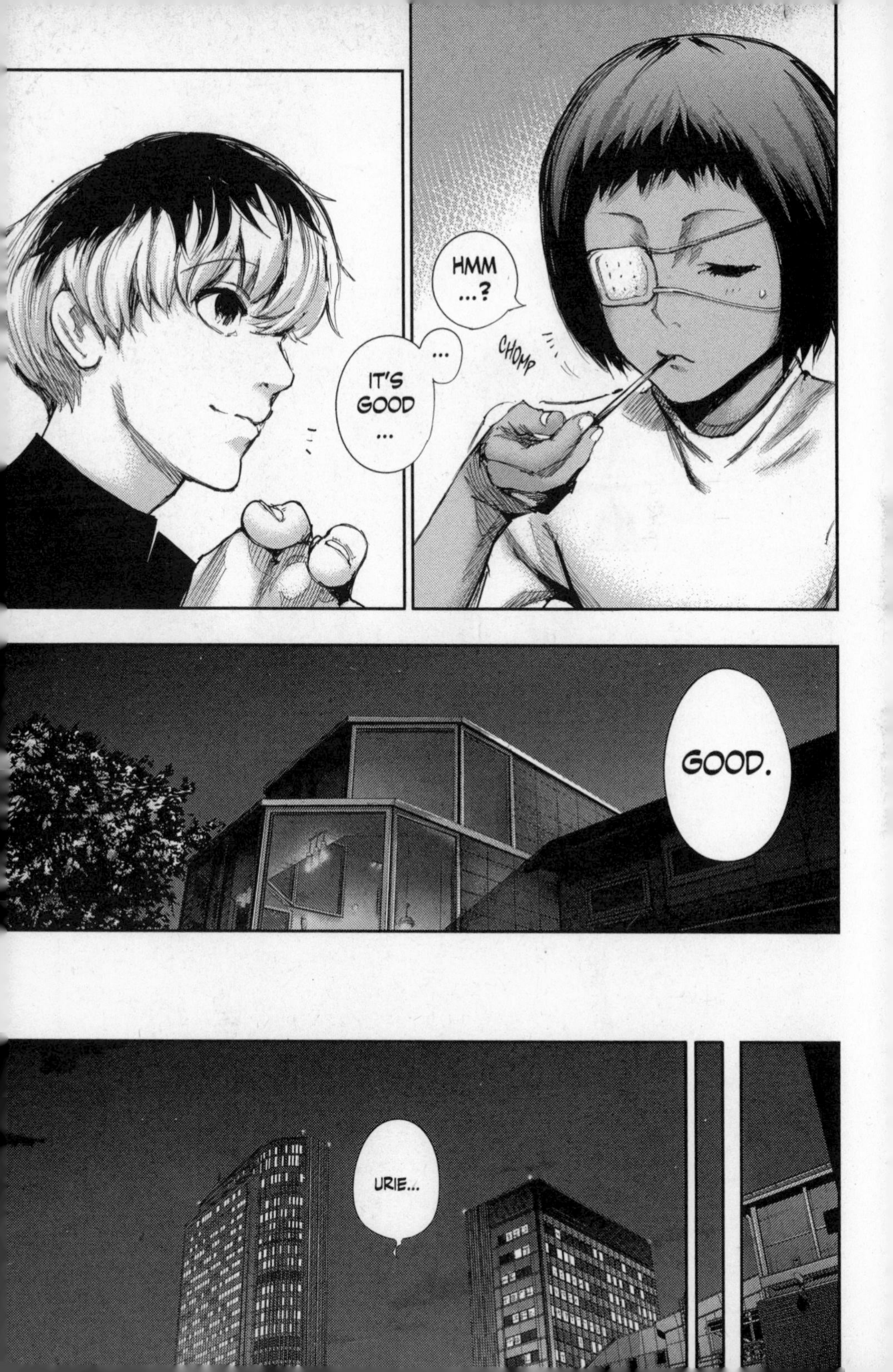

HMM ...?
CHOMP
...
IT'S GOOD ...
GOOD.
URIE...

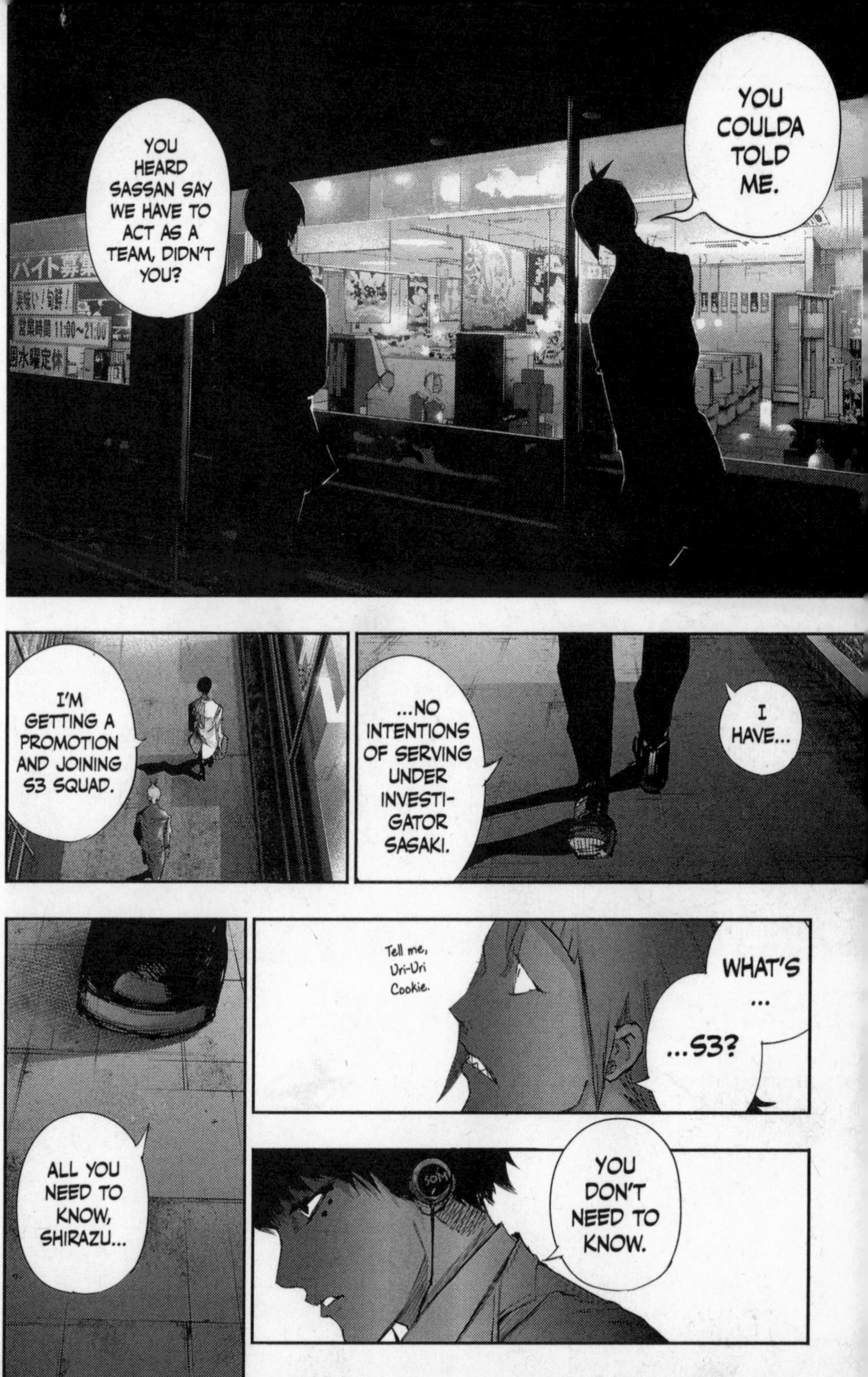
YOU COULDA TOLD ME.
YOU HEARD SASSAN SAY WE HAVE TO ACT AS A TEAM, DIDN'T YOU?
I HAVE...
...NO INTENTIONS OF SERVING UNDER INVESTI-GATOR SASAKI.
I'M GETTING A PROMOTION AND JOINING S3 SQUAD.
WHAT'S ...
...S3?
Tell me, Uri-Uri Cookie.
YOU DON'T NEED TO KNOW.
ALL YOU NEED TO KNOW, SHIRAZU...

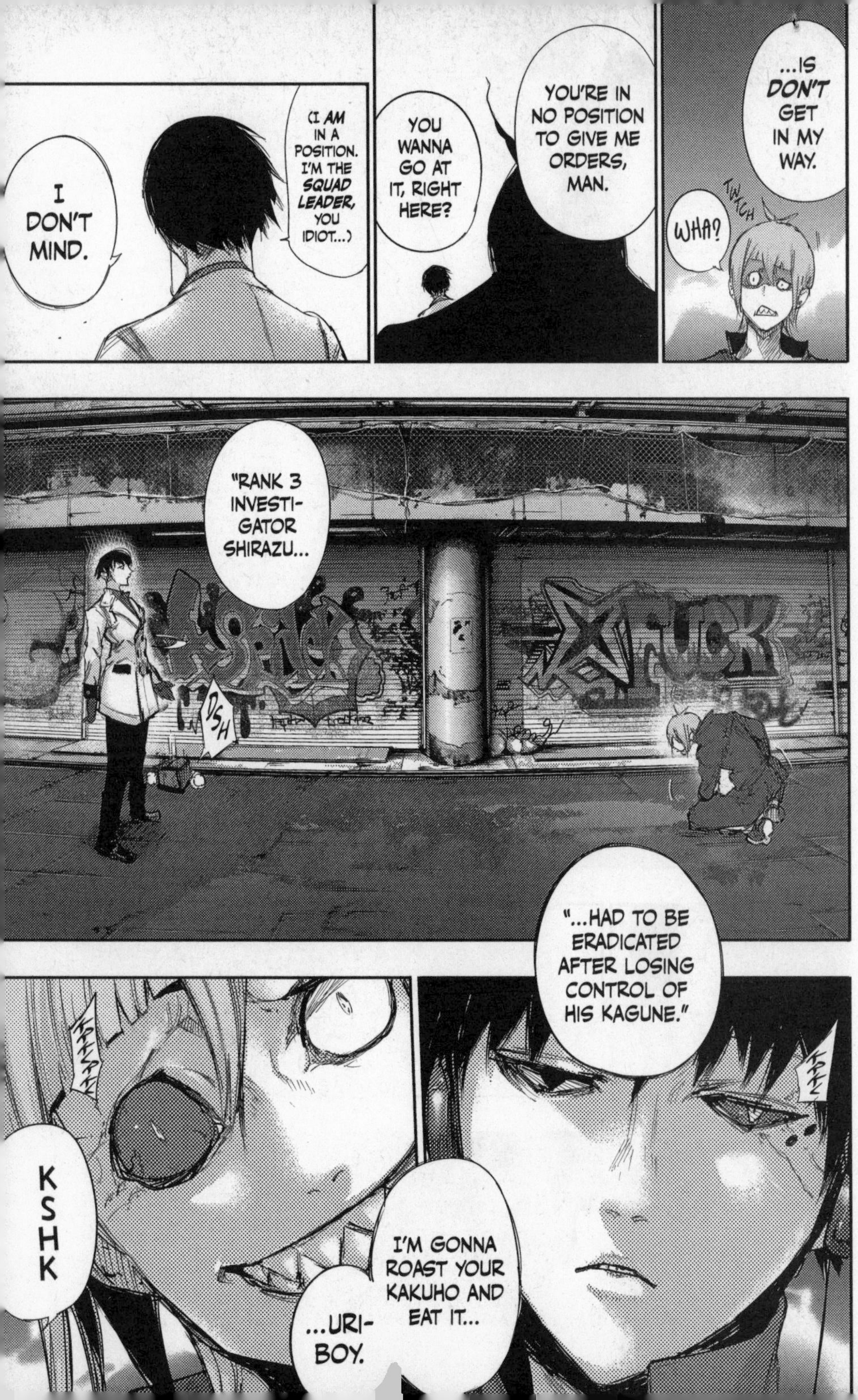
...IS DON'T GET IN MY WAY.
TWICH
WHA?
YOU'RE IN NO POSITION TO GIVE ME ORDERS, MAN.
YOU WANNA GO AT IT, RIGHT HERE?
(I AM IN A POSITION. I'M THE SQUAD LEADER, YOU IDIOT...)
I DON'T MIND.
"RANK 3 INVESTIGATOR SHIRAZU...
DSH
"...HAD TO BE ERADICATED AFTER LOSING CONTROL OF HIS KAGUNE."
KRKL
KRKLRKK
I'M GONNA ROAST YOUR KAKUHO AND EAT IT...
...URI-BOY.
KSHK

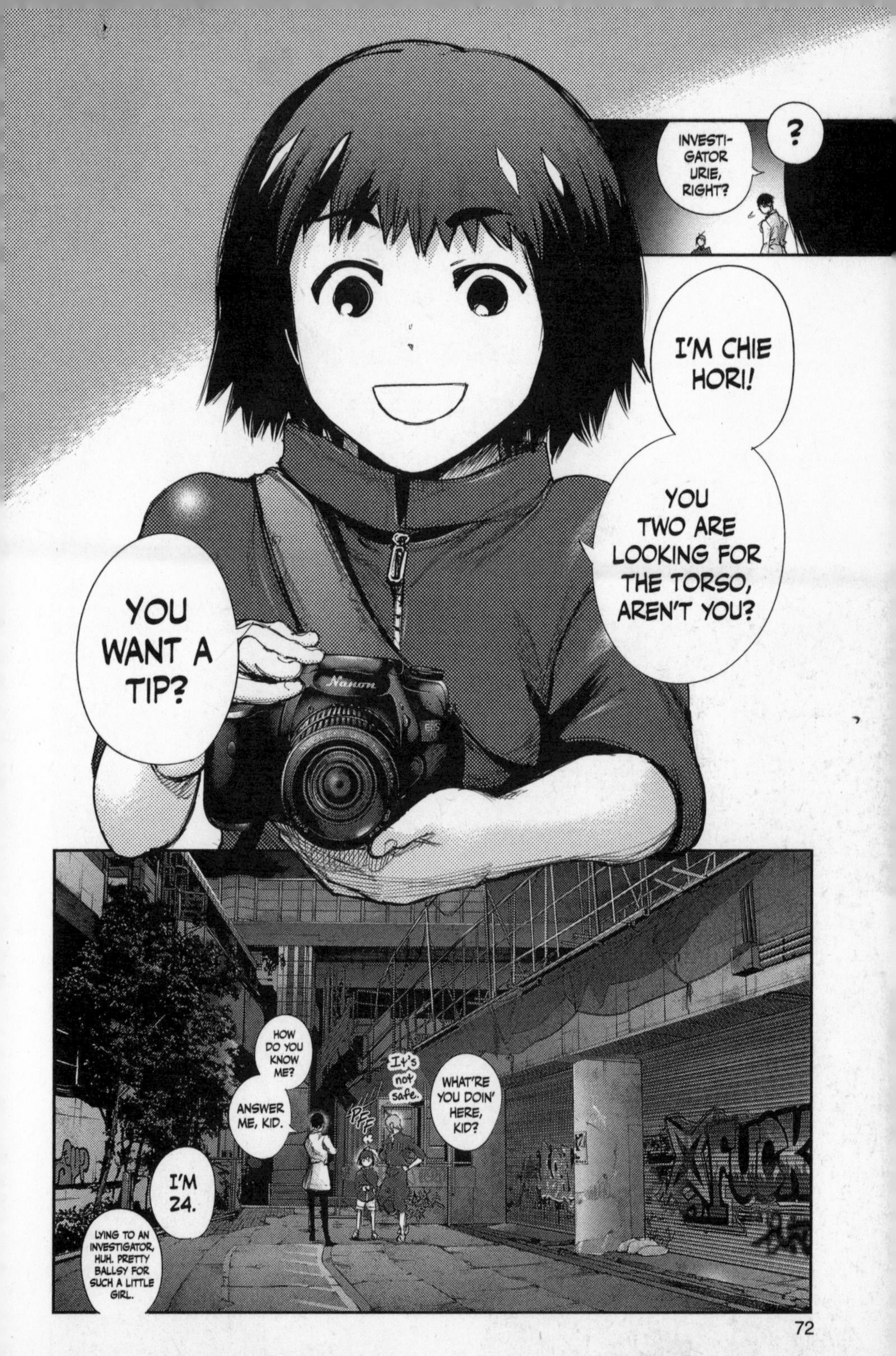
?
INVESTI-GATOR URIE, RIGHT?
I'M CHIE HORI!
YOU TWO ARE LOOKING FOR THE TORSO, AREN'T YOU?
YOU WANT A TIP?
WHAT'RE YOU DOIN' HERE, KID?
It's not safe.
PFF
HOW DO YOU KNOW ME?
ANSWER ME, KID.
I'M 24.
LYING TO AN INVESTIGATOR, HUH. PRETTY BALLSY FOR SUCH A LITTLE GIRL.

Bell :3

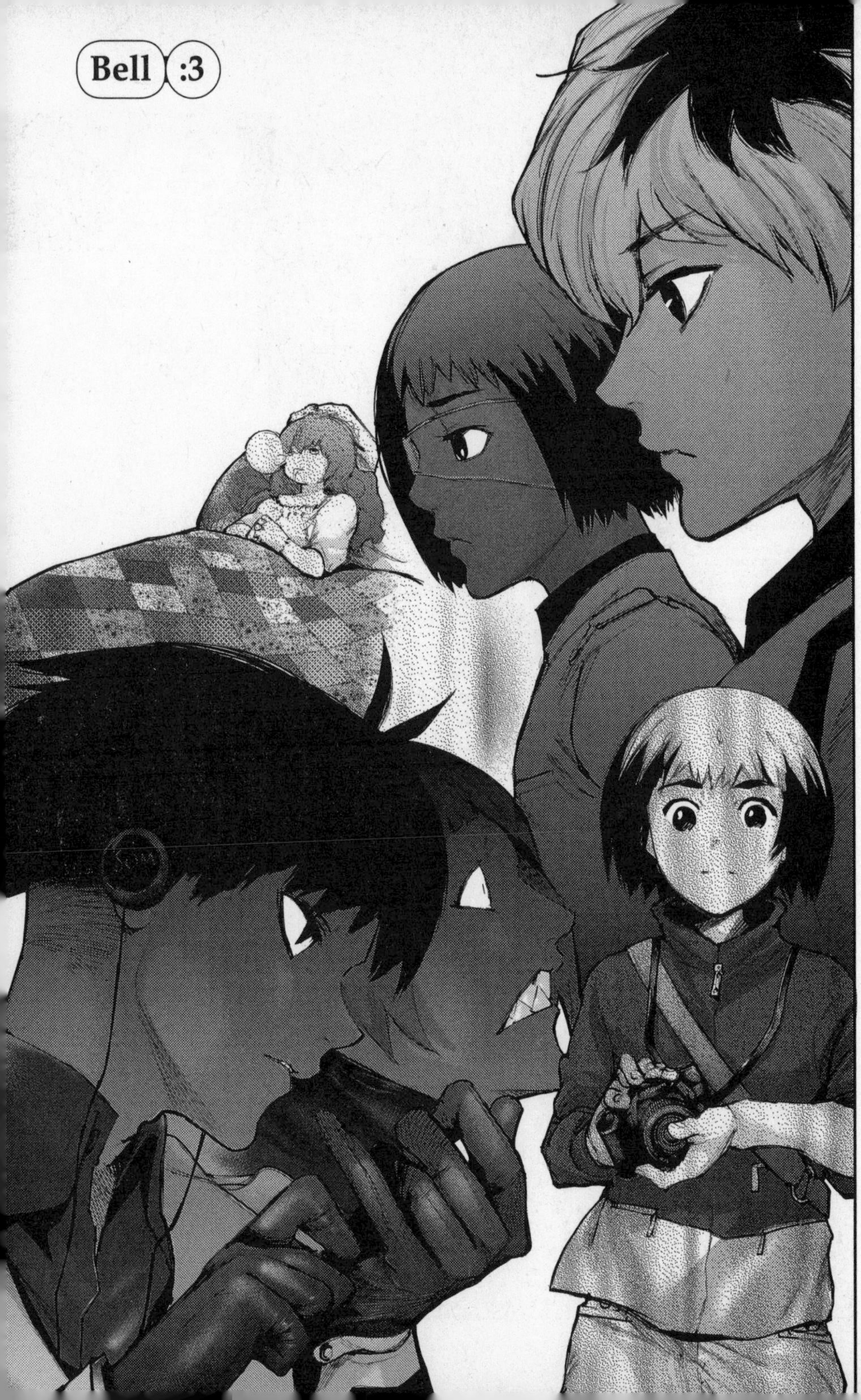

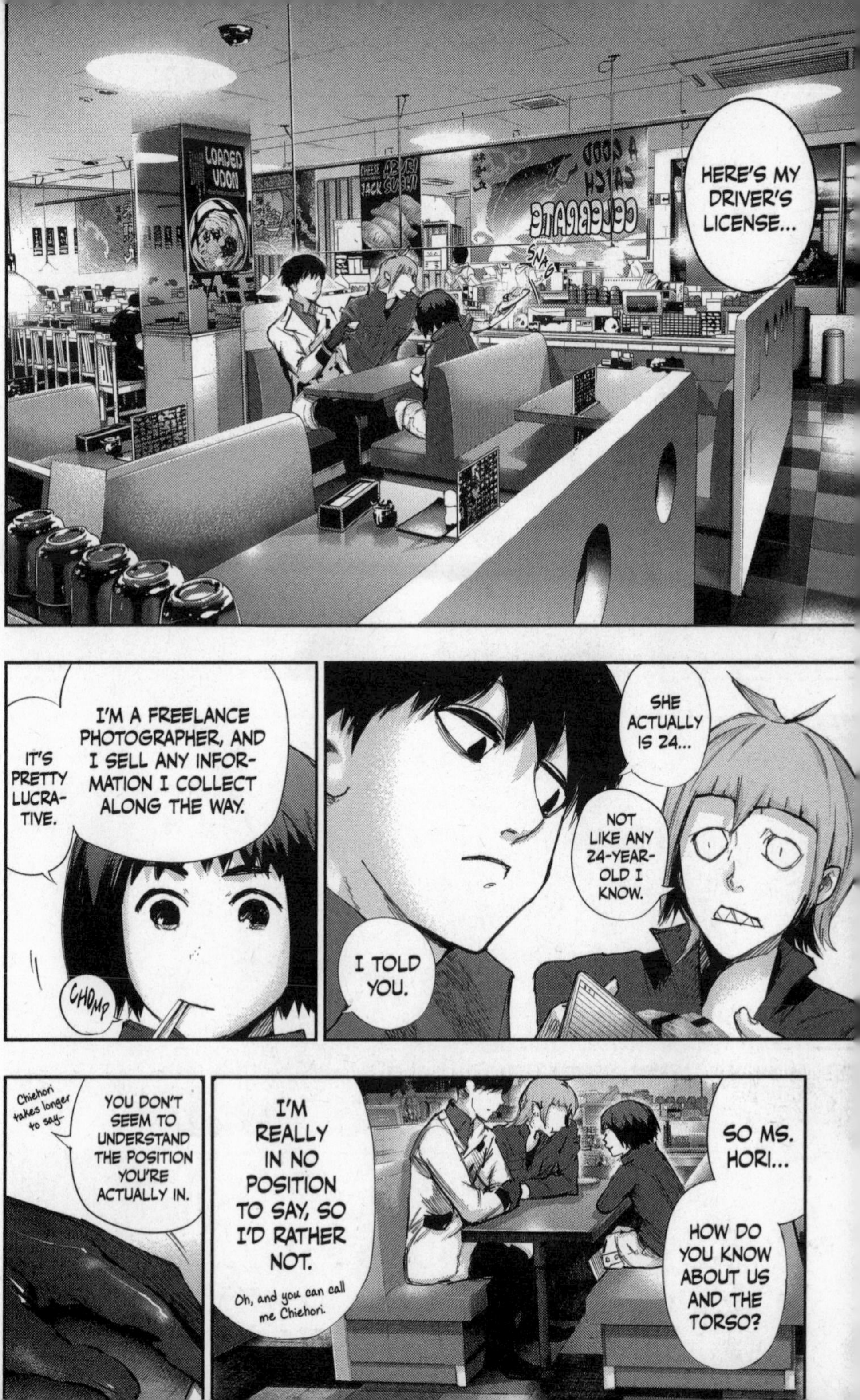
LOADED UDON
ABURI SUSHI
SNAG
HERE'S MY DRIVER'S LICENSE...
SHE ACTUALLY IS 24...
NOT LIKE ANY 24-YEAR-OLD I KNOW.
I TOLD YOU.
I'M A FREELANCE PHOTOGRAPHER, AND I SELL ANY INFORMATION I COLLECT ALONG THE WAY.
IT'S PRETTY LUCRATIVE.
CHOMP
SO MS. HORI...
HOW DO YOU KNOW ABOUT US AND THE TORSO?
I'M REALLY IN NO POSITION TO SAY, SO I'D RATHER NOT.
Oh, and you can call me Chiehori.
YOU DON'T SEEM TO UNDERSTAND THE POSITION YOU'RE ACTUALLY IN.
Chiehori takes longer to say...

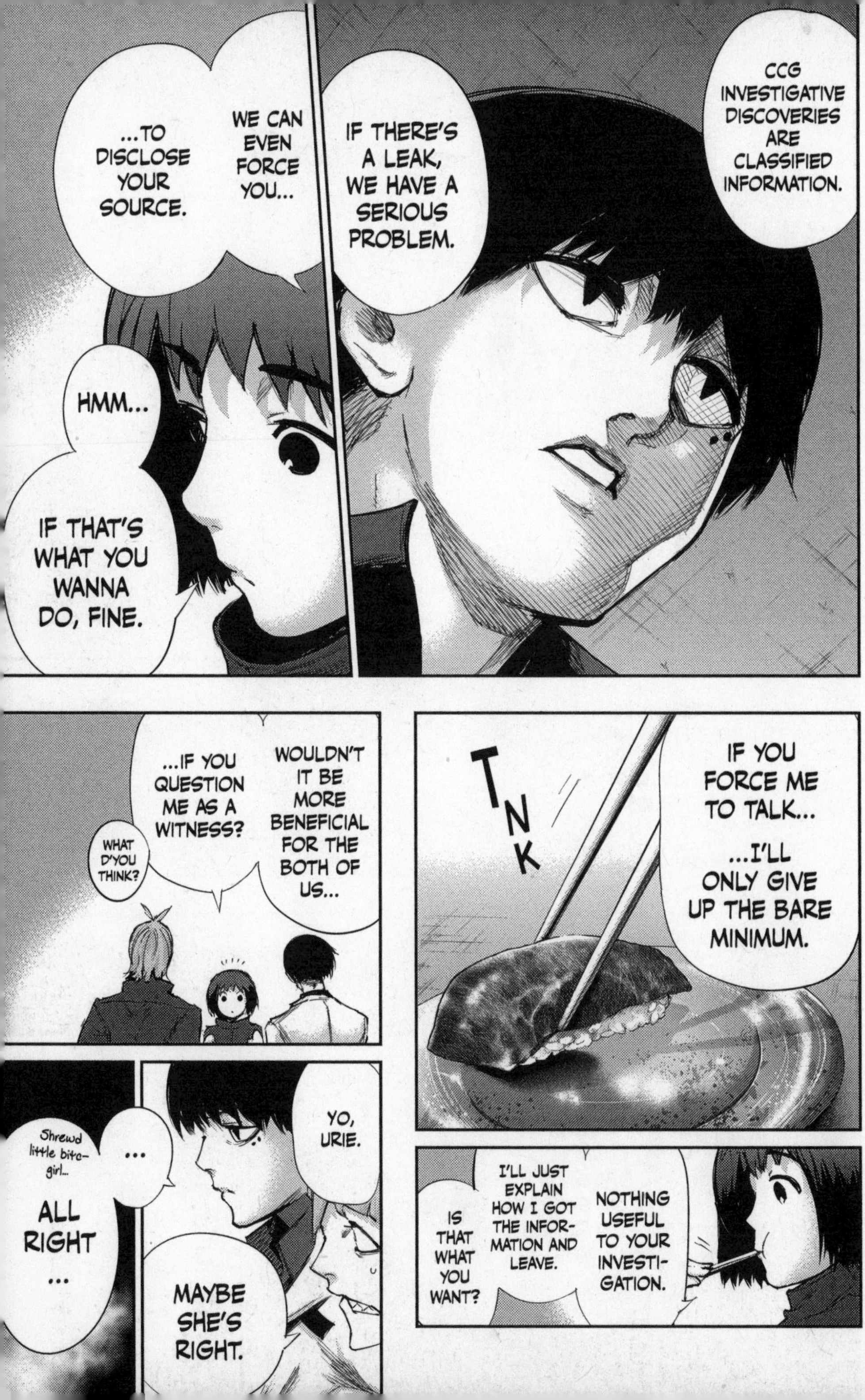
CCG INVESTIGATIVE DISCOVERIES ARE CLASSIFIED INFORMATION.
IF THERE'S A LEAK, WE HAVE A SERIOUS PROBLEM.
WE CAN EVEN FORCE YOU...
...TO DISCLOSE YOUR SOURCE.
HMM...
IF THAT'S WHAT YOU WANNA DO, FINE.
TNK
IF YOU FORCE ME TO TALK...
...I'LL ONLY GIVE UP THE BARE MINIMUM.
NOTHING USEFUL TO YOUR INVESTIGATION.
I'LL JUST EXPLAIN HOW I GOT THE INFORMATION AND LEAVE.
IS THAT WHAT YOU WANT?
WOULDN'T IT BE MORE BENEFICIAL FOR THE BOTH OF US...
...IF YOU QUESTION ME AS A WITNESS?
WHAT D'YOU THINK?
YO, URIE.
...
Shrewd little bite-girl...
MAYBE SHE'S RIGHT.
ALL RIGHT...

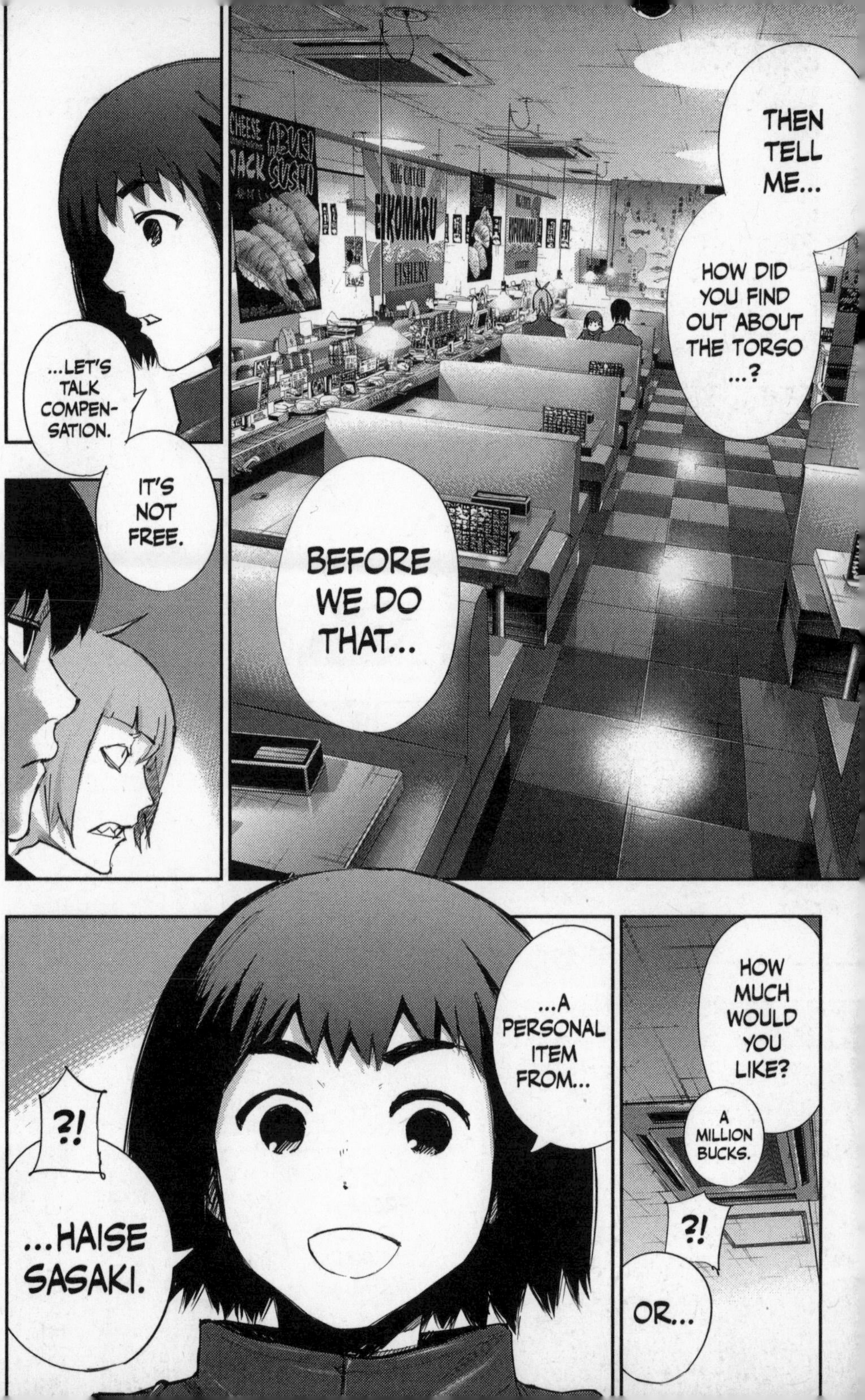
THEN TELL ME...
HOW DID YOU FIND OUT ABOUT THE TORSO ...?
CHEESE JACK
ABURI SUSHI
BIG CATCH EIKOMARU FISHERY
BEFORE WE DO THAT...
...LET'S TALK COMPENSATION.
IT'S NOT FREE.
HOW MUCH WOULD YOU LIKE?
A MILLION BUCKS.
?!
OR...
...A PERSONAL ITEM FROM...
?!
...HAISE SASAKI.

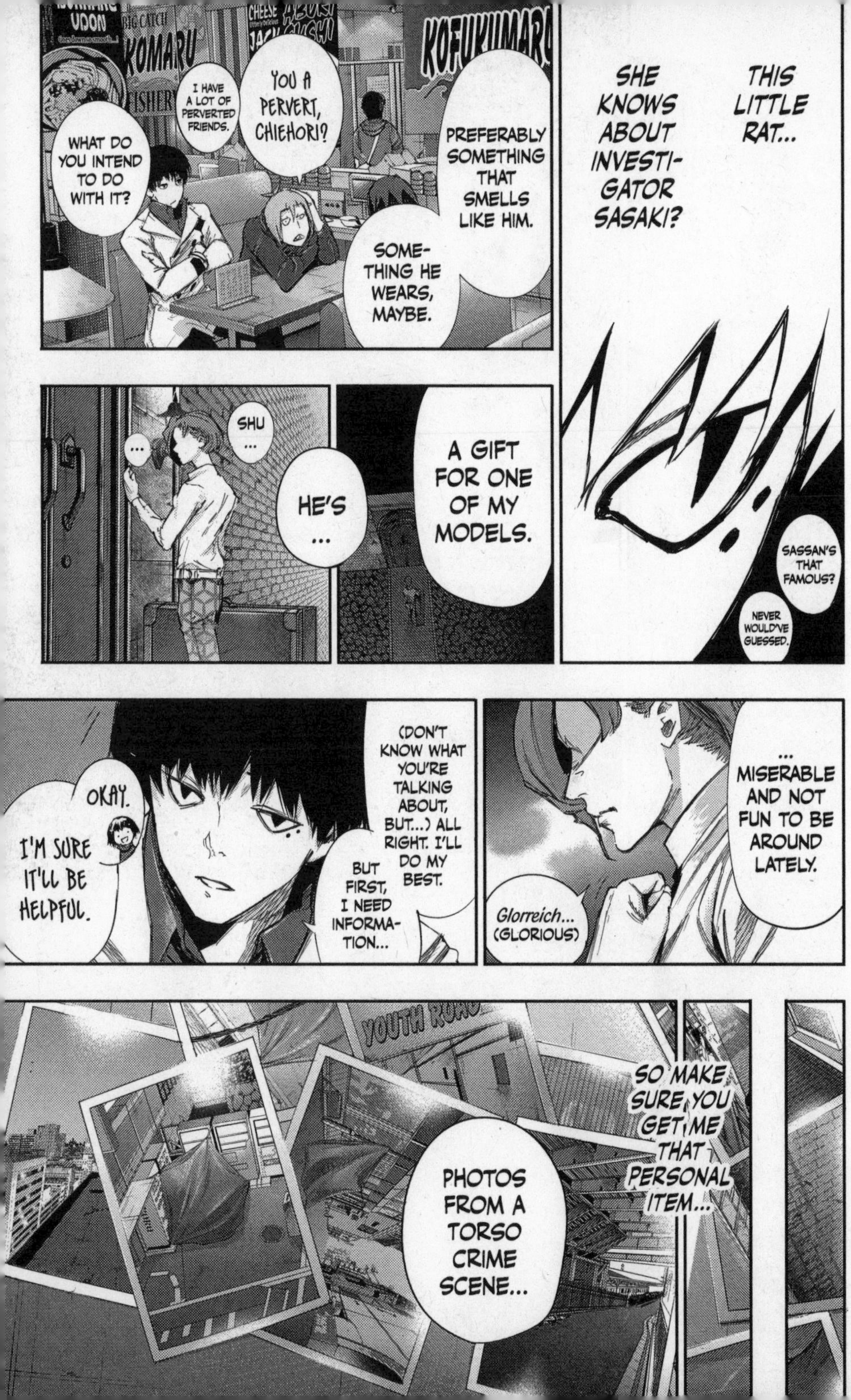
THIS LITTLE RAT...
SHE KNOWS ABOUT INVESTIGATOR SASAKI?
SASSAN'S THAT FAMOUS?
NEVER WOULD'VE GUESSED.
KOFUKUMARU
PREFERABLY SOMETHING THAT SMELLS LIKE HIM.
SOMETHING HE WEARS, MAYBE.
YOU A PERVERT, CHIEHORI?
I HAVE A LOT OF PERVERTED FRIENDS.
WHAT DO YOU INTEND TO DO WITH IT?
A GIFT FOR ONE OF MY MODELS.
SHU ...
HE'S ...
...
... MISERABLE AND NOT FUN TO BE AROUND LATELY.
Glorreich... (GLORIOUS)
(DON'T KNOW WHAT YOU'RE TALKING ABOUT, BUT...) ALL RIGHT. I'LL DO MY BEST.
BUT FIRST, I NEED INFORMATION...
OKAY.
I'M SURE IT'LL BE HELPFUL.
SO MAKE SURE YOU GET ME THAT PERSONAL ITEM...
PHOTOS FROM A TORSO CRIME SCENE...

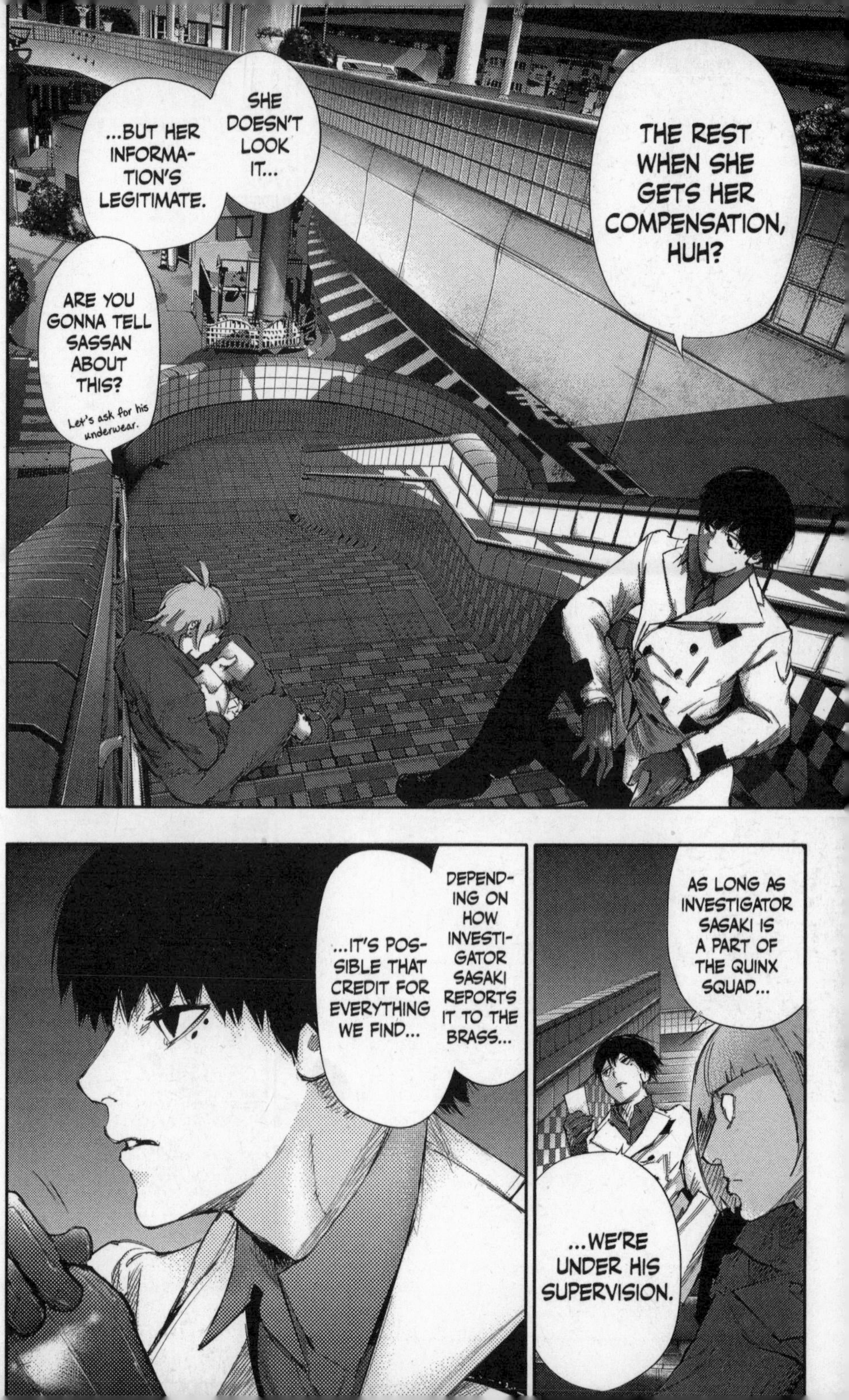
THE REST WHEN SHE GETS HER COMPENSATION, HUH?
SHE DOESN'T LOOK IT...
...BUT HER INFORMATION'S LEGITIMATE.
ARE YOU GONNA TELL SASSAN ABOUT THIS?
Let's ask for his underwear.
AS LONG AS INVESTIGATOR SASAKI IS A PART OF THE QUINX SQUAD...
...WE'RE UNDER HIS SUPERVISION.
DEPENDING ON HOW INVESTIGATOR SASAKI REPORTS IT TO THE BRASS...
...IT'S POSSIBLE THAT CREDIT FOR EVERYTHING WE FIND...

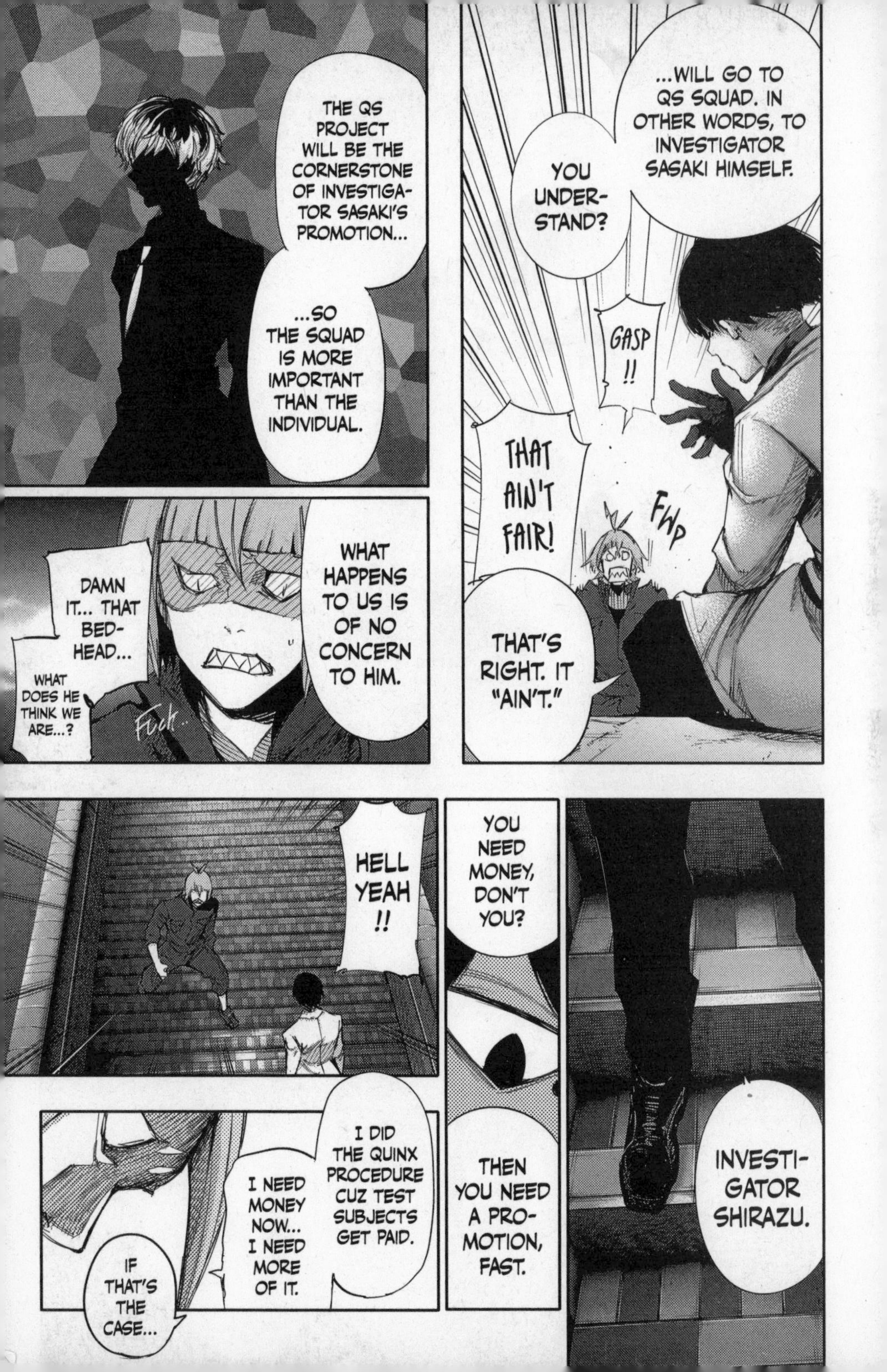
...WILL GO TO QS SQUAD. IN OTHER WORDS, TO INVESTIGATOR SASAKI HIMSELF.
YOU UNDER-STAND?
GASP !!
THAT AIN'T FAIR!
FWP
THAT'S RIGHT. IT "AIN'T."
THE QS PROJECT WILL BE THE CORNERSTONE OF INVESTIGA-TOR SASAKI'S PROMOTION...
...SO THE SQUAD IS MORE IMPORTANT THAN THE INDIVIDUAL.
WHAT HAPPENS TO US IS OF NO CONCERN TO HIM.
DAMN IT... THAT BED-HEAD...
WHAT DOES HE THINK WE ARE...?
Fuck..
INVESTI-GATOR SHIRAZU.
YOU NEED MONEY, DON'T YOU?
THEN YOU NEED A PRO-MOTION, FAST.
HELL YEAH !!
I DID THE QUINX PROCEDURE CUZ TEST SUBJECTS GET PAID.
I NEED MONEY NOW... I NEED MORE OF IT.
IF THAT'S THE CASE...

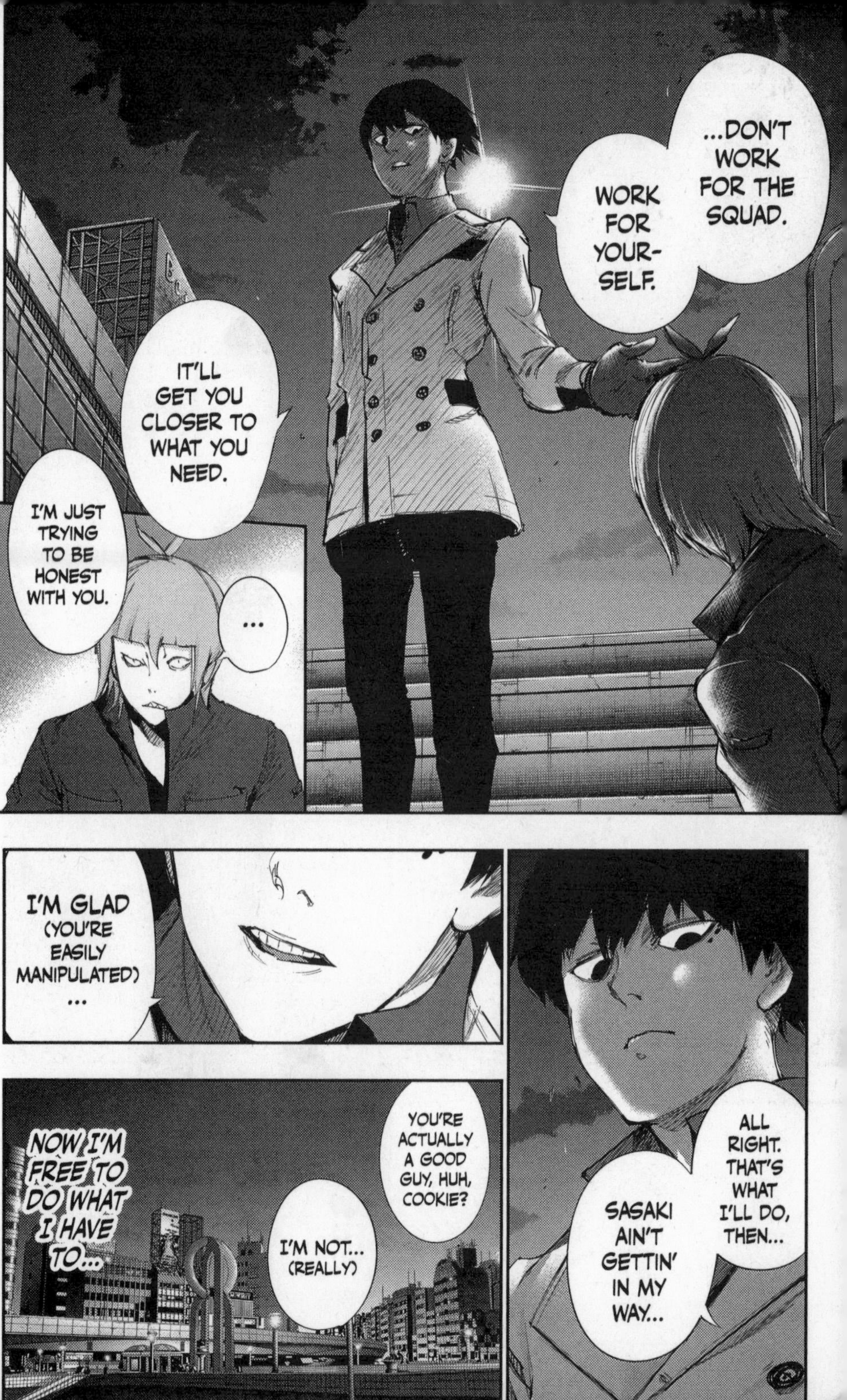
...DON'T WORK FOR THE SQUAD.
WORK FOR YOURSELF.
IT'LL GET YOU CLOSER TO WHAT YOU NEED.
...
I'M JUST TRYING TO BE HONEST WITH YOU.
ALL RIGHT. THAT'S WHAT I'LL DO, THEN...
SASAKI AIN'T GETTIN' IN MY WAY...
I'M GLAD (YOU'RE EASILY MANIPULATED)...
YOU'RE ACTUALLY A GOOD GUY, HUH, COOKIE?
I'M NOT... (REALLY)
NOW I'M FREE TO DO WHAT I HAVE TO...

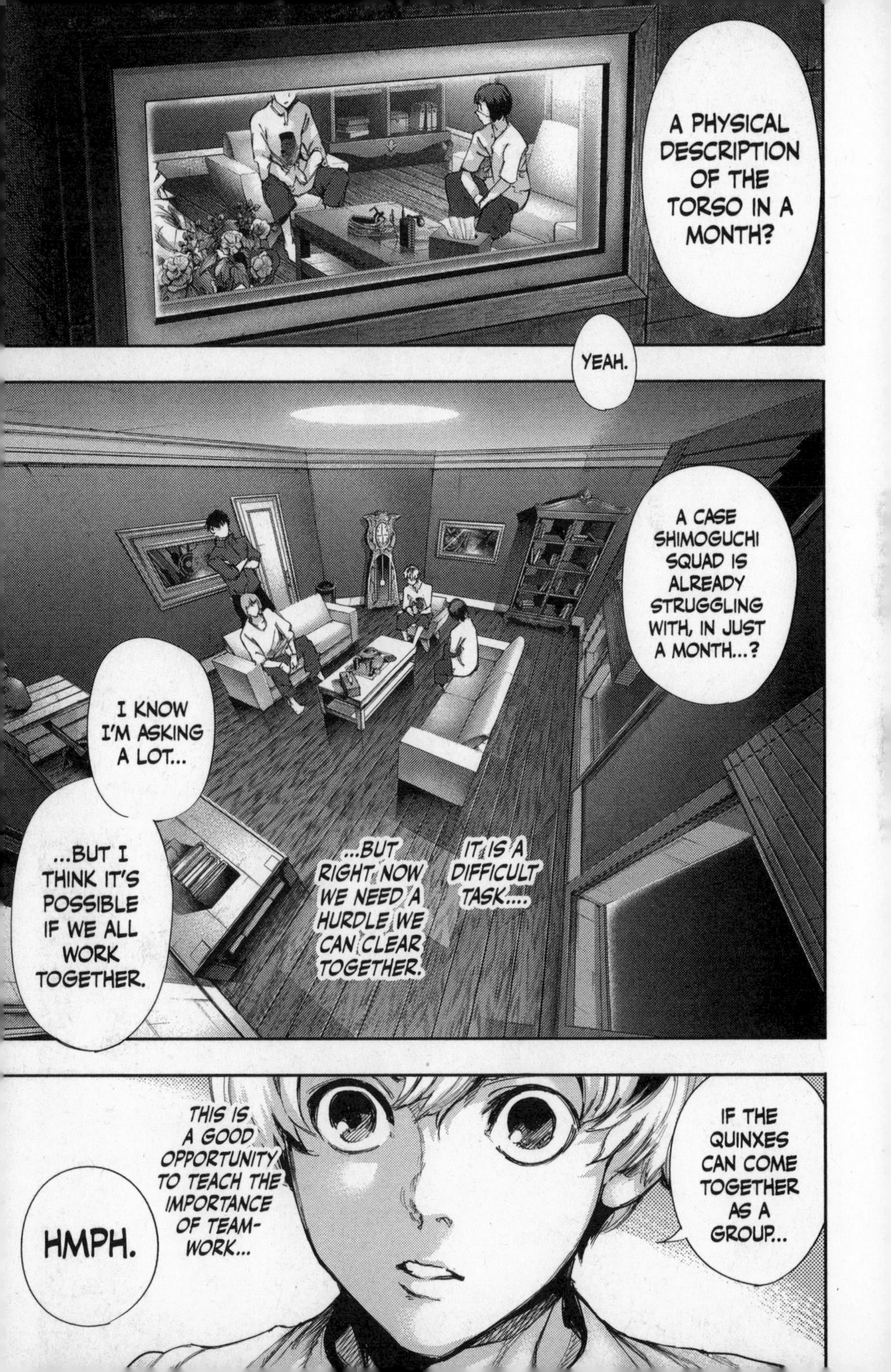

A PHYSICAL DESCRIPTION OF THE TORSO IN A MONTH?
YEAH.
A CASE SHIMOGUCHI SQUAD IS ALREADY STRUGGLING WITH, IN JUST A MONTH...?
IT IS A DIFFICULT TASK....
...BUT RIGHT NOW WE NEED A HURDLE WE CAN CLEAR TOGETHER.
I KNOW I'M ASKING A LOT...
...BUT I THINK IT'S POSSIBLE IF WE ALL WORK TOGETHER.
IF THE QUINXES CAN COME TOGETHER AS A GROUP...
THIS IS A GOOD OPPORTUNITY TO TEACH THE IMPORTANCE OF TEAM-WORK...
HMPH.

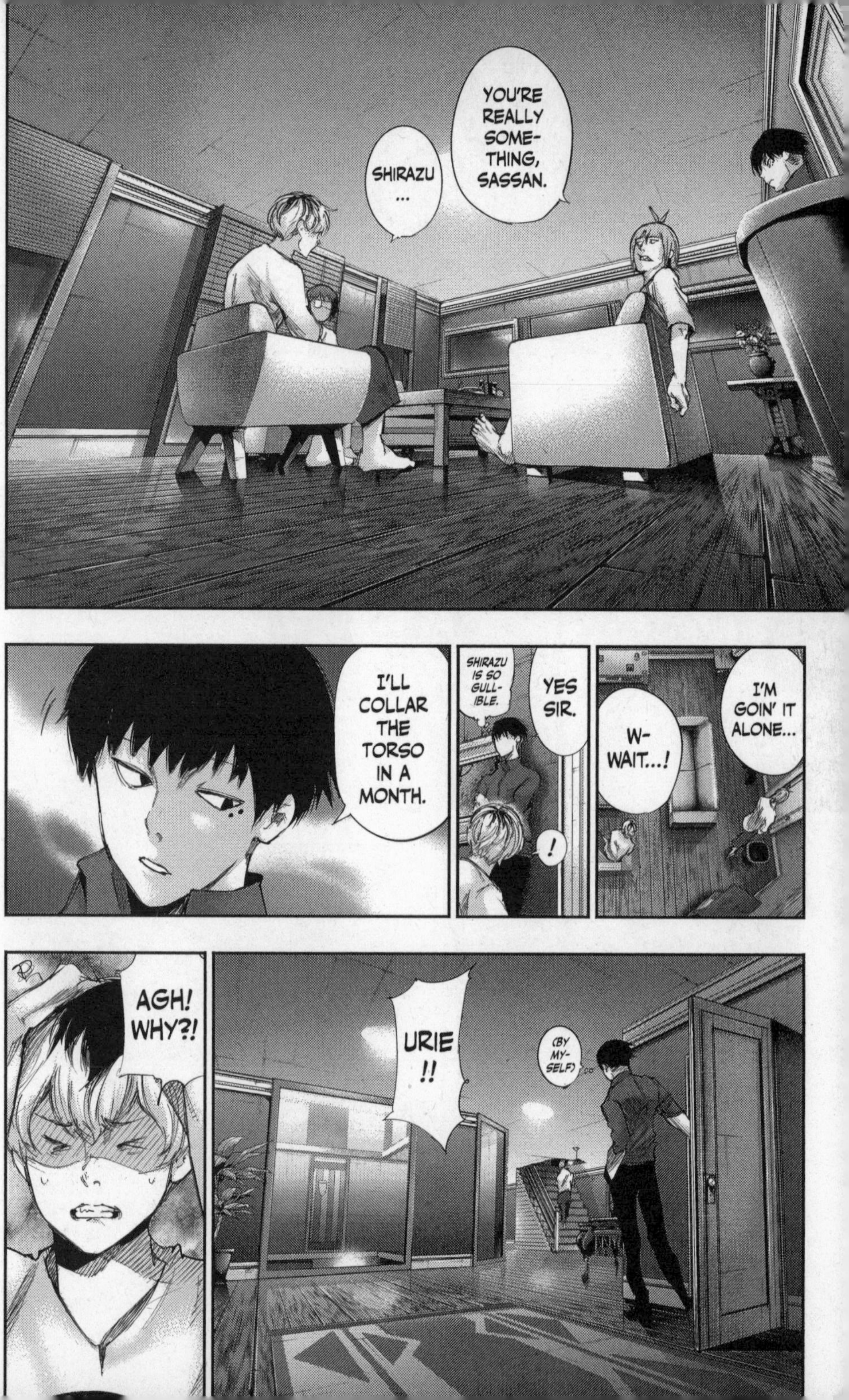
YOU'RE REALLY SOMETHING, SASSAN.
SHIRAZU...
I'M GOIN' IT ALONE...
W-WAIT...!
YES SIR.
SHIRAZU IS SO GULLIBLE.
!
I'LL COLLAR THE TORSO IN A MONTH.
URIE!!
(BY MYSELF)
AGH! WHY?!

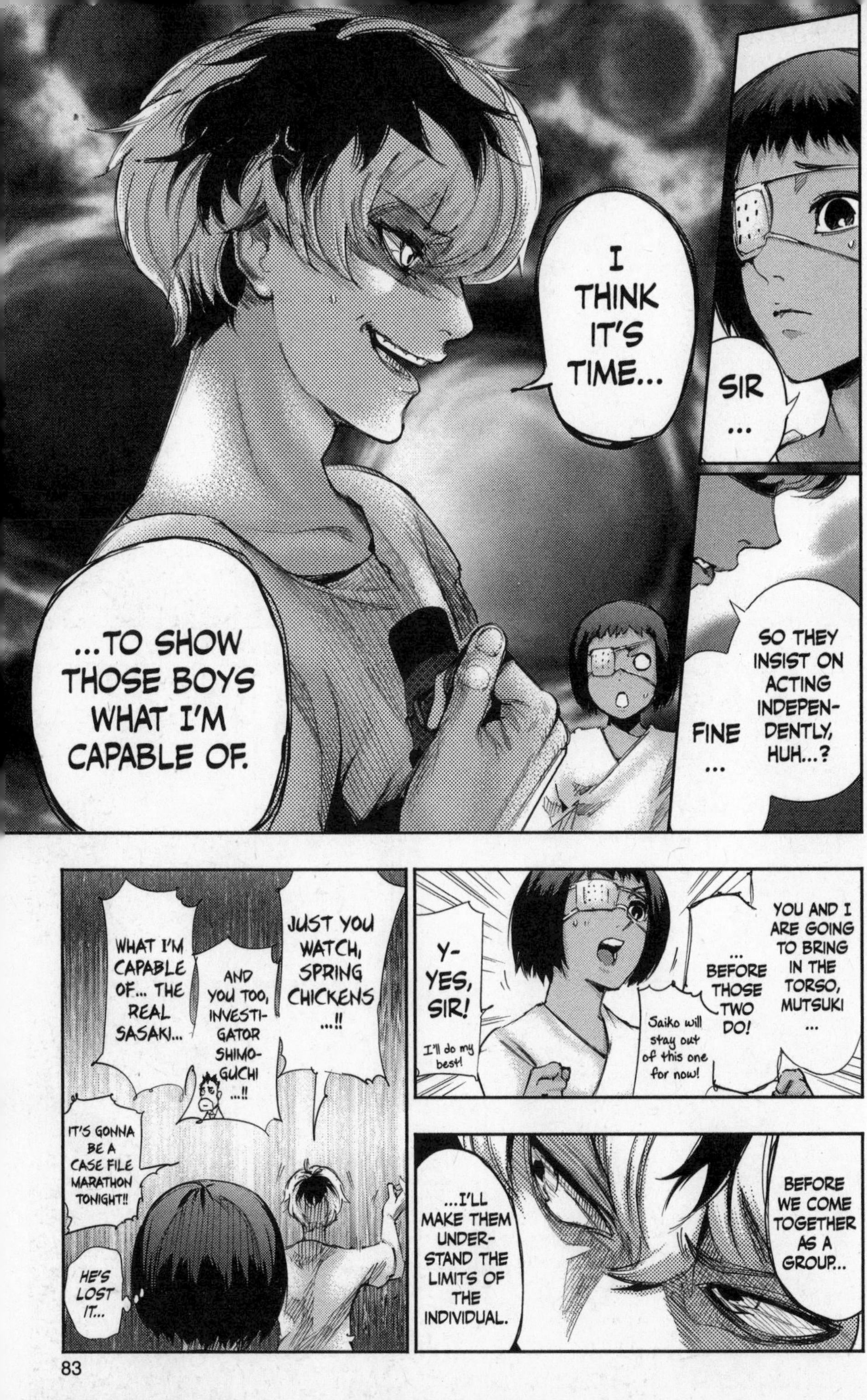
SIR
...
SO THEY INSIST ON ACTING INDEPEN-DENTLY, HUH...?
FINE
...
I THINK IT'S TIME...
...TO SHOW THOSE BOYS WHAT I'M CAPABLE OF.
YOU AND I ARE GOING TO BRING IN THE TORSO, MUTSUKI
...
... BEFORE THOSE TWO DO!
Y- YES, SIR!
I'll do my best!
Saiko will stay out of this one for now!
BEFORE WE COME TOGETHER AS A GROUP...
...I'LL MAKE THEM UNDER-STAND THE LIMITS OF THE INDIVIDUAL.
JUST YOU WATCH, SPRING CHICKENS ...!!
WHAT I'M CAPABLE OF... THE REAL SASAKI...
AND YOU TOO, INVESTI-GATOR SHIMO-GUCHI ...!!
IT'S GONNA BE A CASE FILE MARATHON TONIGHT!!
HE'S LOST IT...

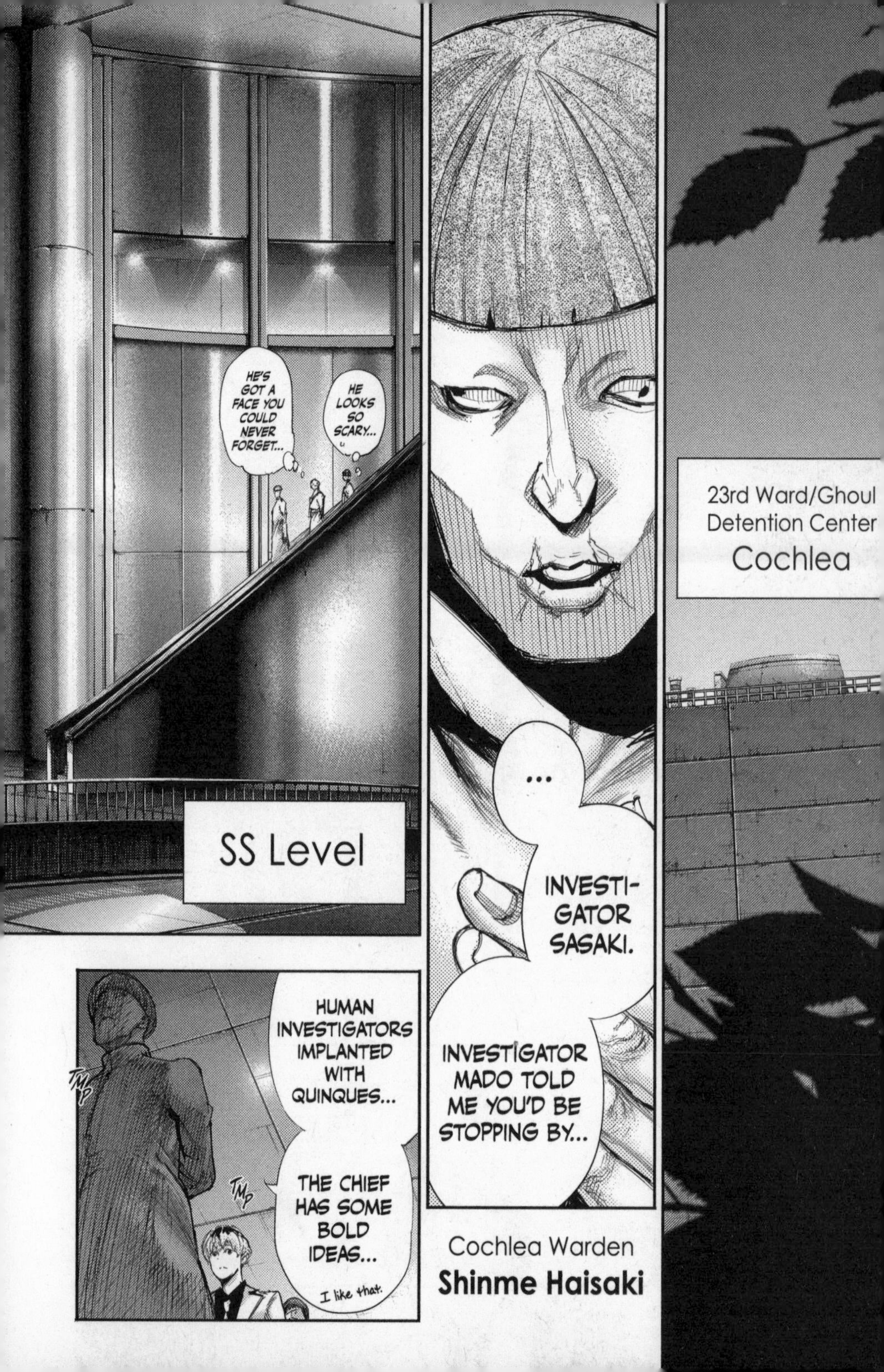
23rd Ward/Ghoul Detention Center
Cochlea
...
INVESTIGATOR SASAKI.
INVESTIGATOR MADO TOLD ME YOU'D BE STOPPING BY...
Cochlea Warden
Shinme Haisaki
HE LOOKS SO SCARY...
HE'S GOT A FACE YOU COULD NEVER FORGET...
SS Level
HUMAN INVESTIGATORS IMPLANTED WITH QUINQUES...
TMP
THE CHIEF HAS SOME BOLD IDEAS...
I like that.
TMP

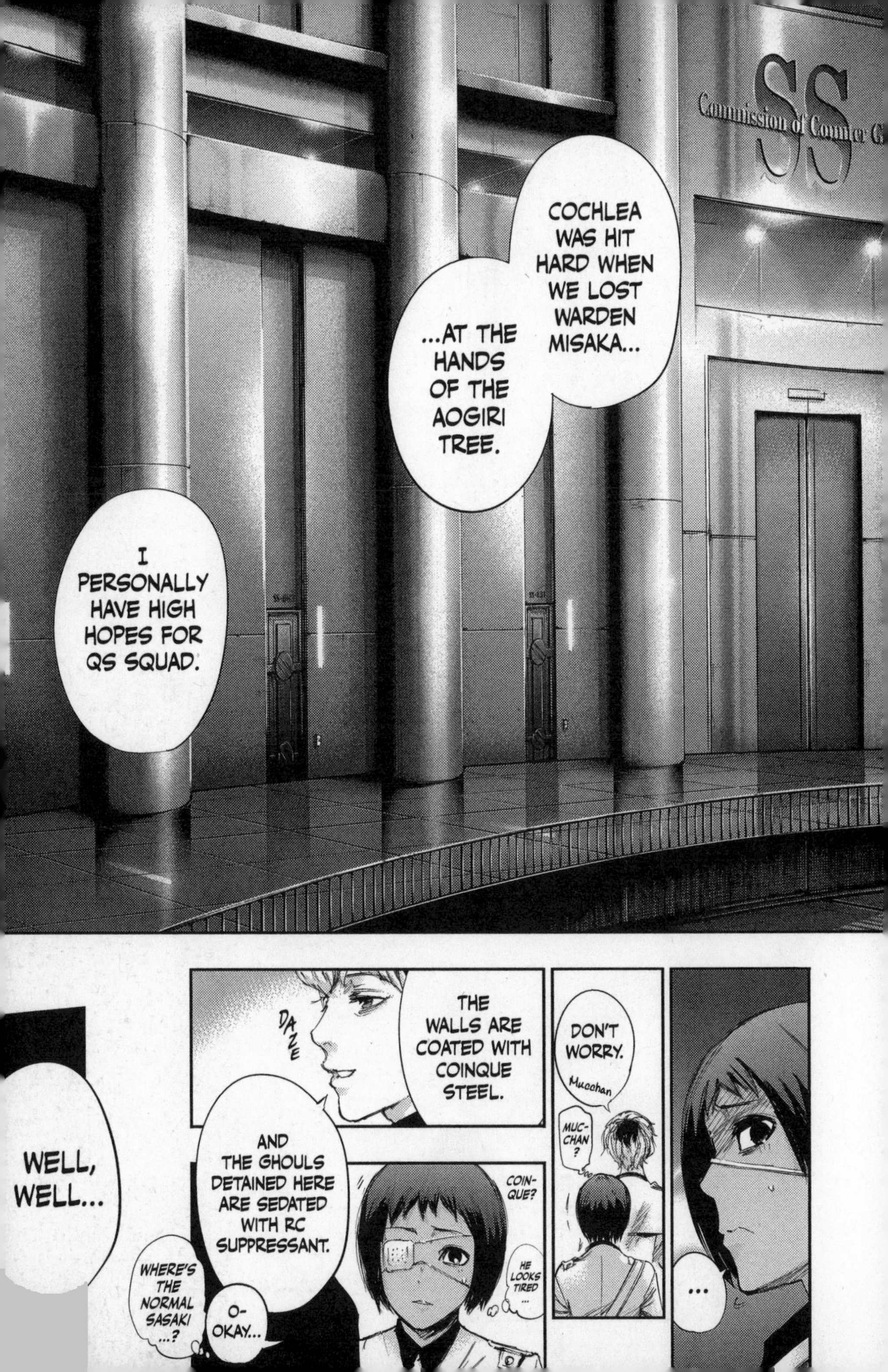
SS
Commission of Counter
COCHLEA WAS HIT HARD WHEN WE LOST WARDEN MISAKA...
...AT THE HANDS OF THE AOGIRI TREE.
I PERSONALLY HAVE HIGH HOPES FOR QS SQUAD.
...
DON'T WORRY.
Mucchan
MUC-CHAN?
HE LOOKS TIRED...
THE WALLS ARE COATED WITH COINQUE STEEL.
DAZE
AND THE GHOULS DETAINED HERE ARE SEDATED WITH RC SUPPRESSANT.
COINQUE?
O-OKAY...
WHERE'S THE NORMAL SASAKI...?
WELL, WELL...

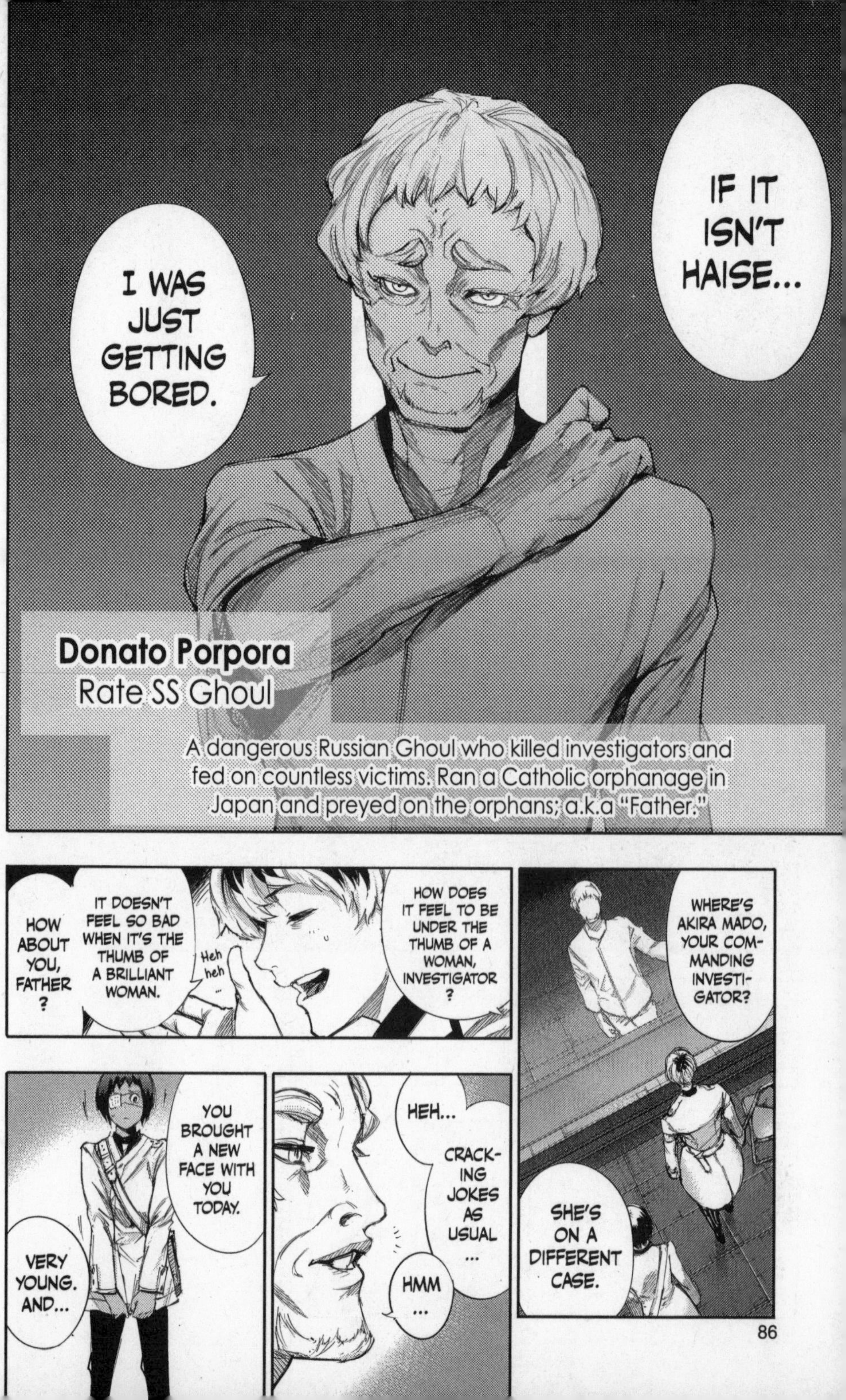
IF IT ISN'T HAISE...
I WAS JUST GETTING BORED.
Donato Porpora
Rate SS Ghoul
A dangerous Russian Ghoul who killed investigators and fed on countless victims. Ran a Catholic orphanage in Japan and preyed on the orphans; a.k.a "Father."
WHERE'S AKIRA MADO, YOUR COMMANDING INVESTIGATOR?
SHE'S ON A DIFFERENT CASE.
HOW DOES IT FEEL TO BE UNDER THE THUMB OF A WOMAN, INVESTIGATOR?
Heh heh...
IT DOESN'T FEEL SO BAD WHEN IT'S THE THUMB OF A BRILLIANT WOMAN.
HOW ABOUT YOU, FATHER?
HEH...
CRACKING JOKES AS USUAL...
HMM...
YOU BROUGHT A NEW FACE WITH YOU TODAY.
VERY YOUNG. AND...

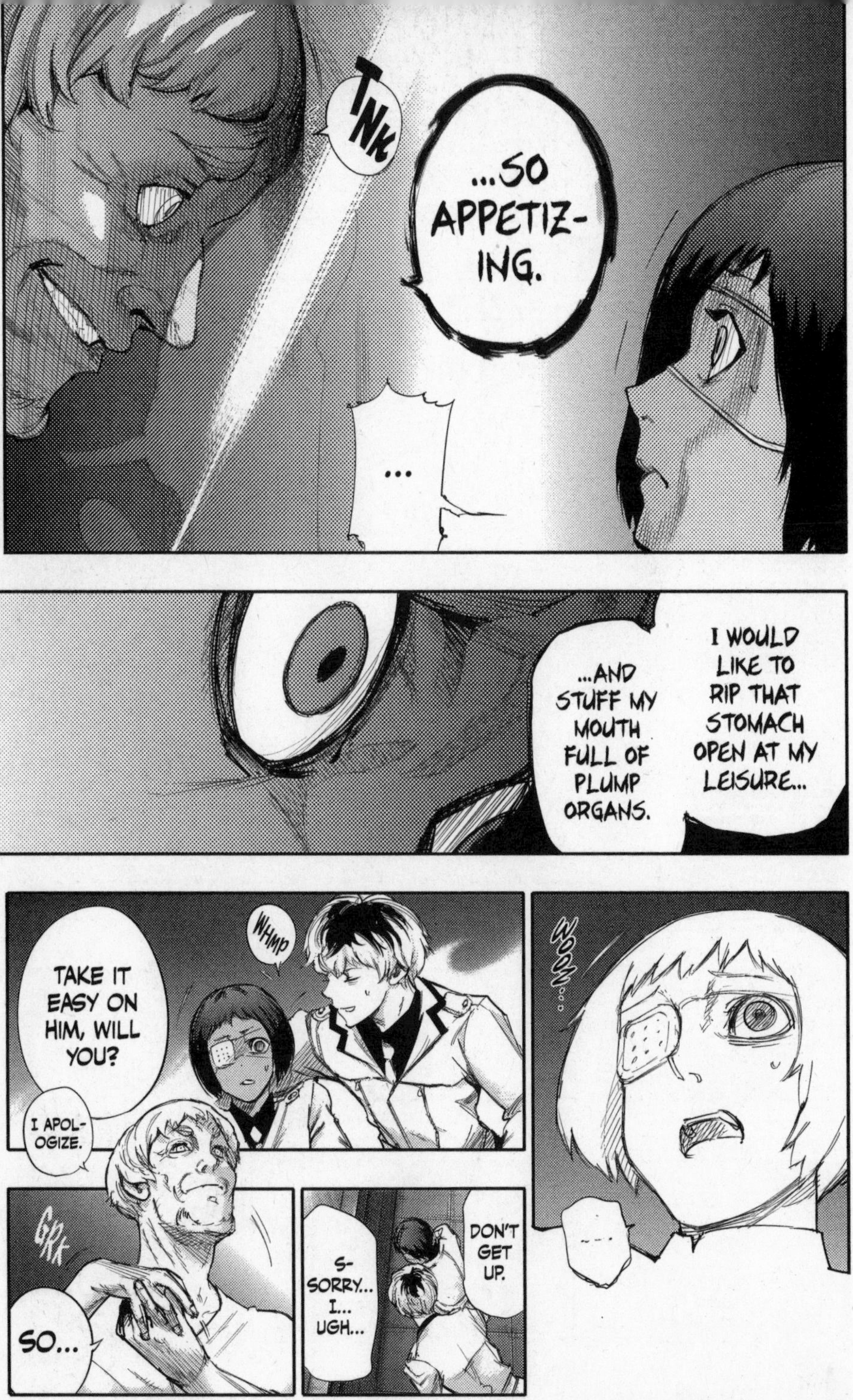
...SO APPETIZ-ING.
TNK
...
I WOULD LIKE TO RIP THAT STOMACH OPEN AT MY LEISURE...
...AND STUFF MY MOUTH FULL OF PLUMP ORGANS.
WOOZ...
...
WHMP
TAKE IT EASY ON HIM, WILL YOU?
I APOL-OGIZE.
DON'T GET UP.
S-SORRY... I... UGH...
GRK
SO...

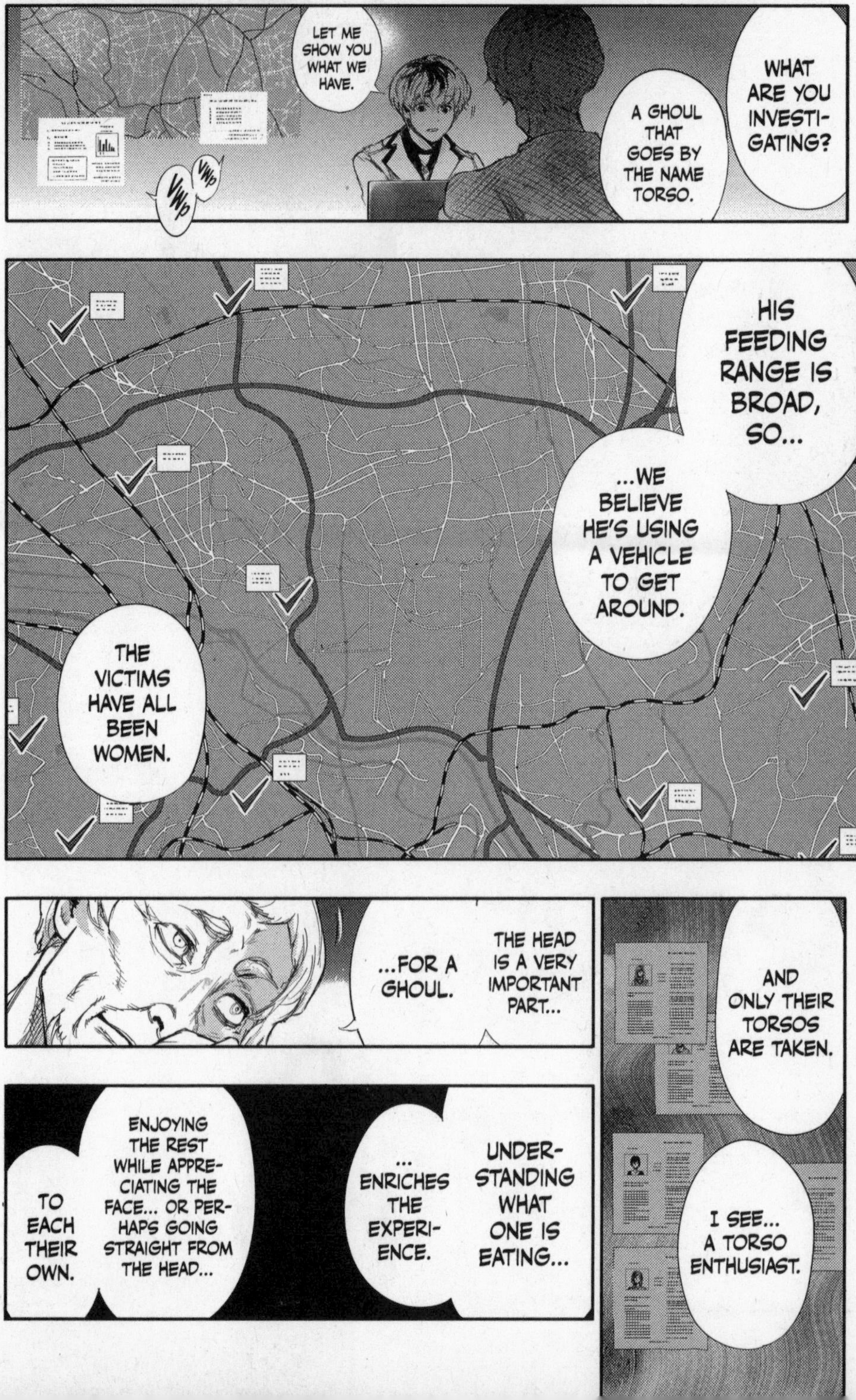
WHAT ARE YOU INVESTI-GATING?
A GHOUL THAT GOES BY THE NAME TORSO.
LET ME SHOW YOU WHAT WE HAVE.
VWp
VWp
HIS FEEDING RANGE IS BROAD, SO...
...WE BELIEVE HE'S USING A VEHICLE TO GET AROUND.
THE VICTIMS HAVE ALL BEEN WOMEN.
AND ONLY THEIR TORSOS ARE TAKEN.
I SEE... A TORSO ENTHUSIAST.
THE HEAD IS A VERY IMPORTANT PART...
...FOR A GHOUL.
UNDER-STANDING WHAT ONE IS EATING...
...ENRICHES THE EXPERI-ENCE.
ENJOYING THE REST WHILE APPRE-CIATING THE FACE... OR PER-HAPS GOING STRAIGHT FROM THE HEAD...
TO EACH THEIR OWN.

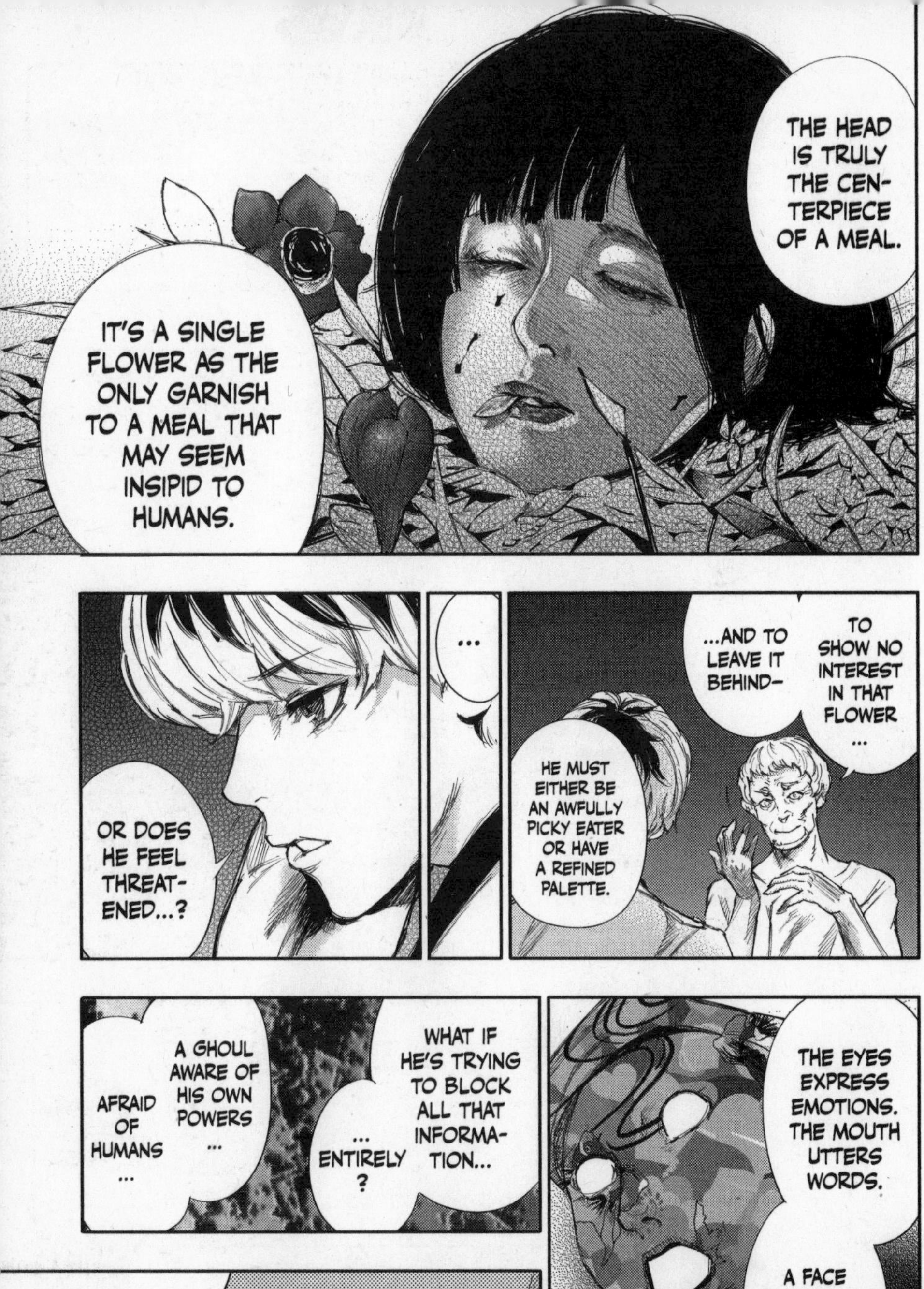
THE HEAD IS TRULY THE CEN-TERPIECE OF A MEAL.
IT'S A SINGLE FLOWER AS THE ONLY GARNISH TO A MEAL THAT MAY SEEM INSIPID TO HUMANS.
TO SHOW NO INTEREST IN THAT FLOWER ...
...AND TO LEAVE IT BEHIND—
HE MUST EITHER BE AN AWFULLY PICKY EATER OR HAVE A REFINED PALETTE.
...
OR DOES HE FEEL THREAT-ENED...?
THE EYES EXPRESS EMOTIONS. THE MOUTH UTTERS WORDS.
A FACE CONTAINS AN ENORMOUS AMOUNT OF INFORMATION.
WHAT IF HE'S TRYING TO BLOCK ALL THAT INFORMA-TION...
... ENTIRELY ?
A GHOUL AWARE OF HIS OWN POWERS ...
AFRAID OF HUMANS ...
BECAUSE ...

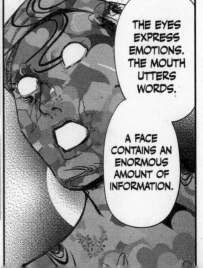

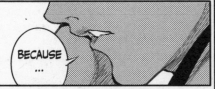

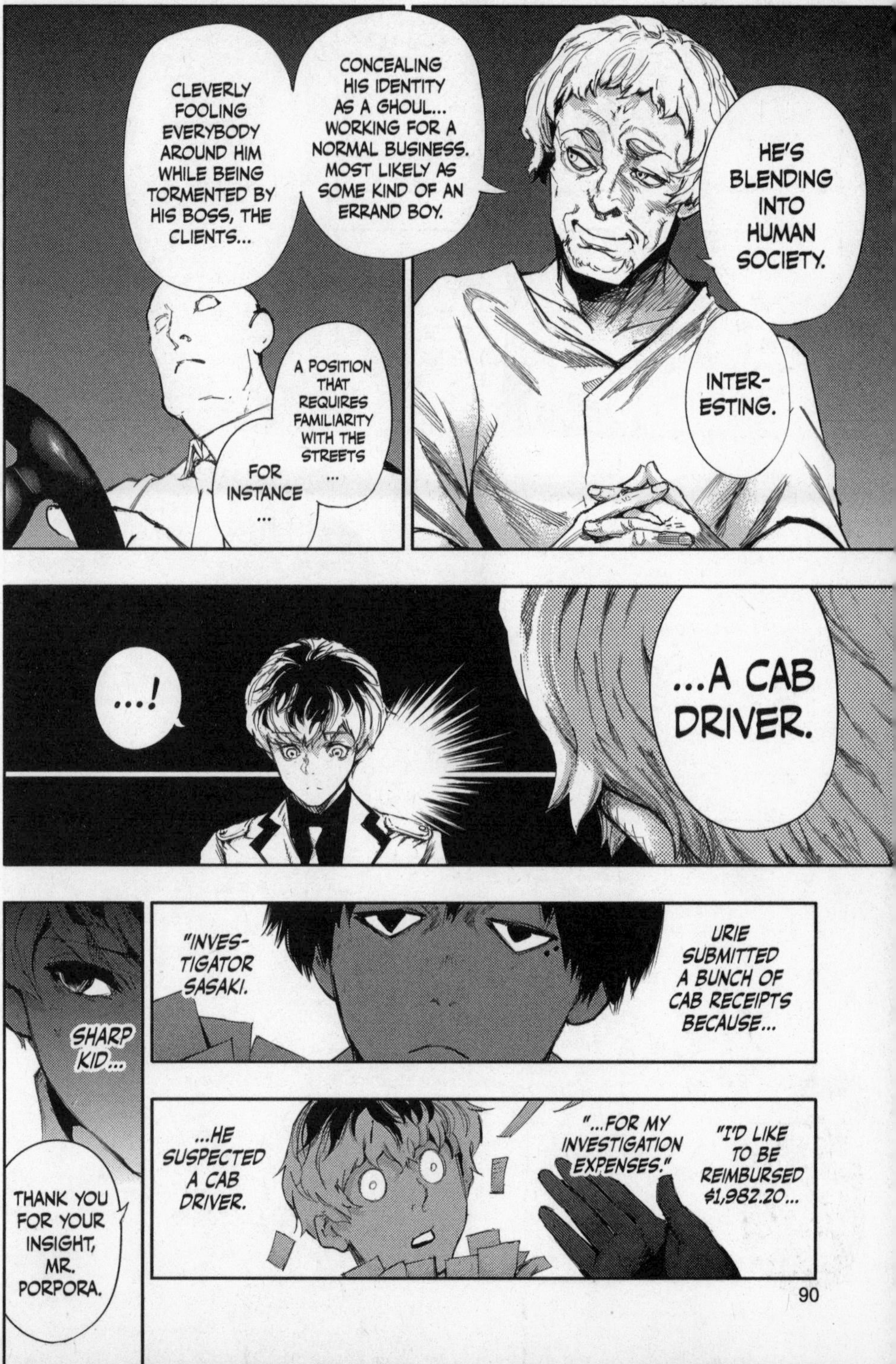
HE'S BLENDING INTO HUMAN SOCIETY.
INTER-ESTING.
CONCEALING HIS IDENTITY AS A GHOUL... WORKING FOR A NORMAL BUSINESS. MOST LIKELY AS SOME KIND OF AN ERRAND BOY.
CLEVERLY FOOLING EVERYBODY AROUND HIM WHILE BEING TORMENTED BY HIS BOSS, THE CLIENTS...
A POSITION THAT REQUIRES FAMILIARITY WITH THE STREETS ...
FOR INSTANCE ...
...A CAB DRIVER.
...!
URIE SUBMITTED A BUNCH OF CAB RECEIPTS BECAUSE...
"INVES-TIGATOR SASAKI.
"I'D LIKE TO BE REIMBURSED $1,982.20...
"...FOR MY INVESTIGATION EXPENSES."
...HE SUSPECTED A CAB DRIVER.
SHARP KID...
THANK YOU FOR YOUR INSIGHT, MR. PORPORA.

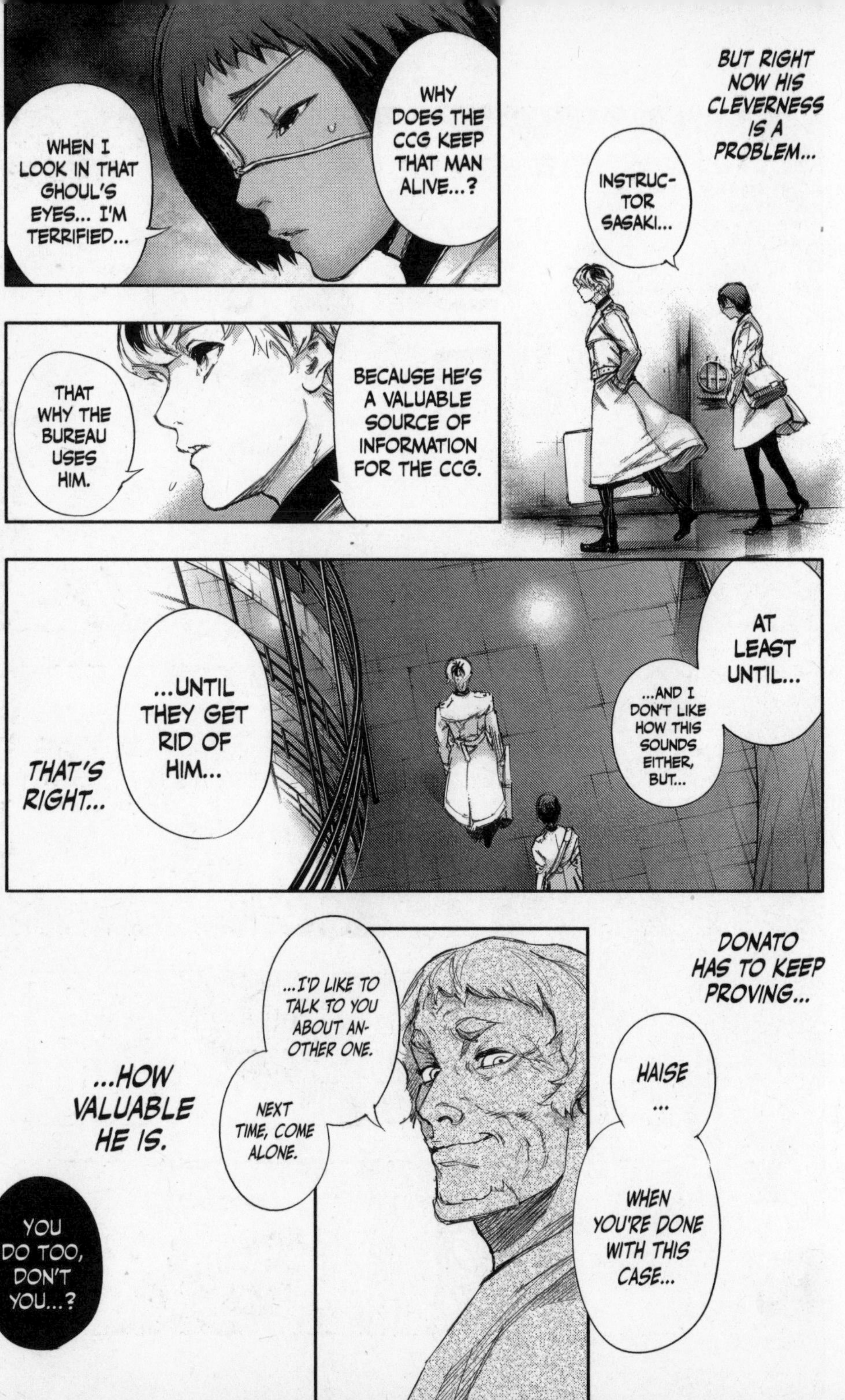
BUT RIGHT NOW HIS CLEVERNESS IS A PROBLEM...
INSTRUCTOR SASAKI...
WHY DOES THE CCG KEEP THAT MAN ALIVE...?
WHEN I LOOK IN THAT GHOUL'S EYES... I'M TERRIFIED...
BECAUSE HE'S A VALUABLE SOURCE OF INFORMATION FOR THE CCG.
THAT WHY THE BUREAU USES HIM.
AT LEAST UNTIL...
...AND I DON'T LIKE HOW THIS SOUNDS EITHER, BUT...
...UNTIL THEY GET RID OF HIM...
THAT'S RIGHT...
DONATO HAS TO KEEP PROVING...
HAISE ...
WHEN YOU'RE DONE WITH THIS CASE...
...I'D LIKE TO TALK TO YOU ABOUT AN-OTHER ONE.
NEXT TIME, COME ALONE.
...HOW VALUABLE HE IS.
YOU DO TOO, DON'T YOU...?

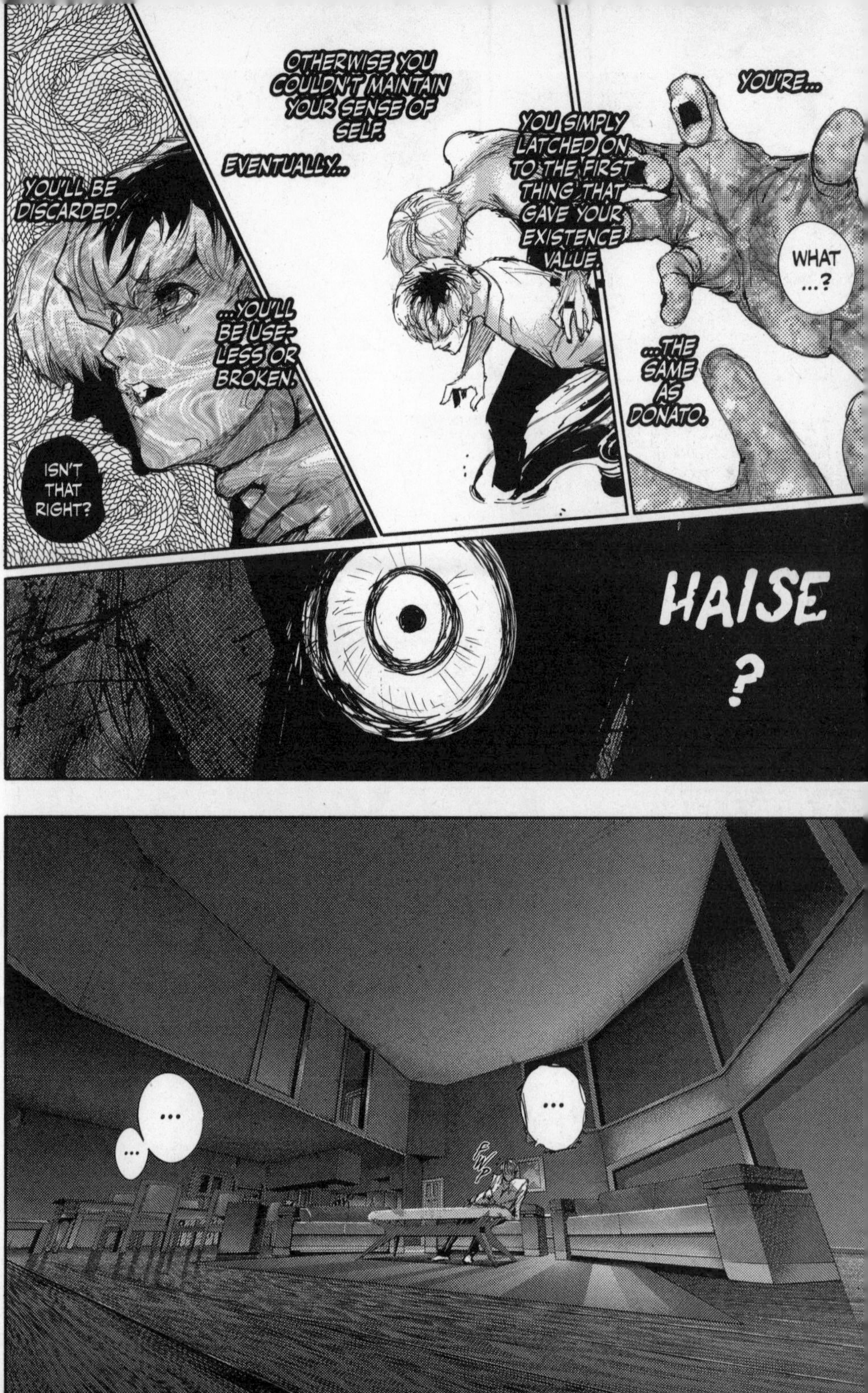
YOU'RE...
WHAT ...?
...THE SAME AS DONATO.
YOU SIMPLY LATCHED ON TO THE FIRST THING THAT GAVE YOUR EXISTENCE VALUE.
OTHERWISE YOU COULDN'T MAINTAIN YOUR SENSE OF SELF.
EVENTUALLY...
...YOU'LL BE USE-LESS OR BROKEN.
YOU'LL BE DISCARDED.
ISN'T THAT RIGHT?
HAISE ?
...
...
...

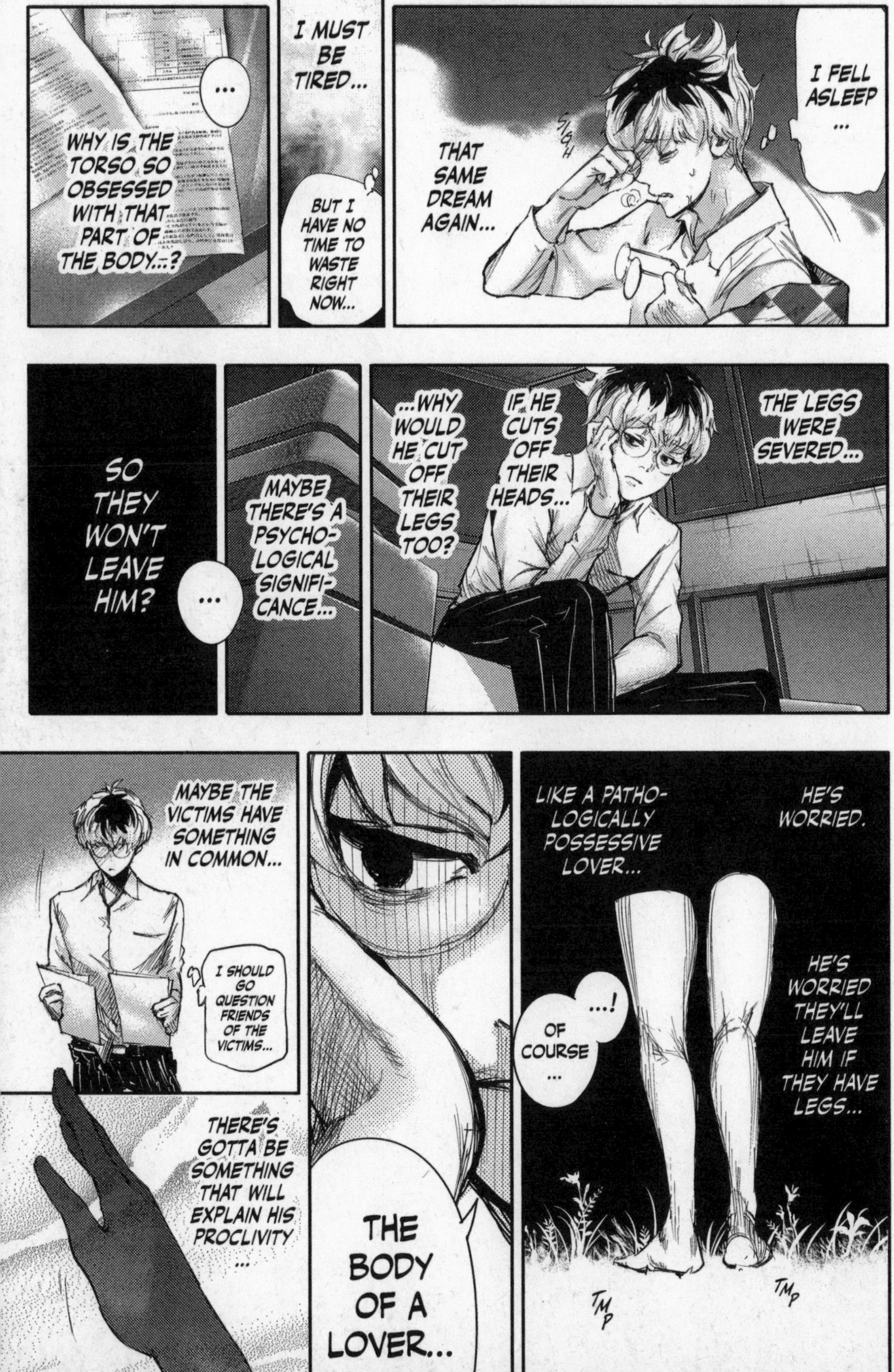
I FELL ASLEEP ...
SIGH
THAT SAME DREAM AGAIN...
I MUST BE TIRED...
BUT I HAVE NO TIME TO WASTE RIGHT NOW...
...
WHY IS THE TORSO SO OBSESSED WITH THAT PART OF THE BODY...?
THE LEGS WERE SEVERED...
IF HE CUTS OFF THEIR HEADS...
...WHY WOULD HE CUT OFF THEIR LEGS TOO?
MAYBE THERE'S A PSYCHOLOGICAL SIGNIFICANCE...
SO THEY WON'T LEAVE HIM?
...
HE'S WORRIED.
LIKE A PATHOLOGICALLY POSSESSIVE LOVER...
HE'S WORRIED THEY'LL LEAVE HIM IF THEY HAVE LEGS...
...!
OF COURSE ...
TMP
TMP
THE BODY OF A LOVER...
MAYBE THE VICTIMS HAVE SOMETHING IN COMMON...
I SHOULD GO QUESTION FRIENDS OF THE VICTIMS...
THERE'S GOTTA BE SOMETHING THAT WILL EXPLAIN HIS PROCLIVITY ...

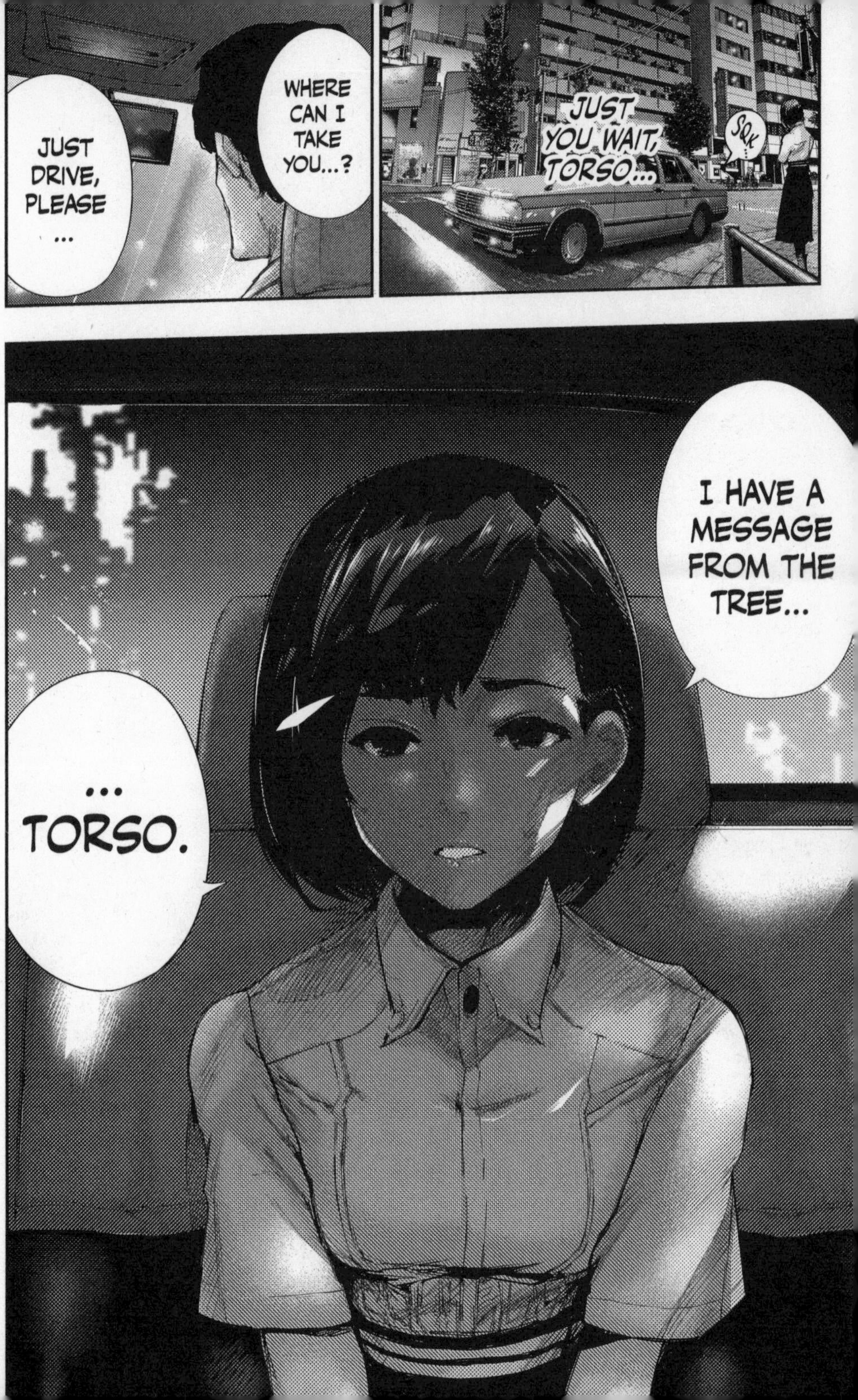
SQK
JUST YOU WAIT, TORSO...
WHERE CAN I TAKE YOU...?
JUST DRIVE, PLEASE ...
I HAVE A MESSAGE FROM THE TREE...
... TORSO.

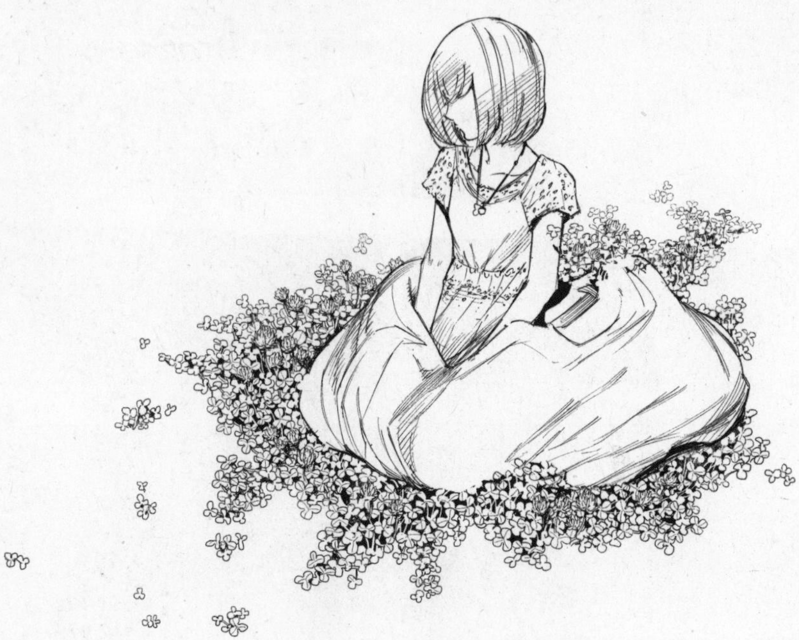

Remit to See, Limit to See :4

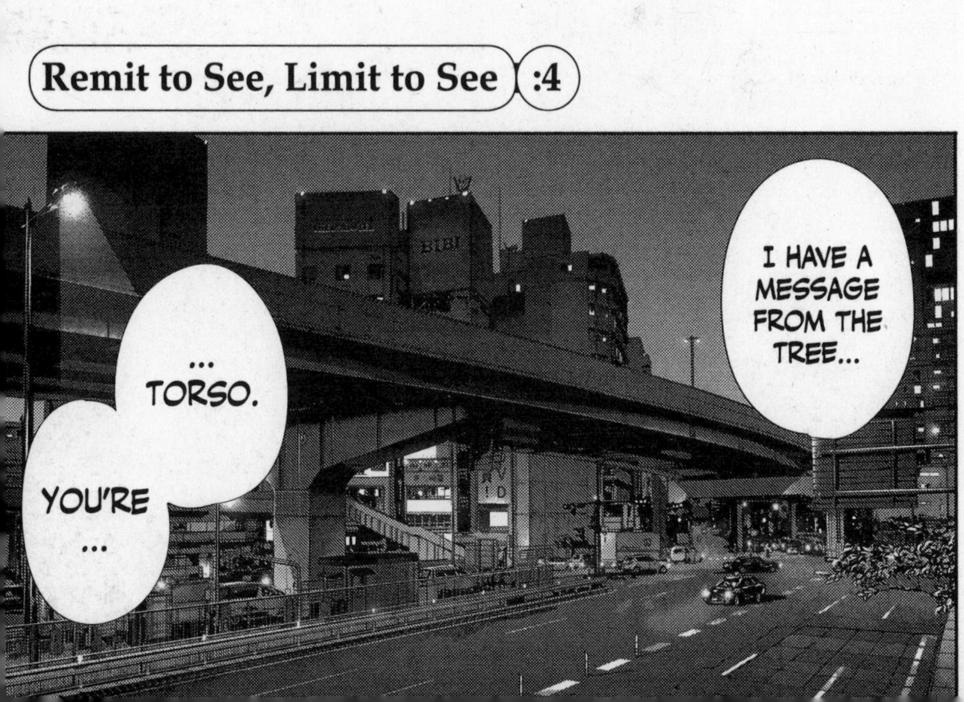
BIBI
I HAVE A MESSAGE FROM THE TREE...
... TORSO.
YOU'RE ...

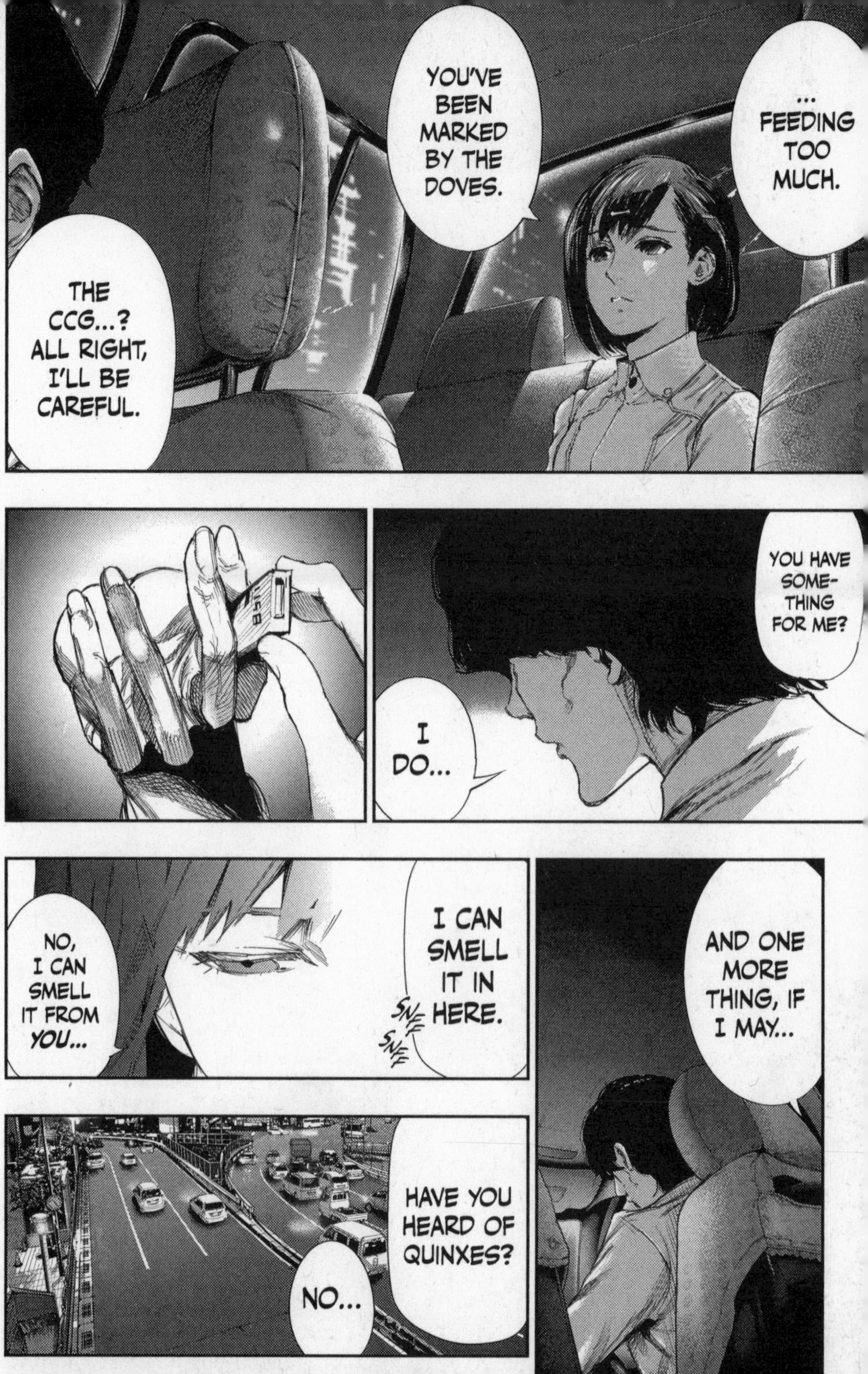
...FEEDING TOO MUCH.
YOU'VE BEEN MARKED BY THE DOVES.
THE CCG...? ALL RIGHT, I'LL BE CAREFUL.
YOU HAVE SOME-THING FOR ME?
I DO...
AND ONE MORE THING, IF I MAY...
I CAN SMELL IT IN HERE.
SNFF SNFF
NO, I CAN SMELL IT FROM *YOU*...
HAVE YOU HEARD OF QUINXES?
NO...

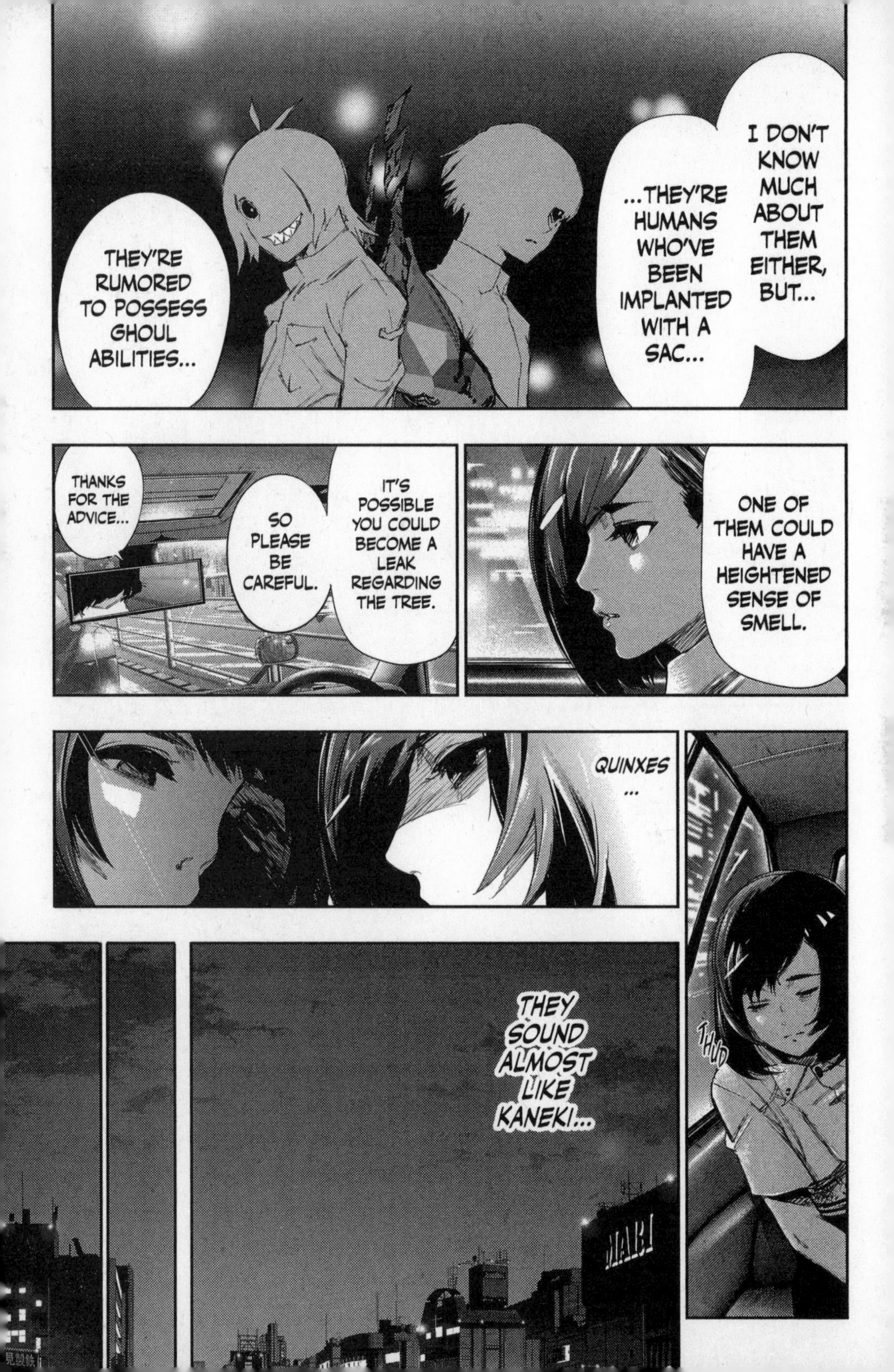
I DON'T KNOW MUCH ABOUT THEM EITHER, BUT...
...THEY'RE HUMANS WHO'VE BEEN IMPLANTED WITH A SAC...
THEY'RE RUMORED TO POSSESS GHOUL ABILITIES...
ONE OF THEM COULD HAVE A HEIGHTENED SENSE OF SMELL.
IT'S POSSIBLE YOU COULD BECOME A LEAK REGARDING THE TREE.
SO PLEASE BE CAREFUL.
THANKS FOR THE ADVICE...
THUD
QUINXES ...
THEY SOUND ALMOST LIKE KANEKI...
MABI

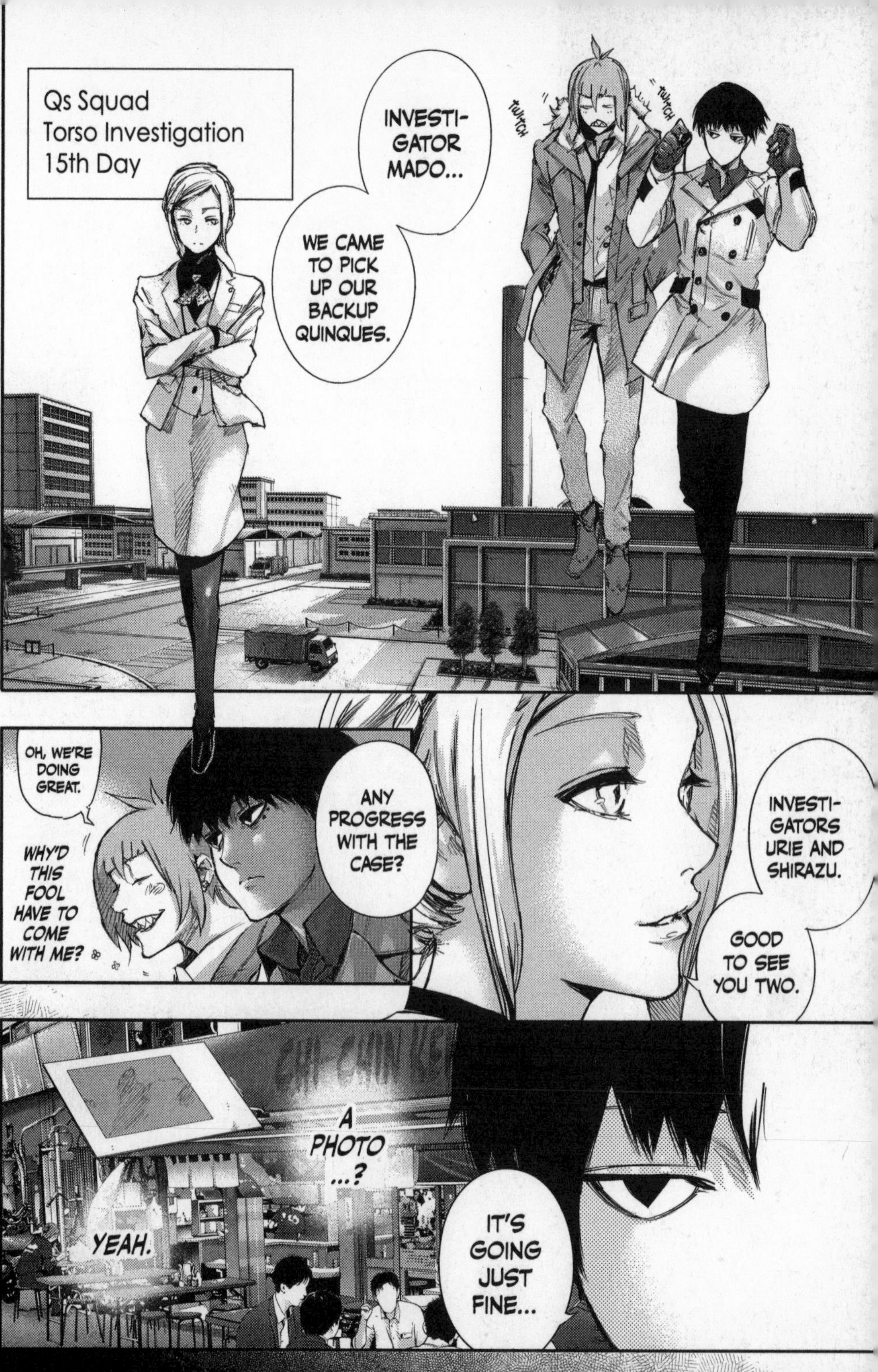
TWITCH
TWITCH
INVESTI-GATOR MADO...
WE CAME TO PICK UP OUR BACKUP QUINQUES.
Qs Squad Torso Investigation 15th Day
INVESTI-GATORS URIE AND SHIRAZU.
GOOD TO SEE YOU TWO.
ANY PROGRESS WITH THE CASE?
OH, WE'RE DOING GREAT.
WHY'D THIS FOOL HAVE TO COME WITH ME?
IT'S GOING JUST FINE...
A PHOTO ...?
YEAH.

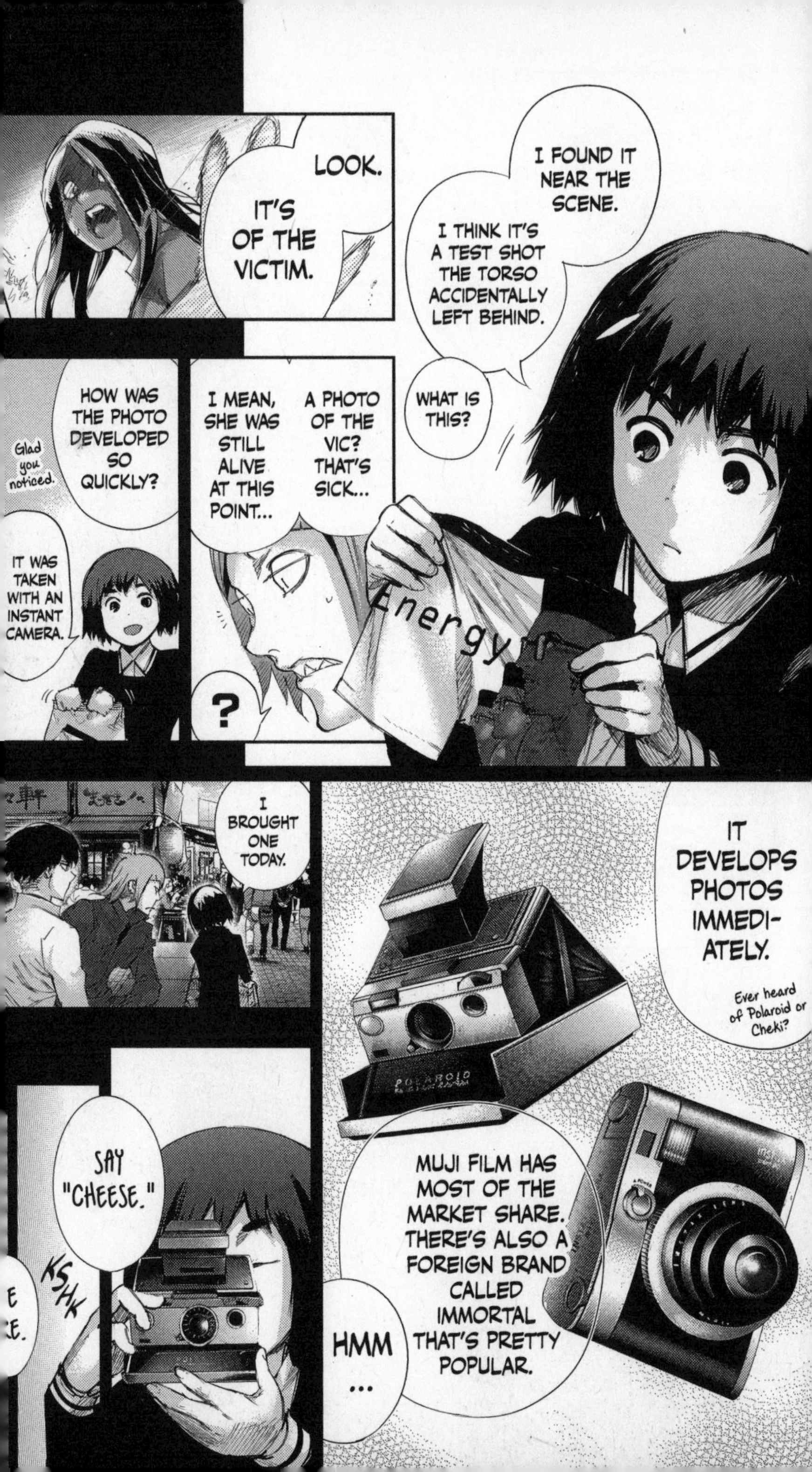
I FOUND IT NEAR THE SCENE.
I THINK IT'S A TEST SHOT THE TORSO ACCIDENTALLY LEFT BEHIND.
WHAT IS THIS?
Energy
LOOK.
IT'S OF THE VICTIM.
A PHOTO OF THE VIC? THAT'S SICK...
I MEAN, SHE WAS STILL ALIVE AT THIS POINT...
?
HOW WAS THE PHOTO DEVELOPED SO QUICKLY?
Glad you noticed.
IT WAS TAKEN WITH AN INSTANT CAMERA.
IT DEVELOPS PHOTOS IMMEDIATELY.
Ever heard of Polaroid or Cheki?
POLAROID
MUJI FILM HAS MOST OF THE MARKET SHARE. THERE'S ALSO A FOREIGN BRAND CALLED IMMORTAL THAT'S PRETTY POPULAR.
HMM...
I BROUGHT ONE TODAY.
SAY "CHEESE."
KSHK

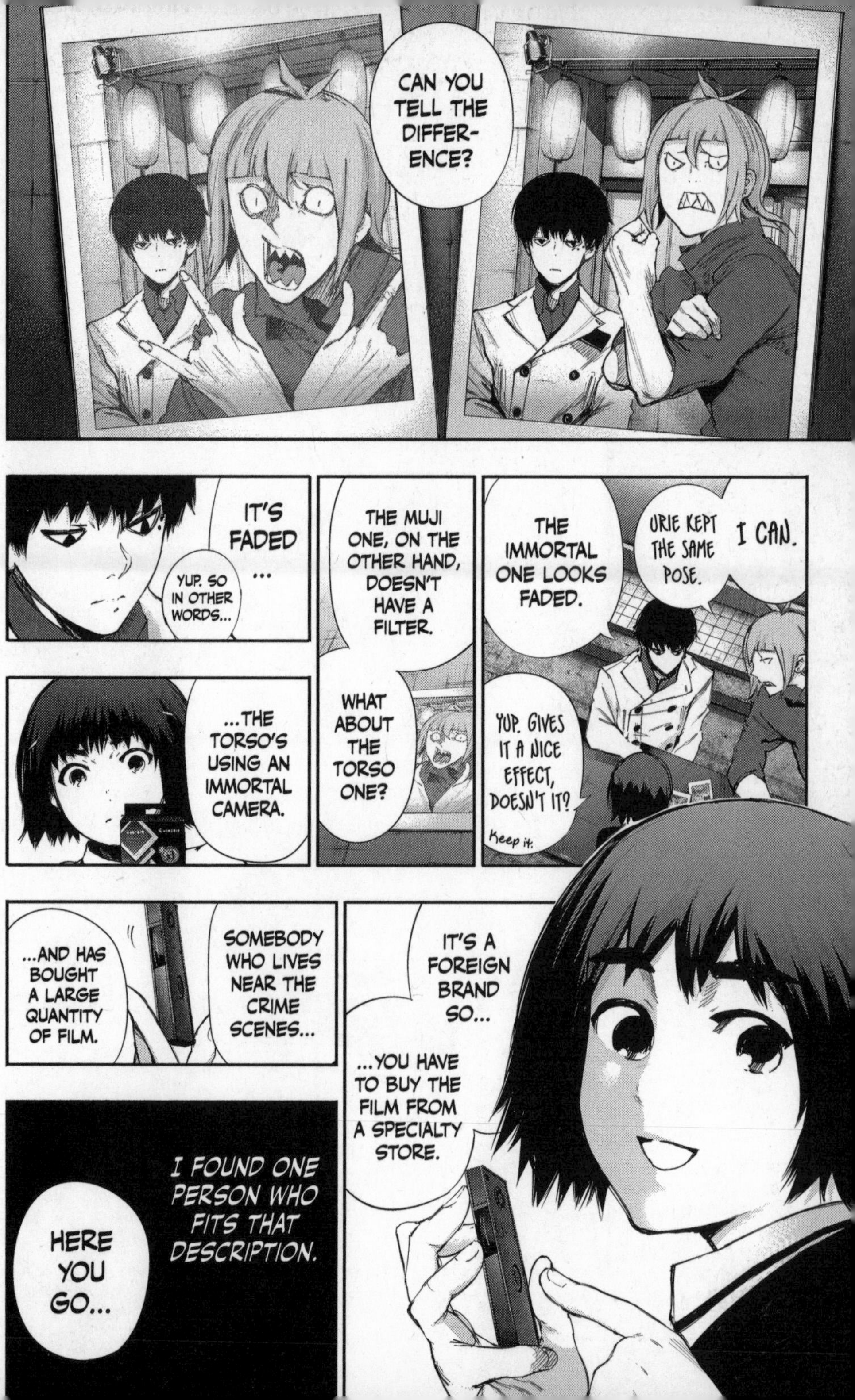
CAN YOU TELL THE DIFFER-ENCE?
I CAN.
URIE KEPT THE SAME POSE.
THE IMMORTAL ONE LOOKS FADED.
YUP. GIVES IT A NICE EFFECT, DOESN'T IT?
Keep it.
THE MUJI ONE, ON THE OTHER HAND, DOESN'T HAVE A FILTER.
WHAT ABOUT THE TORSO ONE?
IT'S FADED...
YUP. SO IN OTHER WORDS...
...THE TORSO'S USING AN IMMORTAL CAMERA.
IT'S A FOREIGN BRAND SO...
...YOU HAVE TO BUY THE FILM FROM A SPECIALTY STORE.
SOMEBODY WHO LIVES NEAR THE CRIME SCENES...
...AND HAS BOUGHT A LARGE QUANTITY OF FILM.
I FOUND ONE PERSON WHO FITS THAT DESCRIPTION.
HERE YOU GO...

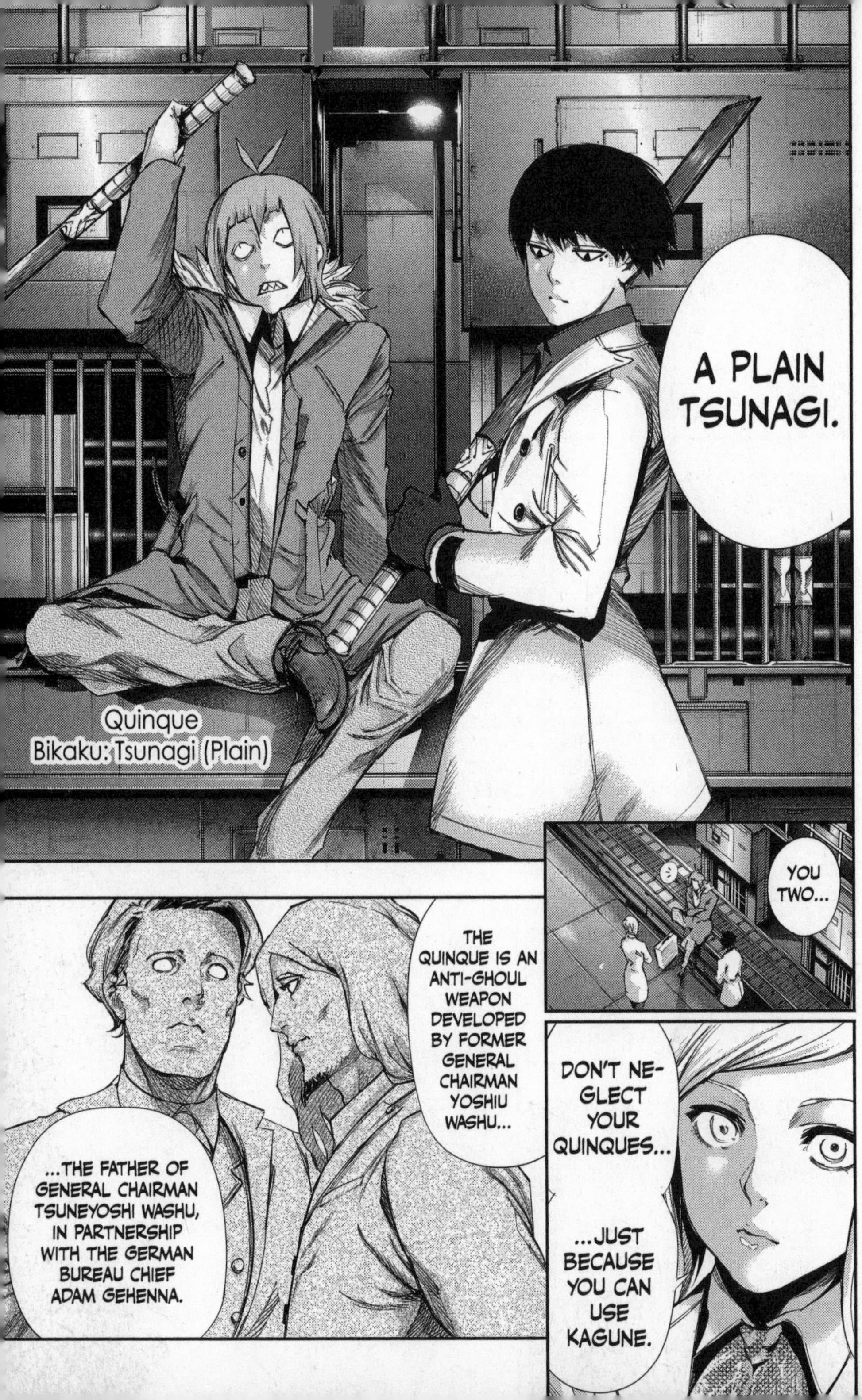
A PLAIN TSUNAGI.
Quinque
Bikaku: Tsunagi (Plain)
YOU TWO...
DON'T NE-GLECT YOUR QUINQUES...
...JUST BECAUSE YOU CAN USE KAGUNE.
THE QUINQUE IS AN ANTI-GHOUL WEAPON DEVELOPED BY FORMER GENERAL CHAIRMAN YOSHIU WASHU...
...THE FATHER OF GENERAL CHAIRMAN TSUNEYOSHI WASHU, IN PARTNERSHIP WITH THE GERMAN BUREAU CHIEF ADAM GEHENNA.

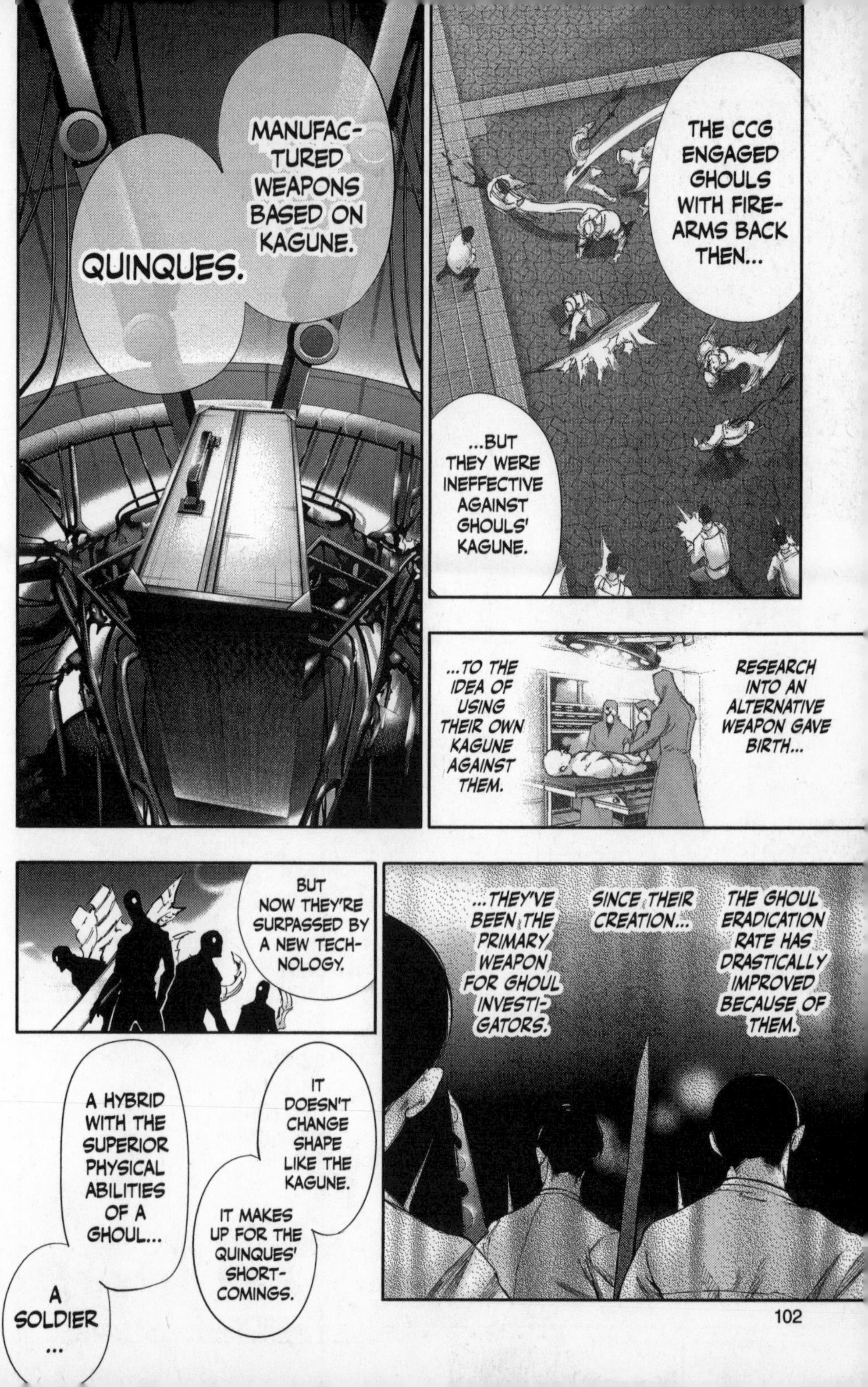
THE CCG ENGAGED GHOULS WITH FIRE-ARMS BACK THEN...
...BUT THEY WERE INEFFECTIVE AGAINST GHOULS' KAGUNE.
RESEARCH INTO AN ALTERNATIVE WEAPON GAVE BIRTH...
...TO THE IDEA OF USING THEIR OWN KAGUNE AGAINST THEM.
MANUFAC-TURED WEAPONS BASED ON KAGUNE.
QUINQUES.
THE GHOUL ERADICATION RATE HAS DRASTICALLY IMPROVED BECAUSE OF THEM.
SINCE THEIR CREATION...
...THEY'VE BEEN THE PRIMARY WEAPON FOR GHOUL INVESTI-GATORS.
BUT NOW THEY'RE SURPASSED BY A NEW TECH-NOLOGY.
IT DOESN'T CHANGE SHAPE LIKE THE KAGUNE.
IT MAKES UP FOR THE QUINQUES' SHORT-COMINGS.
A HYBRID WITH THE SUPERIOR PHYSICAL ABILITIES OF A GHOUL...
A SOLDIER ...

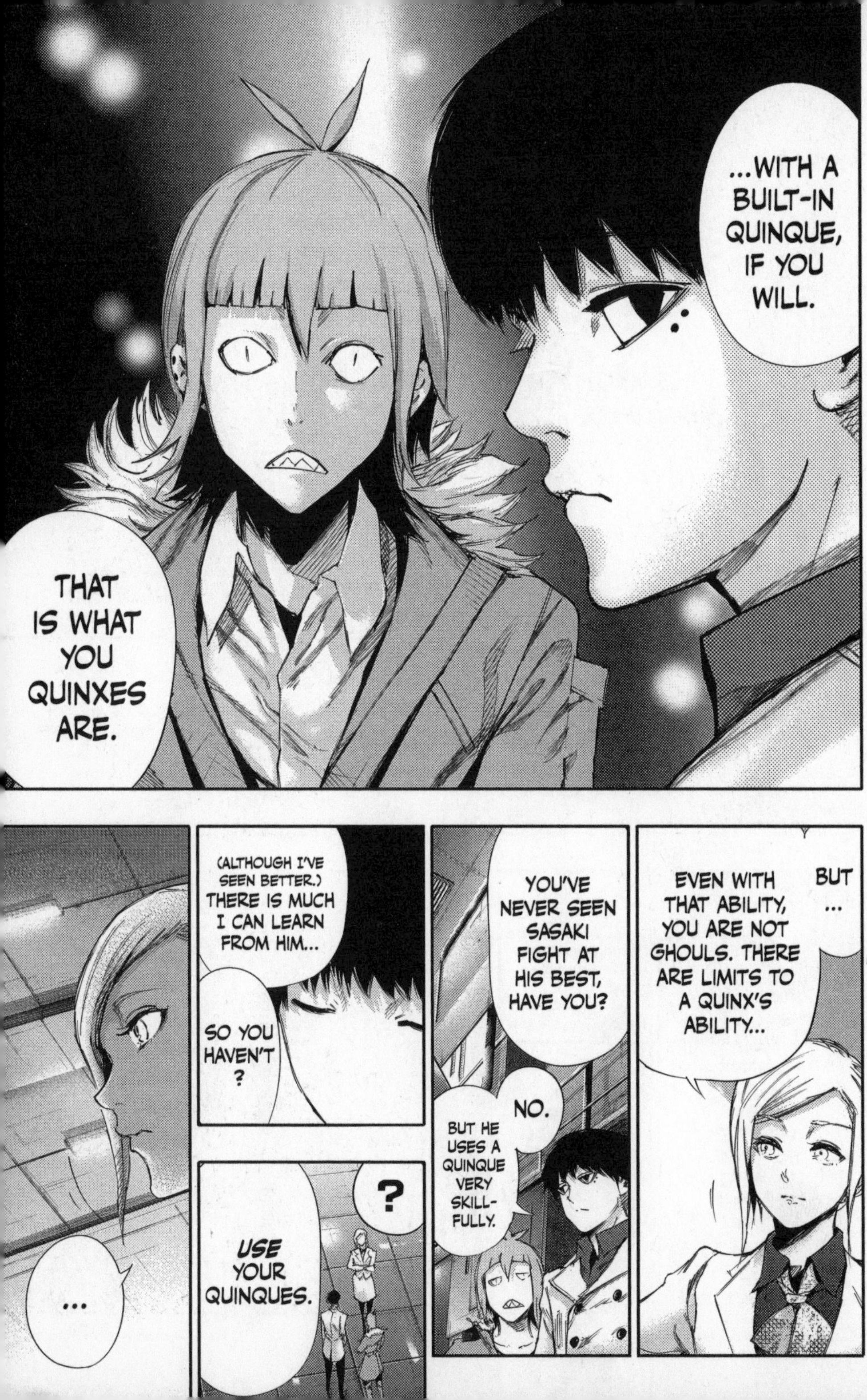
...WITH A BUILT-IN QUINQUE, IF YOU WILL.
THAT IS WHAT YOU QUINXES ARE.
BUT ...
EVEN WITH THAT ABILITY, YOU ARE NOT GHOULS. THERE ARE LIMITS TO A QUINX'S ABILITY...
YOU'VE NEVER SEEN SASAKI FIGHT AT HIS BEST, HAVE YOU?
NO.
BUT HE USES A QUINQUE VERY SKILL-FULLY.
(ALTHOUGH I'VE SEEN BETTER.) THERE IS MUCH I CAN LEARN FROM HIM...
SO YOU HAVEN'T ?
?
USE YOUR QUINQUES.
...

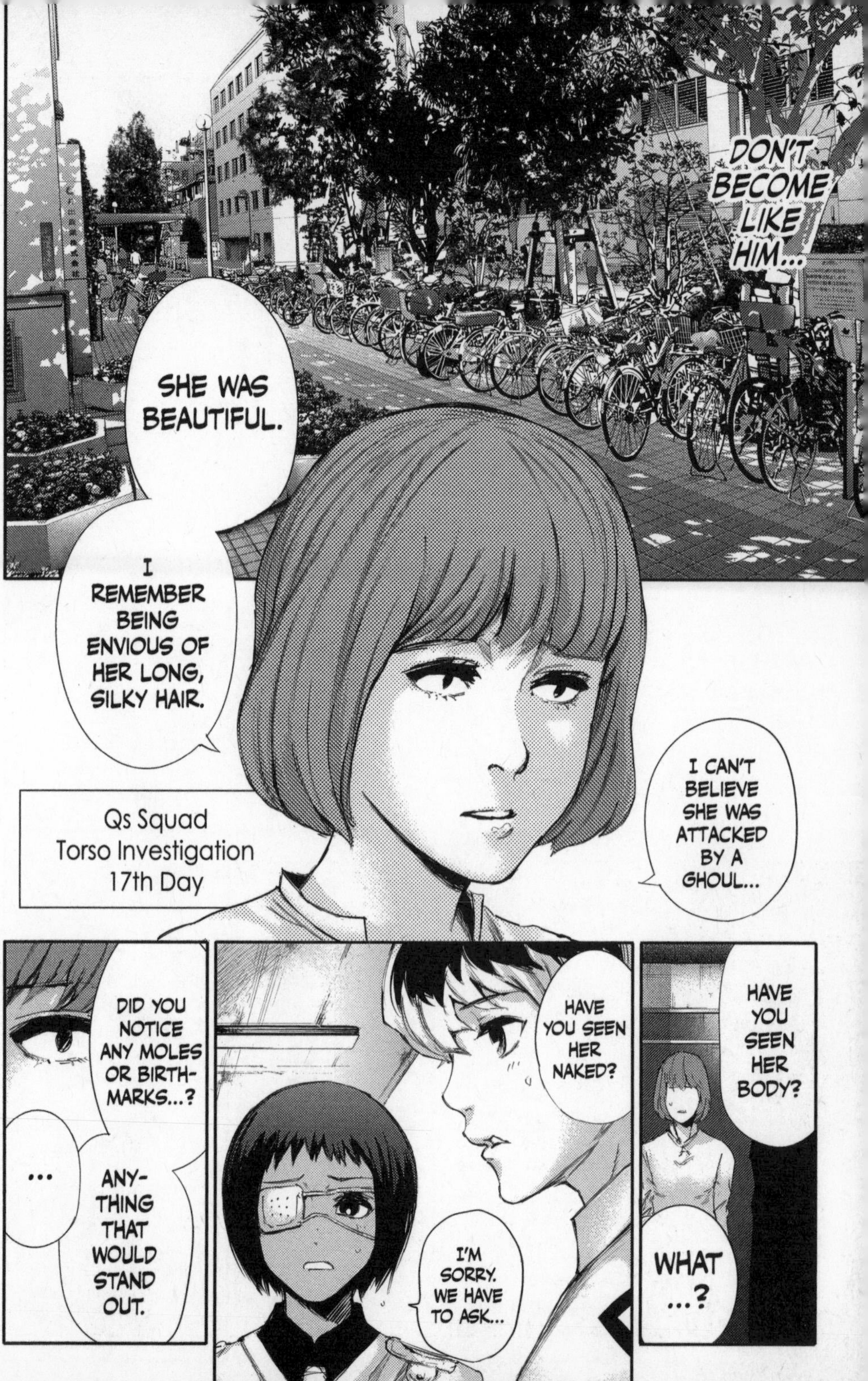
DON'T BECOME LIKE HIM...
SHE WAS BEAUTIFUL.
I REMEMBER BEING ENVIOUS OF HER LONG, SILKY HAIR.
Qs Squad Torso Investigation 17th Day
I CAN'T BELIEVE SHE WAS ATTACKED BY A GHOUL...
HAVE YOU SEEN HER BODY?
WHAT ...?
HAVE YOU SEEN HER NAKED?
I'M SORRY. WE HAVE TO ASK...
DID YOU NOTICE ANY MOLES OR BIRTH-MARKS...?
...
ANY-THING THAT WOULD STAND OUT.

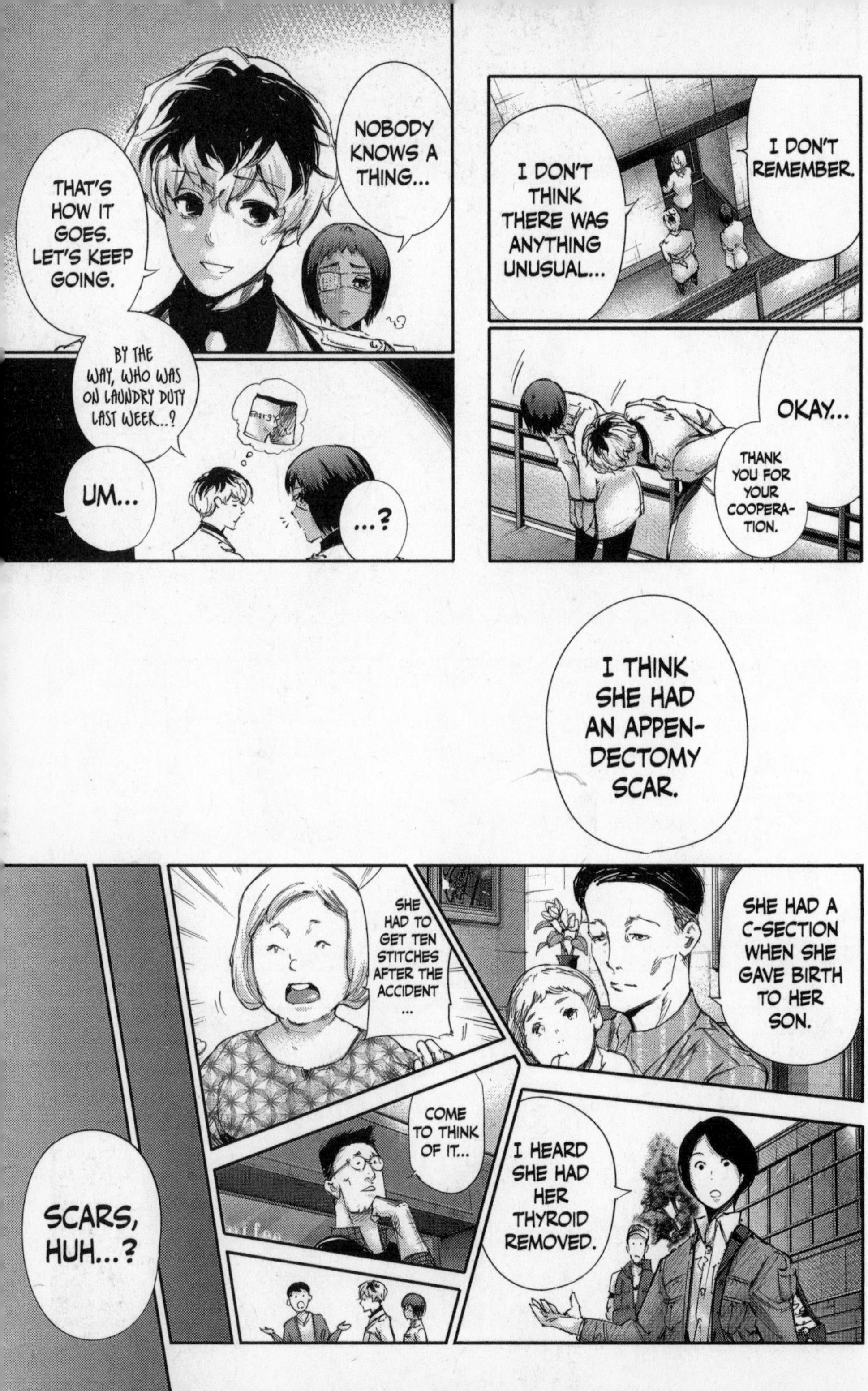
I DON'T REMEMBER.
I DON'T THINK THERE WAS ANYTHING UNUSUAL...
NOBODY KNOWS A THING...
THAT'S HOW IT GOES. LET'S KEEP GOING.
OKAY...
THANK YOU FOR YOUR COOPERATION.
BY THE WAY, WHO WAS ON LAUNDRY DUTY LAST WEEK...?
UM...
...?
I THINK SHE HAD AN APPENDECTOMY SCAR.
SHE HAD A C-SECTION WHEN SHE GAVE BIRTH TO HER SON.
SHE HAD TO GET TEN STITCHES AFTER THE ACCIDENT ...
I HEARD SHE HAD HER THYROID REMOVED.
COME TO THINK OF IT...
SCARS, HUH...?

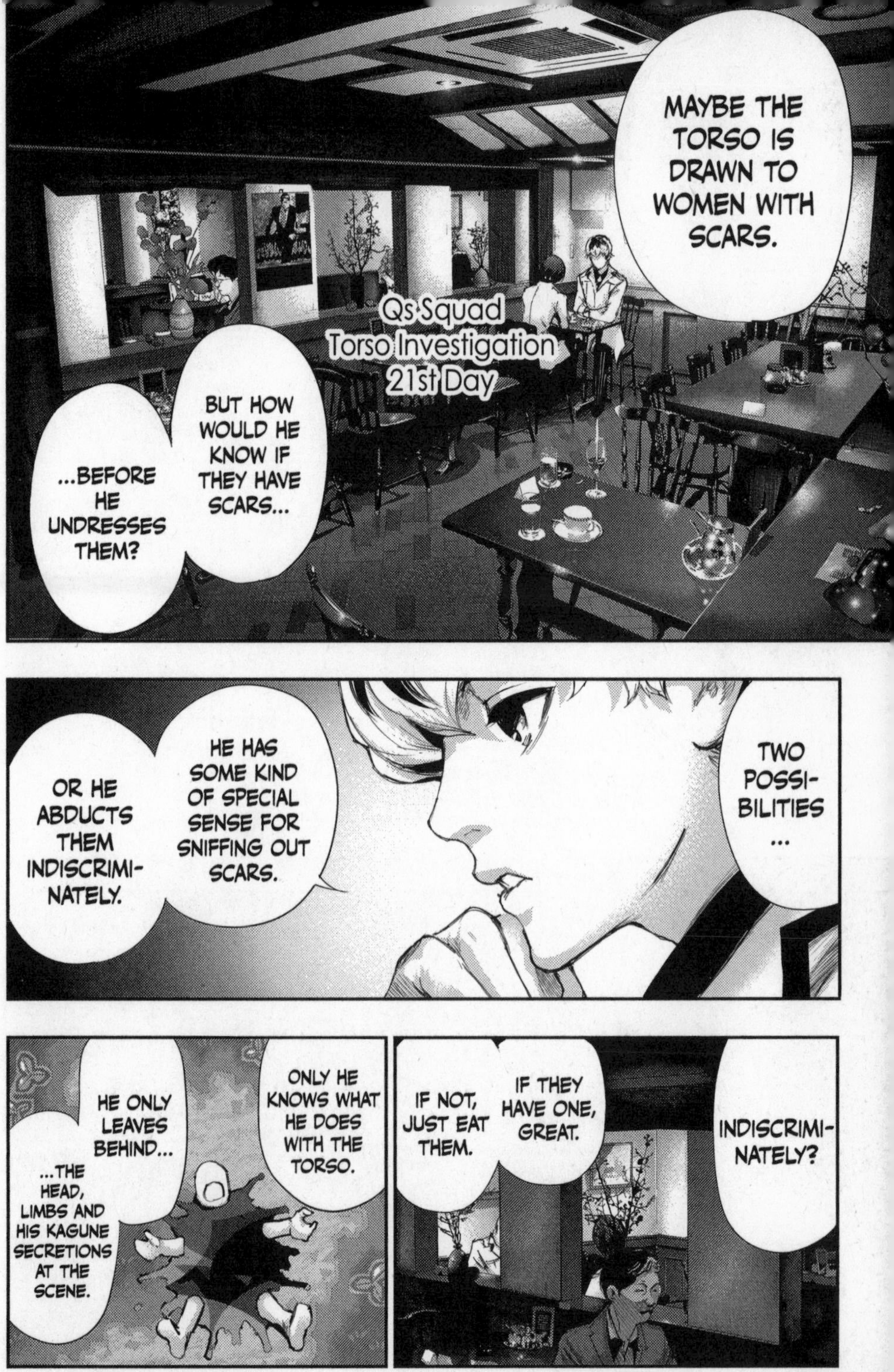
MAYBE THE TORSO IS DRAWN TO WOMEN WITH SCARS.
Qs Squad Torso Investigation 21st Day
BUT HOW WOULD HE KNOW IF THEY HAVE SCARS...
...BEFORE HE UNDRESSES THEM?
TWO POSSI-BILITIES...
HE HAS SOME KIND OF SPECIAL SENSE FOR SNIFFING OUT SCARS.
OR HE ABDUCTS THEM INDISCRIMI-NATELY.
INDISCRIMI-NATELY?
IF THEY HAVE ONE, GREAT.
IF NOT, JUST EAT THEM.
ONLY HE KNOWS WHAT HE DOES WITH THE TORSO.
HE ONLY LEAVES BEHIND...
...THE HEAD, LIMBS AND HIS KAGUNE SECRETIONS AT THE SCENE.

BUT IF HE'S PARTICULAR ABOUT HIS VICTIMS...

...HE SHOULD BE TARGETING AREAS WHERE THEY'D MOST LIKELY BE.

LOOK.

HOSPITAL RECORDS OF ALL THE VICTIMS.

MAINLY SURGICAL HOSPITALS.

IS THAT ...?

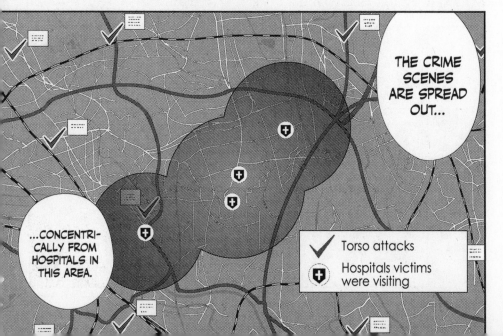

THE CRIME SCENES ARE SPREAD OUT...

...CONCENTRICALLY FROM HOSPITALS IN THIS AREA.

✔ Torso attacks

✚ Hospitals victims were visiting

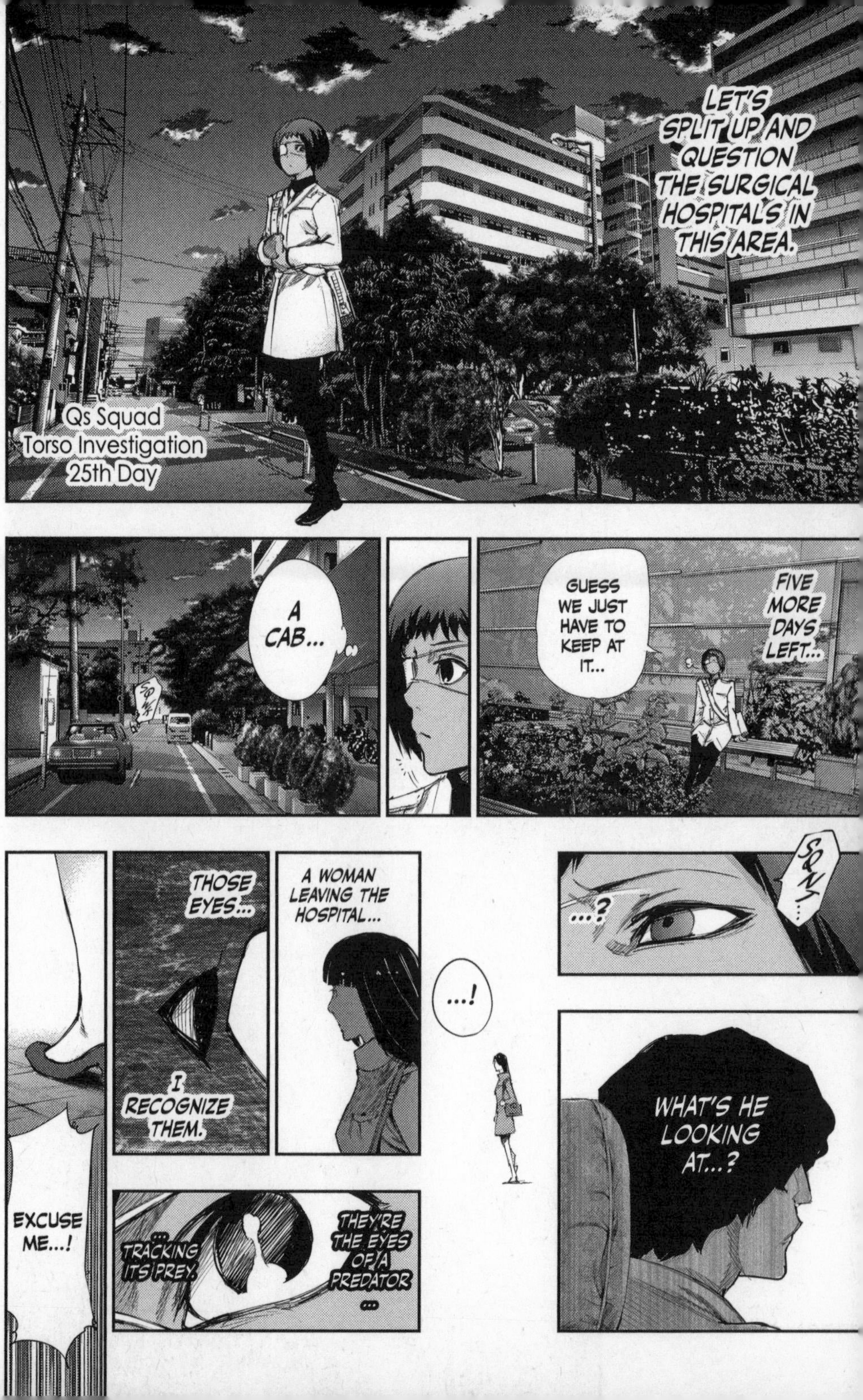
LET'S SPLIT UP AND QUESTION THE SURGICAL HOSPITALS IN THIS AREA.
Qs Squad Torso Investigation 25th Day
FIVE MORE DAYS LEFT...
GUESS WE JUST HAVE TO KEEP AT IT...
A CAB...
SQNT...
...?
...!
WHAT'S HE LOOKING AT...?
A WOMAN LEAVING THE HOSPITAL...
THOSE EYES...
I RECOGNIZE THEM.
THEY'RE THE EYES OF A PREDATOR ...
...TRACKING ITS PREY.
EXCUSE ME...!

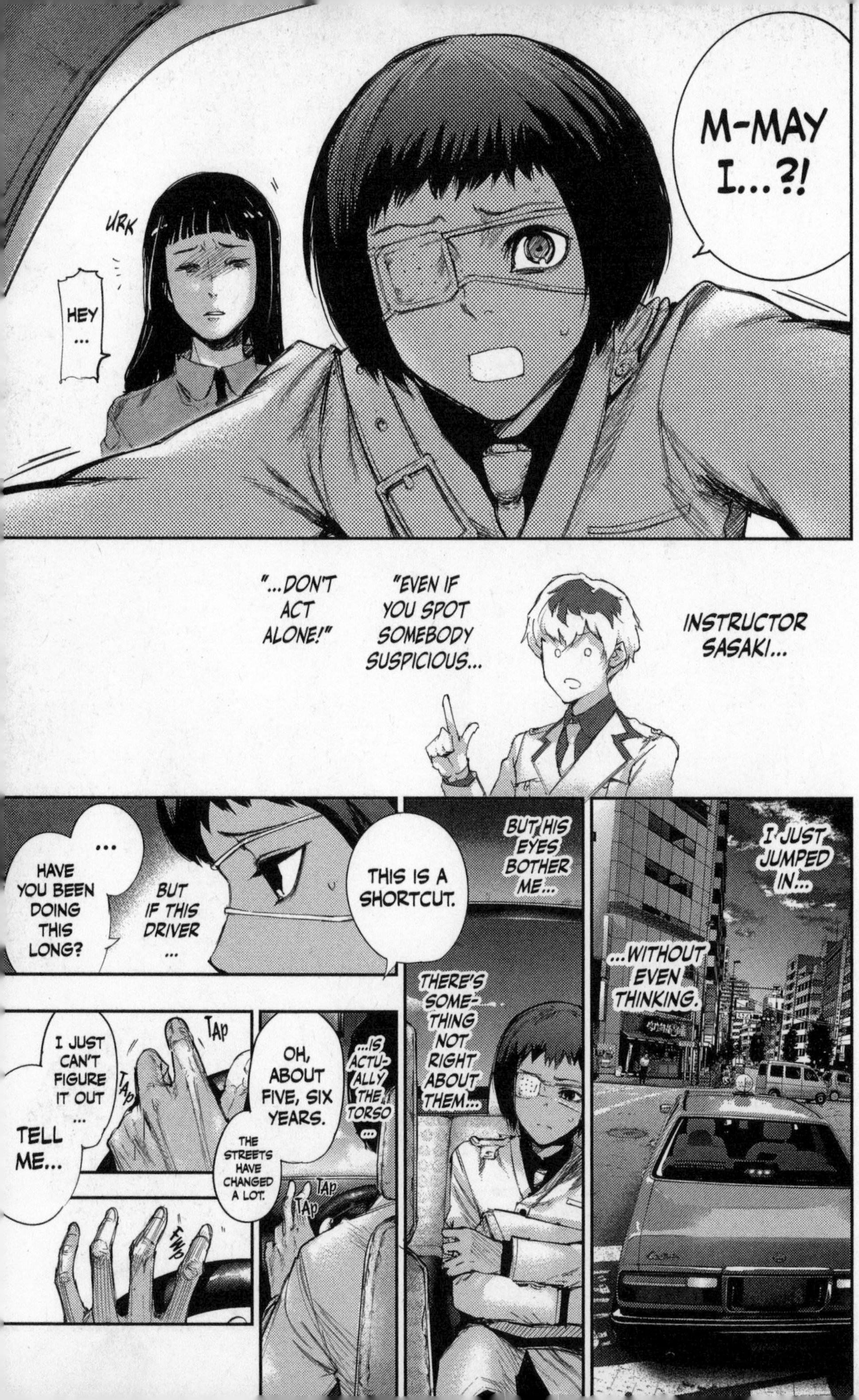
M-MAY I...?!
URK
HEY ...
INSTRUCTOR SASAKI...
"EVEN IF YOU SPOT SOMEBODY SUSPICIOUS...
"...DON'T ACT ALONE!"
I JUST JUMPED IN...
...WITHOUT EVEN THINKING.
BUT HIS EYES BOTHER ME...
THERE'S SOME-THING NOT RIGHT ABOUT THEM...
THIS IS A SHORTCUT.
BUT IF THIS DRIVER ...
... HAVE YOU BEEN DOING THIS LONG?
...IS ACTUALLY THE TORSO ...
OH, ABOUT FIVE, SIX YEARS.
THE STREETS HAVE CHANGED A LOT.
TAP
TAP
TAP
TAP
I JUST CAN'T FIGURE IT OUT ...
TELL ME...
FWIP

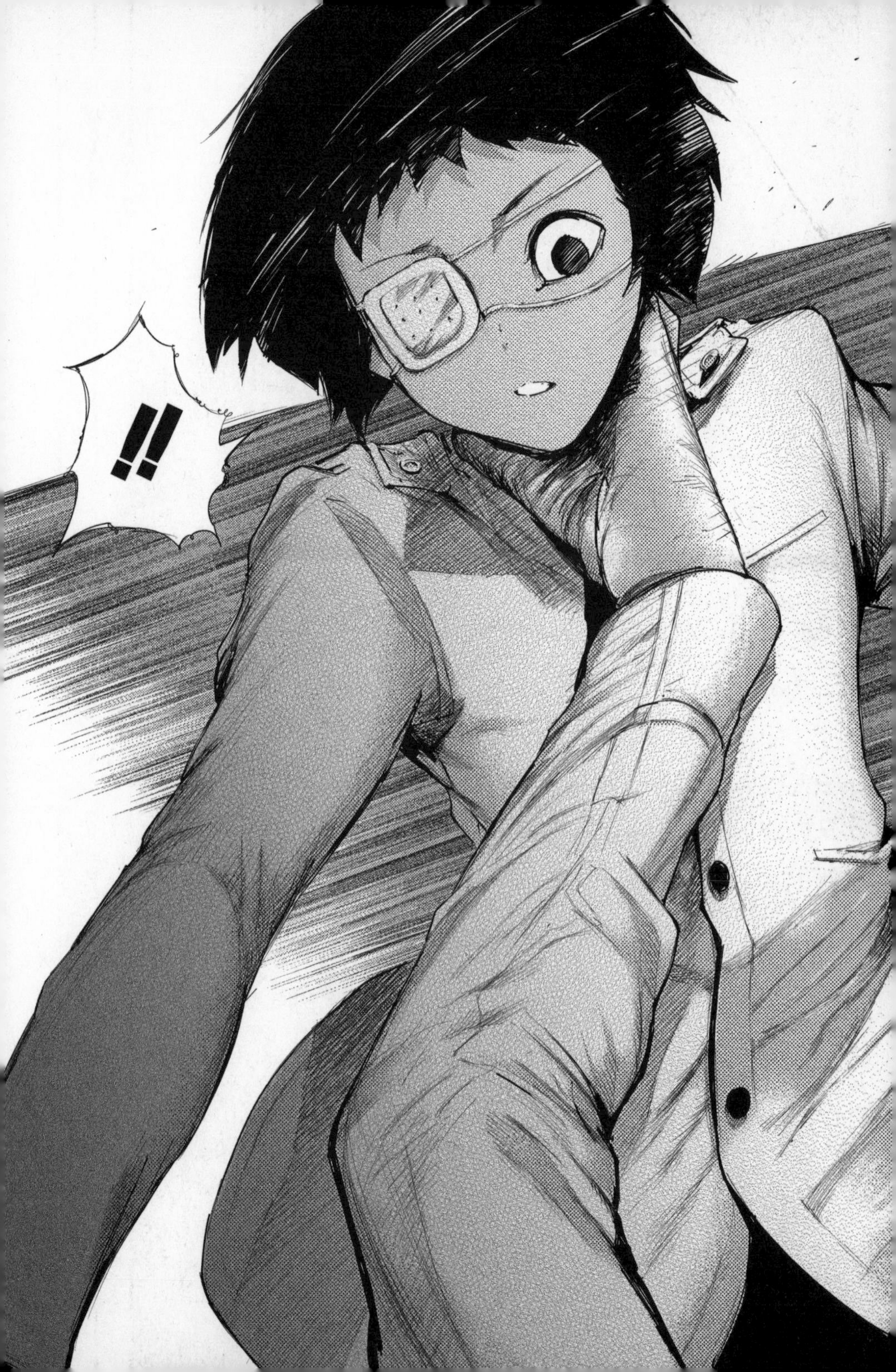
!!

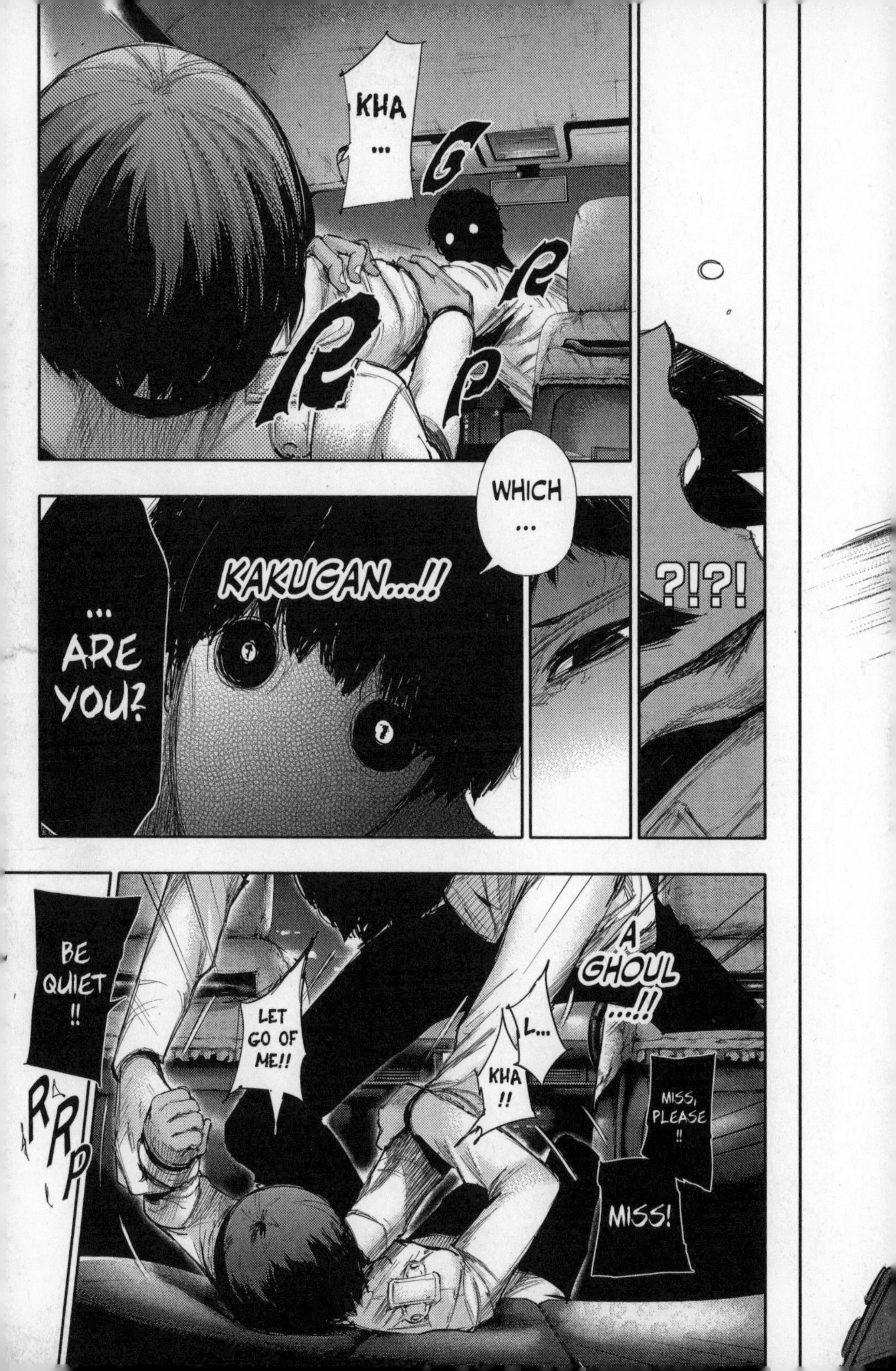
?!?!
KHA ...
GRRP
GRRP
WHICH ...
KAKUGAN...!!
... ARE YOU?
A GHOUL ...!!
MISS, PLEASE !!
MISS!
L...
KHA !!
LET GO OF ME!!
BE QUIET !!
RRP

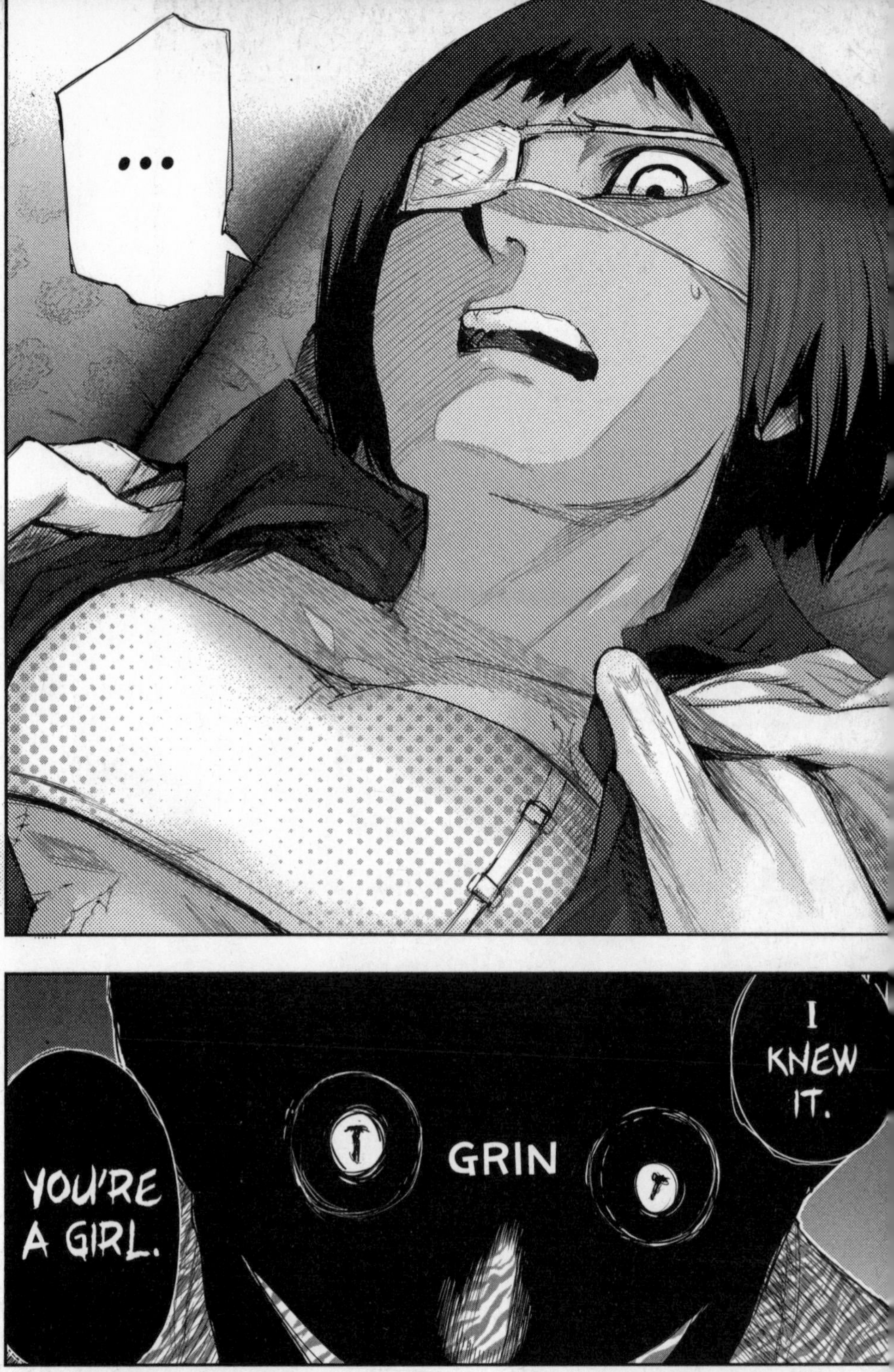
...
I KNEW IT.
GRIN
YOU'RE A GIRL.

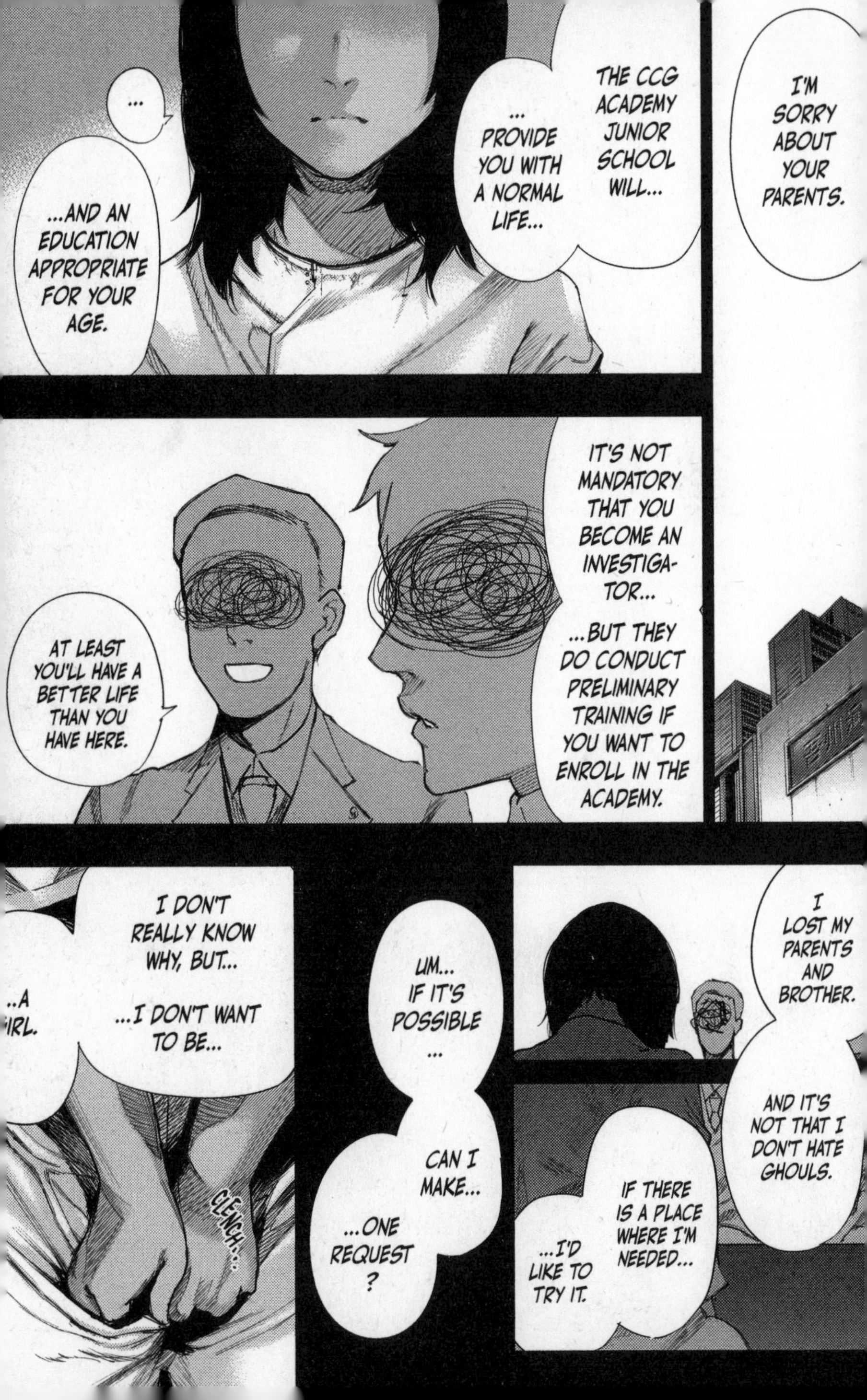
I'M SORRY ABOUT YOUR PARENTS.
THE CCG ACADEMY JUNIOR SCHOOL WILL...
...PROVIDE YOU WITH A NORMAL LIFE...
...
...AND AN EDUCATION APPROPRIATE FOR YOUR AGE.
IT'S NOT MANDATORY THAT YOU BECOME AN INVESTIGA-TOR...
...BUT THEY DO CONDUCT PRELIMINARY TRAINING IF YOU WANT TO ENROLL IN THE ACADEMY.
AT LEAST YOU'LL HAVE A BETTER LIFE THAN YOU HAVE HERE.
I LOST MY PARENTS AND BROTHER.
AND IT'S NOT THAT I DON'T HATE GHOULS.
IF THERE IS A PLACE WHERE I'M NEEDED...
...I'D LIKE TO TRY IT.
UM... IF IT'S POSSIBLE ...
CAN I MAKE...
...ONE REQUEST ?
I DON'T REALLY KNOW WHY, BUT...
...I DON'T WANT TO BE...
..A IRL.
CLENCH...

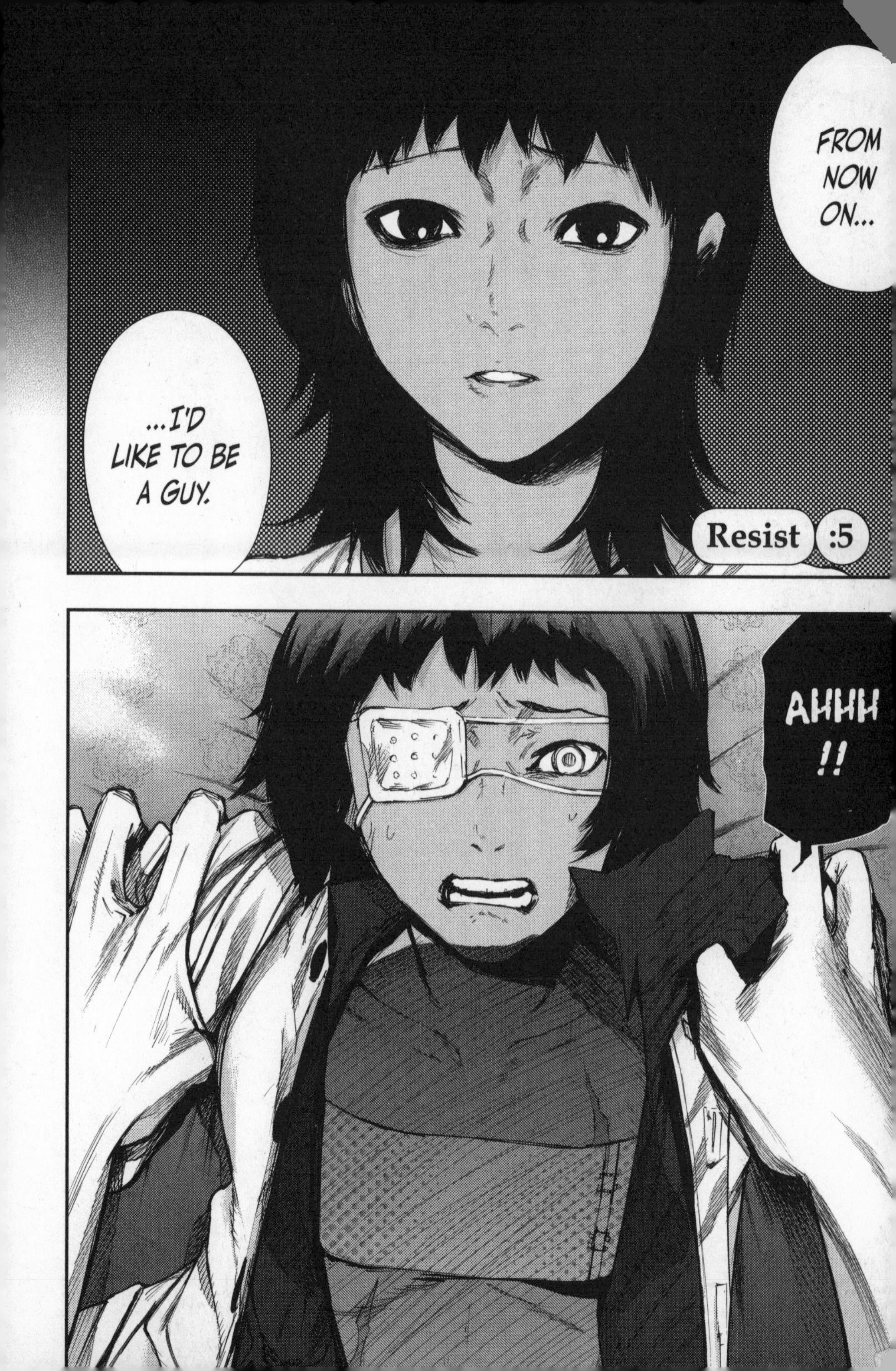
FROM NOW ON...
...I'D LIKE TO BE A GUY.
Resist :5
AHHH !!

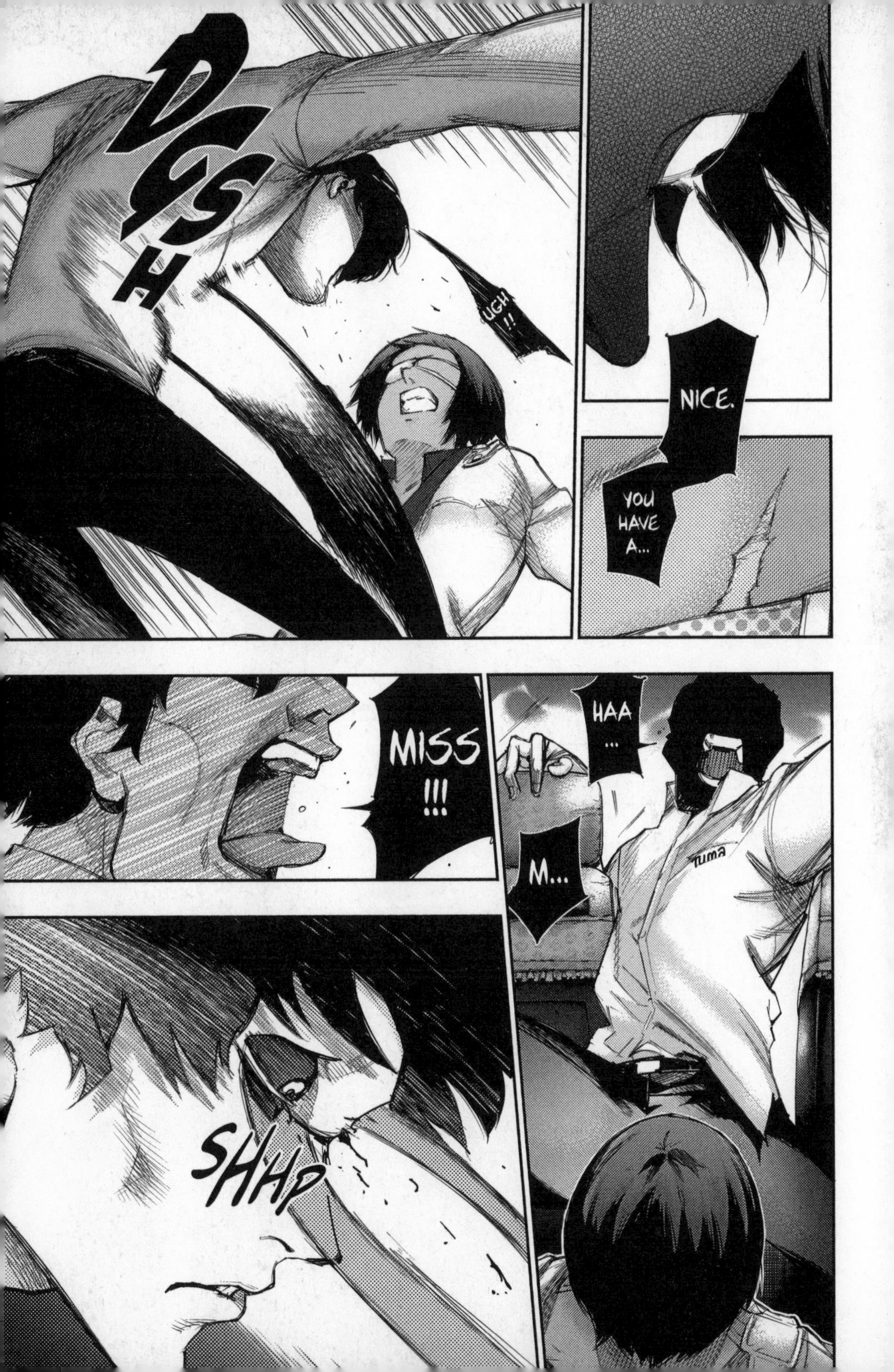
NICE.
YOU HAVE A...
DGSH
UGH!!
HAA...
M...
MISS!!!
SHHP

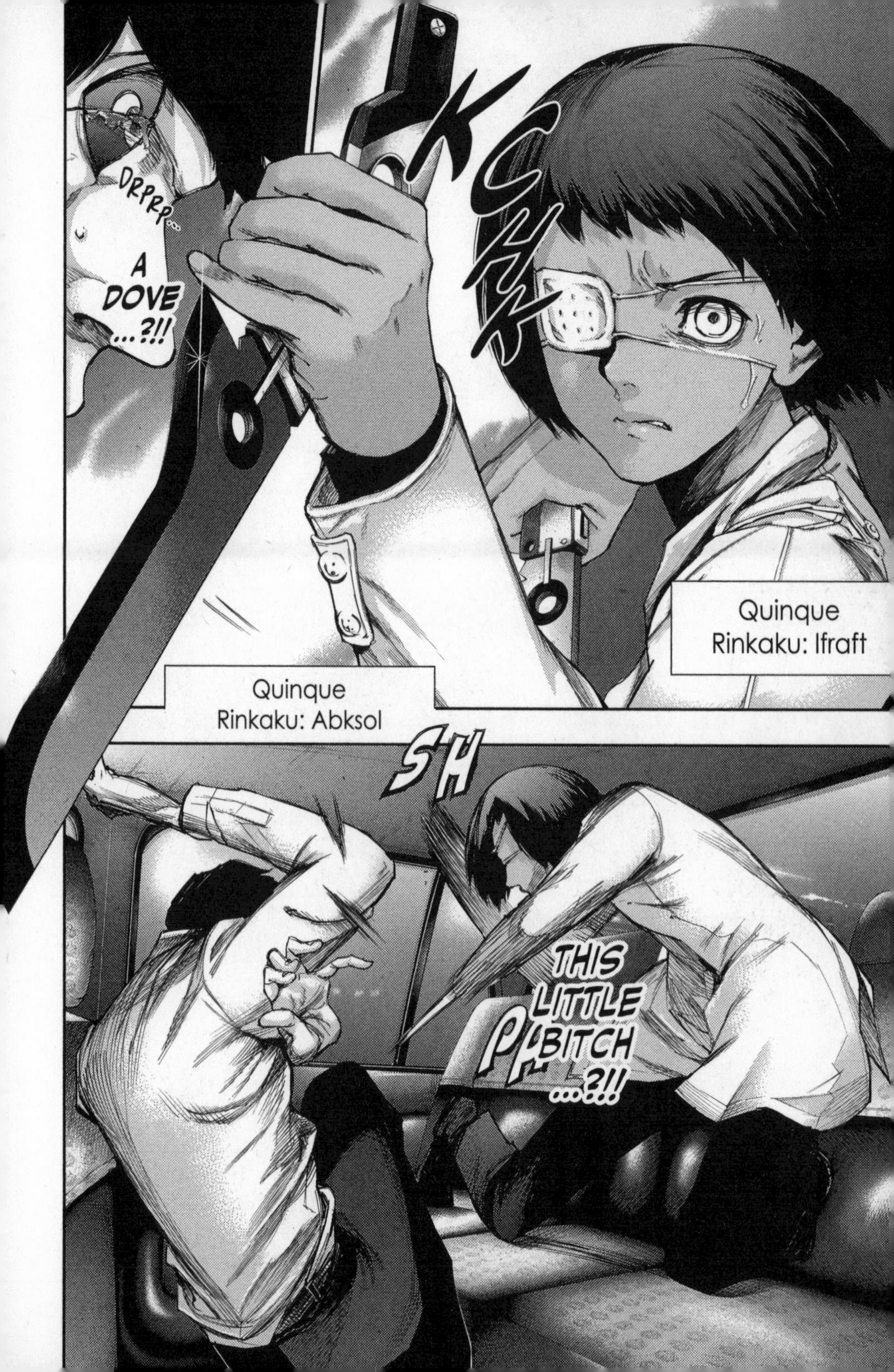
KCHAK
DRPRP...
A DOVE...?!!
Quinque
Rinkaku: Ifraft
Quinque
Rinkaku: Abksol
SH
THIS LITTLE BITCH...?!!

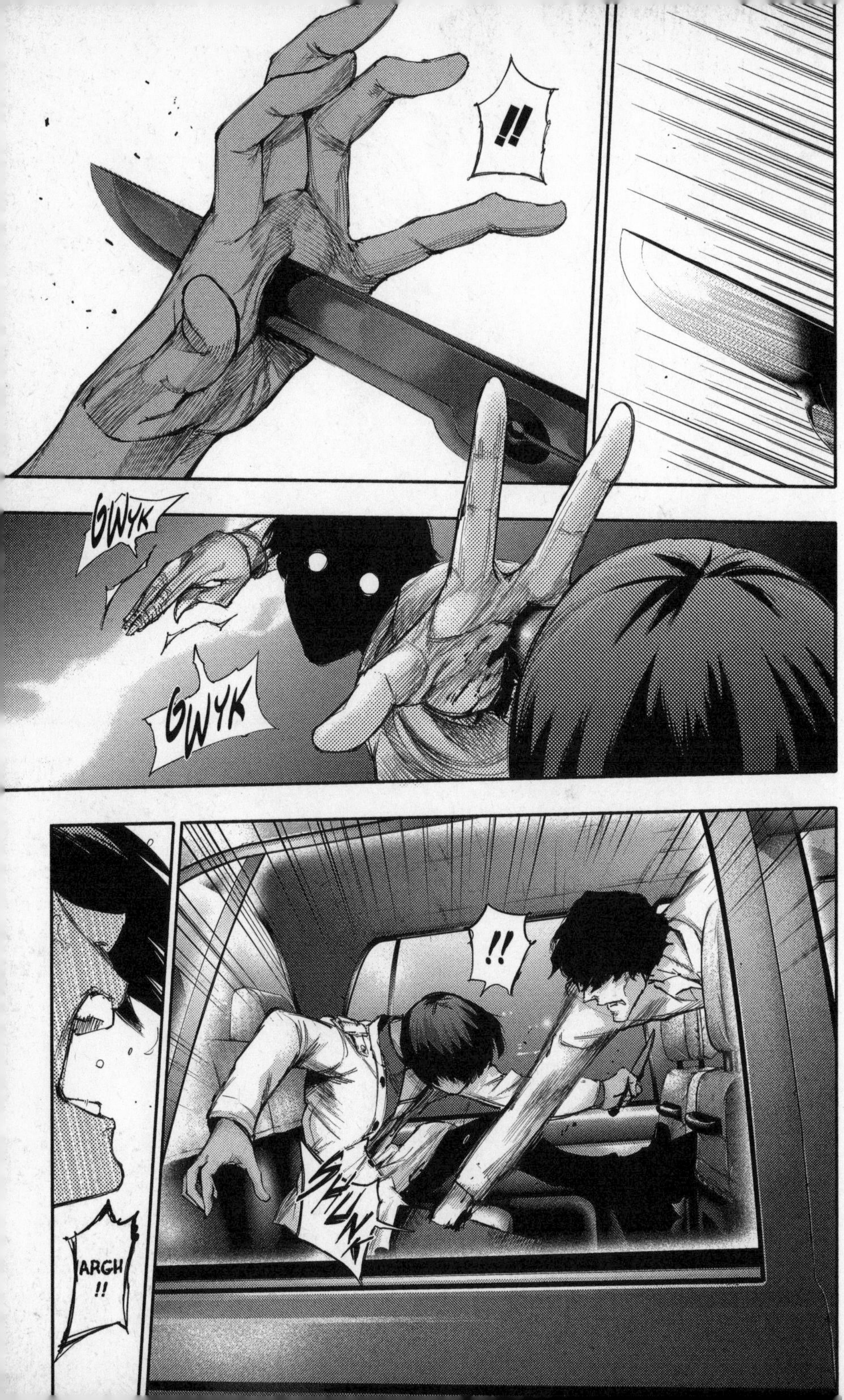
!!
GWYK
GWYK
!!
SKUNK
ARGH !!

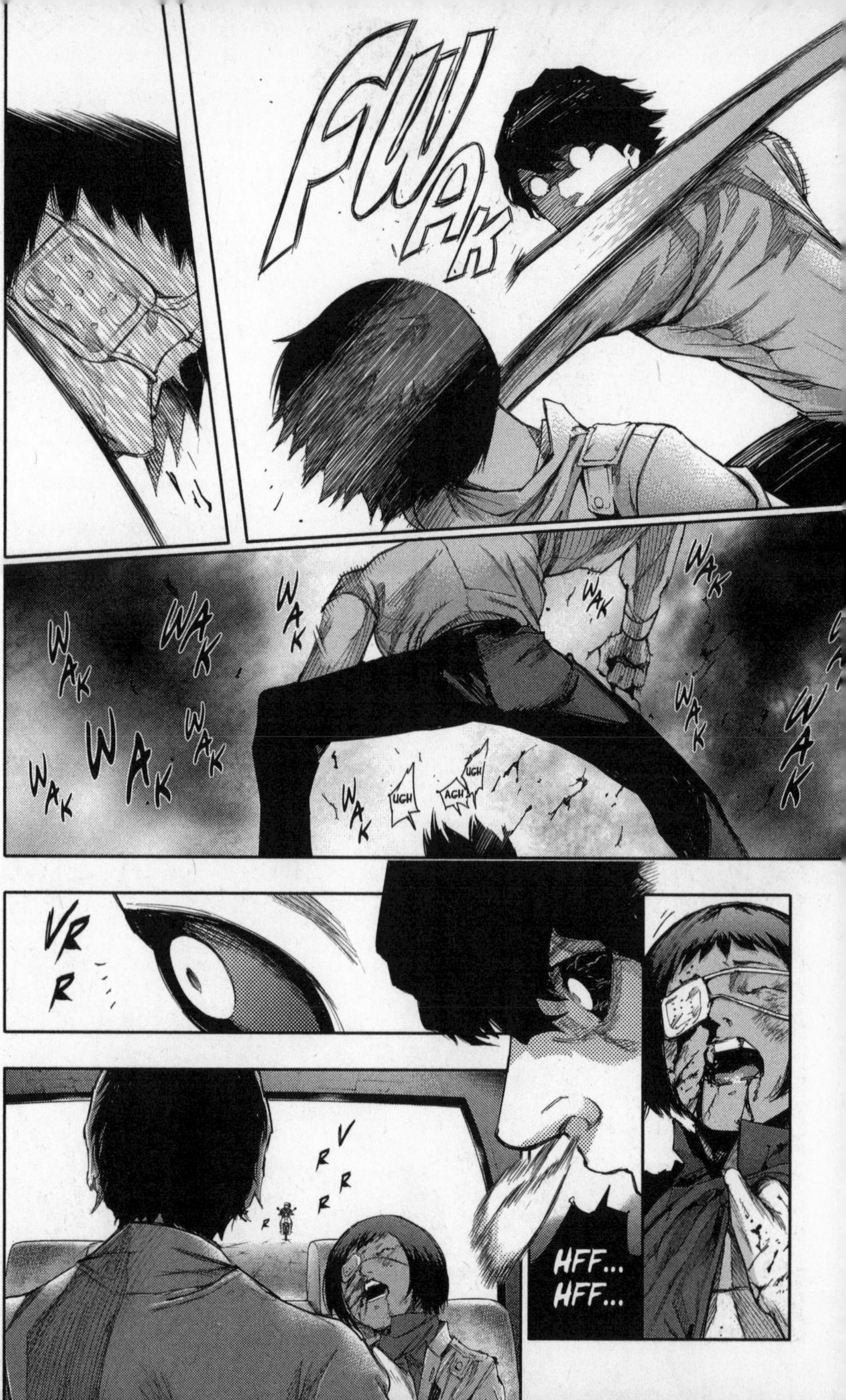
FWAK
WAK
WAK
WAK
WAK
WAK
WAK
WAK
WAK
WAK
WAK
UGH
AGH
UGH
HFF... HFF...
VRR
R
VRRR
RRR

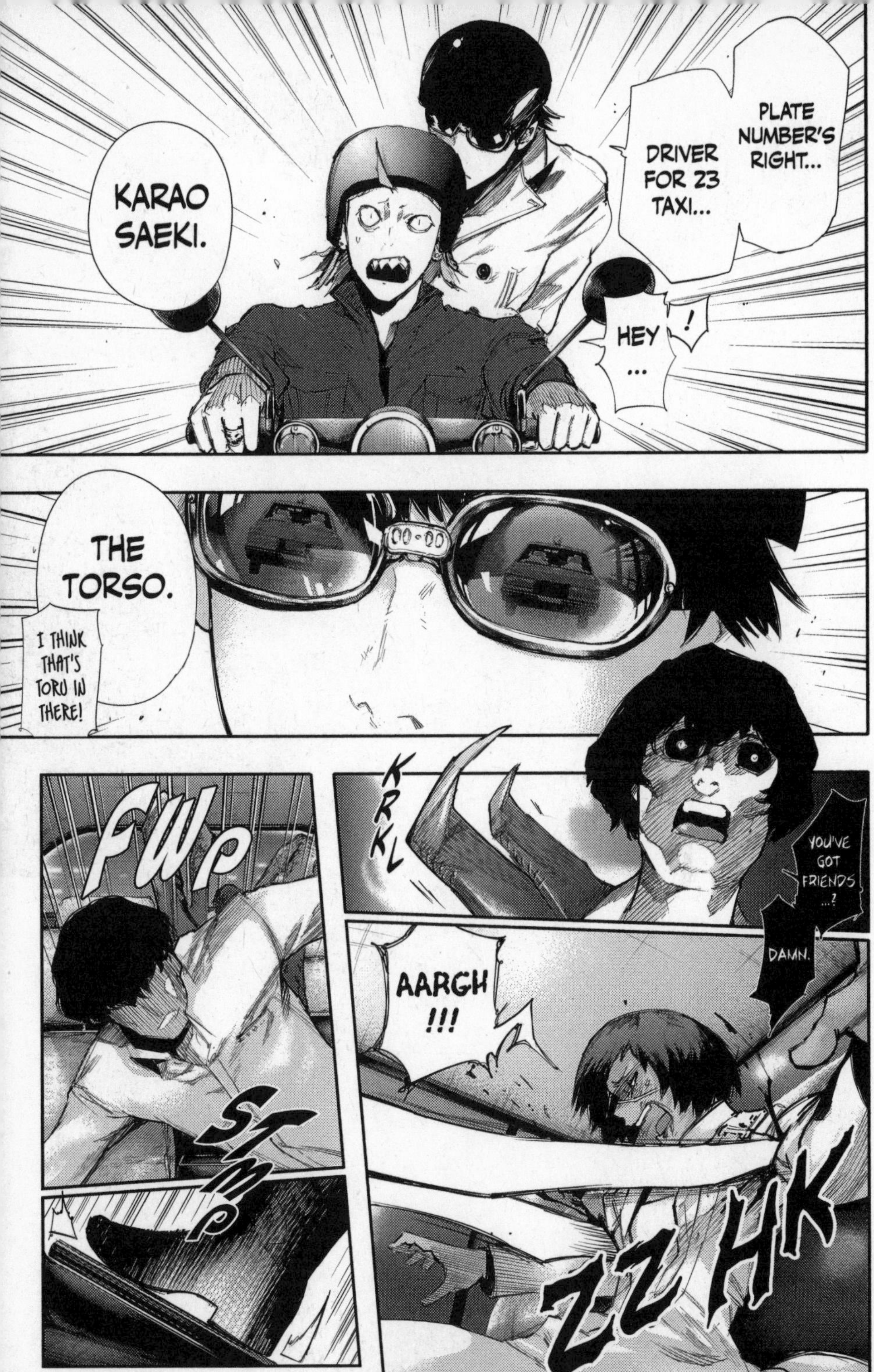
PLATE NUMBER'S RIGHT...
DRIVER FOR 23 TAXI...
KARAO SAEKI.
HEY ...
!
THE TORSO.
I THINK THAT'S TORU IN THERE!
KRKL
YOU'VE GOT FRIENDS ...?
DAMN.
AARGH !!!
ZZHK
FWP
STMP

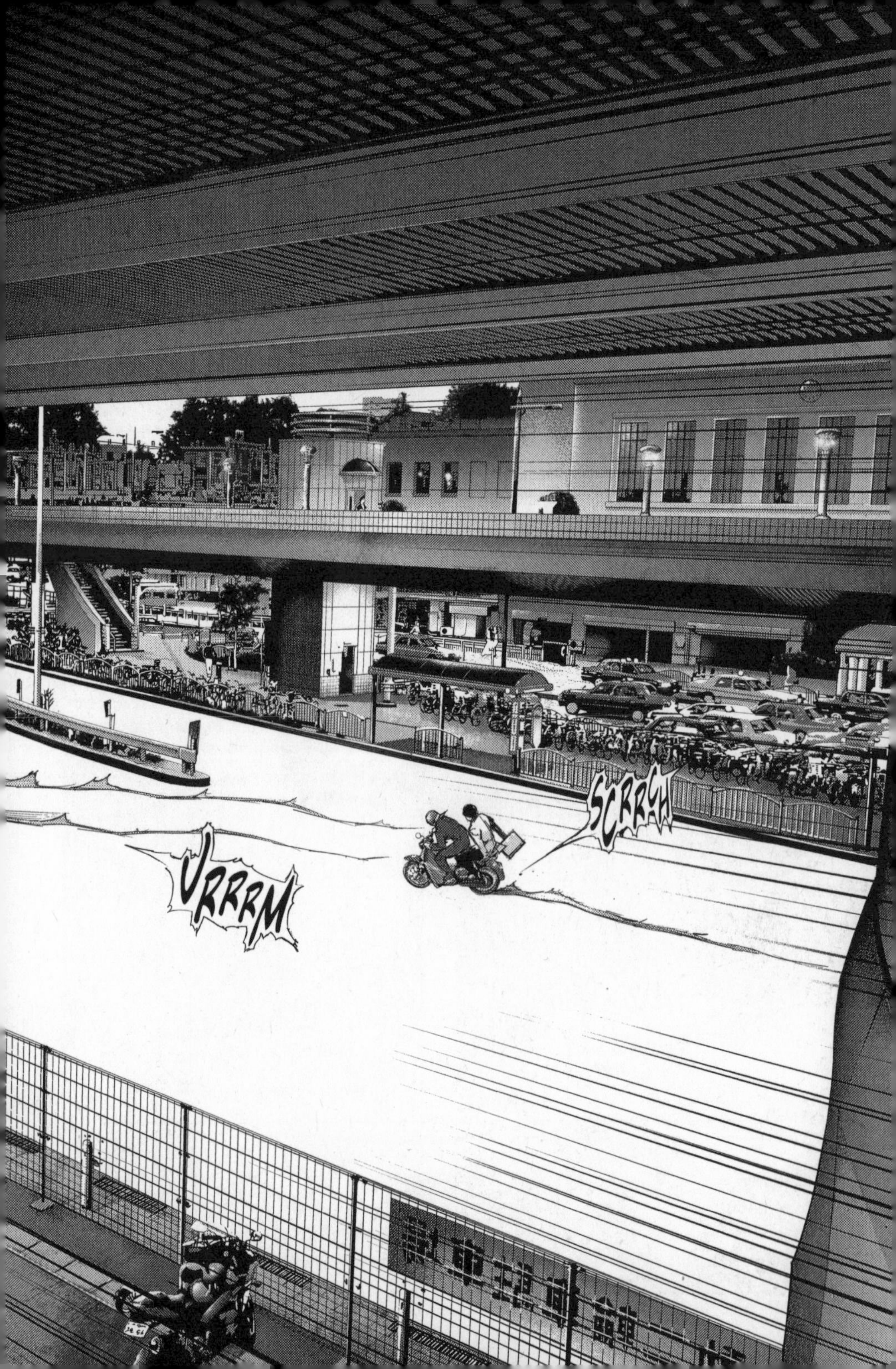
SCRRCH
VRRRM

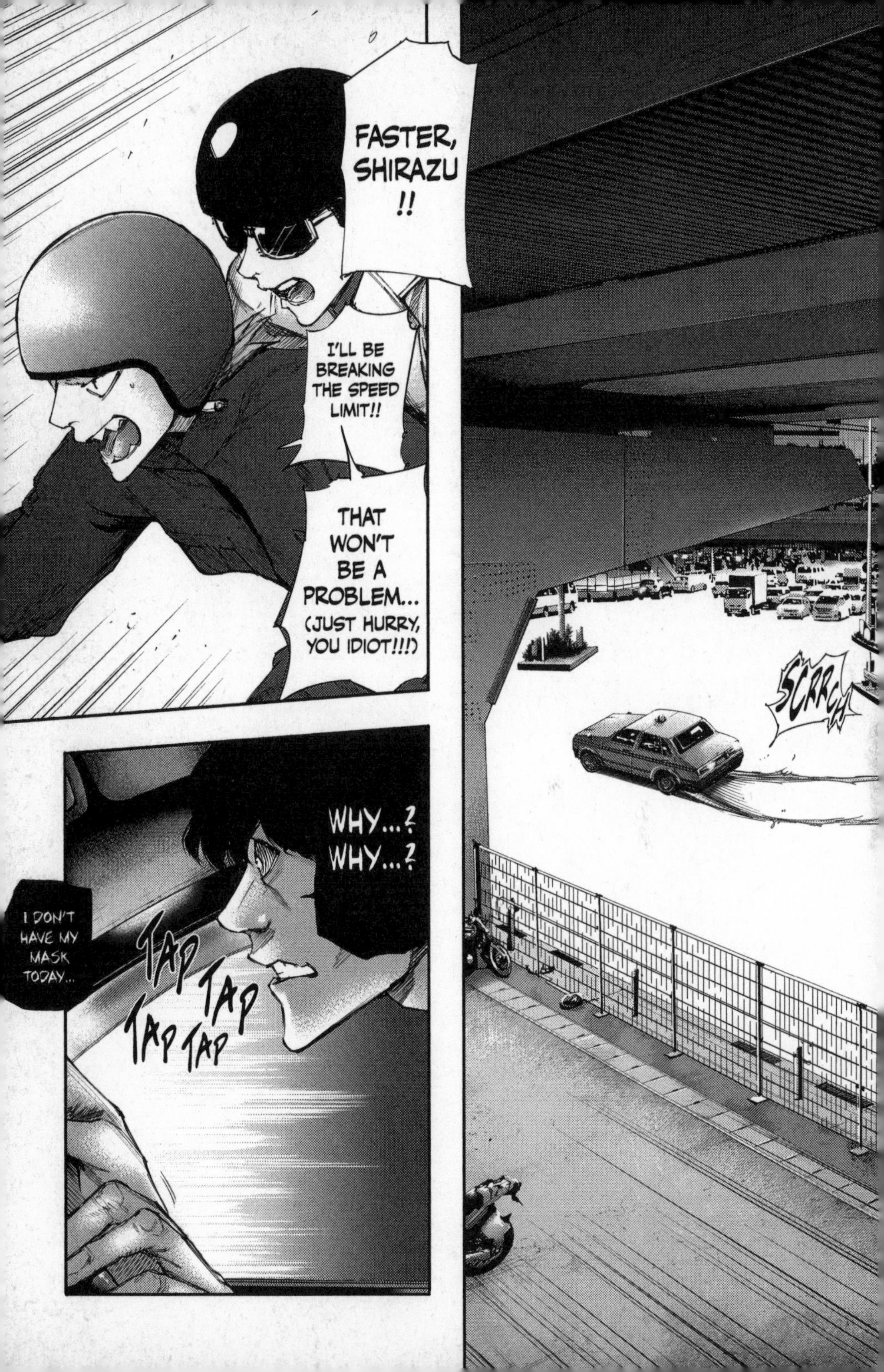
SCRRCH
FASTER, SHIRAZU!!
I'LL BE BREAKING THE SPEED LIMIT!!
THAT WON'T BE A PROBLEM... (JUST HURRY, YOU IDIOT!!!)
WHY...? WHY...?
TAP TAP TAP TAP
I DON'T HAVE MY MASK TODAY...

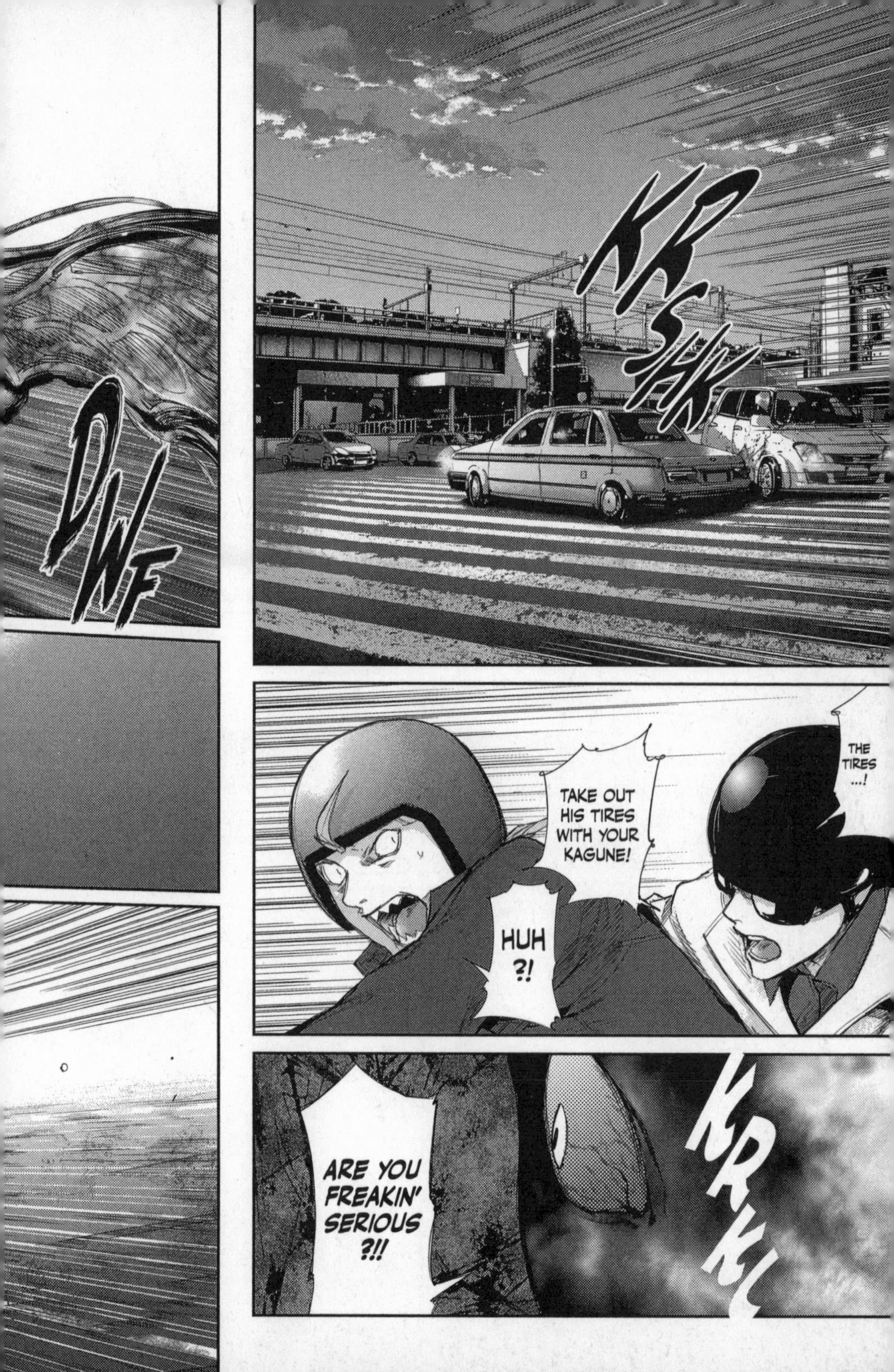
KRSHK
DWF
THE TIRES ...!
TAKE OUT HIS TIRES WITH YOUR KAGUNE!
HUH ?!
KRKL
ARE YOU FREAKIN' SERIOUS ?!!

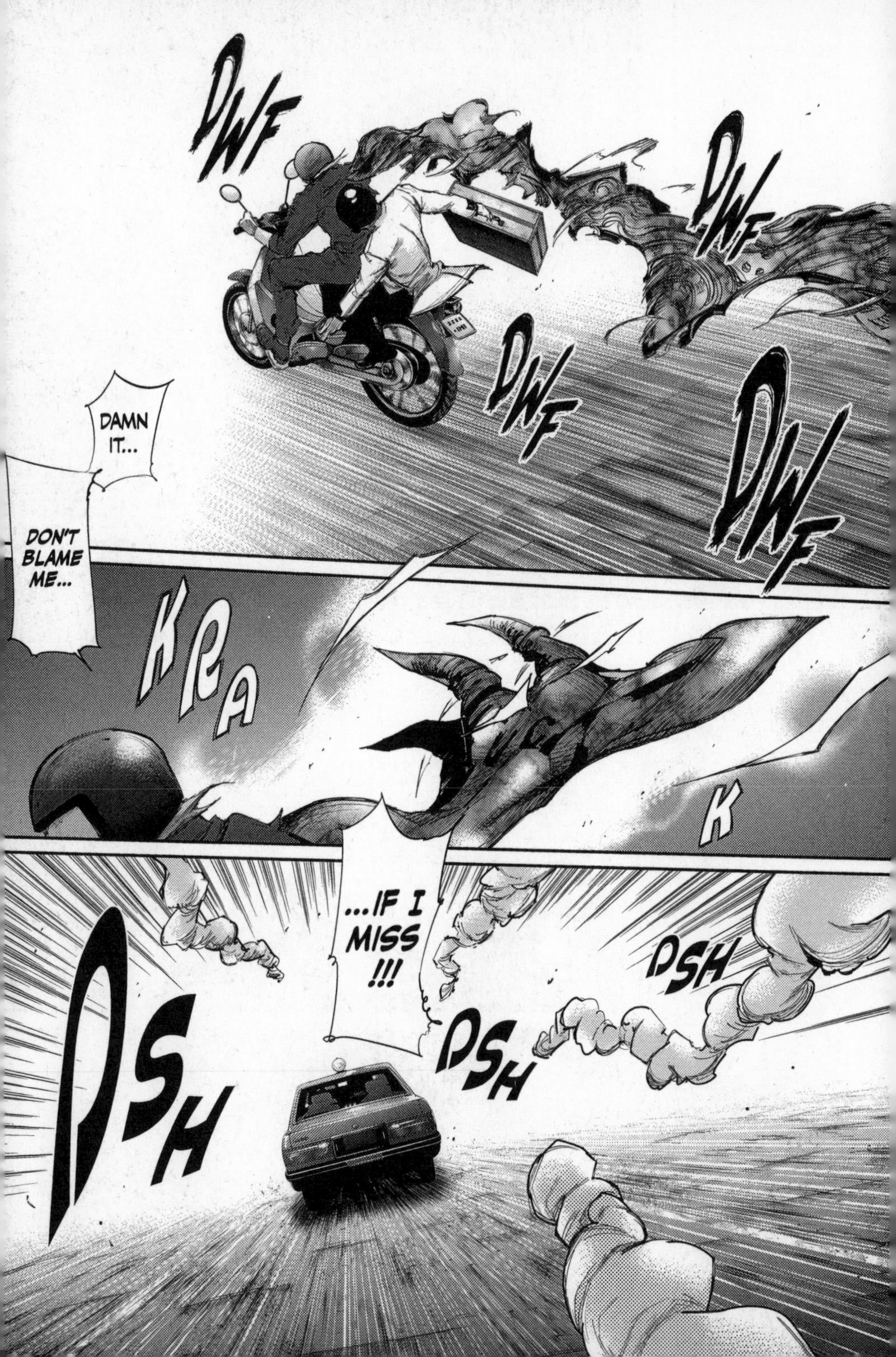
DWF
DWF
DWF
DWF
DAMN IT...
DON'T BLAME ME...
K
KRA
...IF I MISS!!!
DSH
DSH
DSH

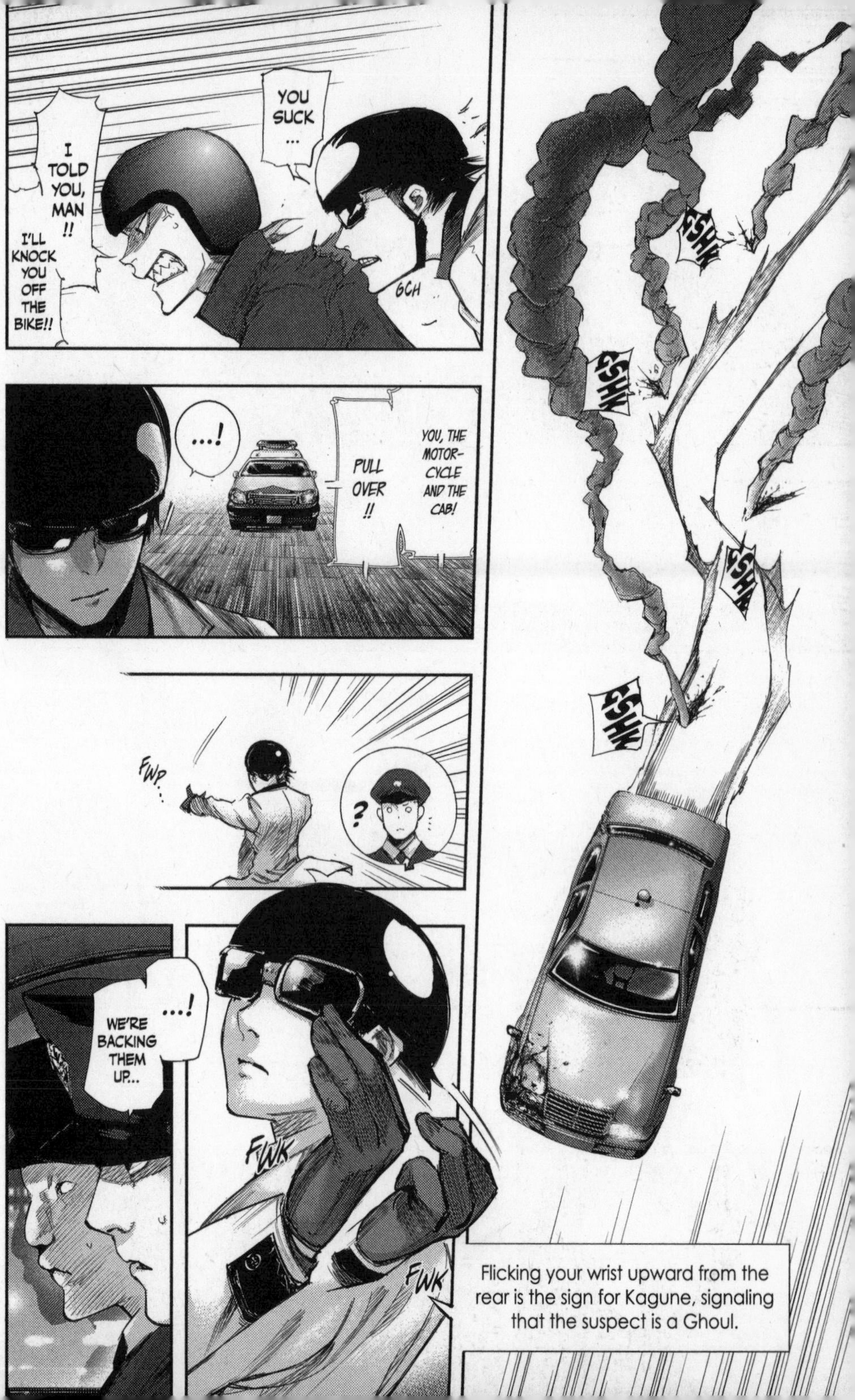
GSHK
GSHK
GSHK
GSHK
Flicking your wrist upward from the rear is the sign for Kagune, signaling that the suspect is a Ghoul.
YOU SUCK ...
GCH
I TOLD YOU, MAN !!
I'LL KNOCK YOU OFF THE BIKE!!
YOU, THE MOTOR-CYCLE AND THE CAB!
PULL OVER !!
...!
?
FWP...
FWK
FWK
...!
WE'RE BACKING THEM UP...

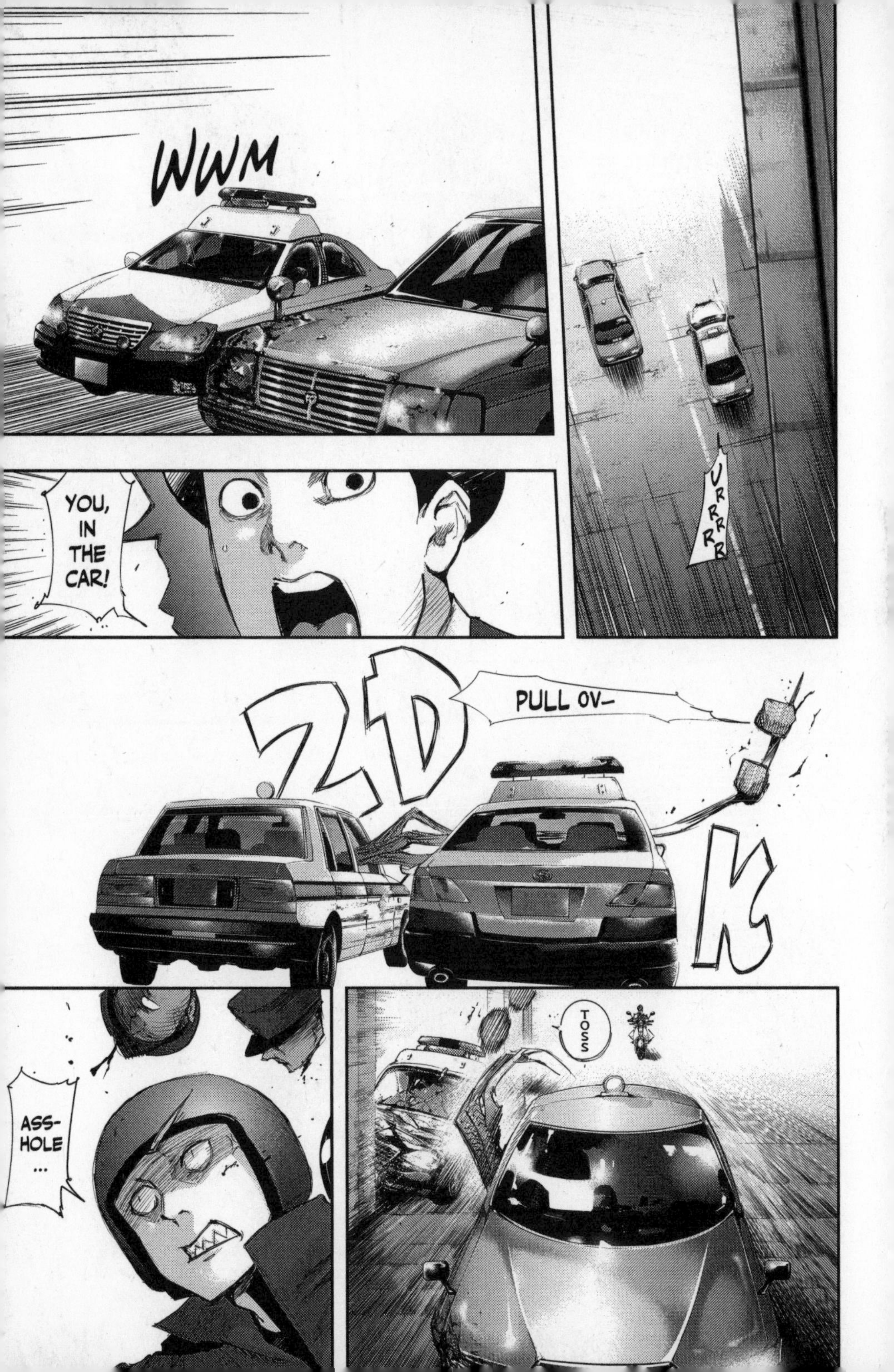
URRRR
WWM
YOU, IN THE CAR!
PULL OV—
ZDK
TOSS
ASS-HOLE ...

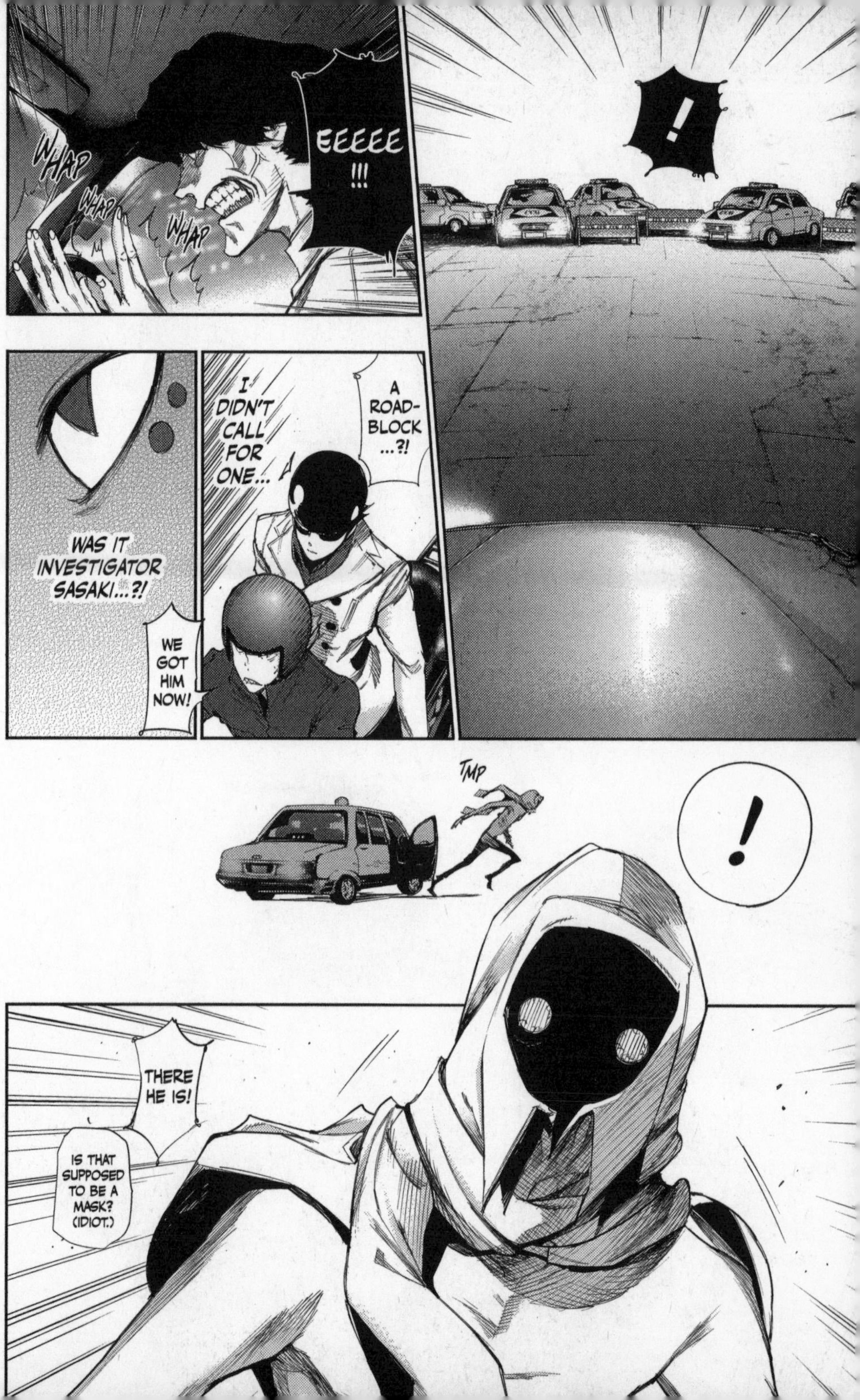
!
WHAP
WHAP
WHAP
EEEEE !!!
A ROAD-BLOCK ...?!
I DIDN'T CALL FOR ONE...
WE GOT HIM NOW!
WAS IT INVESTIGATOR SASAKI...?!
TMP
!
THERE HE IS!
IS THAT SUPPOSED TO BE A MASK? (IDIOT.)

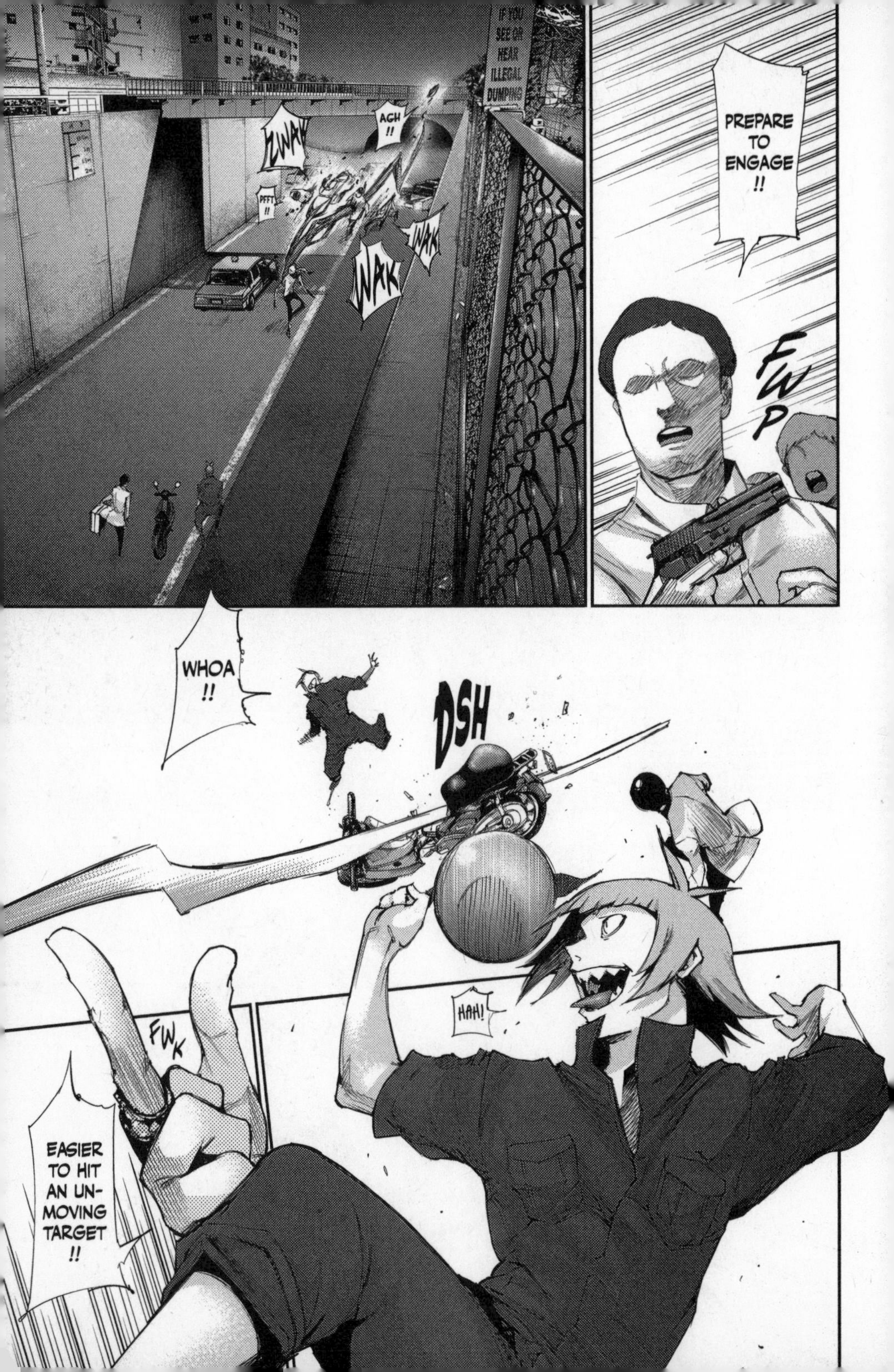
PREPARE TO ENGAGE !!
FWP
IF YOU SEE OR HEAR ILLEGAL DUMPING
AGH !!
ZWAK
PFFT !!
WAK
WAK
WHOA !!
DSH
HAH!
FWK
EASIER TO HIT AN UN-MOVING TARGET !!

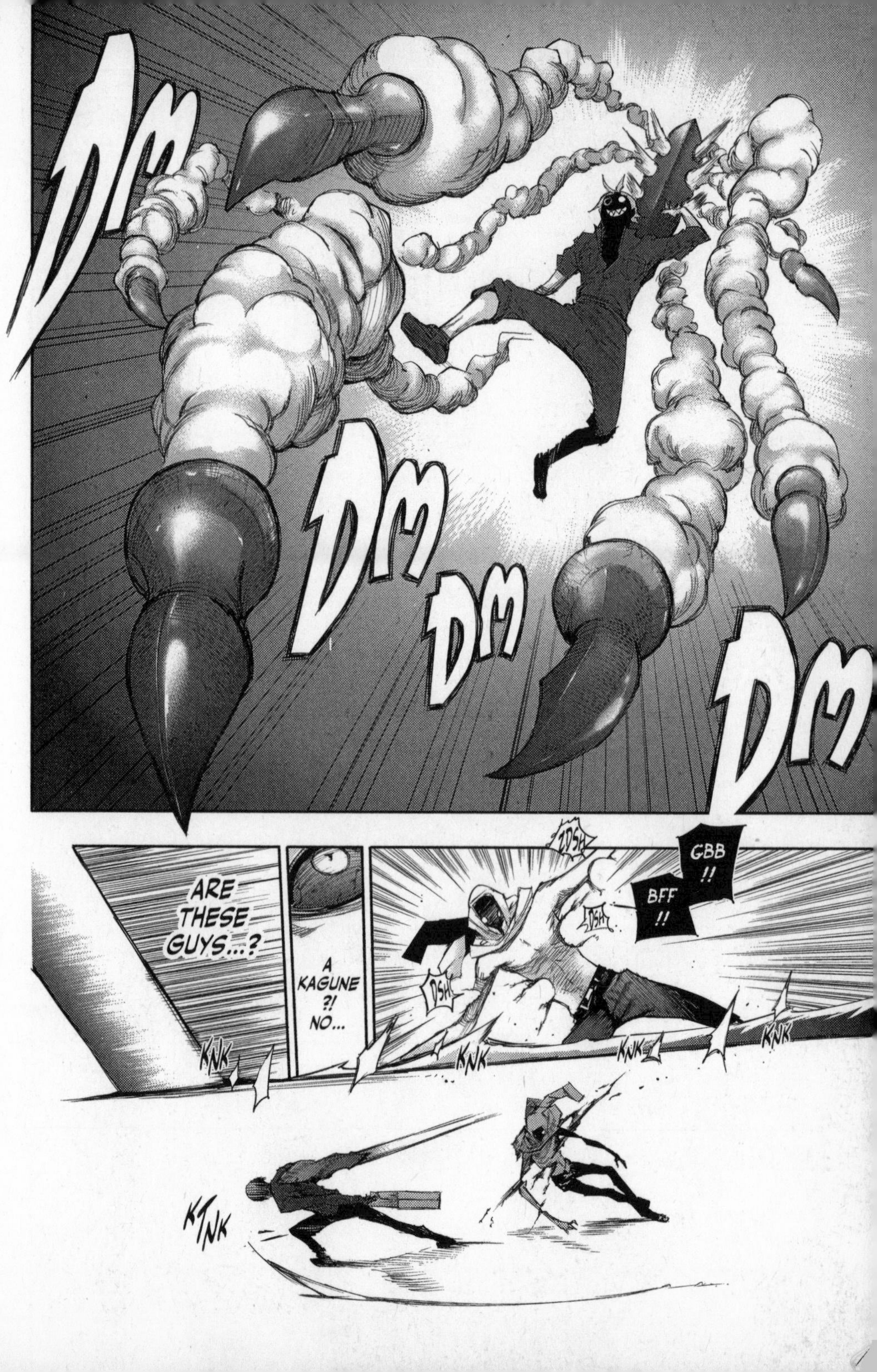
DM
DM
DM
DM
ZDSH
GBB!!
BFF!!
DSH
DSH
KNK
KNK
KNK
KNK
A KAGUNE?! NO...
ARE THESE GUYS...?
KTINK

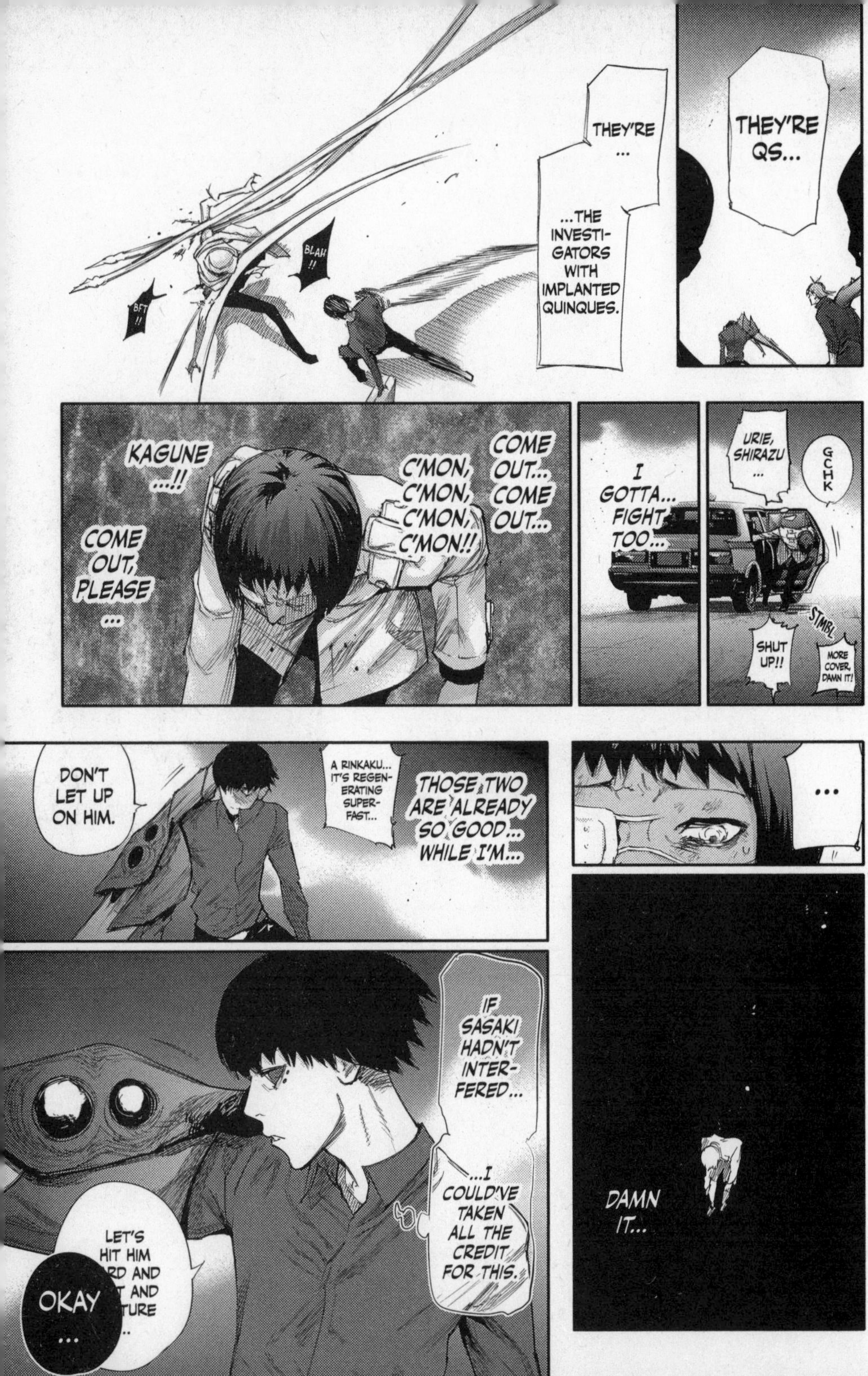

THEY'RE QS...
THEY'RE ...
...THE INVESTIGATORS WITH IMPLANTED QUINQUES.
BLAH !!
BFT !!
URIE, SHIRAZU ...
GCHK
STMBL
SHUT UP!!
MORE COVER, DAMN IT!
I GOTTA... FIGHT TOO...
COME OUT... COME OUT...
C'MON, C'MON, C'MON, C'MON!!
KAGUNE ...!!
COME OUT, PLEASE ...
...
DAMN IT...
DON'T LET UP ON HIM.
A RINKAKU... IT'S REGENERATING SUPER-FAST...
THOSE TWO ARE ALREADY SO GOOD... WHILE I'M...
IF SASAKI HADN'T INTERFERED...
...I COULD'VE TAKEN ALL THE CREDIT FOR THIS.
LET'S HIT HIM
OKAY ...

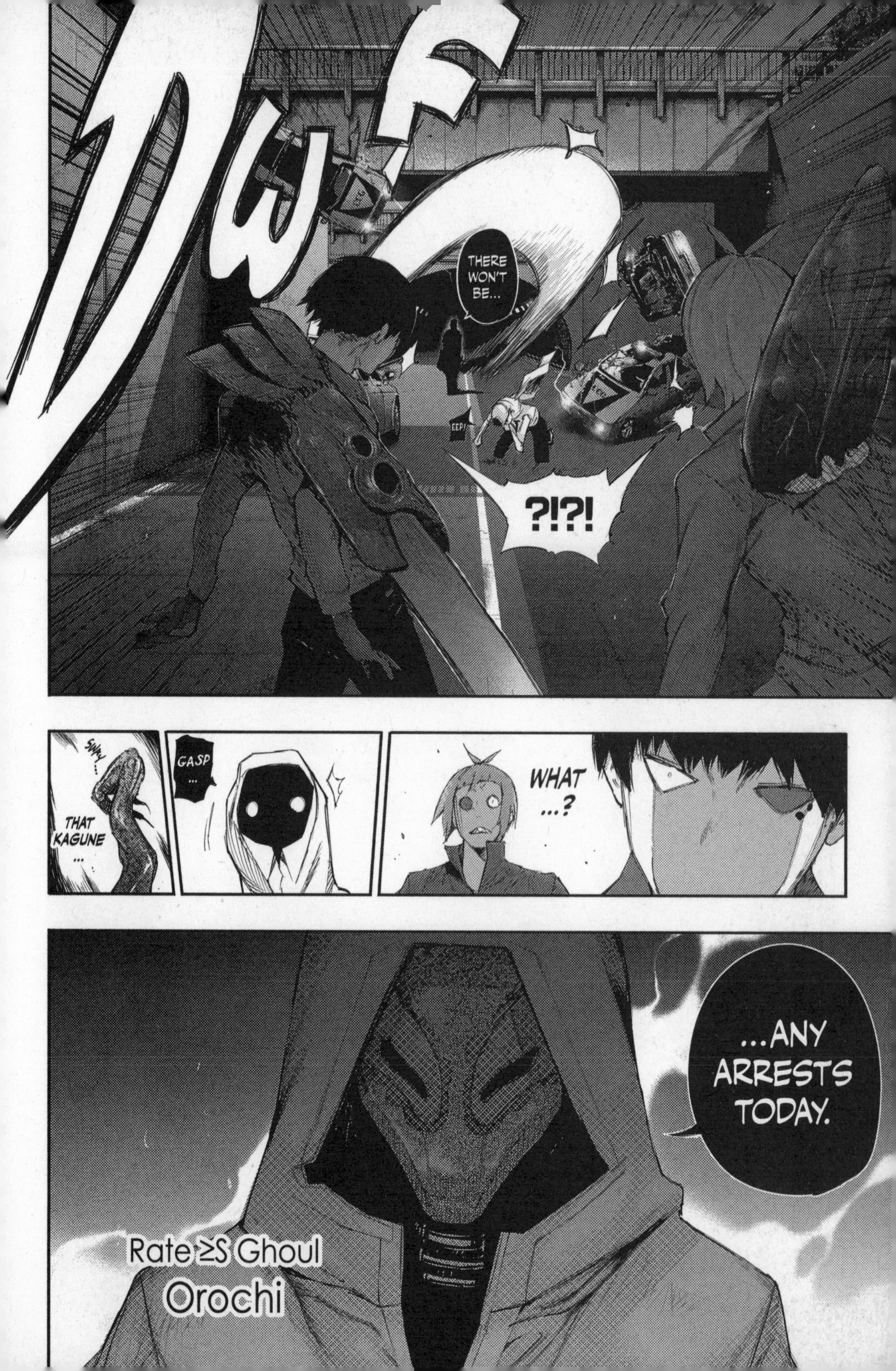
THERE WON'T BE...
EEP!
?!?!
WHAT ...?
GASP ...
SWAY ...
THAT KAGUNE ...
...ANY ARRESTS TODAY.
Rate ≥S Ghoul
Orochi

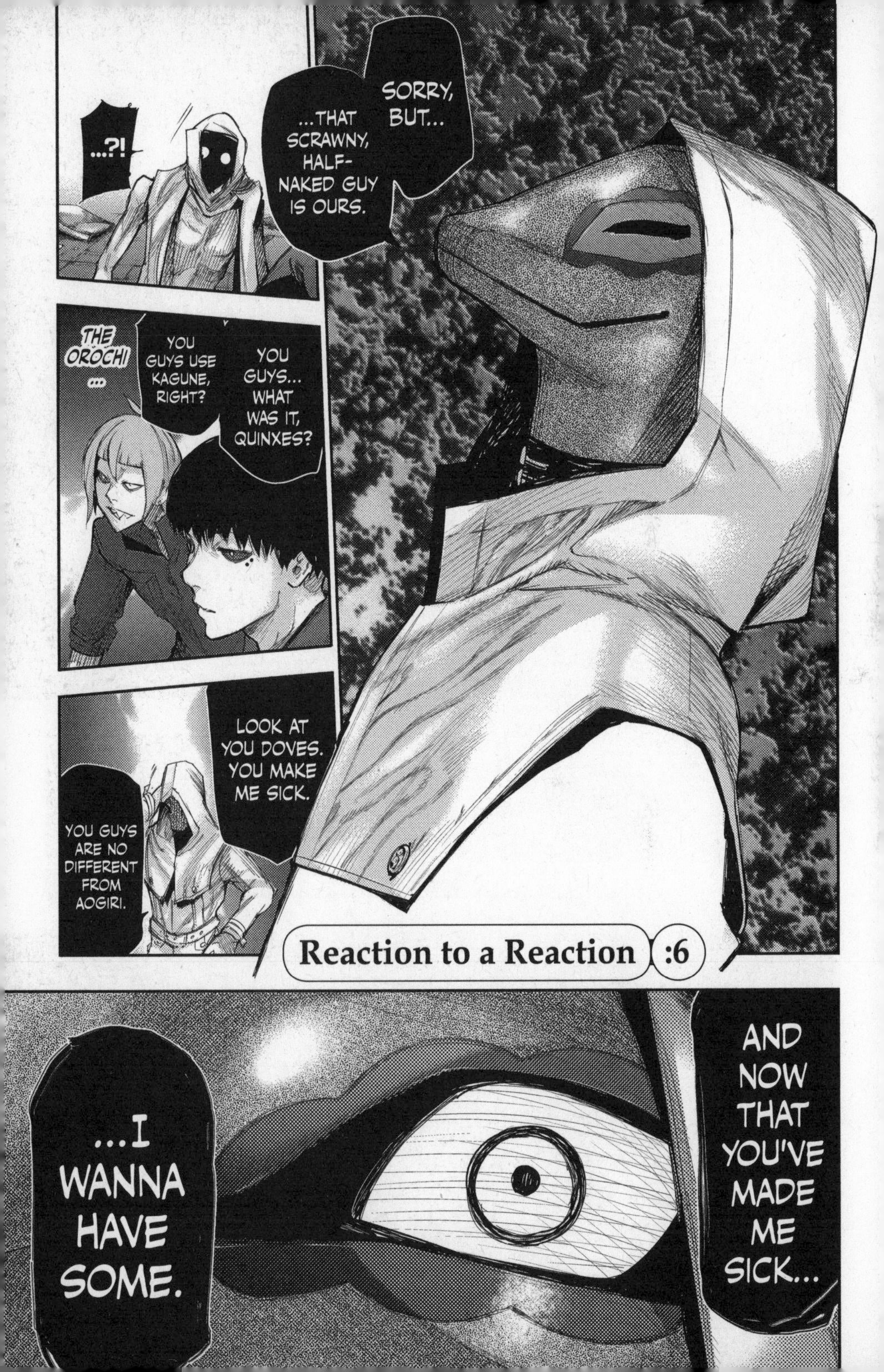
SORRY, BUT... ...THAT SCRAWNY, HALF-NAKED GUY IS OURS.
...?!
YOU GUYS... WHAT WAS IT, QUINXES?
YOU GUYS USE KAGUNE, RIGHT?
THE OROCHI...
LOOK AT YOU DOVES. YOU MAKE ME SICK.
YOU GUYS ARE NO DIFFERENT FROM AOGIRI.
Reaction to a Reaction :6
AND NOW THAT YOU'VE MADE ME SICK...
...I WANNA HAVE SOME.

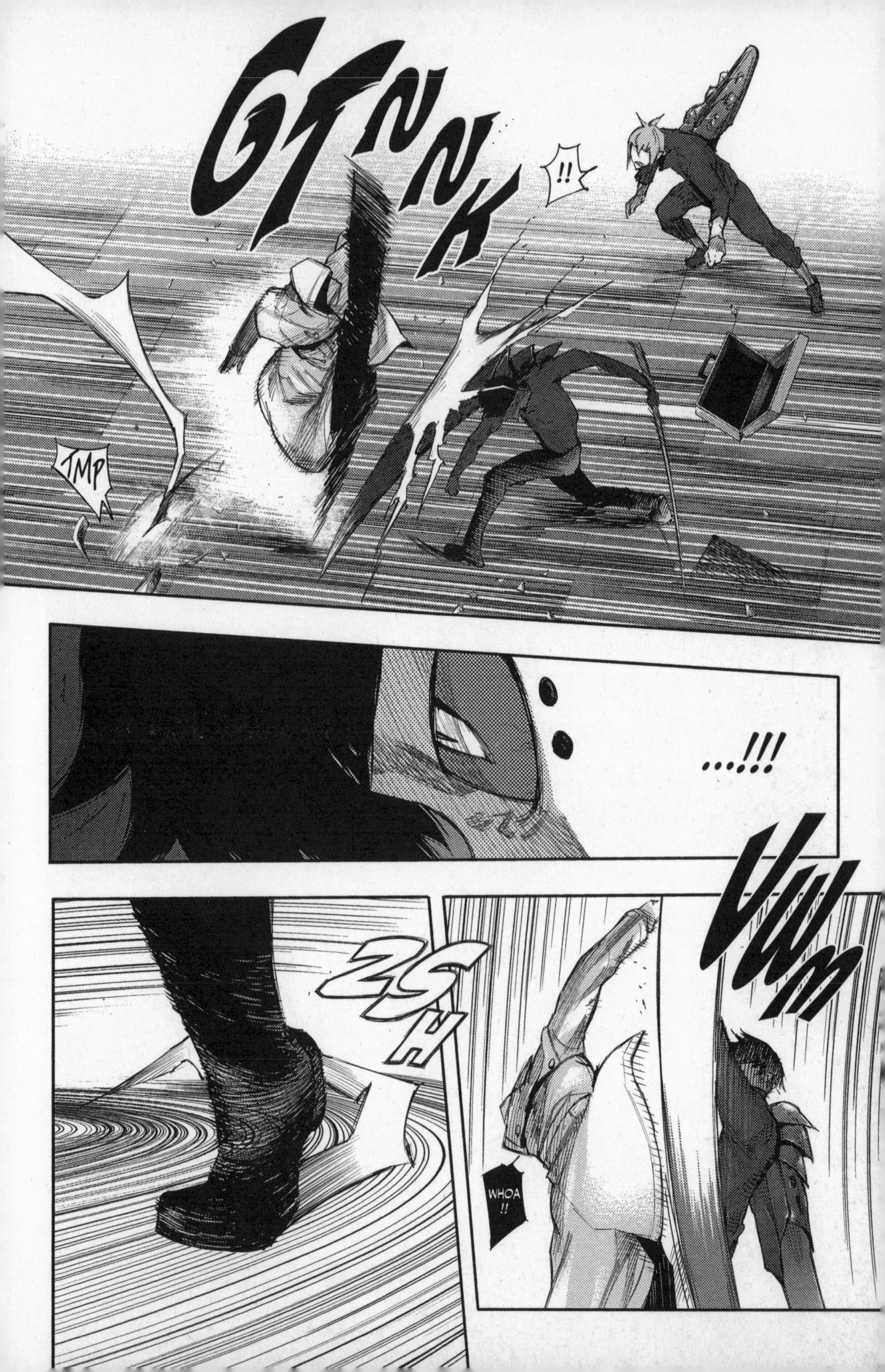
GTNNK
!!
TMP
...!!!
VUUM
WHOA !!
ZSH

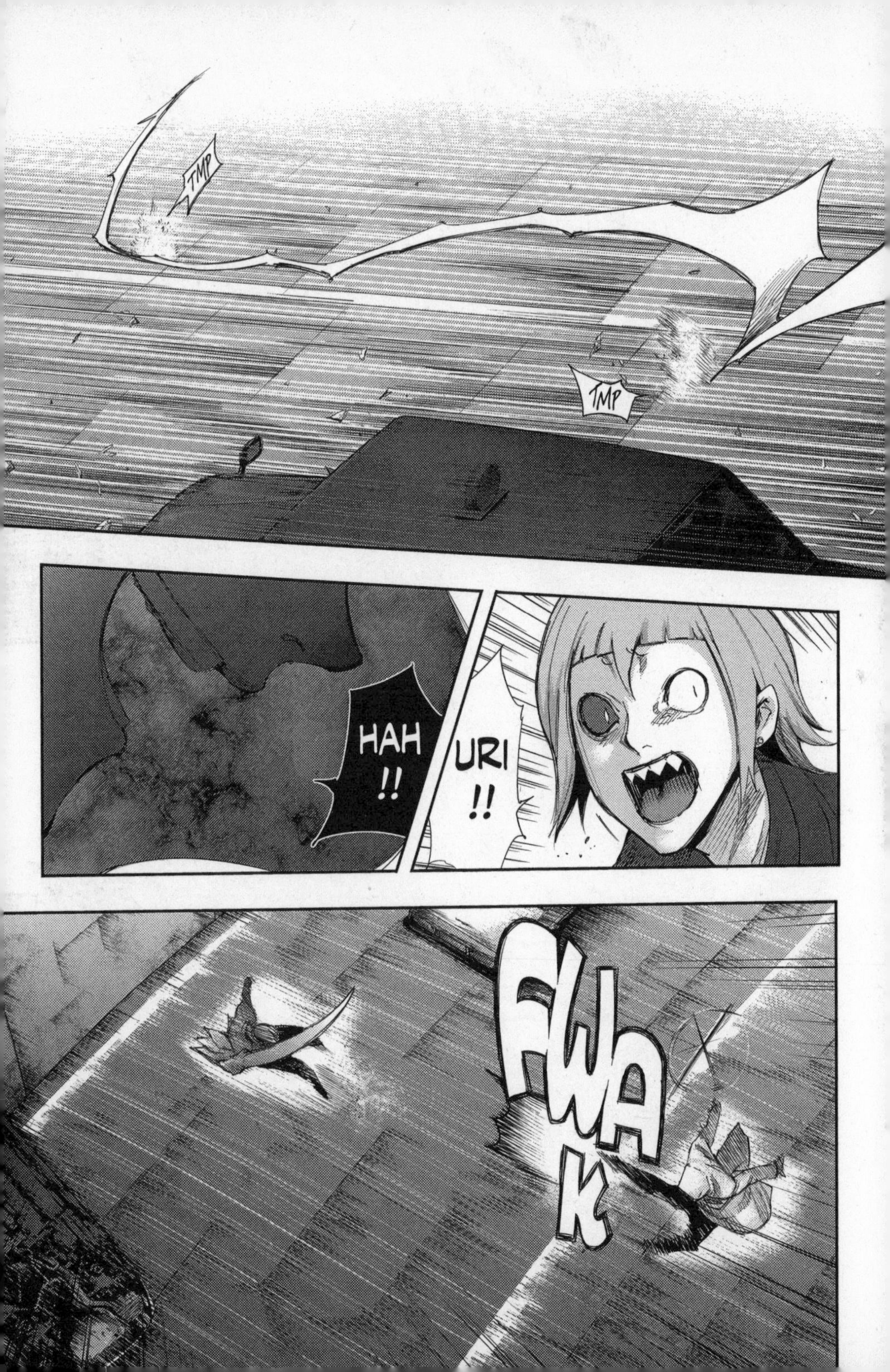
TMP
TMP
URI !!
HAH !!
FWAK

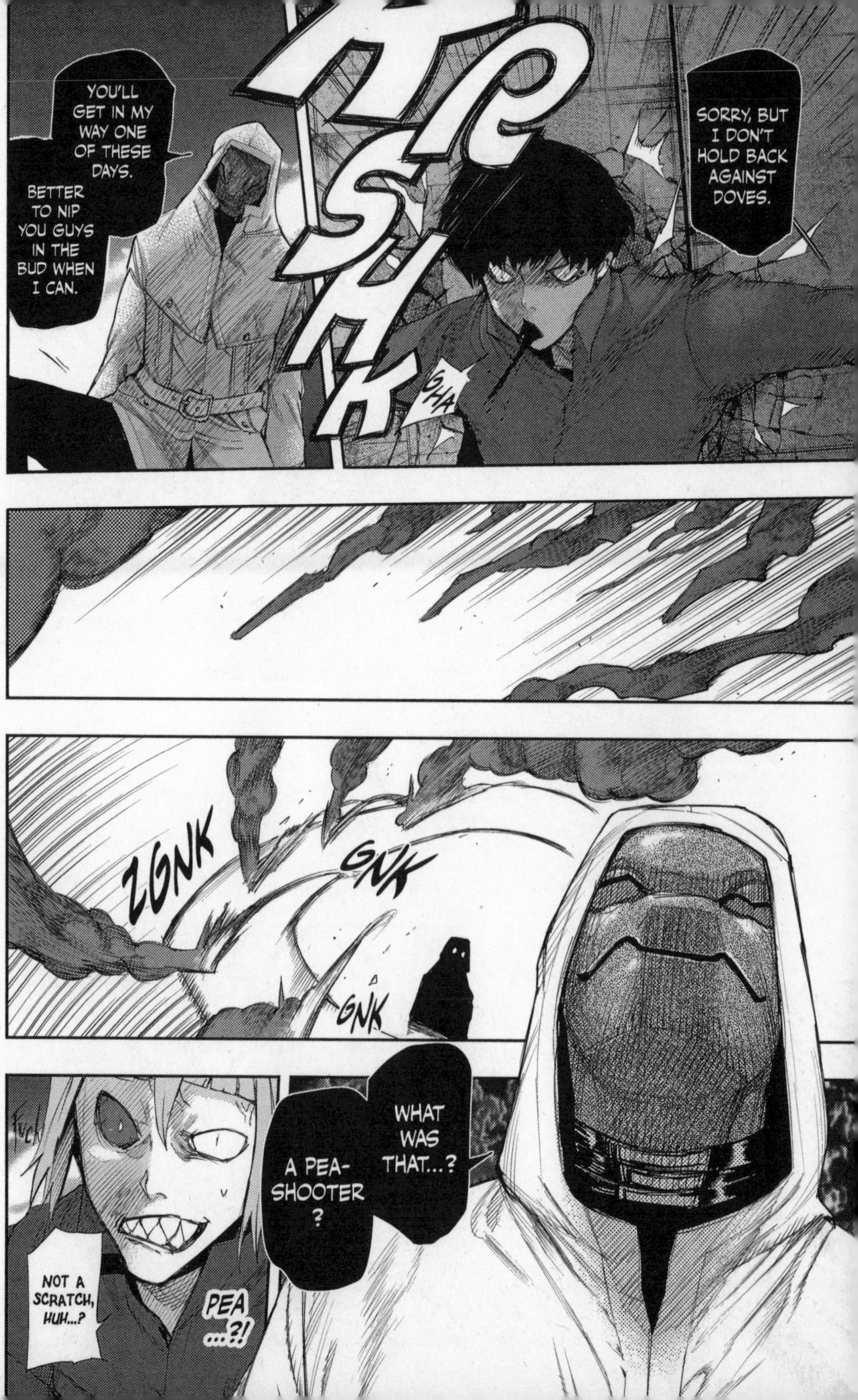
SORRY, BUT I DON'T HOLD BACK AGAINST DOVES.
GHA
YOU'LL GET IN MY WAY ONE OF THESE DAYS.
BETTER TO NIP YOU GUYS IN THE BUD WHEN I CAN.
GNK
ZGNK
GNK
WHAT WAS THAT...?
A PEA-SHOOTER?
PEA...?!
NOT A SCRATCH, HUH...?
FUCK

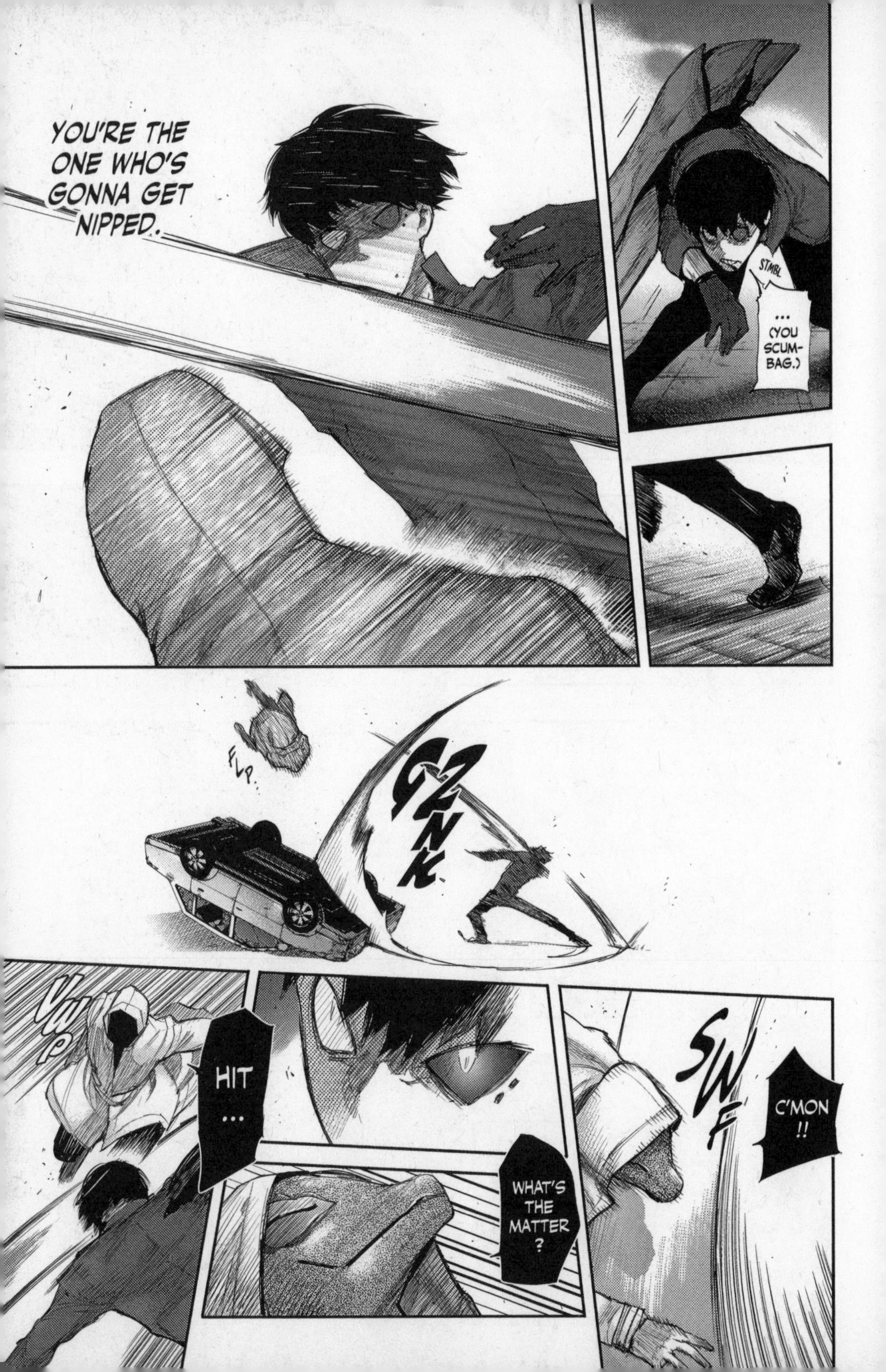
STMBL
... (YOU SCUM-BAG.)
YOU'RE THE ONE WHO'S GONNA GET NIPPED.
FLP.
GZNK
SWF
C'MON!!
HIT ...
WHAT'S THE MATTER?
VWP

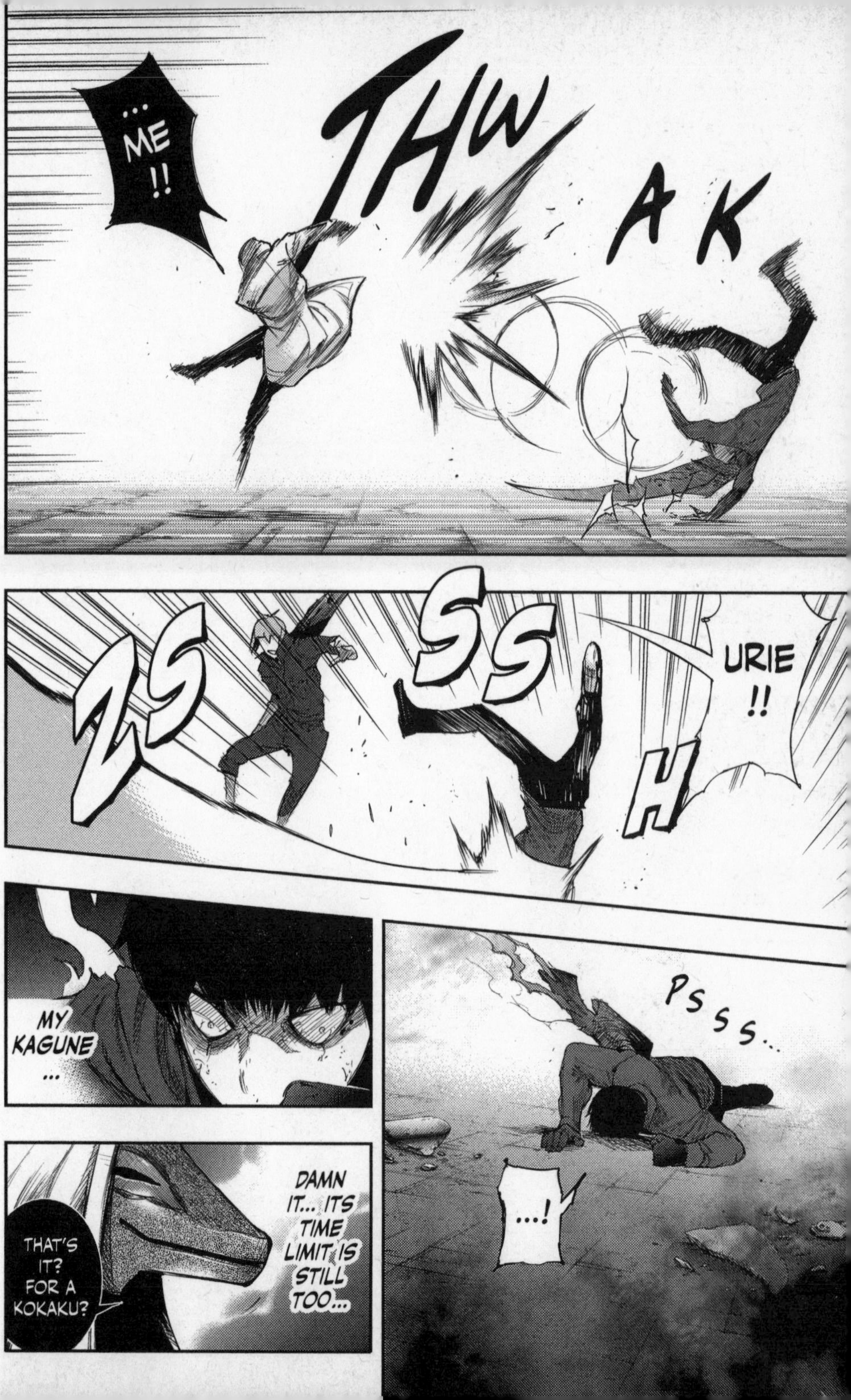
... ME !!
THWAK
URIE !!
ZSSSH
PSSS...
...!
MY KAGUNE ...
DAMN IT... ITS TIME LIMIT IS STILL TOO...
THAT'S IT? FOR A KOKAKU?

ALL IT TOOK WAS A KICK?
SO THIS IS A RATE ΣS GHOUL...
GUESS IT'S JUST AN IMITATION AFTER ALL.
...
QVR
QVR
NOT EVEN URIE...
...STOOD A CHANCE AGAINST HIM.
I CAN'T MOVE...
I'M SCARED...
DO I...
MMM?
...STAND A CHANCE?
WHAT? THERE'S ONE MORE?
I'LL TAKE YOU OUT FIRST THEN...

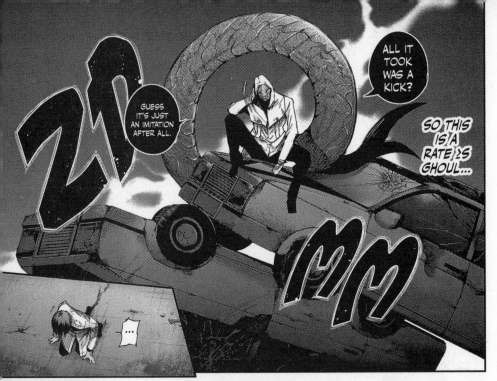

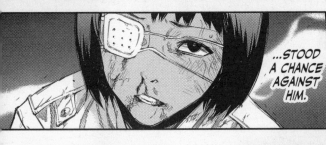

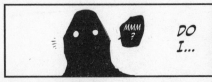

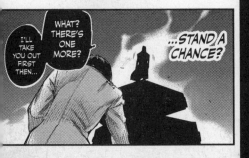

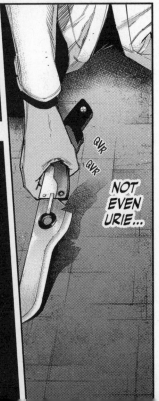

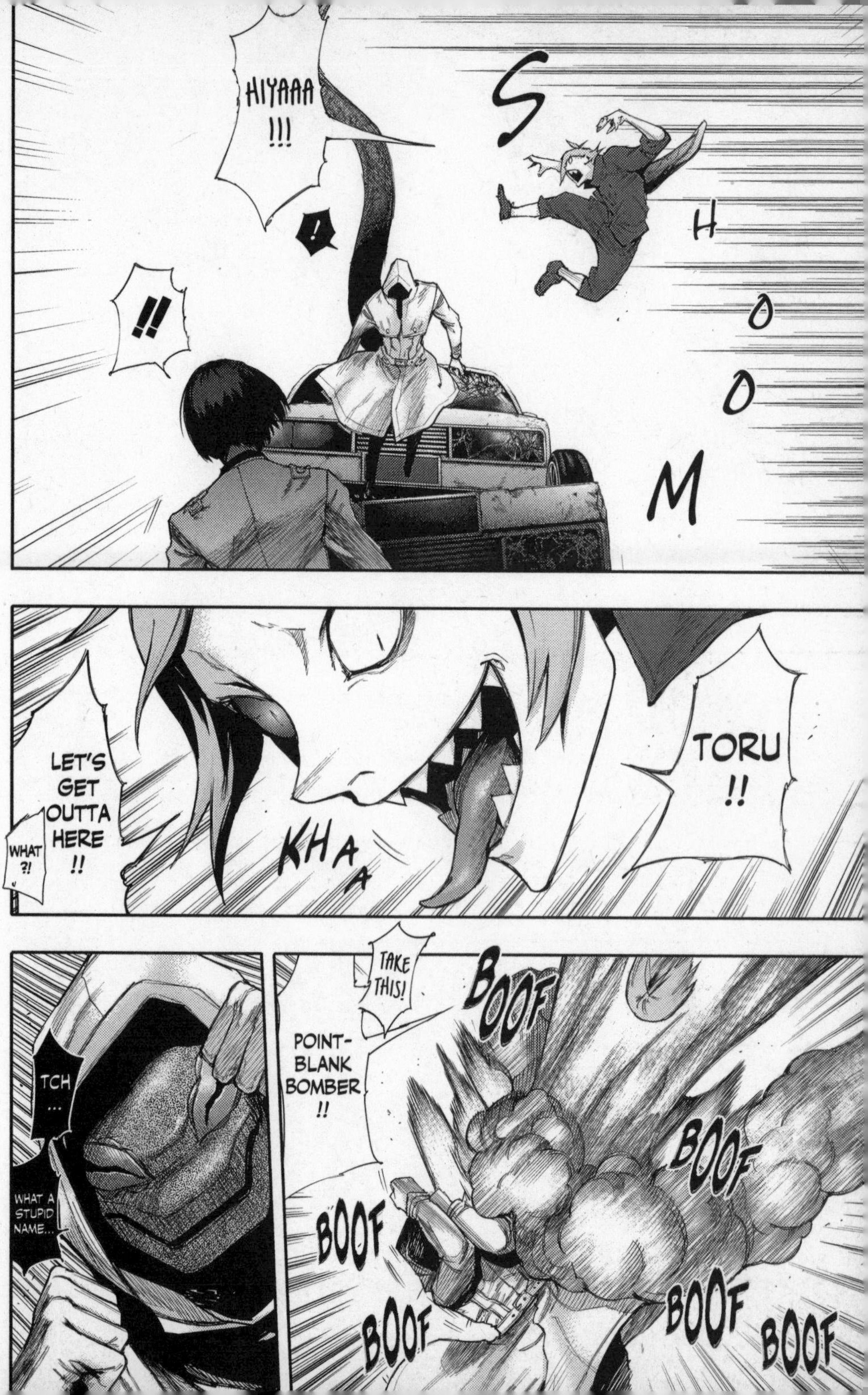
SHOOM
HIYAAA!!!
!
!!
TORU!!
KHAA
LET'S GET OUTTA HERE!!
WHAT?!
BOOF
TAKE THIS!
POINT-BLANK BOMBER!!
BOOF
BOOF
BOOF
BOOF
BOOF
BOOF
TCH...
WHAT A STUPID NAME...

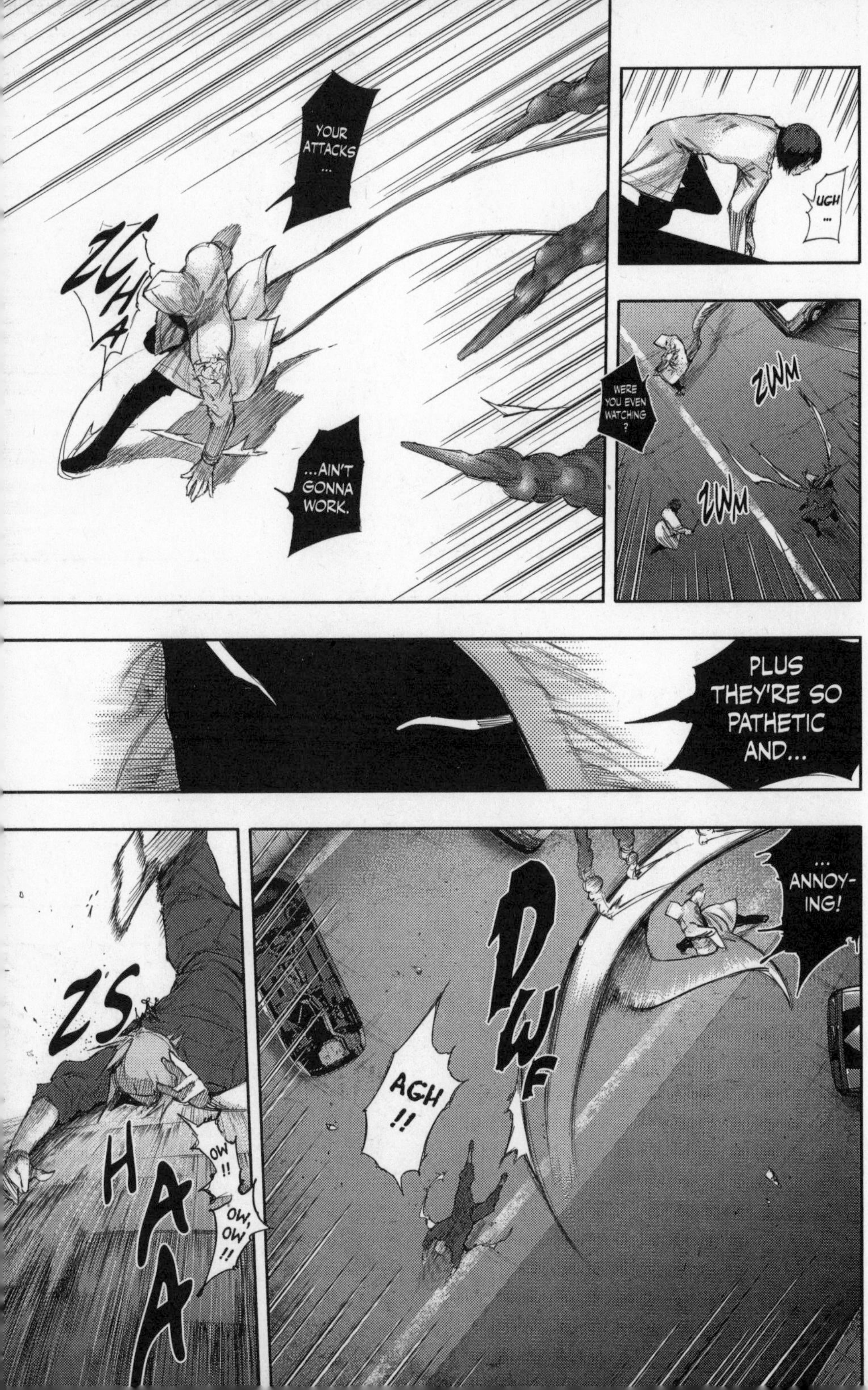

UGH ...
WERE YOU EVEN WATCHING ?
ZWM
ZWM
YOUR ATTACKS ...
ZCHA
...AIN'T GONNA WORK.
PLUS THEY'RE SO PATHETIC AND...
... ANNOY-ING!
DWF
AGH !!
ZS
HAHA
OW !!
OW, OW !!

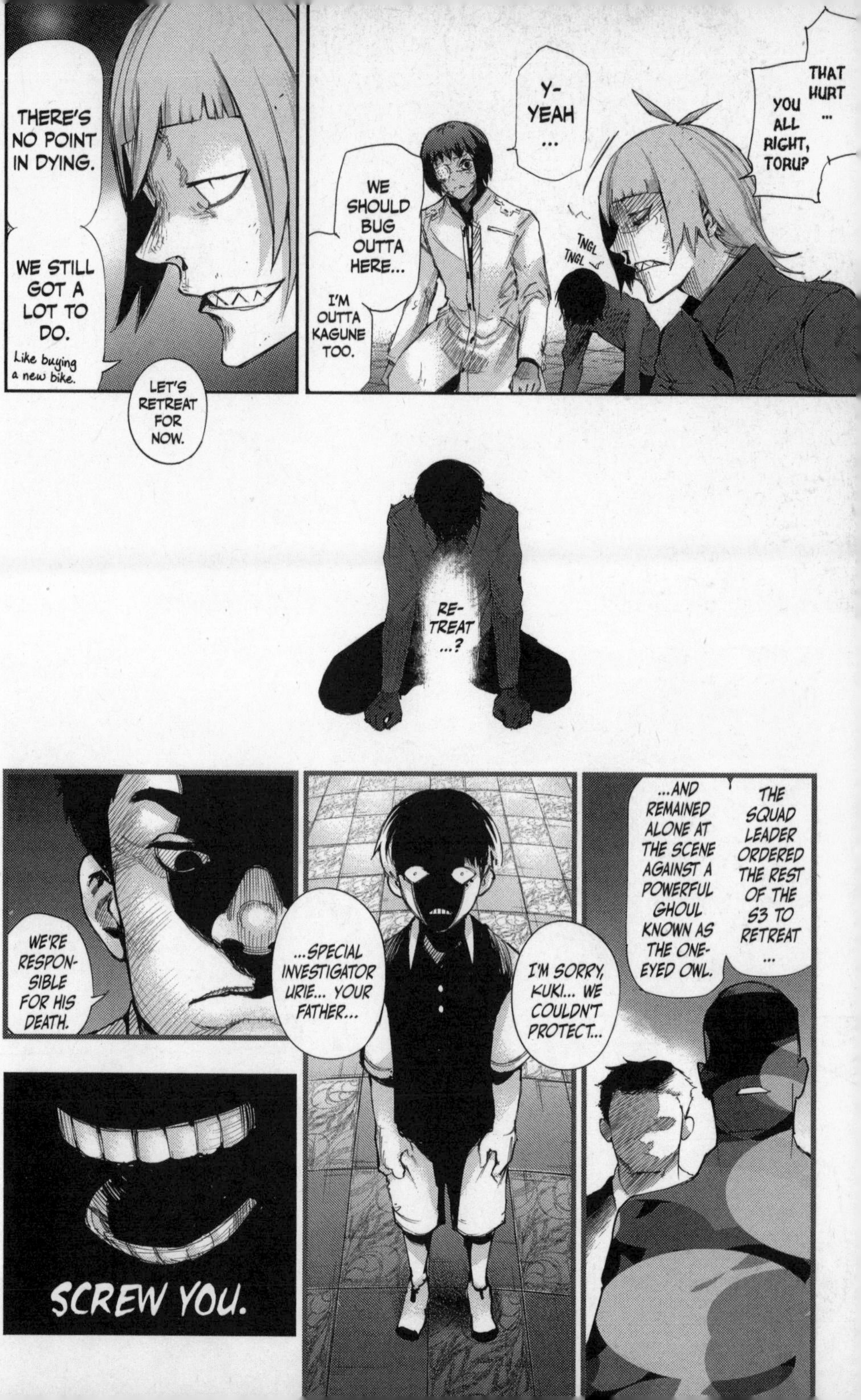
THAT HURT...
YOU ALL RIGHT, TORU?
TNGL TNGL
Y-YEAH...
WE SHOULD BUG OUTTA HERE...
I'M OUTTA KAGUNE TOO.
THERE'S NO POINT IN DYING.
WE STILL GOT A LOT TO DO.
Like buying a new bike.
LET'S RETREAT FOR NOW.
RE-TREAT...?
THE SQUAD LEADER ORDERED THE REST OF THE S3 TO RETREAT...
...AND REMAINED ALONE AT THE SCENE AGAINST A POWERFUL GHOUL KNOWN AS THE ONE-EYED OWL.
I'M SORRY, KUKI... WE COULDN'T PROTECT...
...SPECIAL INVESTIGATOR URIE... YOUR FATHER...
WE'RE RESPONSIBLE FOR HIS DEATH.
SCREW YOU.

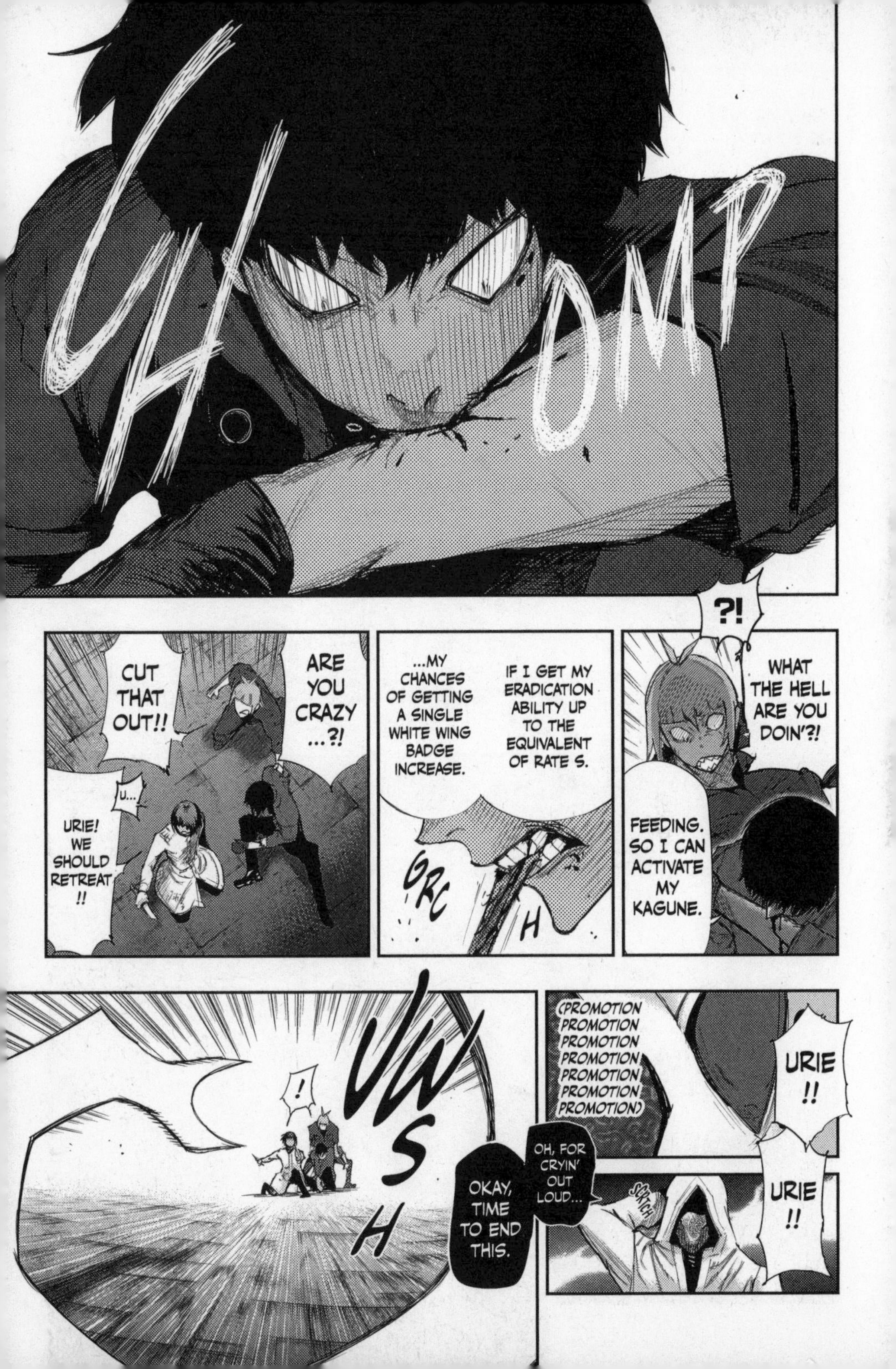
CHOMP
?!
WHAT THE HELL ARE YOU DOIN'?!
FEEDING. SO I CAN ACTIVATE MY KAGUNE.
IF I GET MY ERADICATION ABILITY UP TO THE EQUIVALENT OF RATE S.
...MY CHANCES OF GETTING A SINGLE WHITE WING BADGE INCREASE.
GRCH
ARE YOU CRAZY ...?!
CUT THAT OUT!!
U...
URIE! WE SHOULD RETREAT !!
(PROMOTION PROMOTION PROMOTION PROMOTION PROMOTION PROMOTION PROMOTION)
URIE !!
URIE !!
OH, FOR CRYIN' OUT LOUD...
OKAY, TIME TO END THIS.
!
VWSH

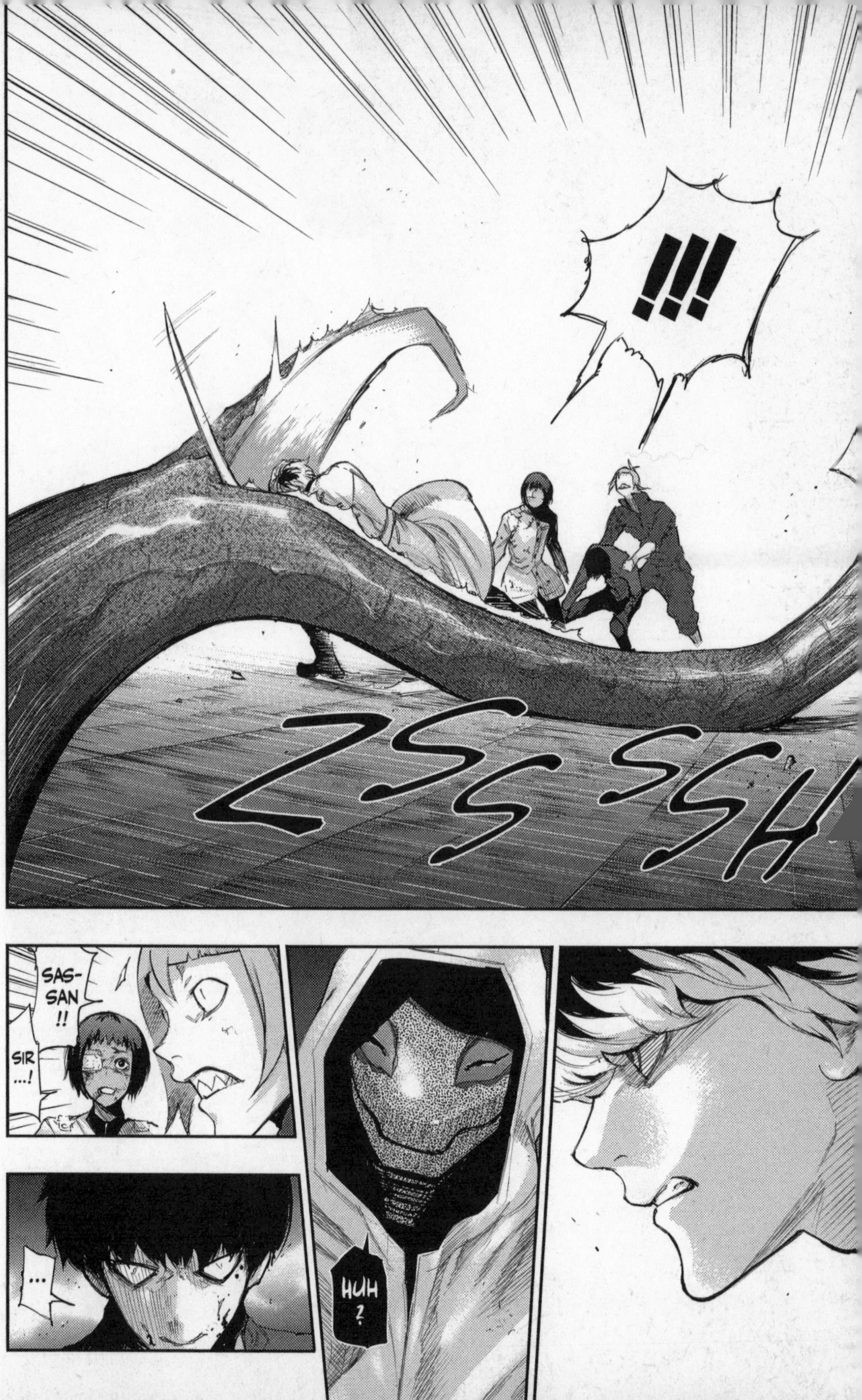
!!!
ZSSSSH
HUH?
SAS-SAN!!
SIR...!
...

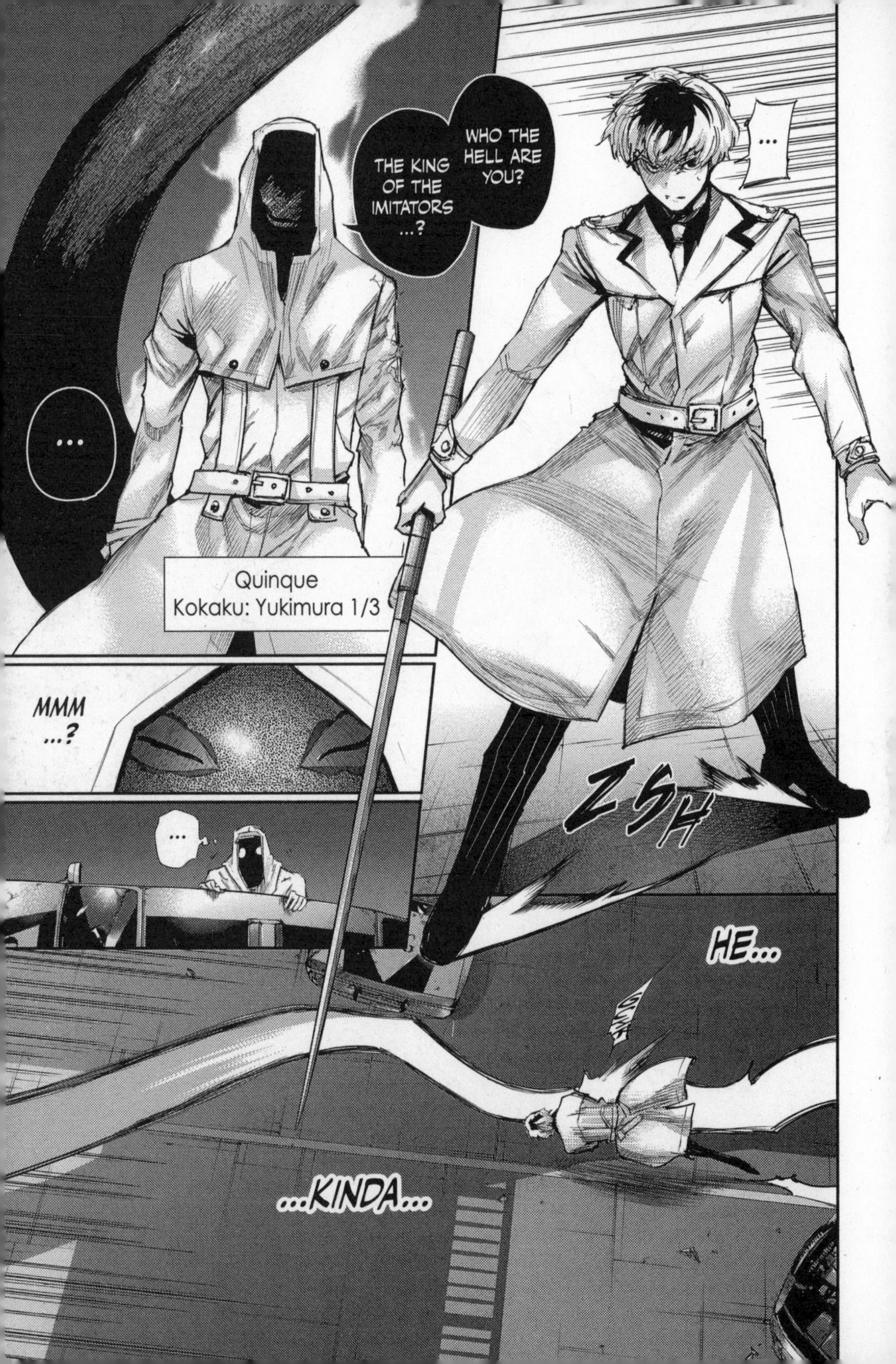
...
WHO THE HELL ARE YOU?
THE KING OF THE IMITATORS ...?
...
Quinque Kokaku: Yukimura 1/3
ZSH
MMM ...?
...
HE...
...KINDA...

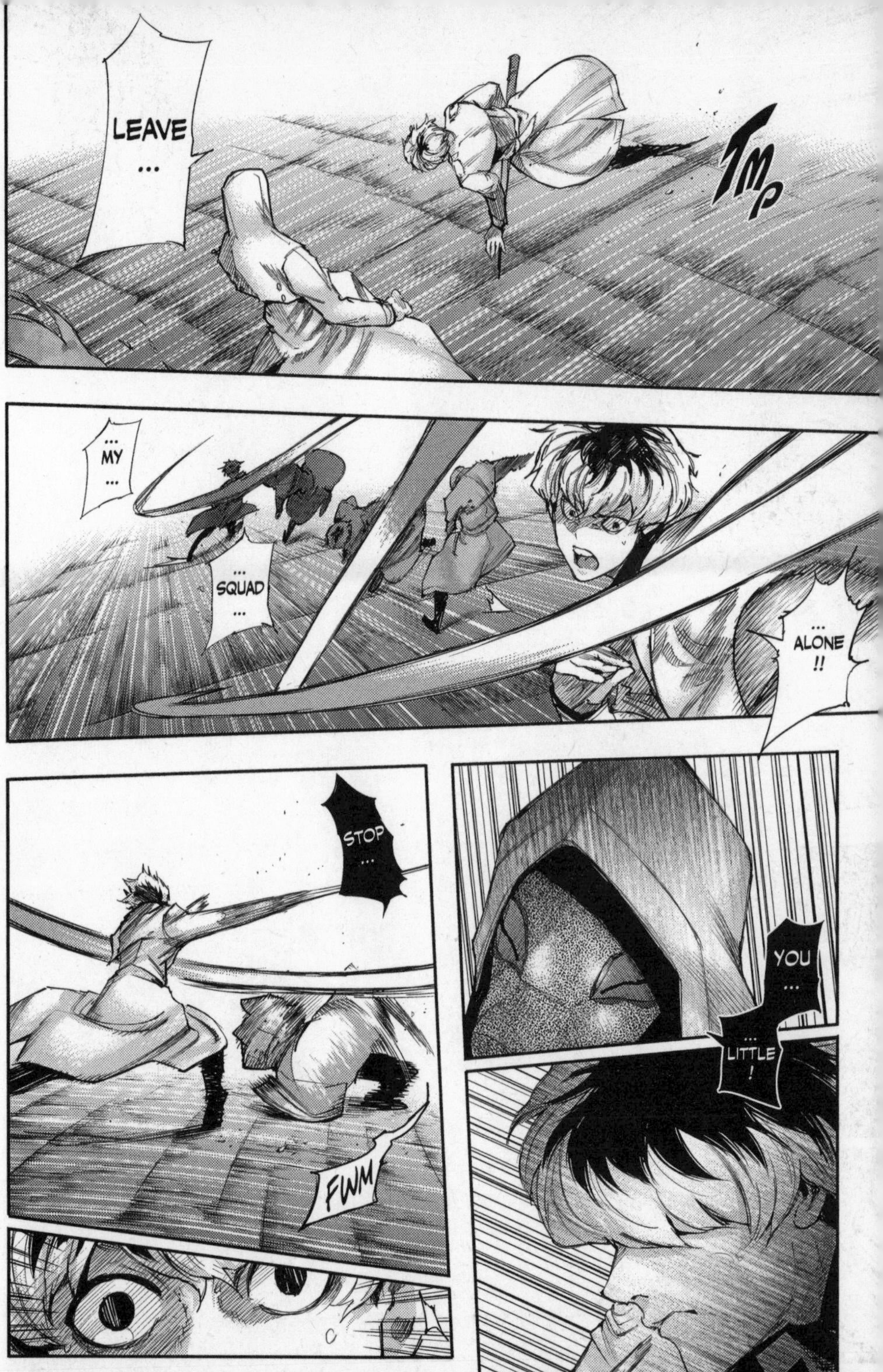

TMP
LEAVE ...
... MY ...
... SQUAD ...
... ALONE !!
YOU ...
... LITTLE !
STOP ...
FWM

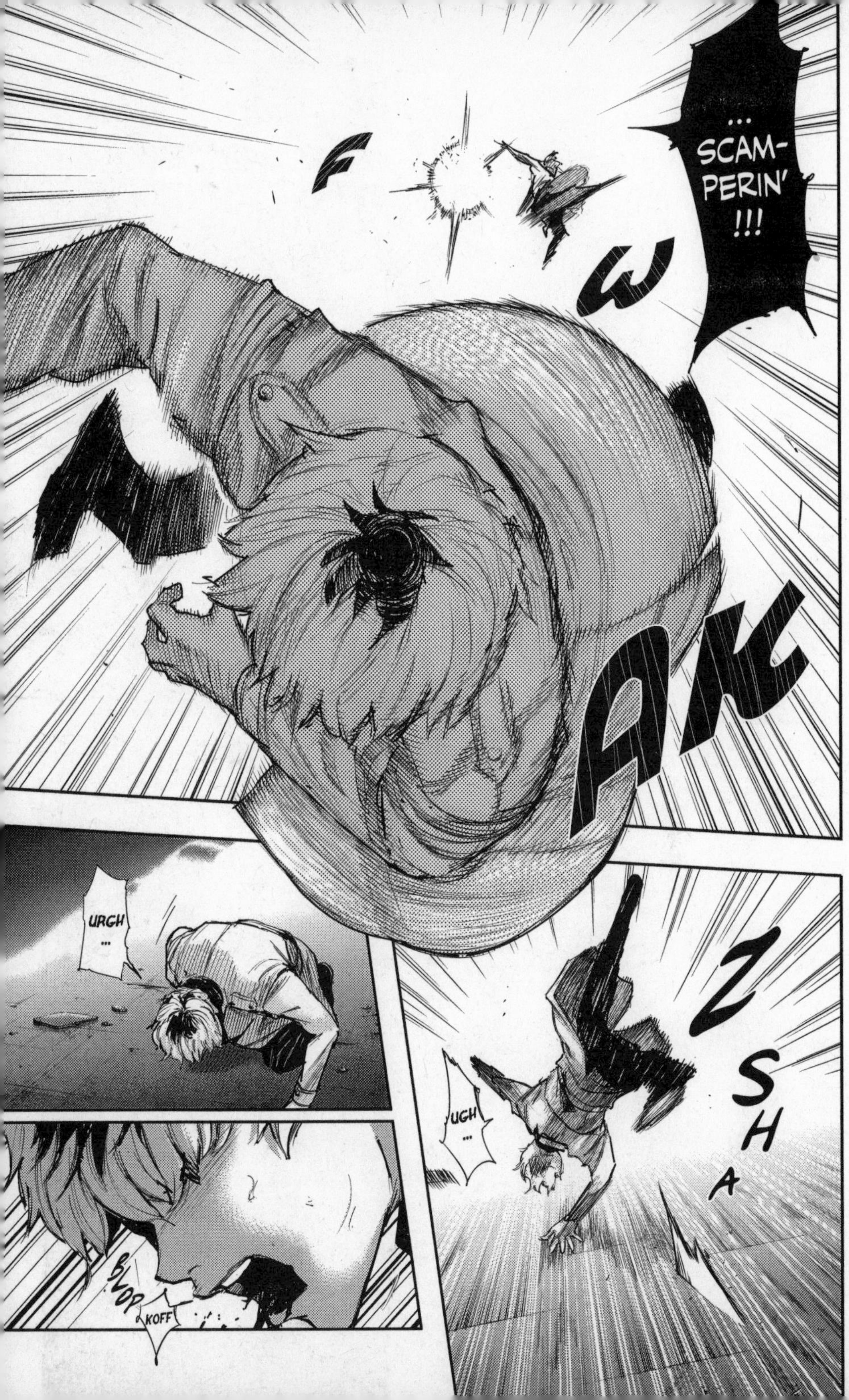

...SCAMPERIN'!!!
FWAK
ZSHA
UGH...
URGH...
BLOP
KOFF

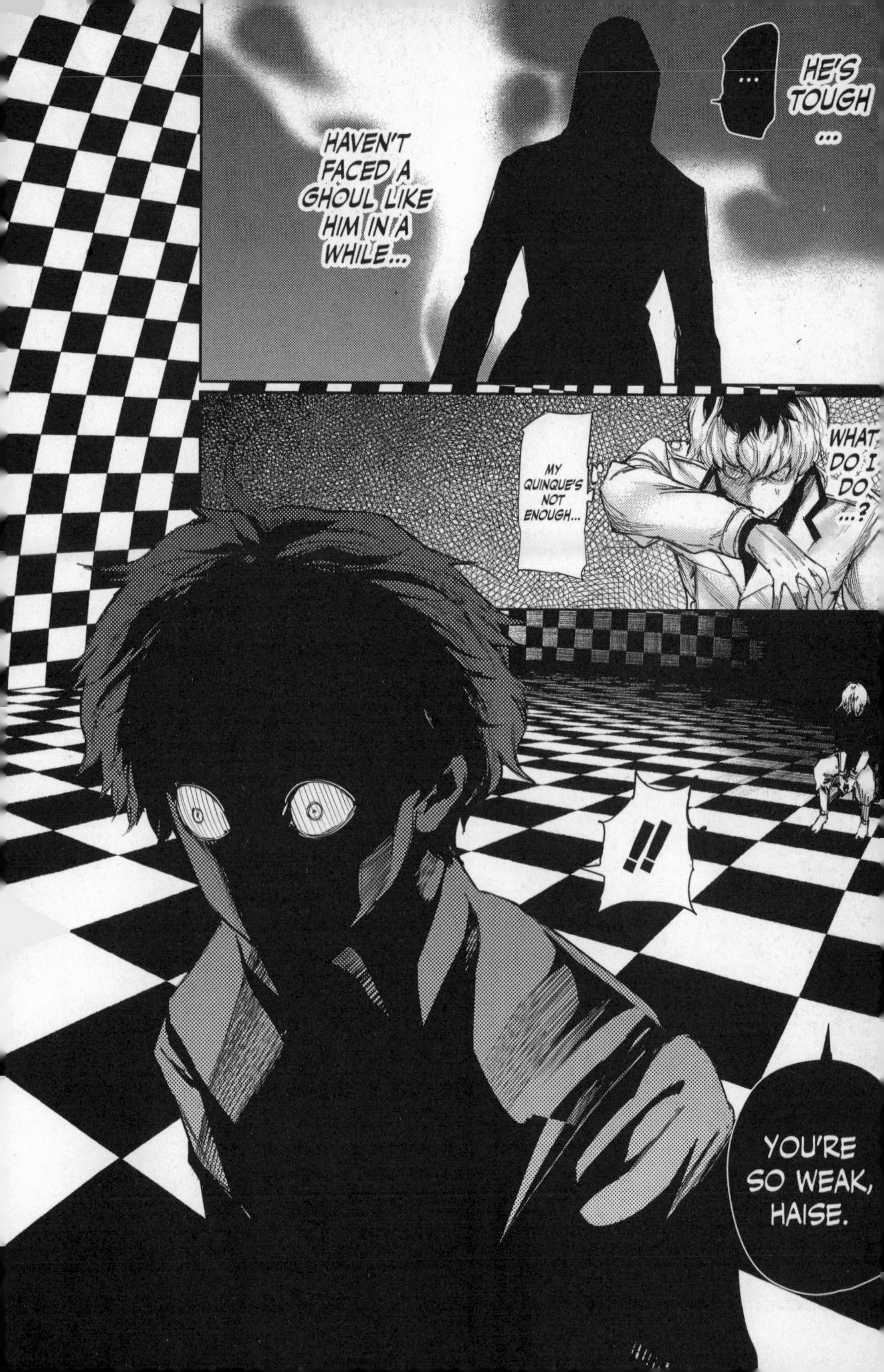
HE'S TOUGH...
...
HAVEN'T FACED A GHOUL LIKE HIM IN A WHILE...
WHAT DO I DO...?
MY QUINQUE'S NOT ENOUGH...
!!
YOU'RE SO WEAK, HAISE.

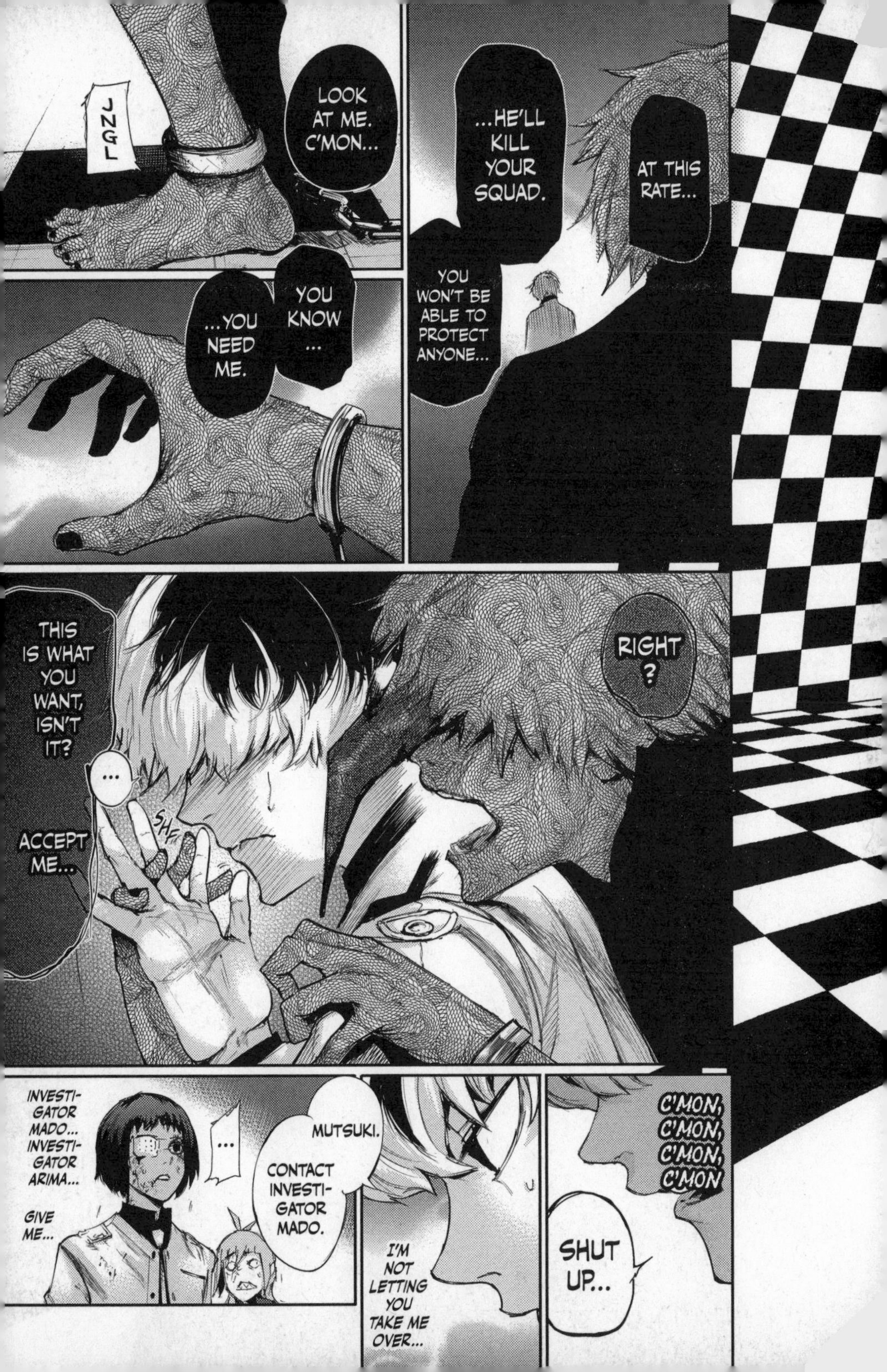
AT THIS RATE...
...HE'LL KILL YOUR SQUAD.
YOU WON'T BE ABLE TO PROTECT ANYONE...
JNGL
LOOK AT ME. C'MON...
YOU KNOW ...
...YOU NEED ME.
RIGHT?
THIS IS WHAT YOU WANT, ISN'T IT?
...
SHF
ACCEPT ME...
C'MON, C'MON, C'MON, C'MON
SHUT UP...
I'M NOT LETTING YOU TAKE ME OVER...
MUTSUKI.
CONTACT INVESTIGATOR MADO.
...
INVESTIGATOR MADO... INVESTIGATOR ARIMA...
GIVE ME...

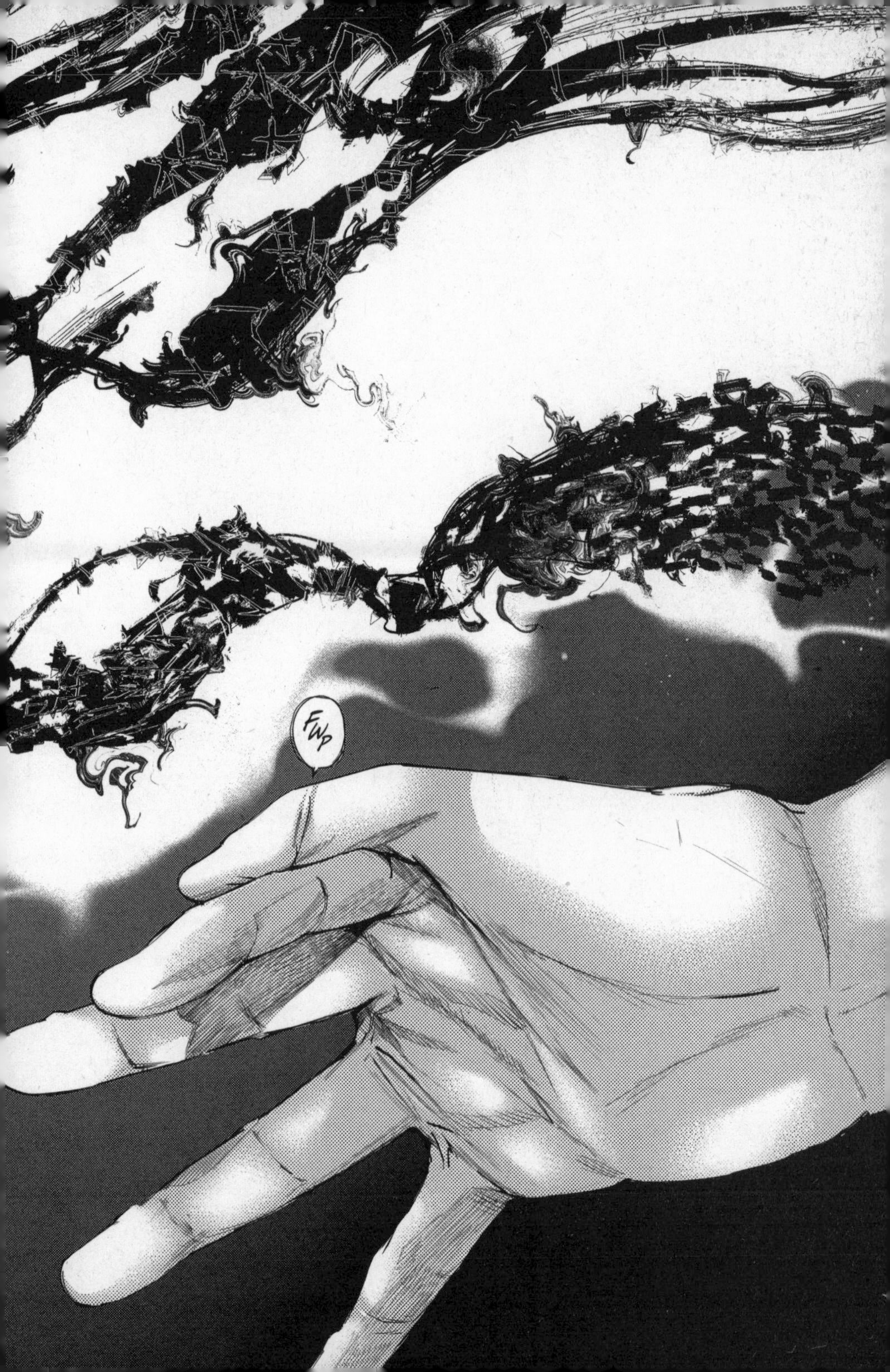
FWP

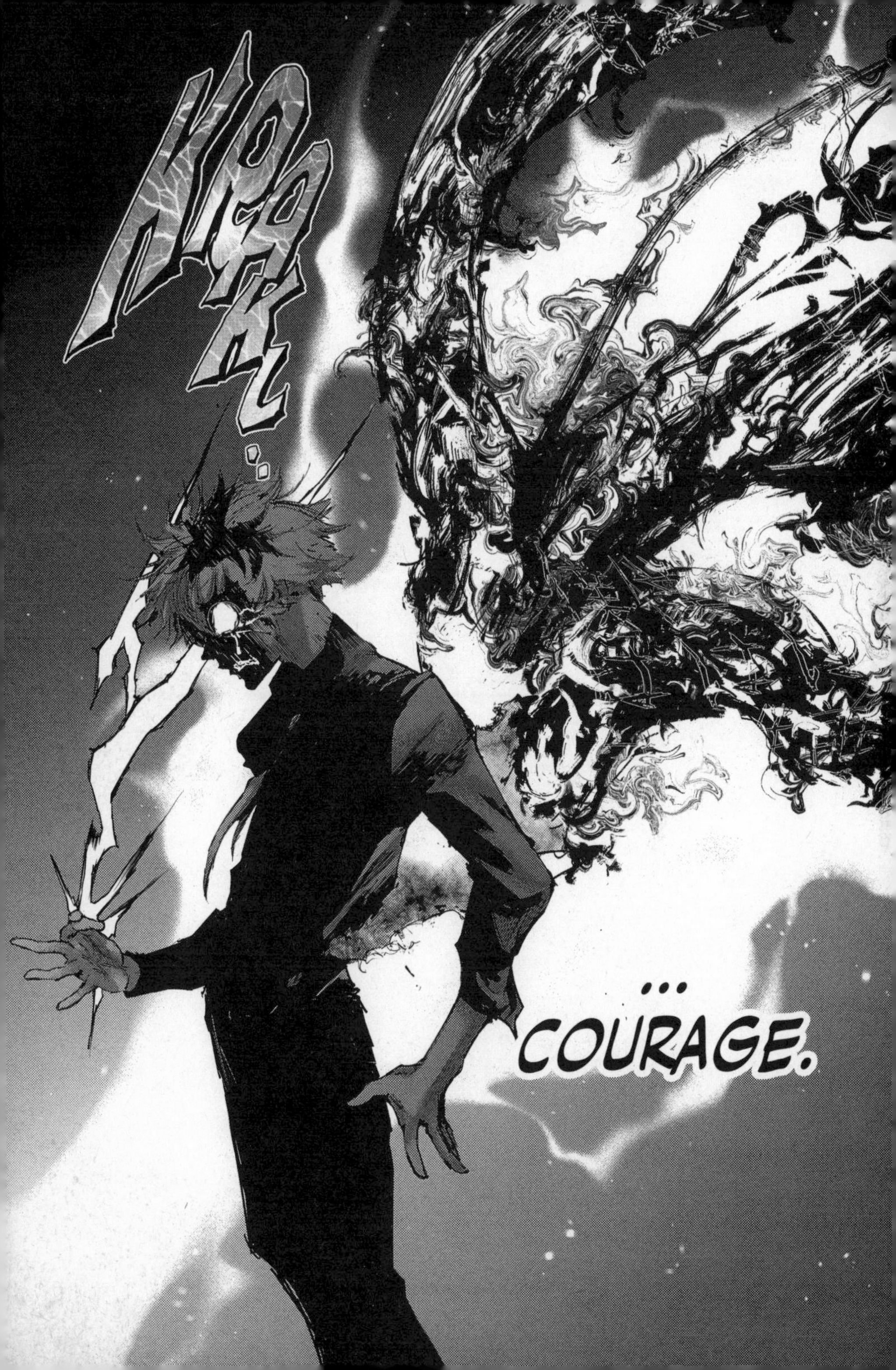
... COURAGE.

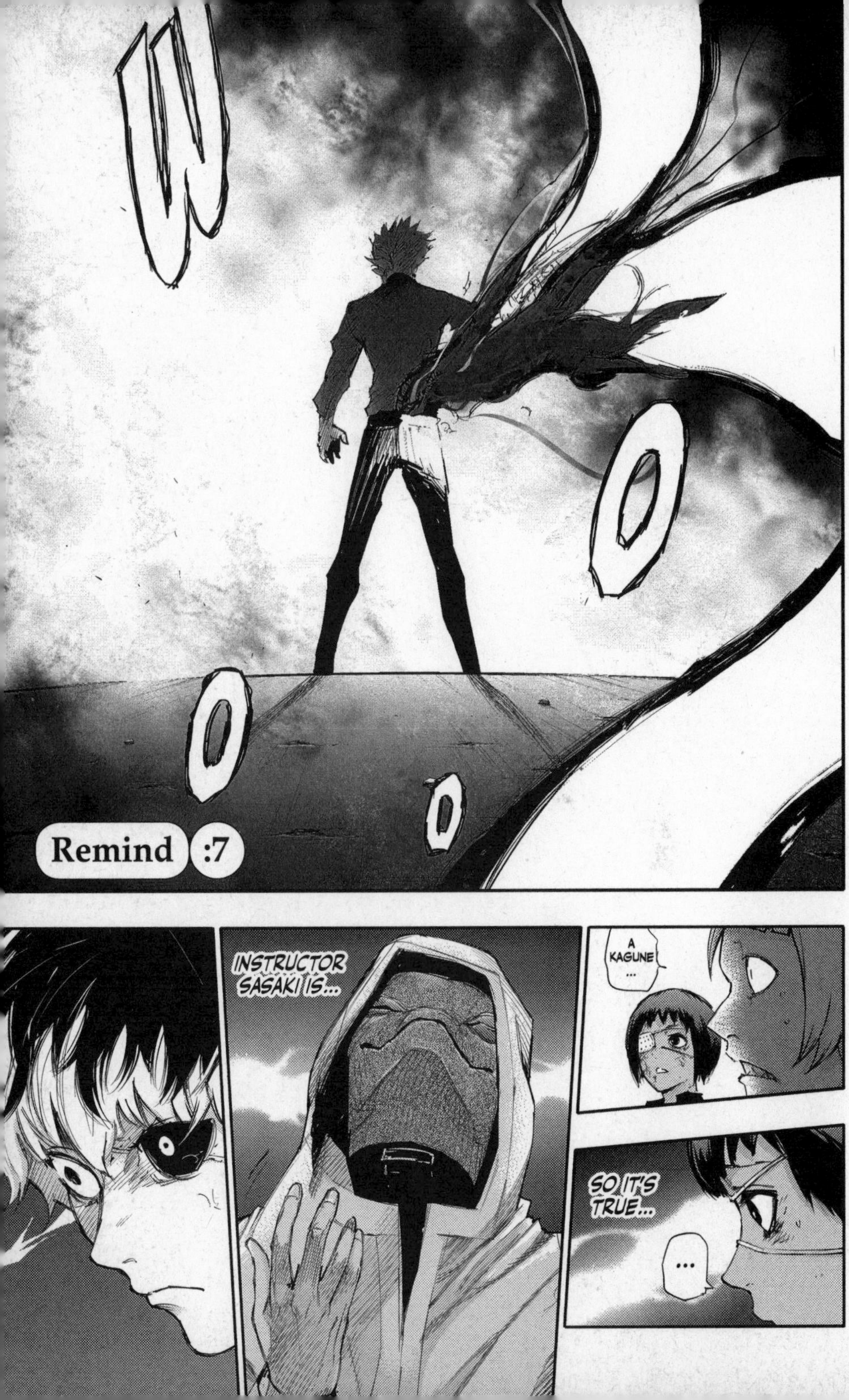
Remind :7
A KAGUNE ...
SO IT'S TRUE...
...
INSTRUCTOR SASAKI IS...

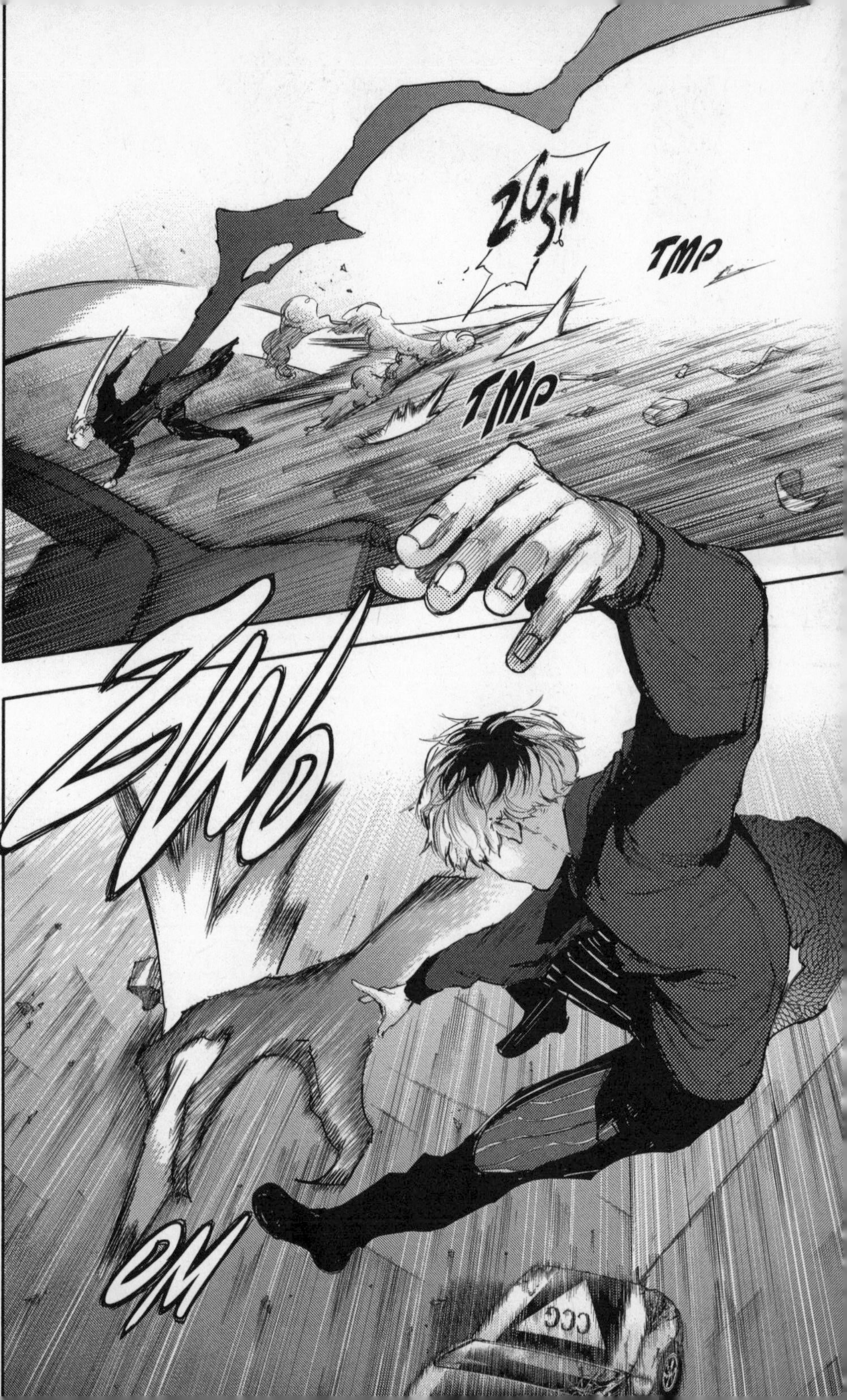
ZGSH
TMP
TMP
ZWO
OM

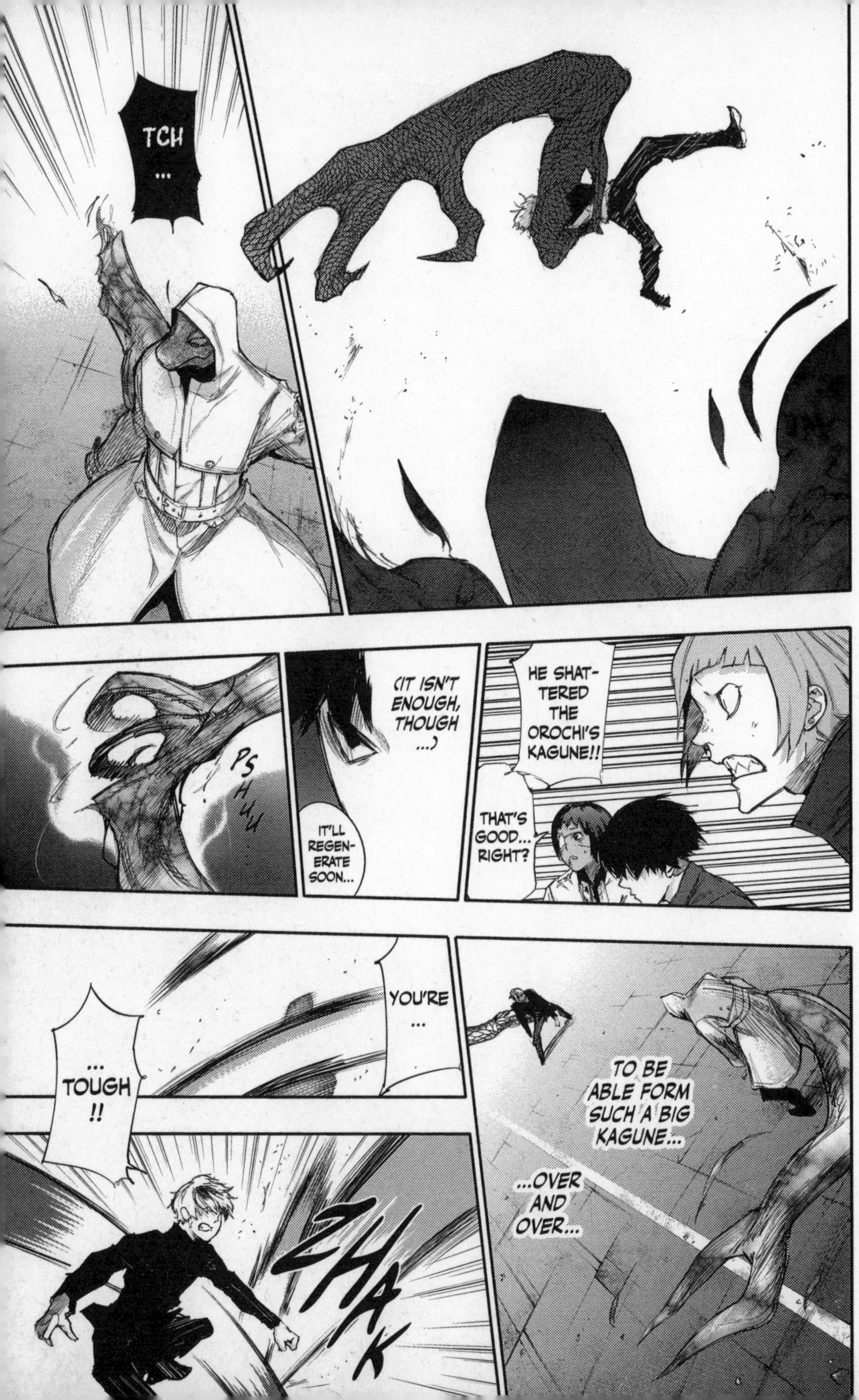
TCH ...
HE SHATTERED THE OROCHI'S KAGUNE!!
THAT'S GOOD... RIGHT?
(IT ISN'T ENOUGH, THOUGH ...)
IT'LL REGENERATE SOON...
PSHUU...
TO BE ABLE FORM SUCH A BIG KAGUNE...
...OVER AND OVER...
YOU'RE ...
... TOUGH !!
ZHAK

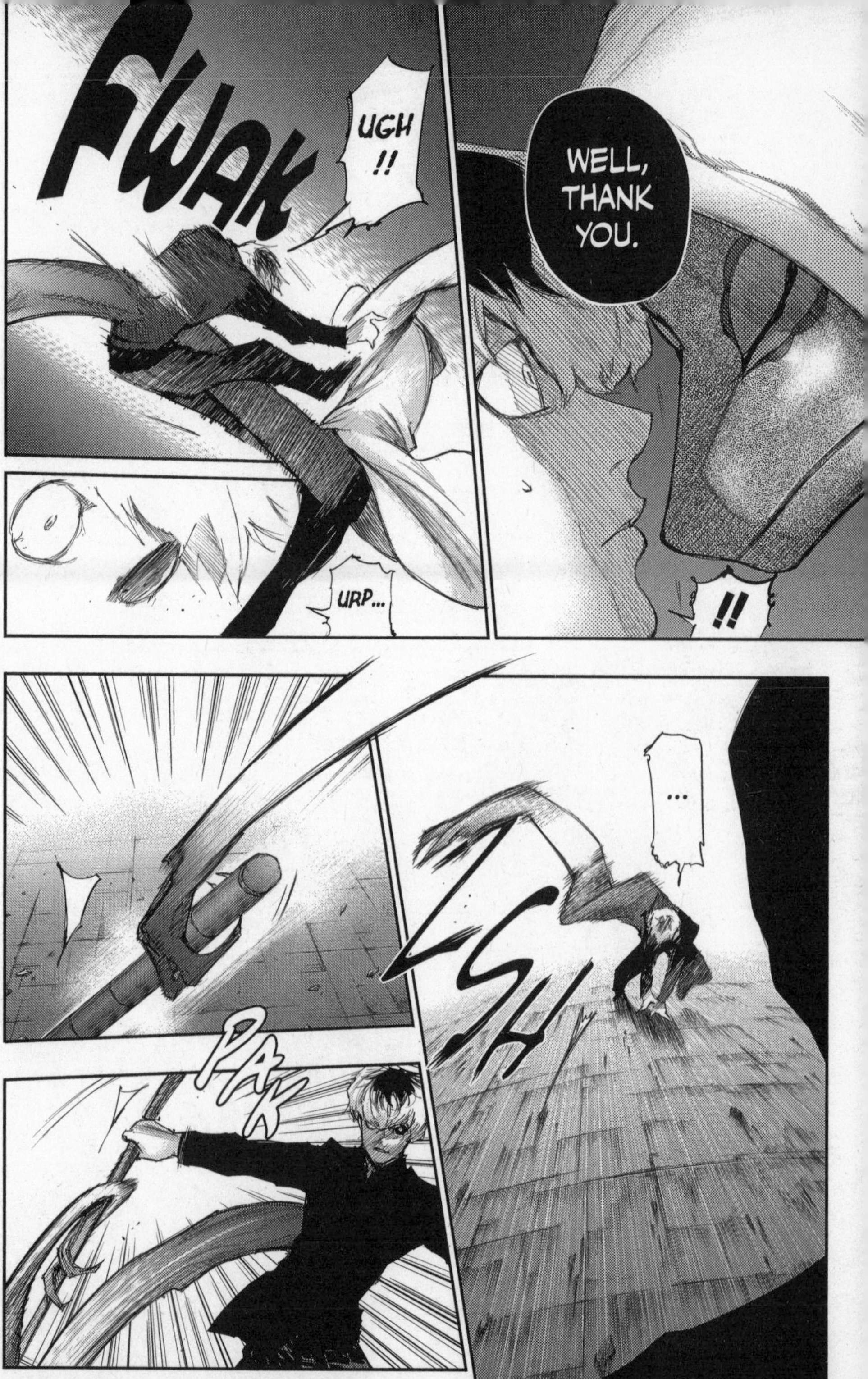
WELL, THANK YOU.
!!
FWAK
UGH !!
URP...
...
LSH
PAK

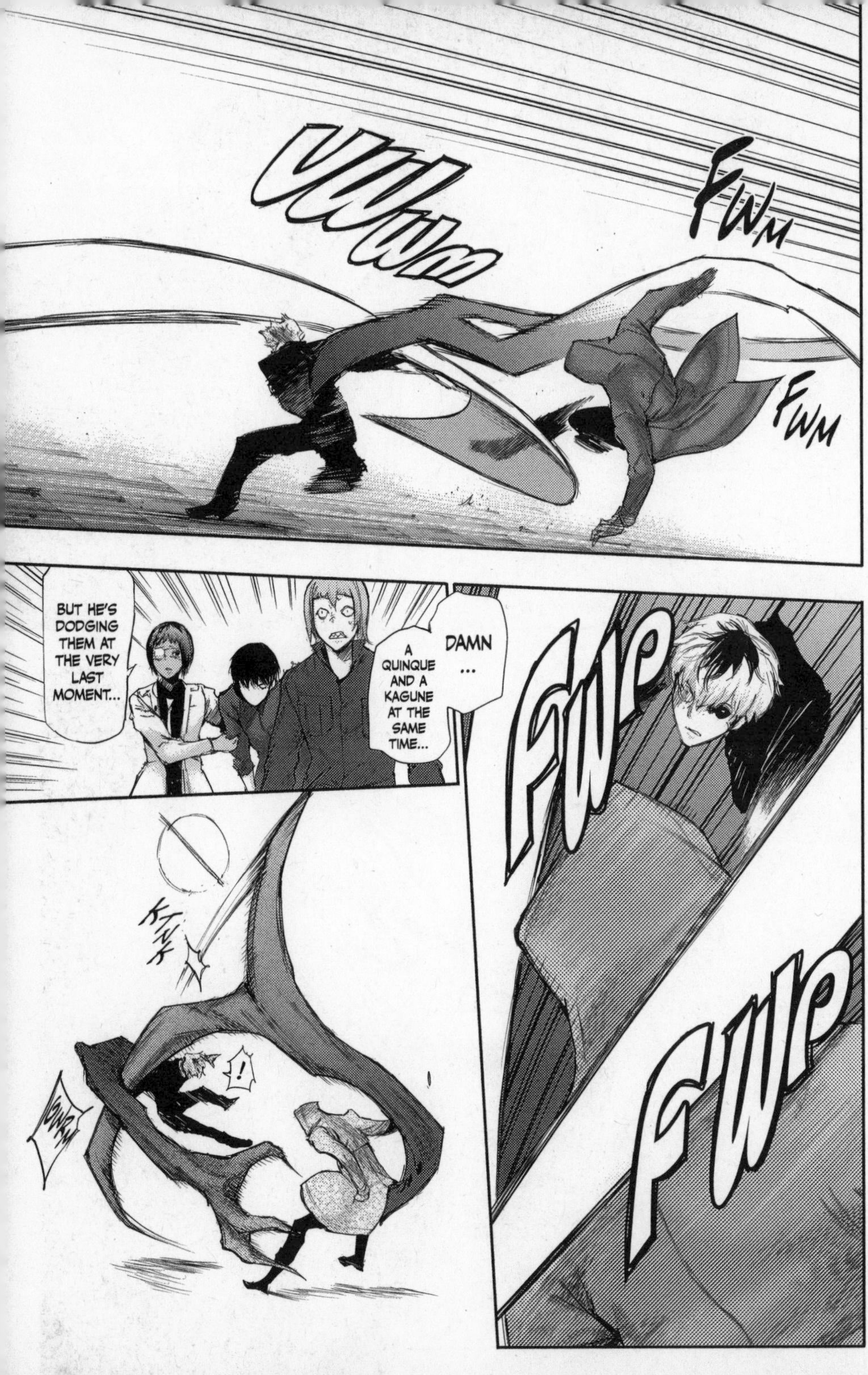
FWM
FWM
DAMN...
A QUINQUE AND A KAGUNE AT THE SAME TIME...
BUT HE'S DODGING THEM AT THE VERY LAST MOMENT...
FWP
FWP
KANK
!

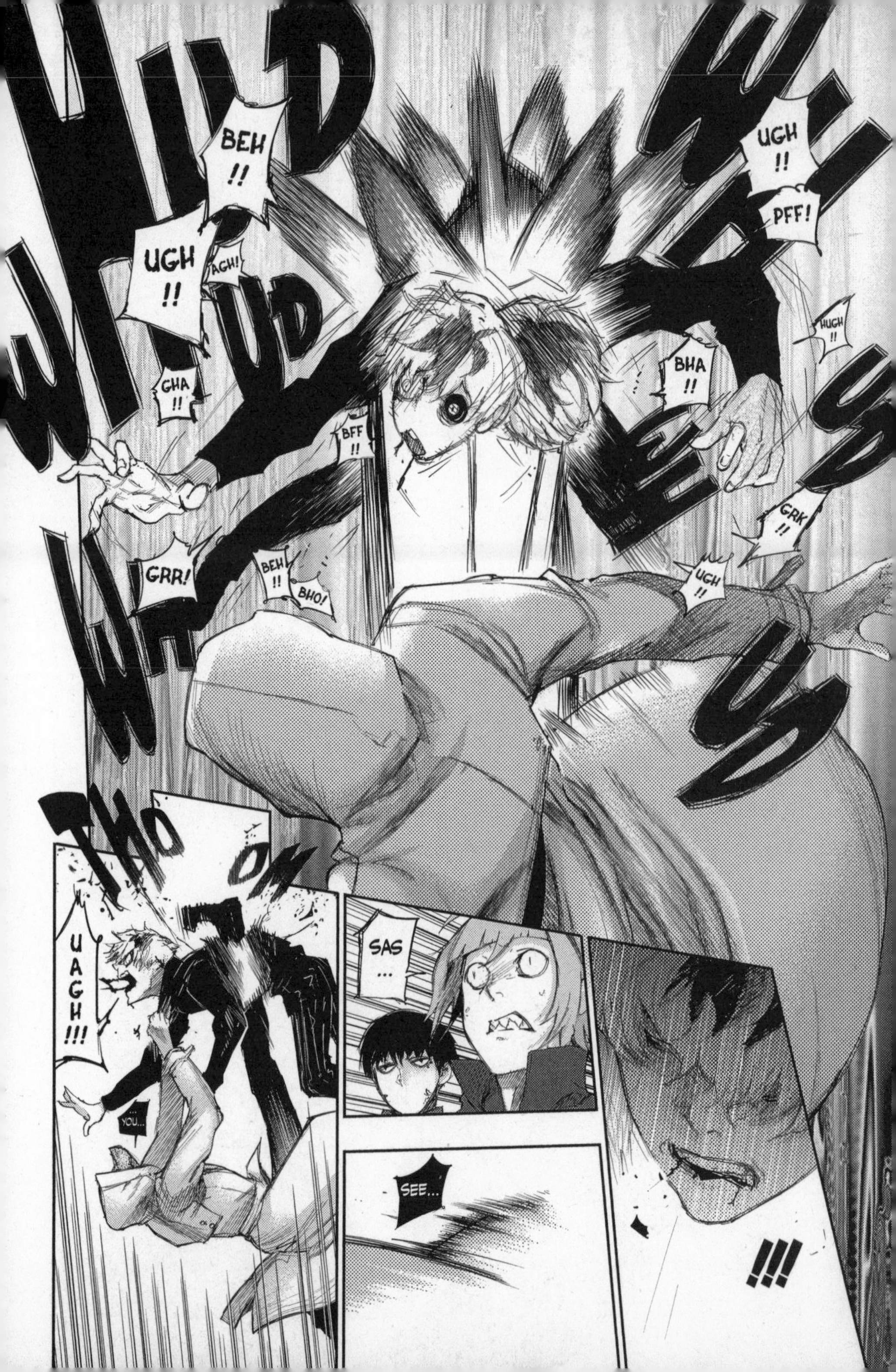
UGH!!
PFF!
HUGH!!
BHA!!
GRK!!
UGH!!
BEH!!
UGH!!
AGH!
GHA!!
BFF!!
GRR!
BEH!!
BHO!
!!!
SAS...
SEE...
THOOM
UAGH!!!
...YOU...

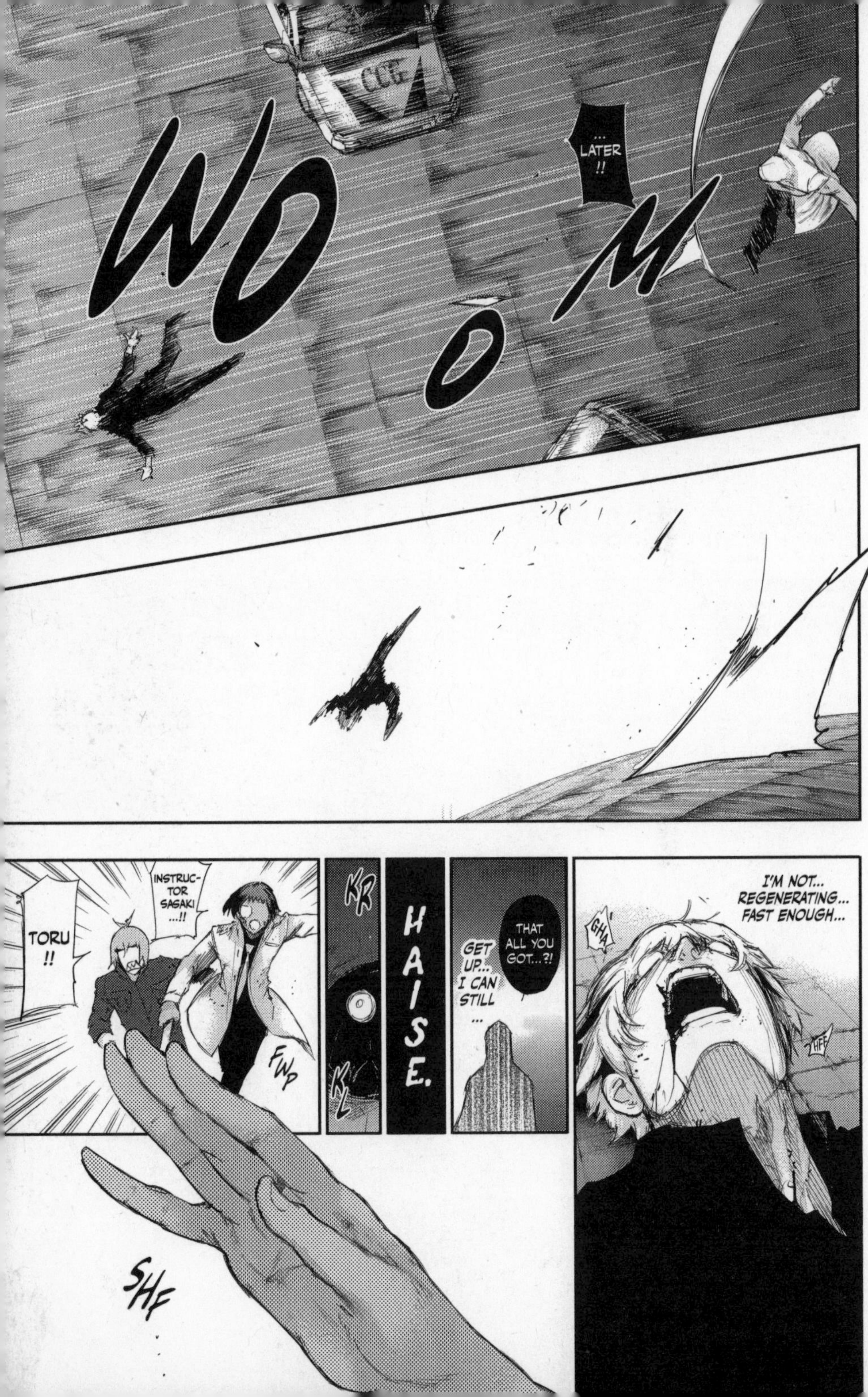

... LATER !!
WOOM
I'M NOT... REGENERATING... FAST ENOUGH...
GHA
HFF
THAT ALL YOU GOT...?!
GET UP... I CAN STILL ...
HAISE.
KR
KL
INSTRUCTOR SASAKI ...!!
TORU !!
FWP
SHF

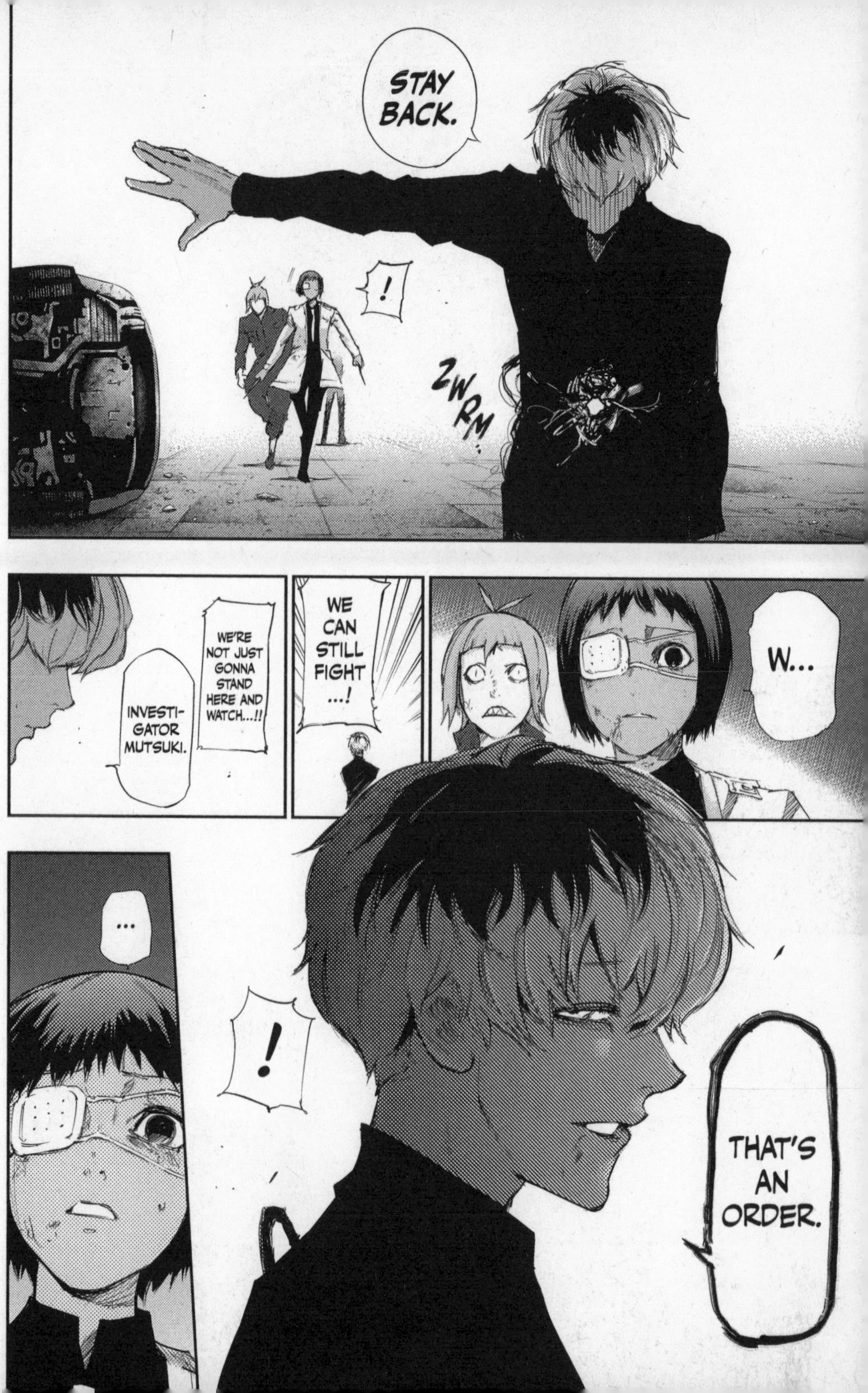
STAY BACK.
!
ZWRM
W...
WE CAN STILL FIGHT ...!
WE'RE NOT JUST GONNA STAND HERE AND WATCH...!!
INVESTI-GATOR MUTSUKI.
THAT'S AN ORDER.
!
...

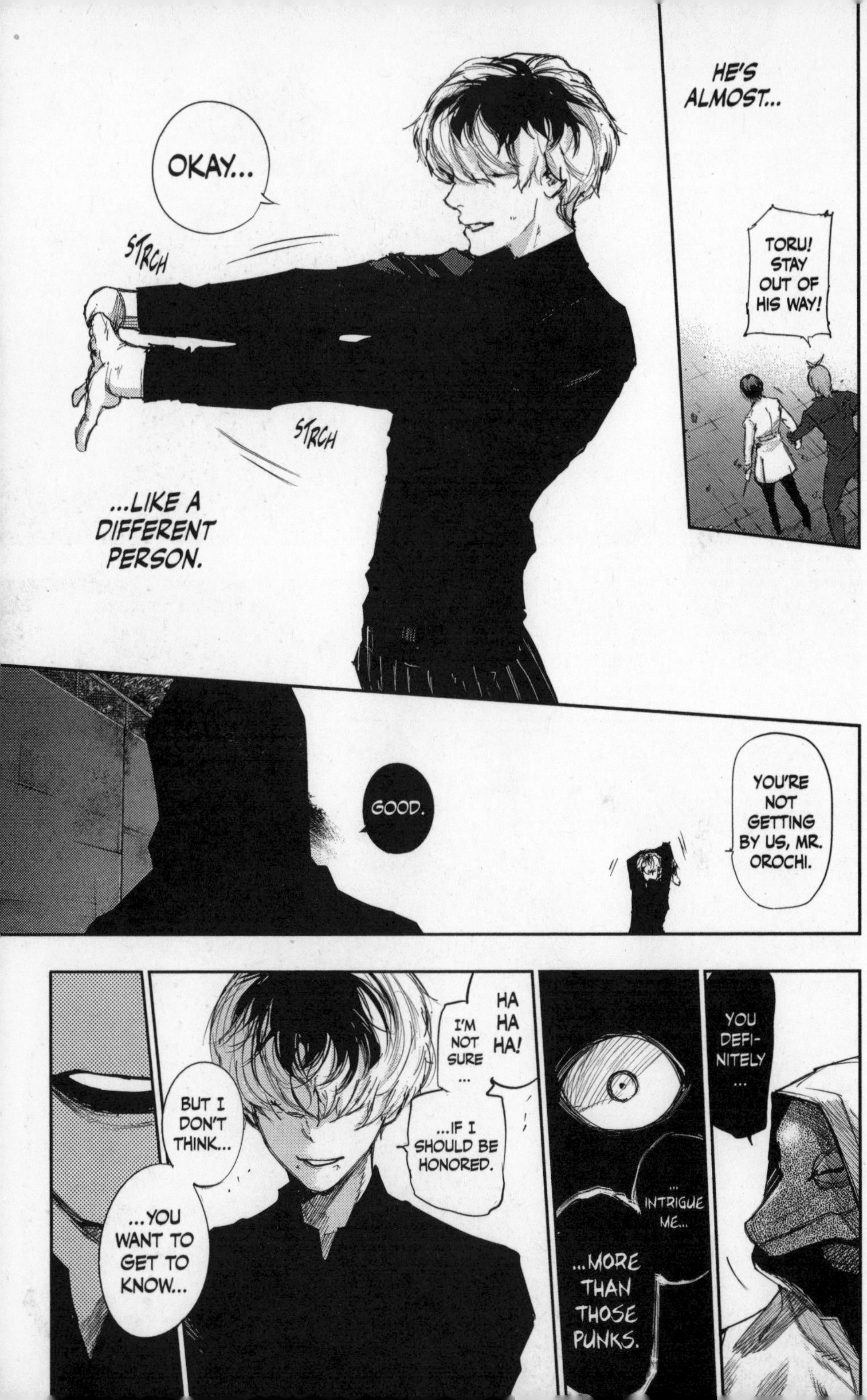
HE'S ALMOST...
TORU! STAY OUT OF HIS WAY!
OKAY...
STRCH
STRCH
...LIKE A DIFFERENT PERSON.
YOU'RE NOT GETTING BY US, MR. OROCHI.
GOOD.
YOU DEFINITELY...
...INTRIGUE ME...
...MORE THAN THOSE PUNKS.
HA HA HA!
I'M NOT SURE...
...IF I SHOULD BE HONORED.
BUT I DON'T THINK...
...YOU WANT TO GET TO KNOW...

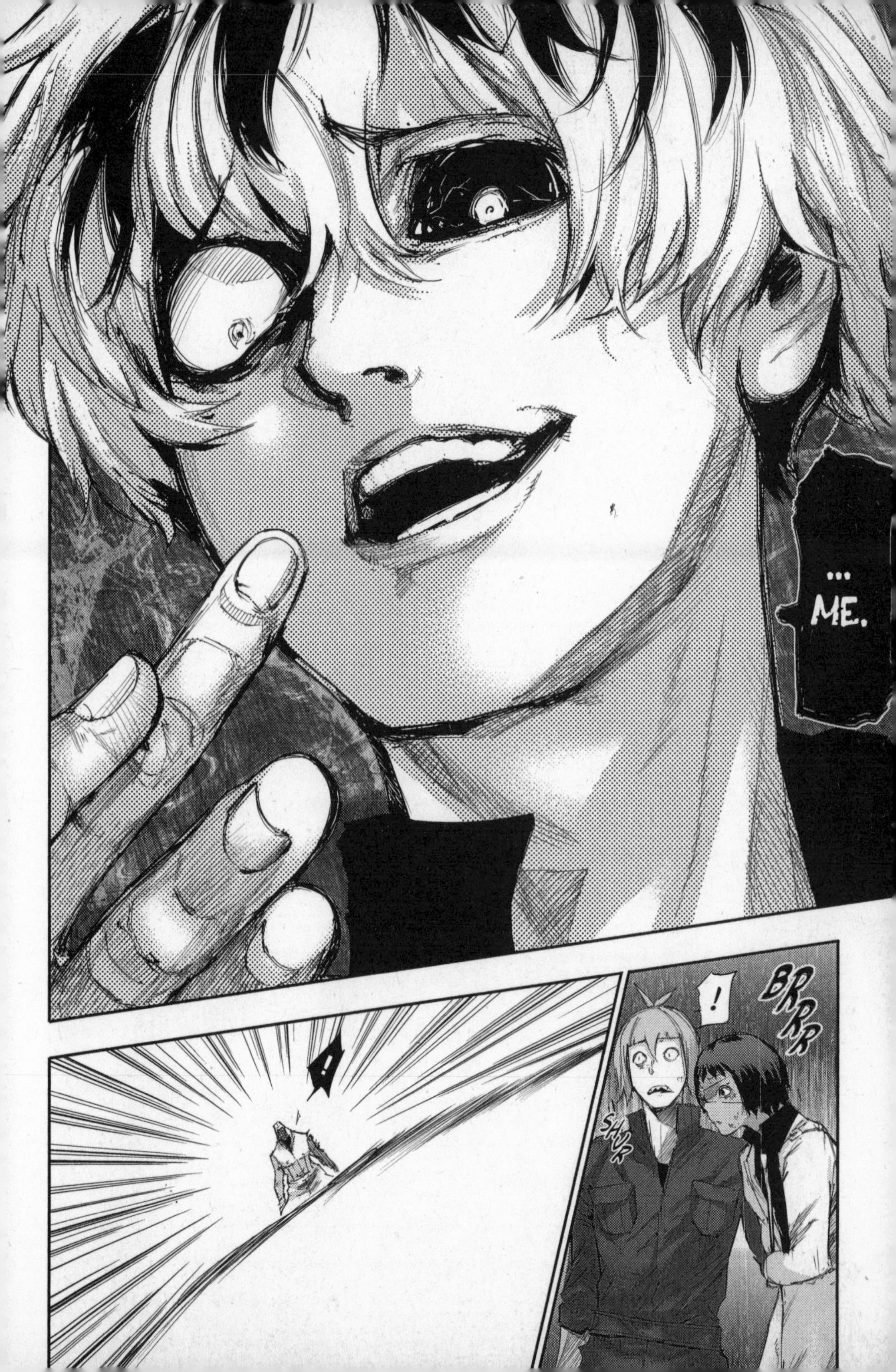
... ME.
BRRR
!
SHUR
!

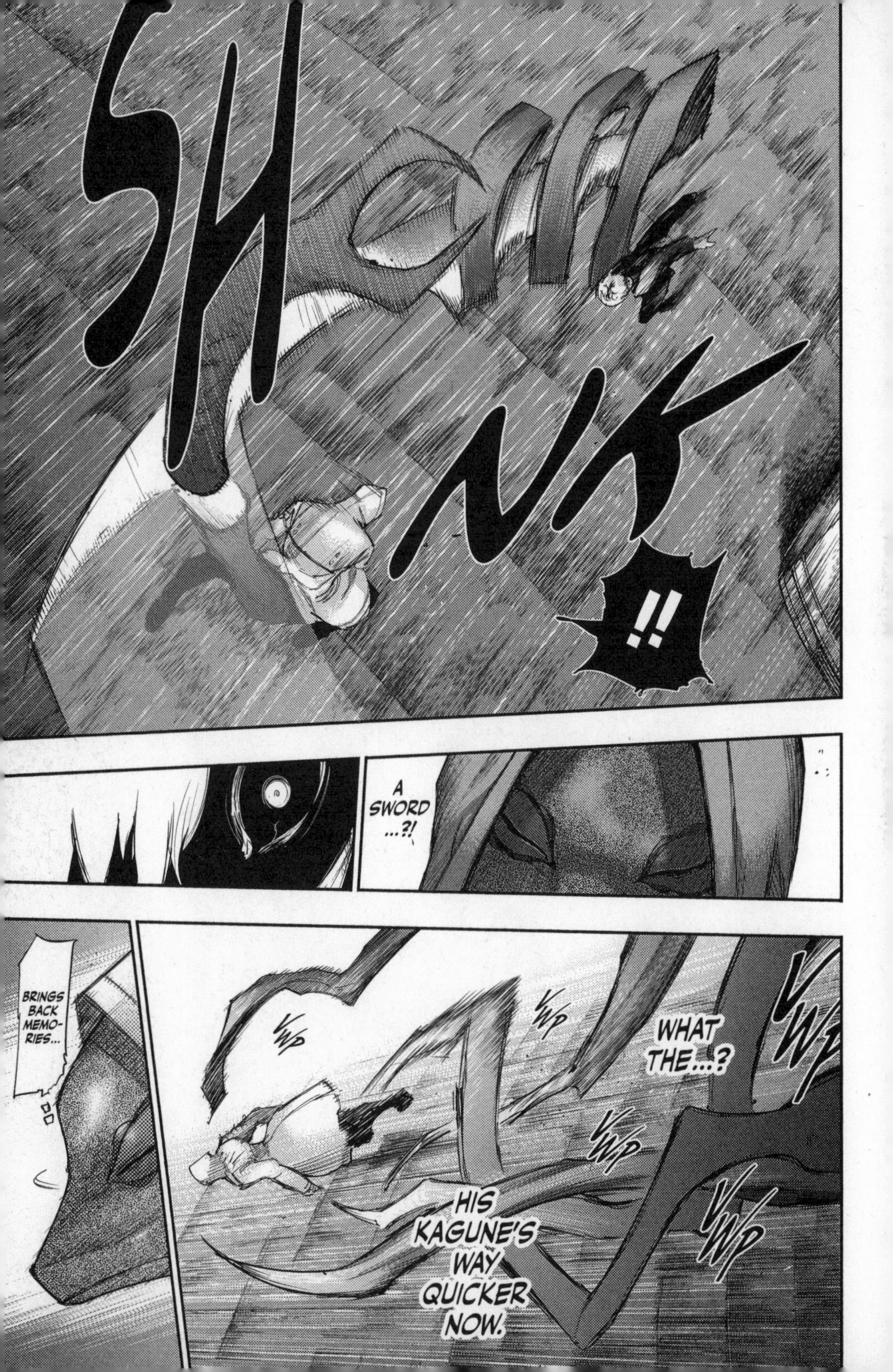
SHNK
!!
A SWORD ...?!
VWP
WHAT THE...?
VWP
VWP
VWP
VWP
HIS KAGUNE'S WAY QUICKER NOW.
BRINGS BACK MEMORIES...

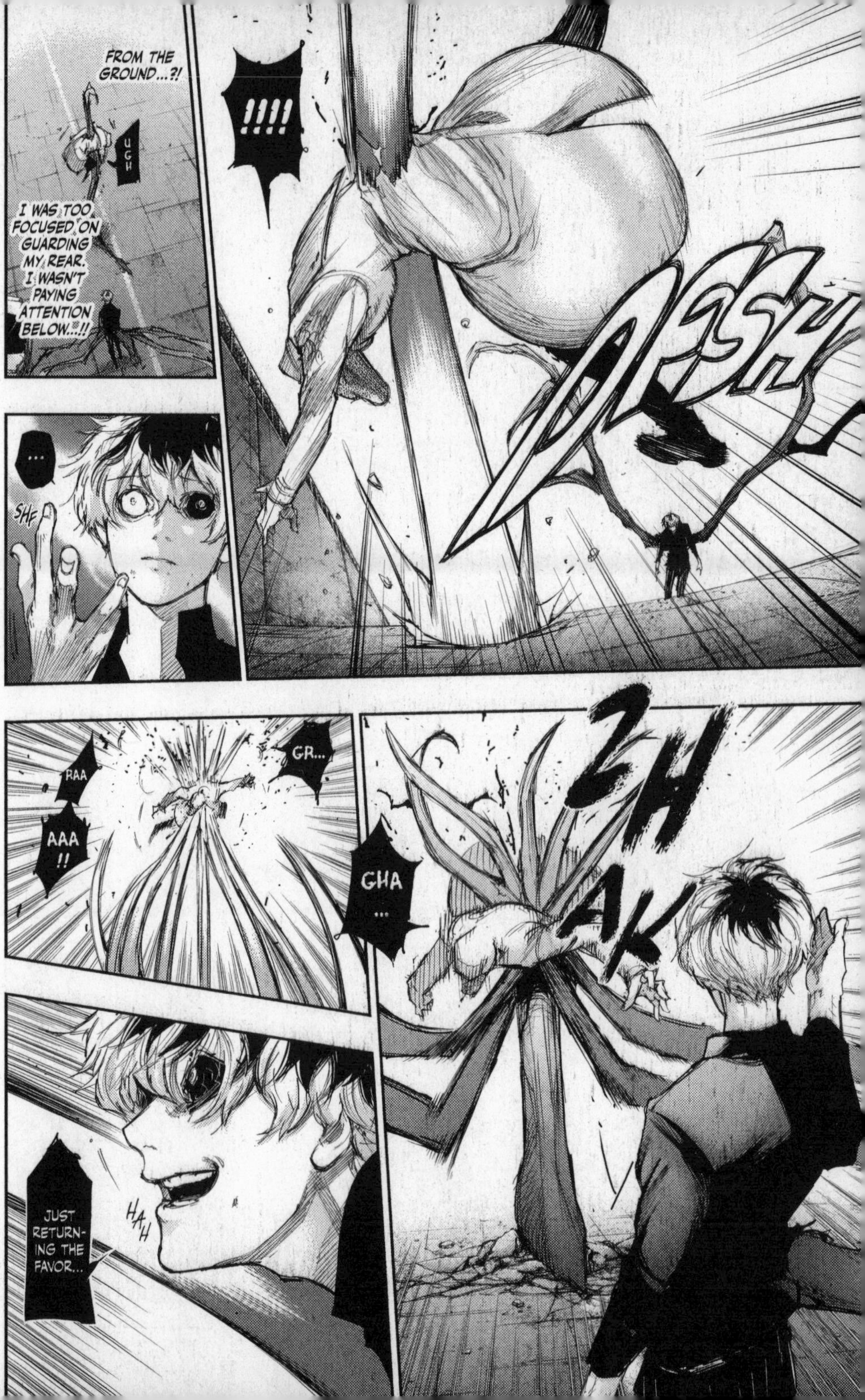
!!!!
FROM THE GROUND...?!
UGH
I WAS TOO FOCUSED ON GUARDING MY REAR. I WASN'T PAYING ATTENTION BELOW...!!
...
SHF
ZH AK
GHA ...
GR...
RAA AAA !!
HAH
JUST RETURNING THE FAVOR...

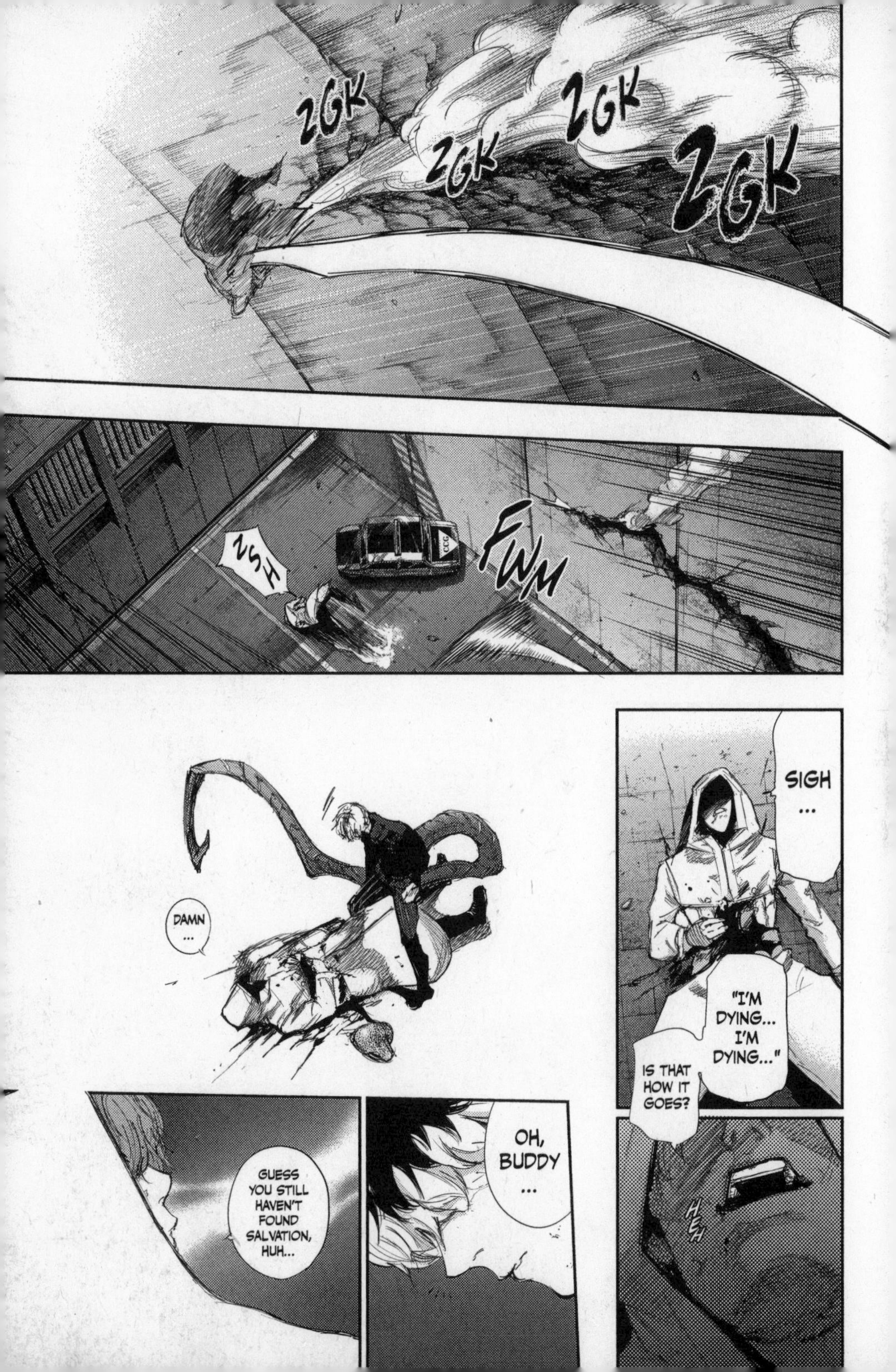
ZGK
ZGK
ZGK
ZGK
FWM
NSH
SIGH...
"I'M DYING... I'M DYING..."
IS THAT HOW IT GOES?
DAMN...
HEH
OH, BUDDY...
GUESS YOU STILL HAVEN'T FOUND SALVATION, HUH...

... KANEKI?

NISHIO...?

?!

WAIT, WHO'S THAT?!

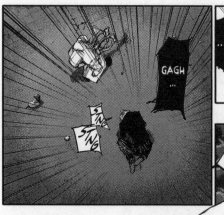

GAGH...

...?!

NISHIO...?

...?

WHAT'S UP WITH HIS VOICE...?

...JUST SAY?

WAIT... WHAT DID I...

SORRY...

AARGH!!

EEE...!!

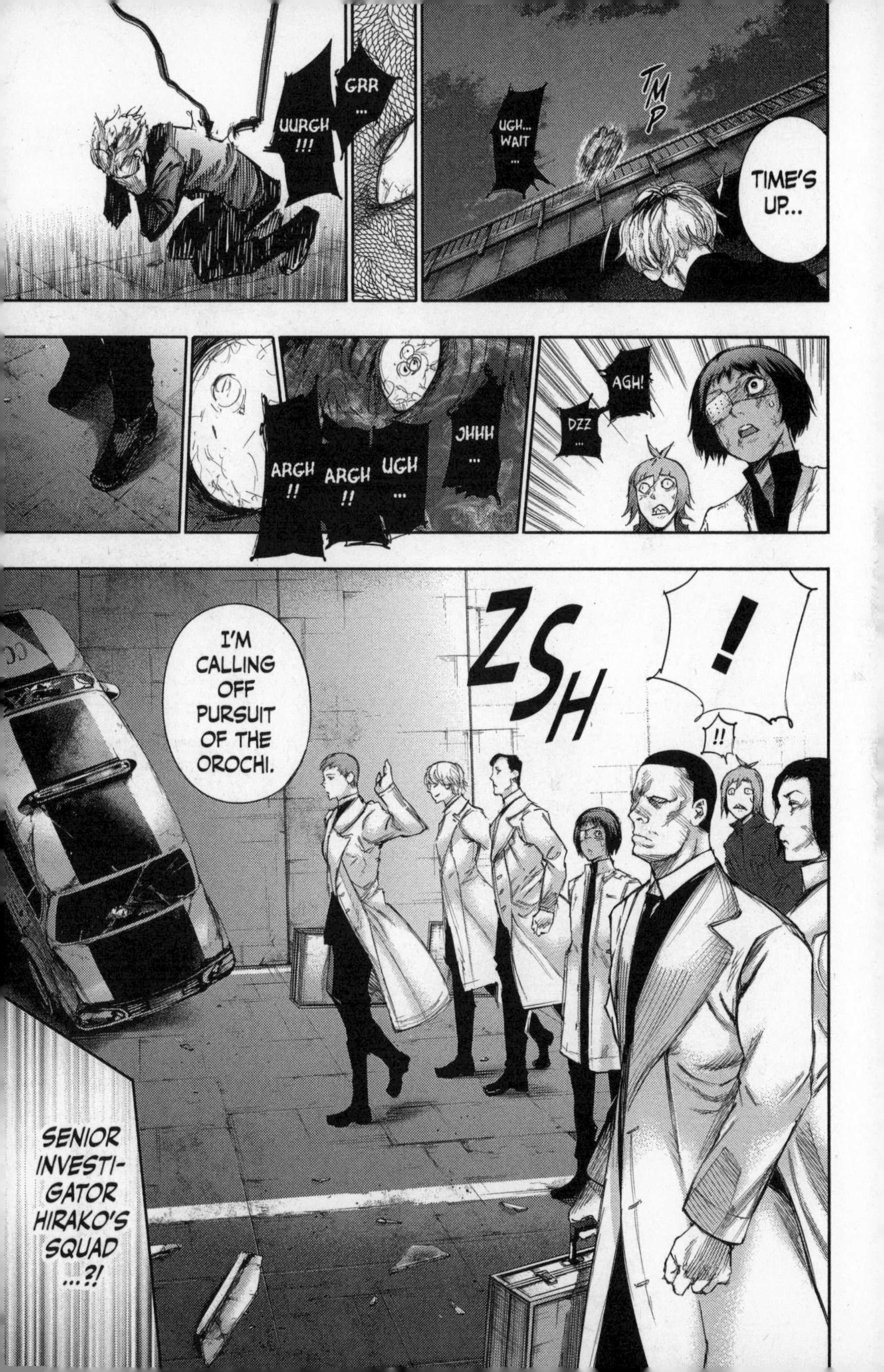
TMP
TIME'S UP...
UGH... WAIT ...
GRR ...
UURGH !!!
AGH!
DZZ ...
JHHH ...
UGH ...
ARGH !!
ARGH !!
!
ZSH
!!
I'M CALLING OFF PURSUIT OF THE OROCHI.
SENIOR INVESTI-GATOR HIRAKO'S SQUAD ...?!

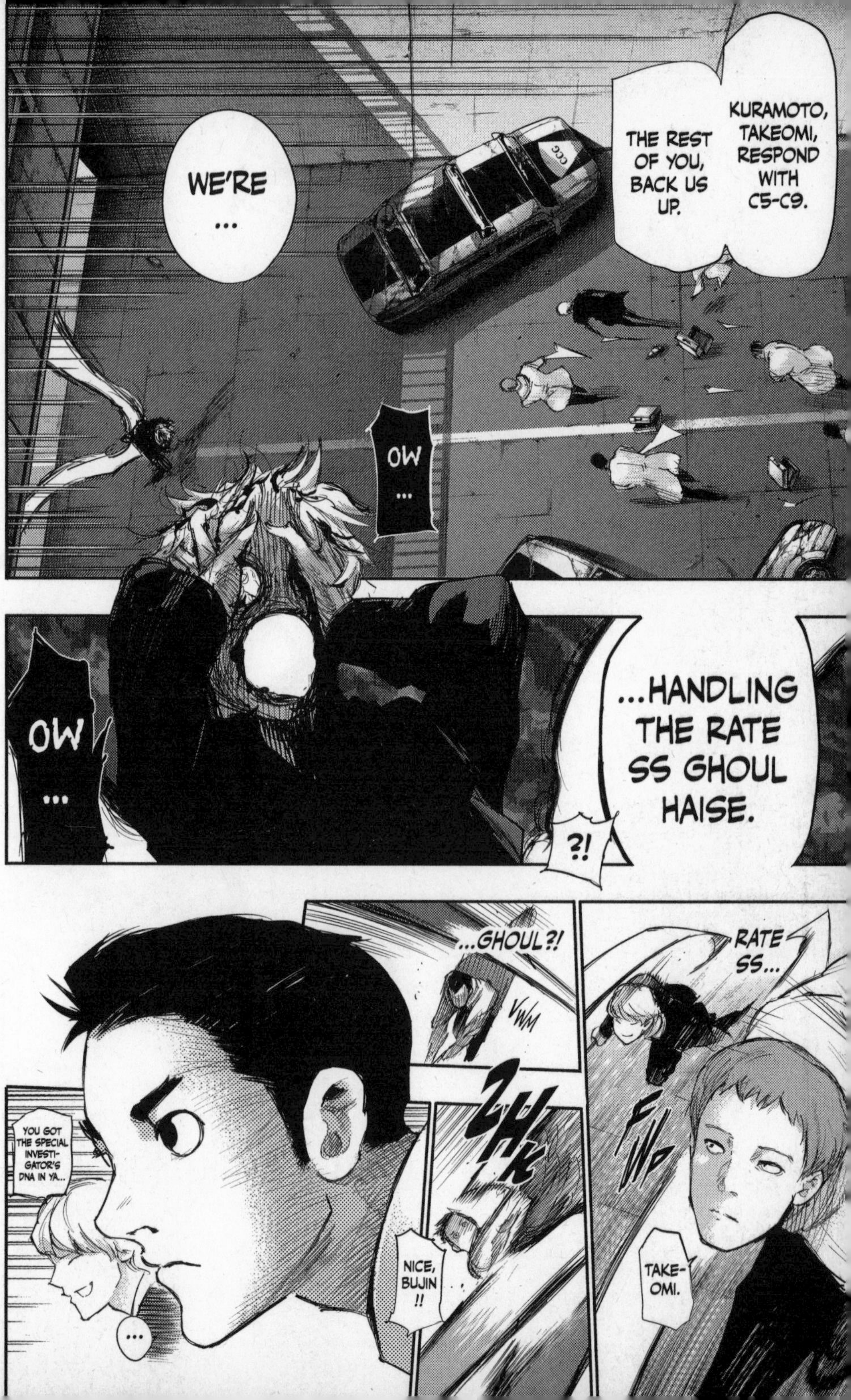
KURAMOTO, TAKEOMI, RESPOND WITH C5-C9.
THE REST OF YOU, BACK US UP.
WE'RE ...
OW ...
...HANDLING THE RATE SS GHOUL HAISE.
?!
OW ...
RATE SS...
TAKE-OMI.
...GHOUL?!
VWM
ZHK
NICE, BUJIN !!
YOU GOT THE SPECIAL INVESTI-GATOR'S DNA IN YA...
...

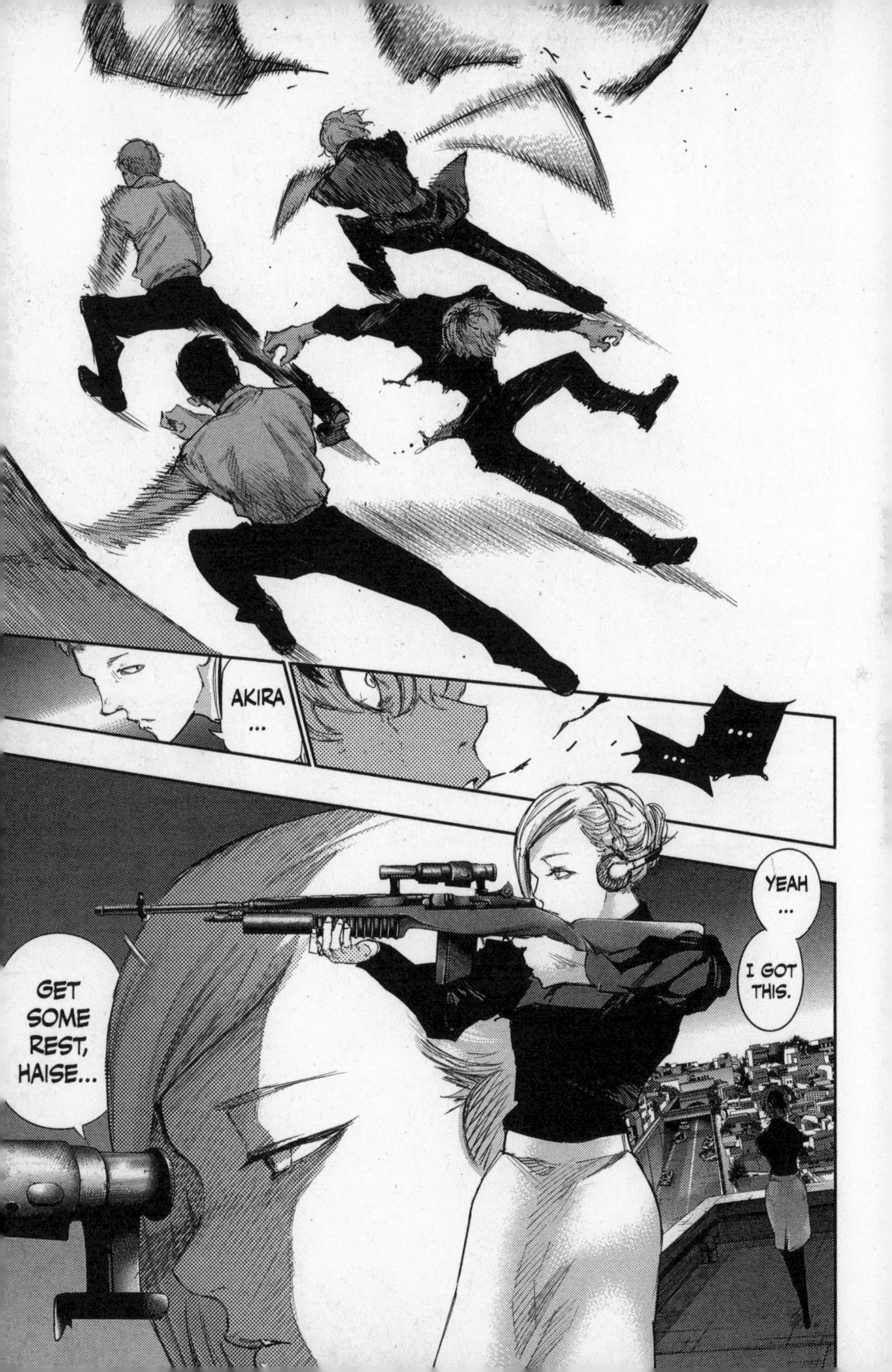
...
...
AKIRA ...
YEAH ...
I GOT THIS.
GET SOME REST, HAISE...

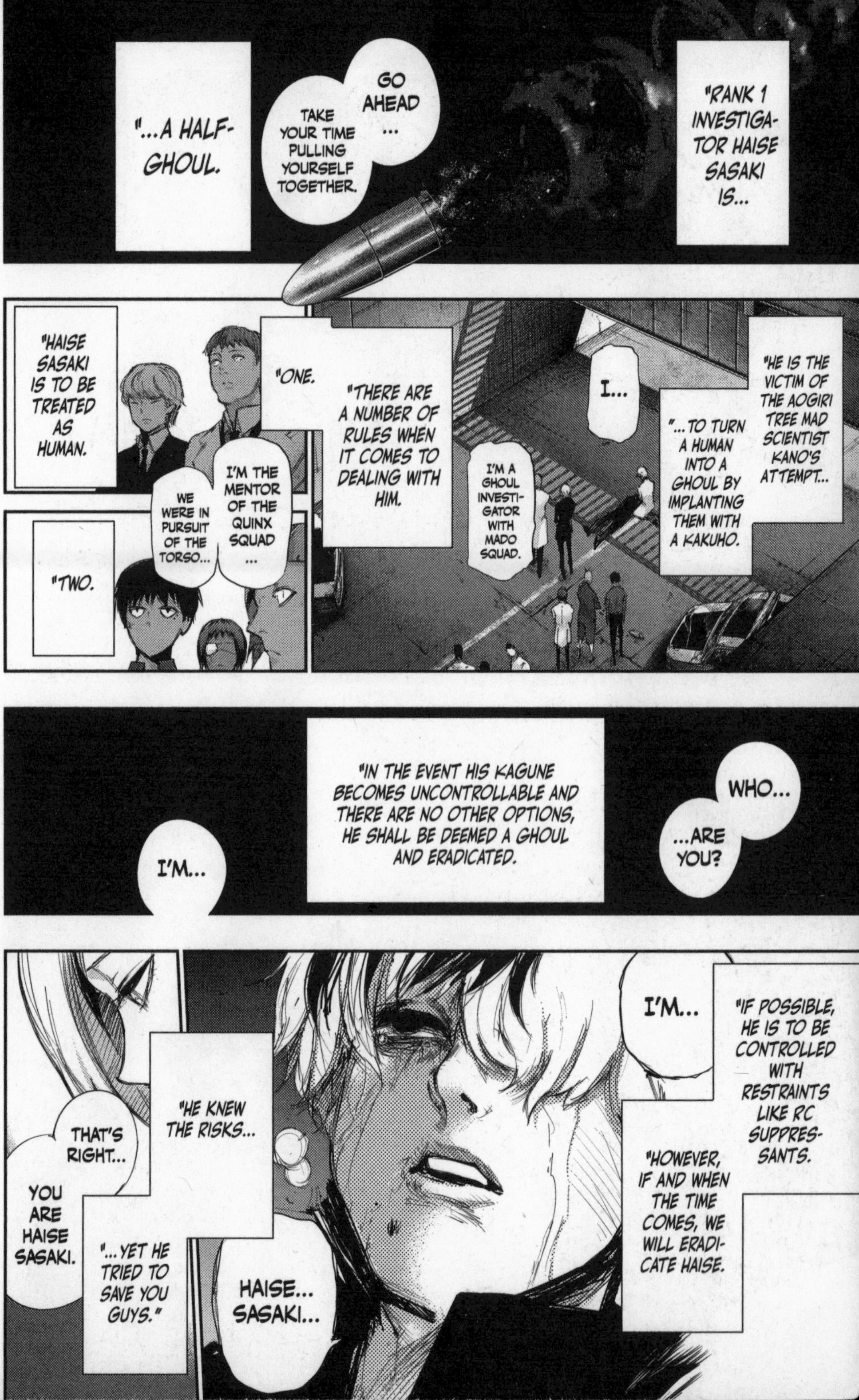
"RANK 1 INVESTIGATOR HAISE SASAKI IS...
GO AHEAD...
TAKE YOUR TIME PULLING YOURSELF TOGETHER.
"...A HALF-GHOUL.
"HE IS THE VICTIM OF THE AOGIRI TREE MAD SCIENTIST KANO'S ATTEMPT...
"...TO TURN A HUMAN INTO A GHOUL BY IMPLANTING THEM WITH A KAKUHO.
I...
I'M A GHOUL INVESTIGATOR WITH MADO SQUAD.
"THERE ARE A NUMBER OF RULES WHEN IT COMES TO DEALING WITH HIM.
"ONE.
"HAISE SASAKI IS TO BE TREATED AS HUMAN.
I'M THE MENTOR OF THE QUINX SQUAD...
WE WERE IN PURSUIT OF THE TORSO...
"TWO.
WHO...
...ARE YOU?
"IN THE EVENT HIS KAGUNE BECOMES UNCONTROLLABLE AND THERE ARE NO OTHER OPTIONS, HE SHALL BE DEEMED A GHOUL AND ERADICATED.
I'M...
I'M...
"IF POSSIBLE, HE IS TO BE CONTROLLED WITH RESTRAINTS LIKE RC SUPPRESSANTS.
"HOWEVER, IF AND WHEN THE TIME COMES, WE WILL ERADICATE HAISE.
HAISE... SASAKI...
"HE KNEW THE RISKS...
"...YET HE TRIED TO SAVE YOU GUYS."
THAT'S RIGHT...
YOU ARE HAISE SASAKI.

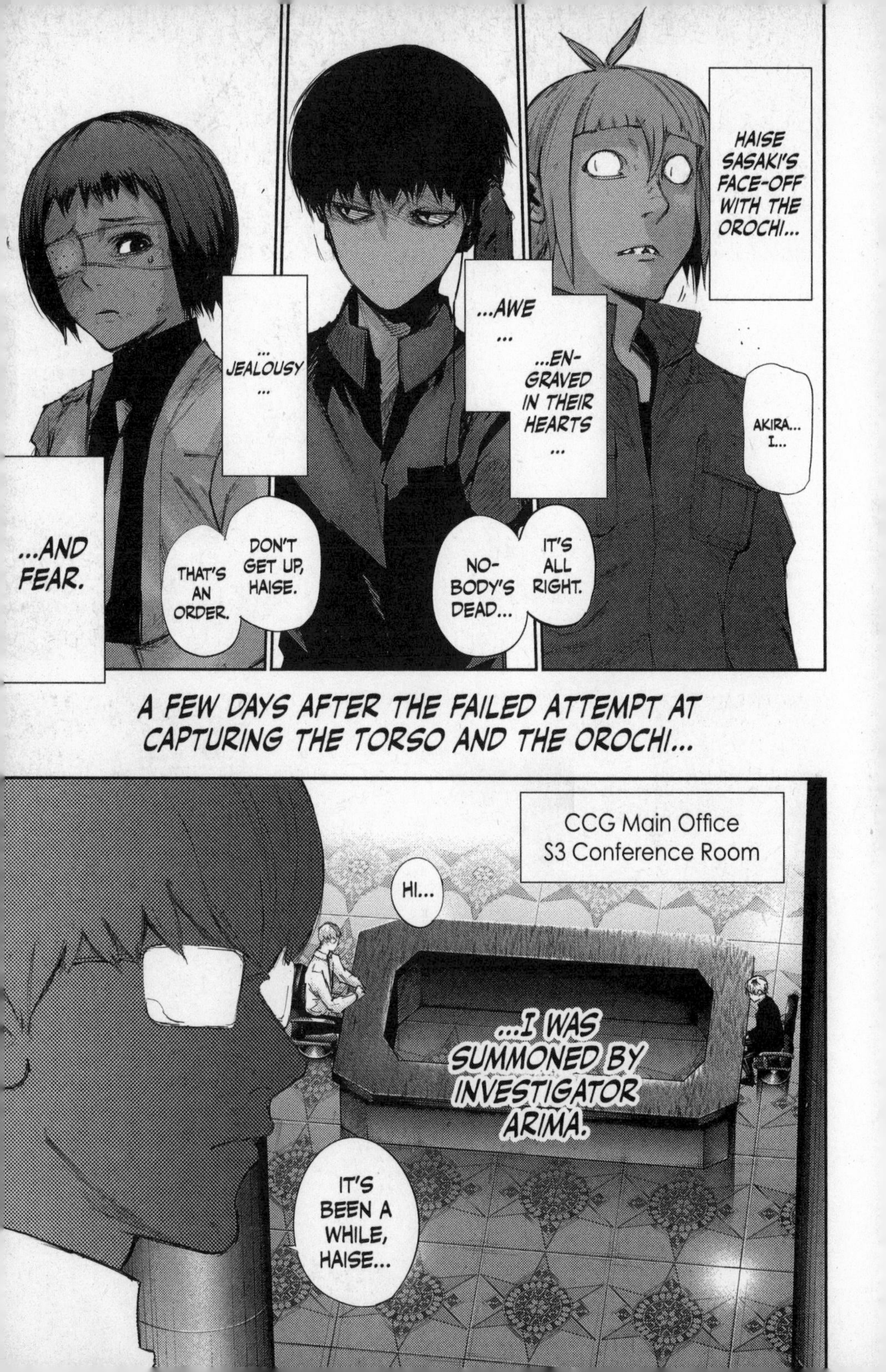
HAISE SASAKI'S FACE-OFF WITH THE OROCHI...
...AWE ... ...EN-GRAVED IN THEIR HEARTS ...
AKIRA... I...
IT'S ALL RIGHT.
NO-BODY'S DEAD...
... JEALOUSY ...
DON'T GET UP, HAISE.
THAT'S AN ORDER.
...AND FEAR.
A FEW DAYS AFTER THE FAILED ATTEMPT AT CAPTURING THE TORSO AND THE OROCHI...
CCG Main Office
S3 Conference Room
HI...
...I WAS SUMMONED BY INVESTIGATOR ARIMA.
IT'S BEEN A WHILE, HAISE...

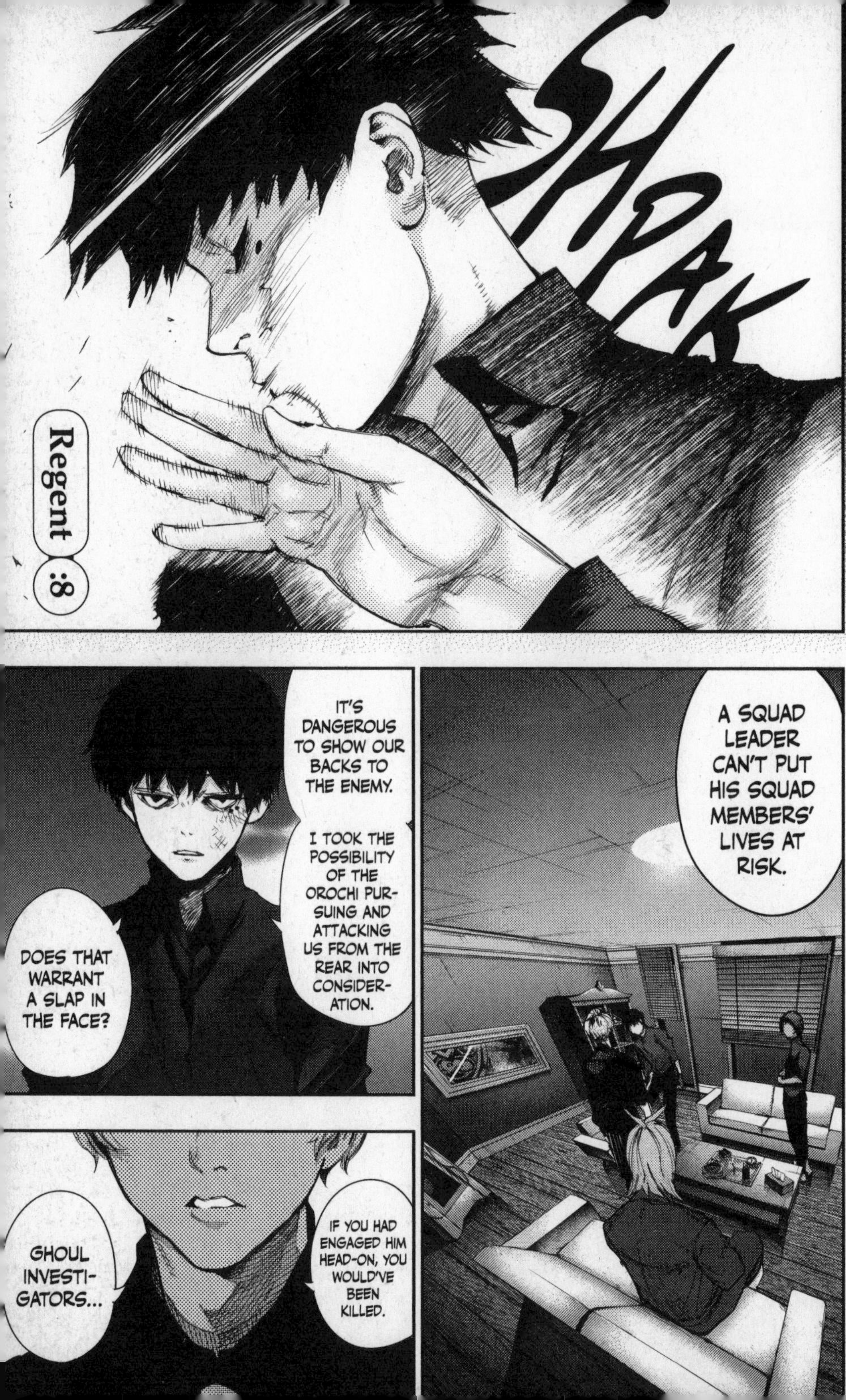
SHPAK
Regent :8
A SQUAD LEADER CAN'T PUT HIS SQUAD MEMBERS' LIVES AT RISK.
IT'S DANGEROUS TO SHOW OUR BACKS TO THE ENEMY.
I TOOK THE POSSIBILITY OF THE OROCHI PURSUING AND ATTACKING US FROM THE REAR INTO CONSIDERATION.
DOES THAT WARRANT A SLAP IN THE FACE?
IF YOU HAD ENGAGED HIM HEAD-ON, YOU WOULD'VE BEEN KILLED.
GHOUL INVESTIGATORS...

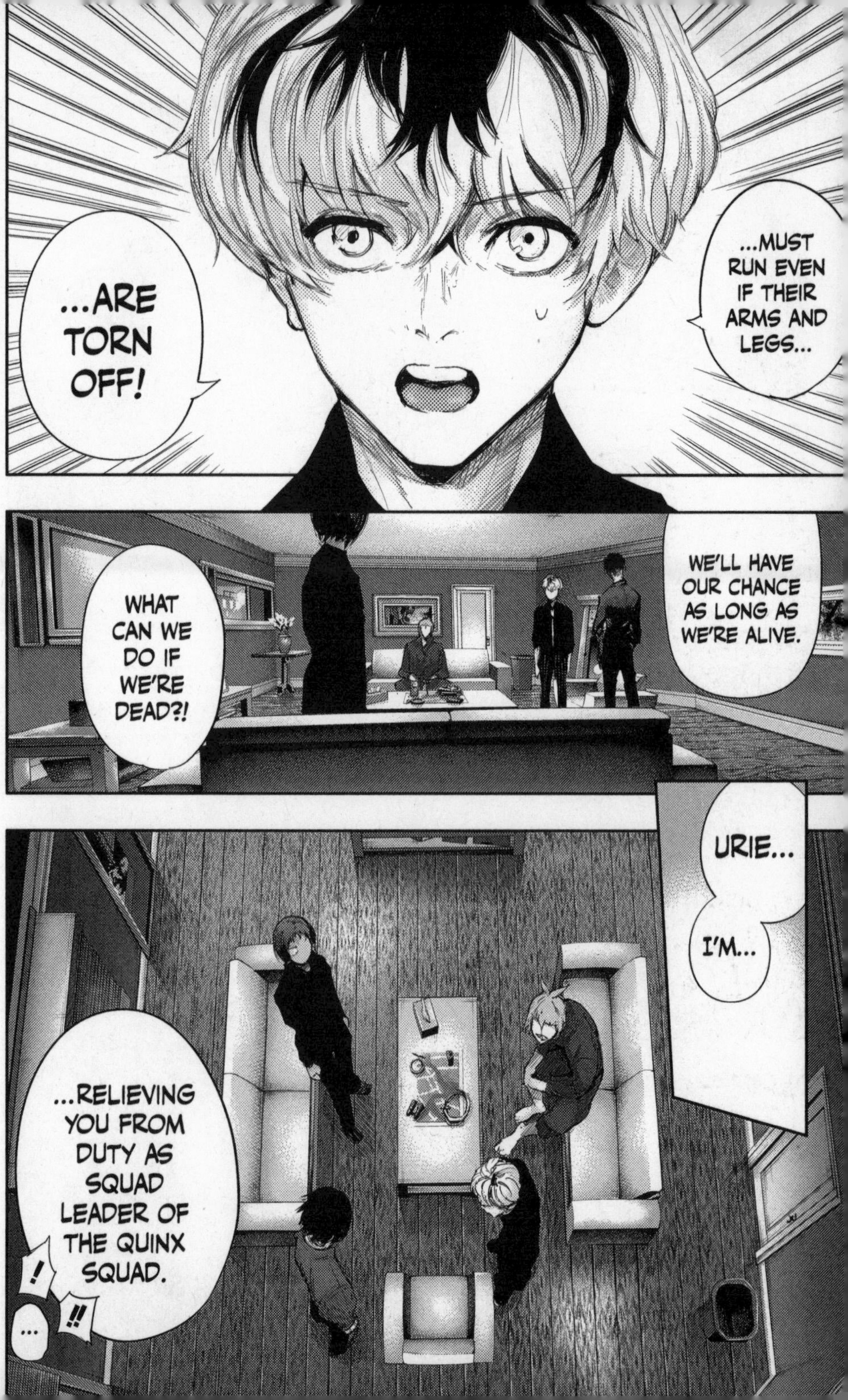
...MUST RUN EVEN IF THEIR ARMS AND LEGS...
...ARE TORN OFF!
WE'LL HAVE OUR CHANCE AS LONG AS WE'RE ALIVE.
WHAT CAN WE DO IF WE'RE DEAD?!
URIE...
I'M...
...RELIEVING YOU FROM DUTY AS SQUAD LEADER OF THE QUINX SQUAD.
!
!!
...

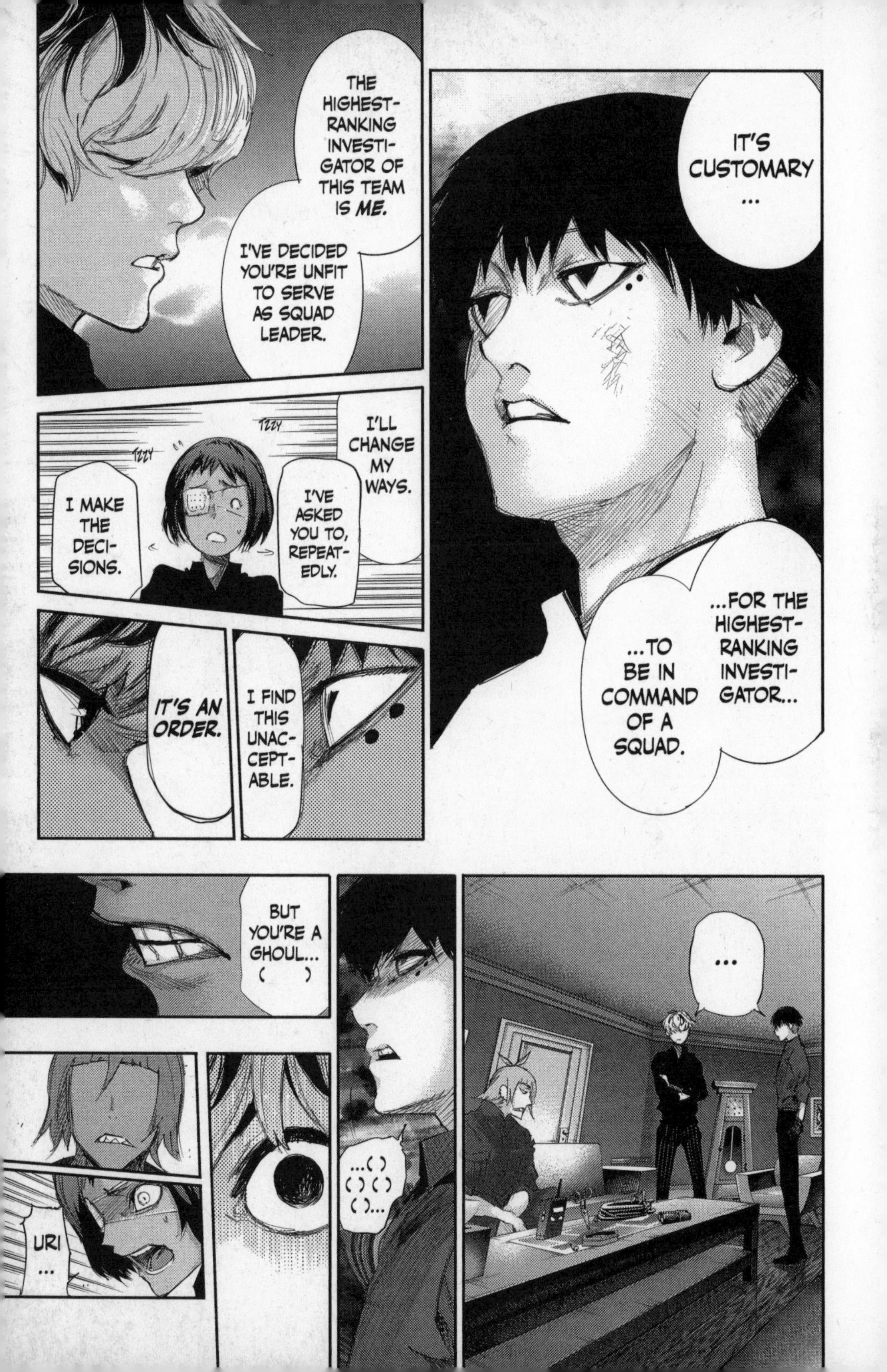
IT'S CUSTOMARY ...
...FOR THE HIGHEST-RANKING INVESTIGATOR...
...TO BE IN COMMAND OF A SQUAD.
THE HIGHEST-RANKING INVESTIGATOR OF THIS TEAM IS *ME.*
I'VE DECIDED YOU'RE UNFIT TO SERVE AS SQUAD LEADER.
TZZY
I'LL CHANGE MY WAYS.
I'VE ASKED YOU TO, REPEATEDLY.
TZZY
I MAKE THE DECISIONS.
I FIND THIS UNACCEPTABLE.
IT'S AN ORDER.
...
BUT YOU'RE A GHOUL... ( )
...( ) ( ) ( ) ( )...
URI ...

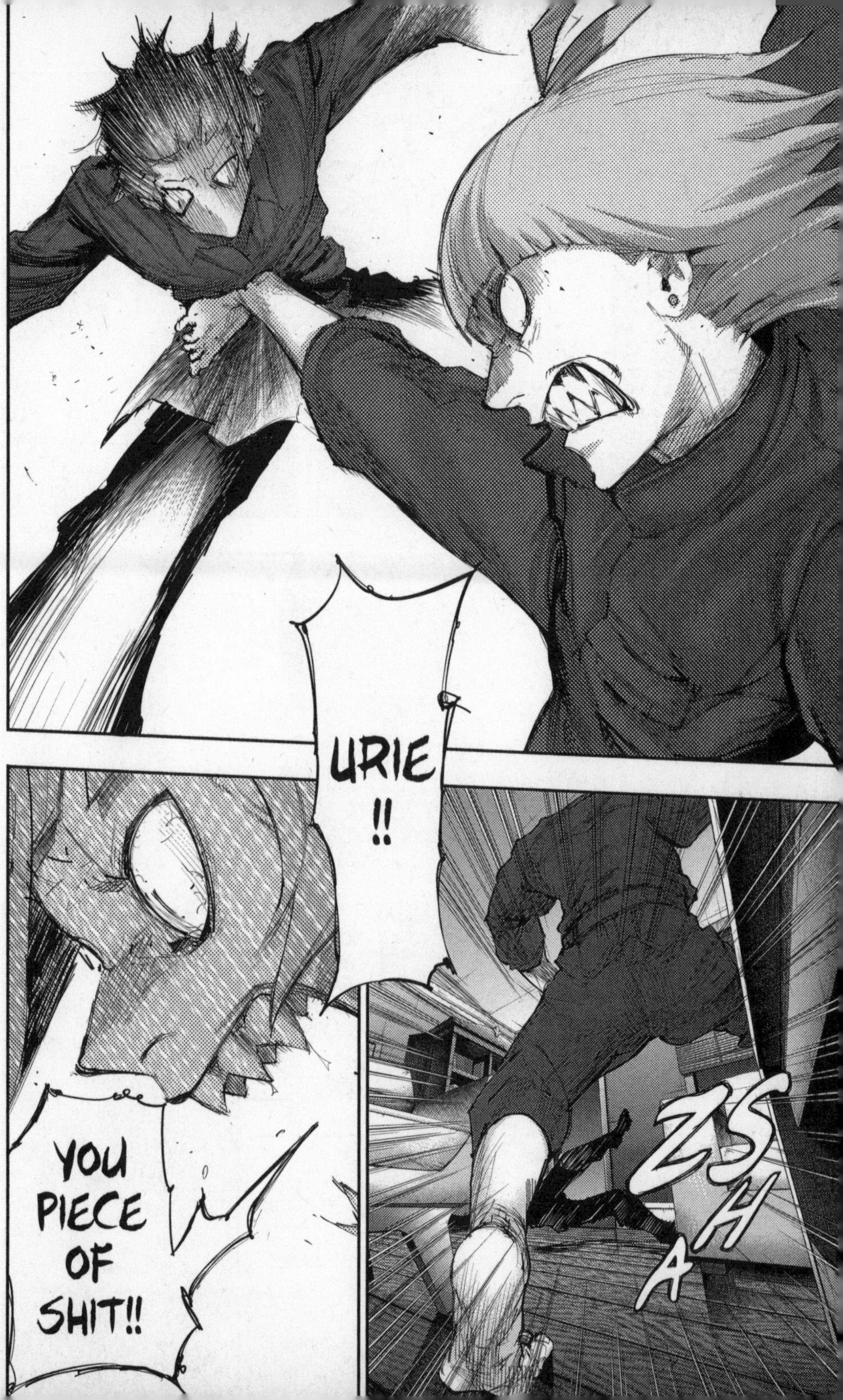
URIE !!
ZSHA
YOU PIECE OF SHIT!!

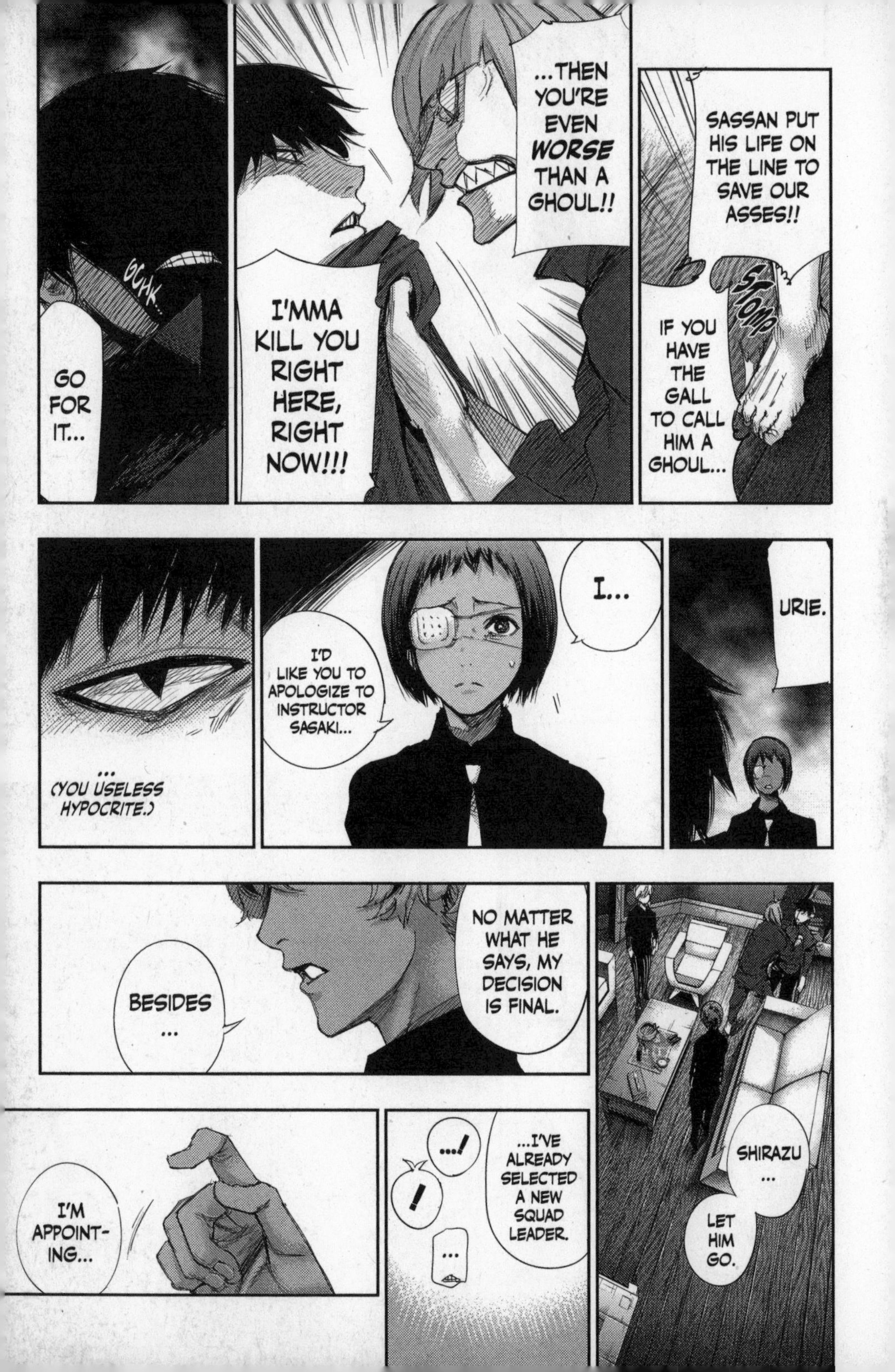
SASSAN PUT HIS LIFE ON THE LINE TO SAVE OUR ASSES!!
STOMP
IF YOU HAVE THE GALL TO CALL HIM A GHOUL...
...THEN YOU'RE EVEN *WORSE* THAN A GHOUL!!
I'MMA KILL YOU RIGHT HERE, RIGHT NOW!!!
GCHK...
GO FOR IT...
URIE.
I...
I'D LIKE YOU TO APOLOGIZE TO INSTRUCTOR SASAKI...
... (YOU USELESS HYPOCRITE.)
SHIRAZU...
LET HIM GO.
NO MATTER WHAT HE SAYS, MY DECISION IS FINAL.
BESIDES...
...I'VE ALREADY SELECTED A NEW SQUAD LEADER.
...!
!
...
I'M APPOINTING...

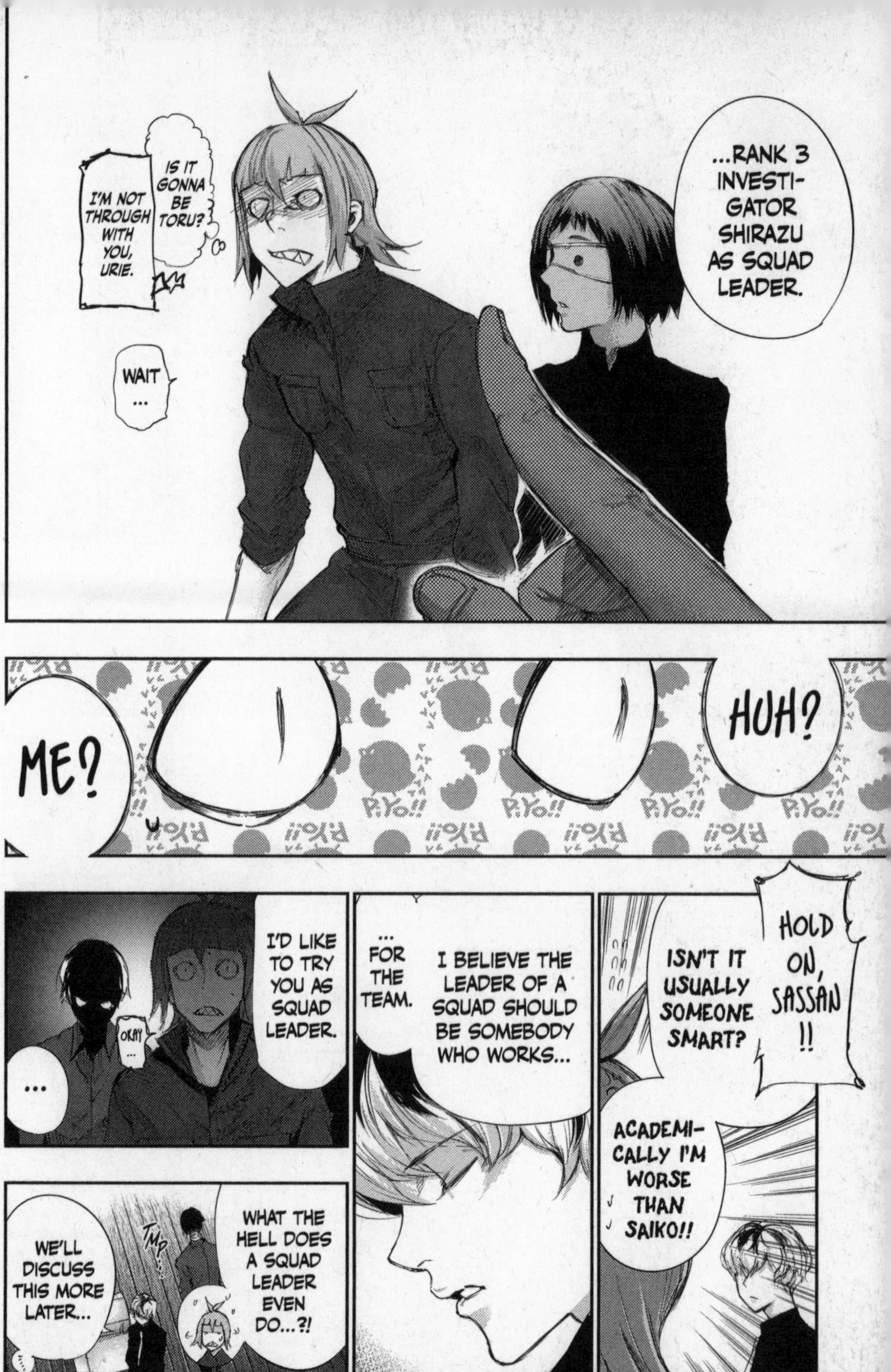
...RANK 3 INVESTIGATOR SHIRAZU AS SQUAD LEADER.
IS IT GONNA BE TORU?
I'M NOT THROUGH WITH YOU, URIE.
WAIT...
HUH?
ME?
P.YO!!
HOLD ON, SASSAN!!
ISN'T IT USUALLY SOMEONE SMART?
ACADEMICALLY I'M WORSE THAN SAIKO!!
I BELIEVE THE LEADER OF A SQUAD SHOULD BE SOMEBODY WHO WORKS...
...FOR THE TEAM.
I'D LIKE TO TRY YOU AS SQUAD LEADER.
OKAY...
...
WHAT THE HELL DOES A SQUAD LEADER EVEN DO...?!
TMP...
WE'LL DISCUSS THIS MORE LATER...

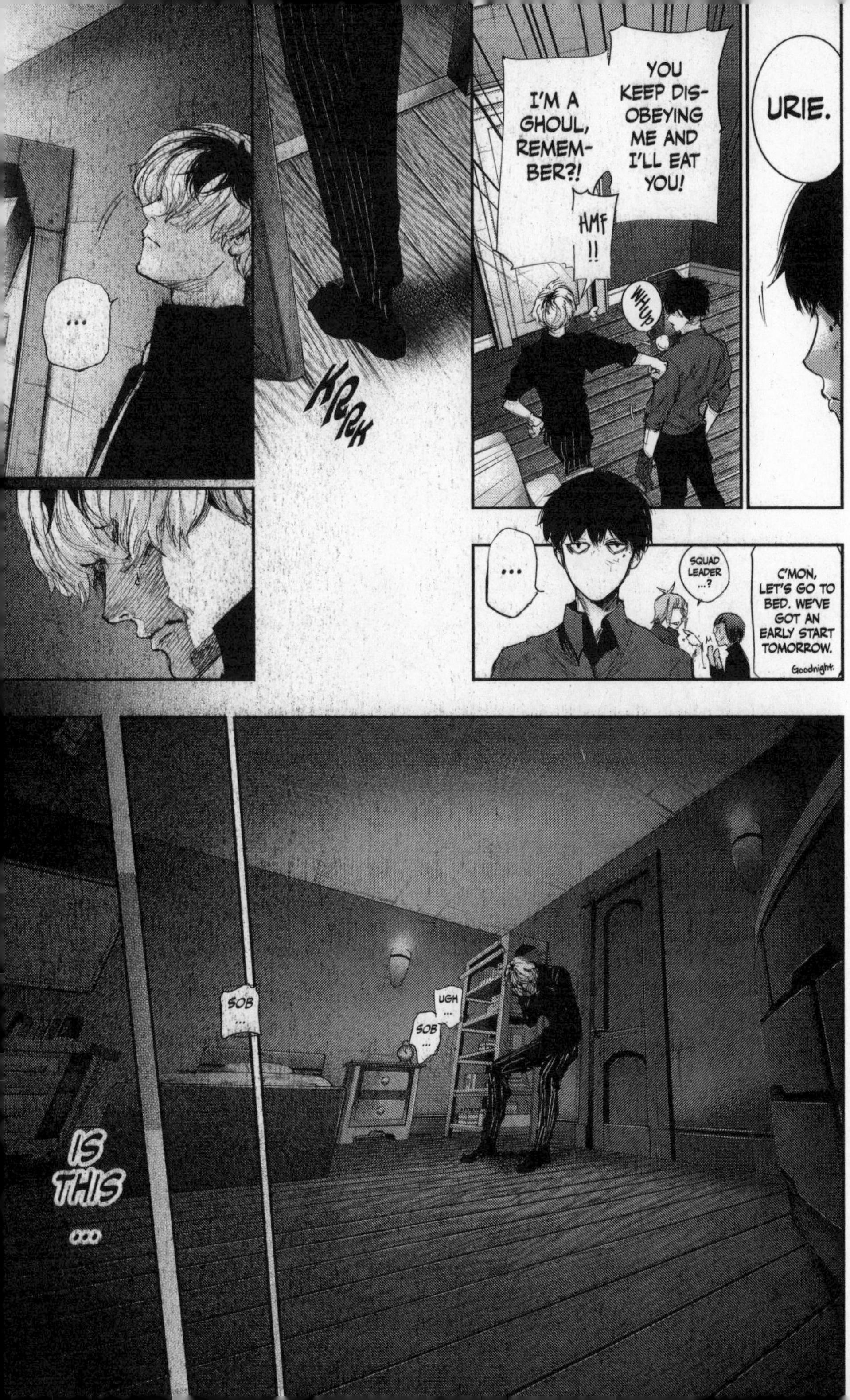
URIE.
YOU KEEP DIS-OBEYING ME AND I'LL EAT YOU!
I'M A GHOUL, REMEMBER?!
HMF !!
WHUP
C'MON, LET'S GO TO BED. WE'VE GOT AN EARLY START TOMORROW.
Goodnight.
SQUAD LEADER ...?
...
KRRK
...
UGH ...
SOB ...
SOB ...
IS THIS ...

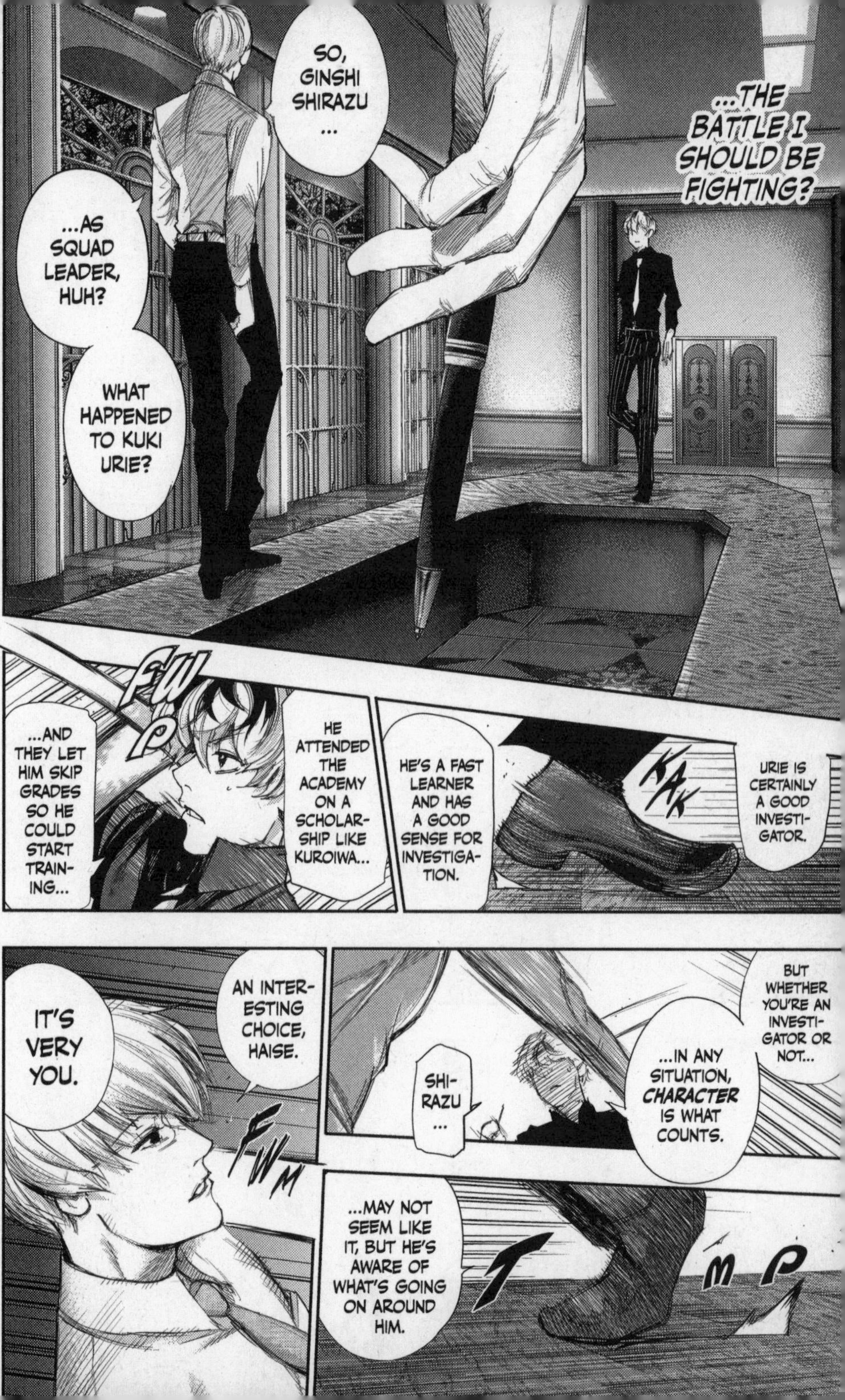
...THE BATTLE I SHOULD BE FIGHTING?
SO, GINSHI SHIRAZU ...
...AS SQUAD LEADER, HUH?
WHAT HAPPENED TO KUKI URIE?
URIE IS CERTAINLY A GOOD INVESTIGATOR.
KAK
HE'S A FAST LEARNER AND HAS A GOOD SENSE FOR INVESTIGATION.
HE ATTENDED THE ACADEMY ON A SCHOLARSHIP LIKE KUROIWA...
FWP
...AND THEY LET HIM SKIP GRADES SO HE COULD START TRAINING...
BUT WHETHER YOU'RE AN INVESTIGATOR OR NOT...
...IN ANY SITUATION, **CHARACTER** IS WHAT COUNTS.
SHIRAZU ...
TMP
...MAY NOT SEEM LIKE IT, BUT HE'S AWARE OF WHAT'S GOING ON AROUND HIM.
AN INTERESTING CHOICE, HAISE.
FWM
IT'S VERY YOU.

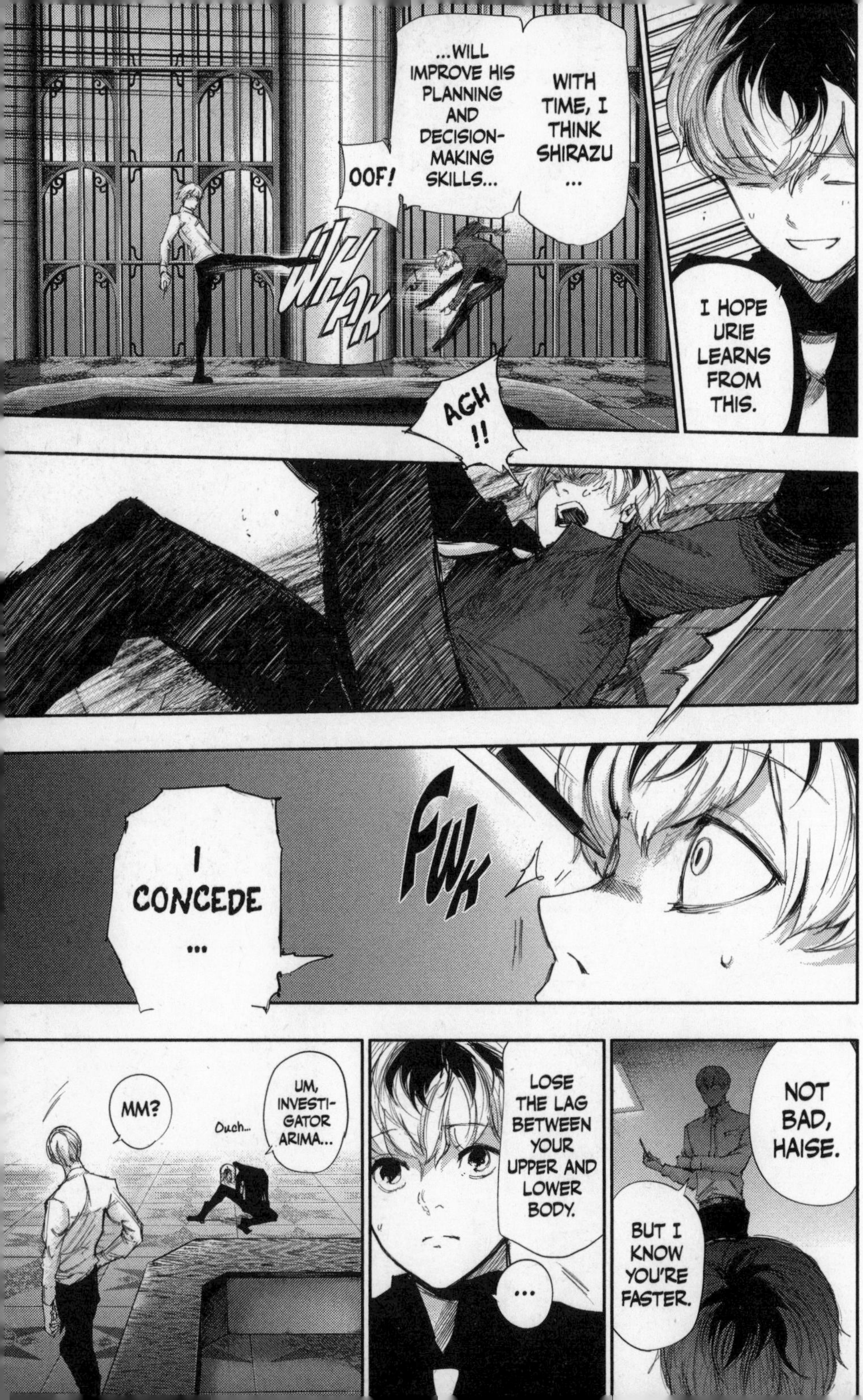
WITH TIME, I THINK SHIRAZU ...
...WILL IMPROVE HIS PLANNING AND DECISION-MAKING SKILLS...
I HOPE URIE LEARNS FROM THIS.
OOF!
WHAK
AGH !!
FWK
I CONCEDE ...
NOT BAD, HAISE.
BUT I KNOW YOU'RE FASTER.
LOSE THE LAG BETWEEN YOUR UPPER AND LOWER BODY.
...
UM, INVESTI-GATOR ARIMA...
Ouch...
MM?

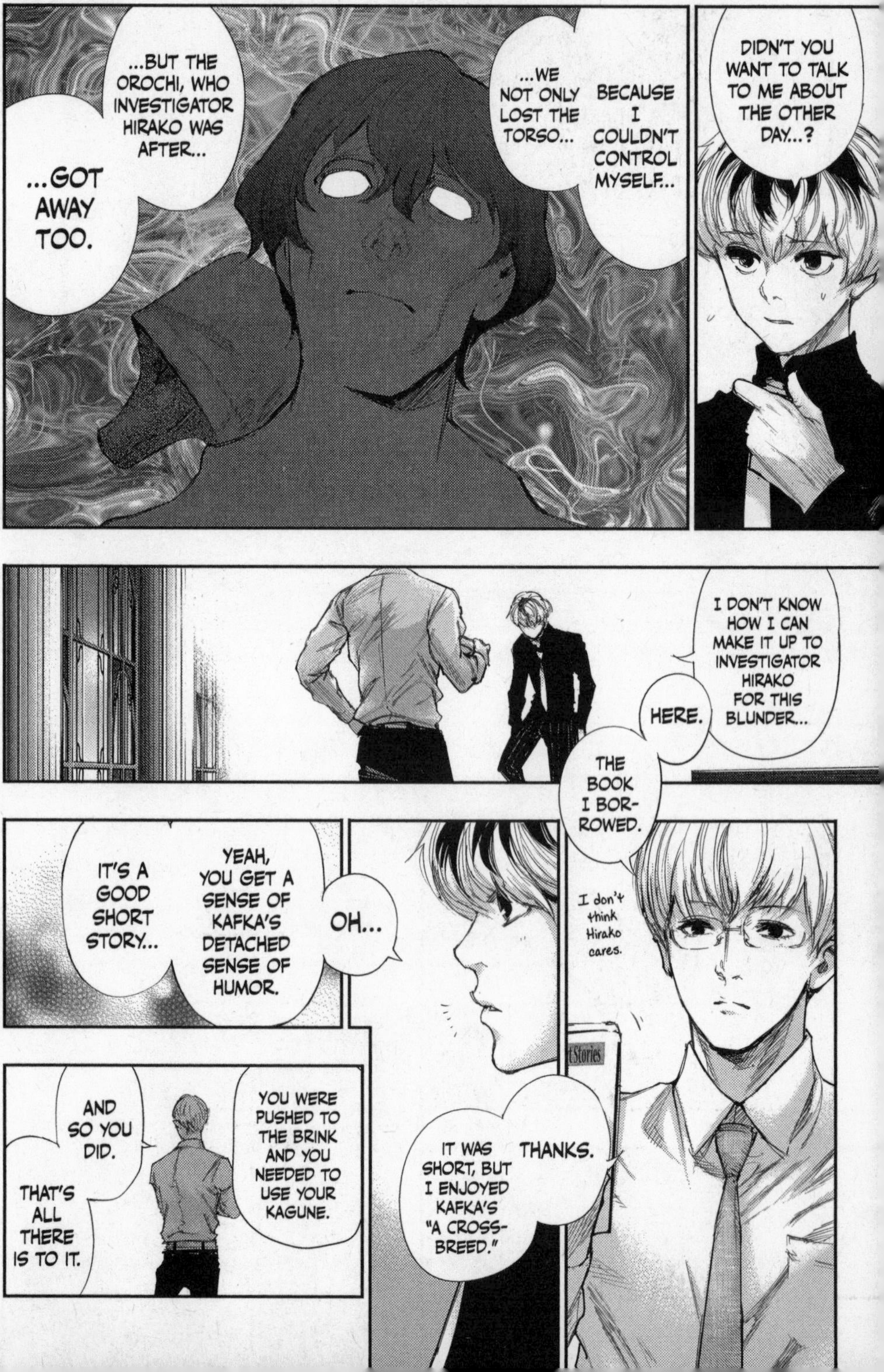
DIDN'T YOU WANT TO TALK TO ME ABOUT THE OTHER DAY...?
BECAUSE I COULDN'T CONTROL MYSELF...
...WE NOT ONLY LOST THE TORSO...
...BUT THE OROCHI, WHO INVESTIGATOR HIRAKO WAS AFTER...
...GOT AWAY TOO.
I DON'T KNOW HOW I CAN MAKE IT UP TO INVESTIGATOR HIRAKO FOR THIS BLUNDER...
HERE.
THE BOOK I BORROWED.
I don't think Hirako cares.
THANKS.
IT WAS SHORT, BUT I ENJOYED KAFKA'S "A CROSS-BREED."
OH...
YEAH, YOU GET A SENSE OF KAFKA'S DETACHED SENSE OF HUMOR.
IT'S A GOOD SHORT STORY...
YOU WERE PUSHED TO THE BRINK AND YOU NEEDED TO USE YOUR KAGUNE.
AND SO YOU DID.
THAT'S ALL THERE IS TO IT.

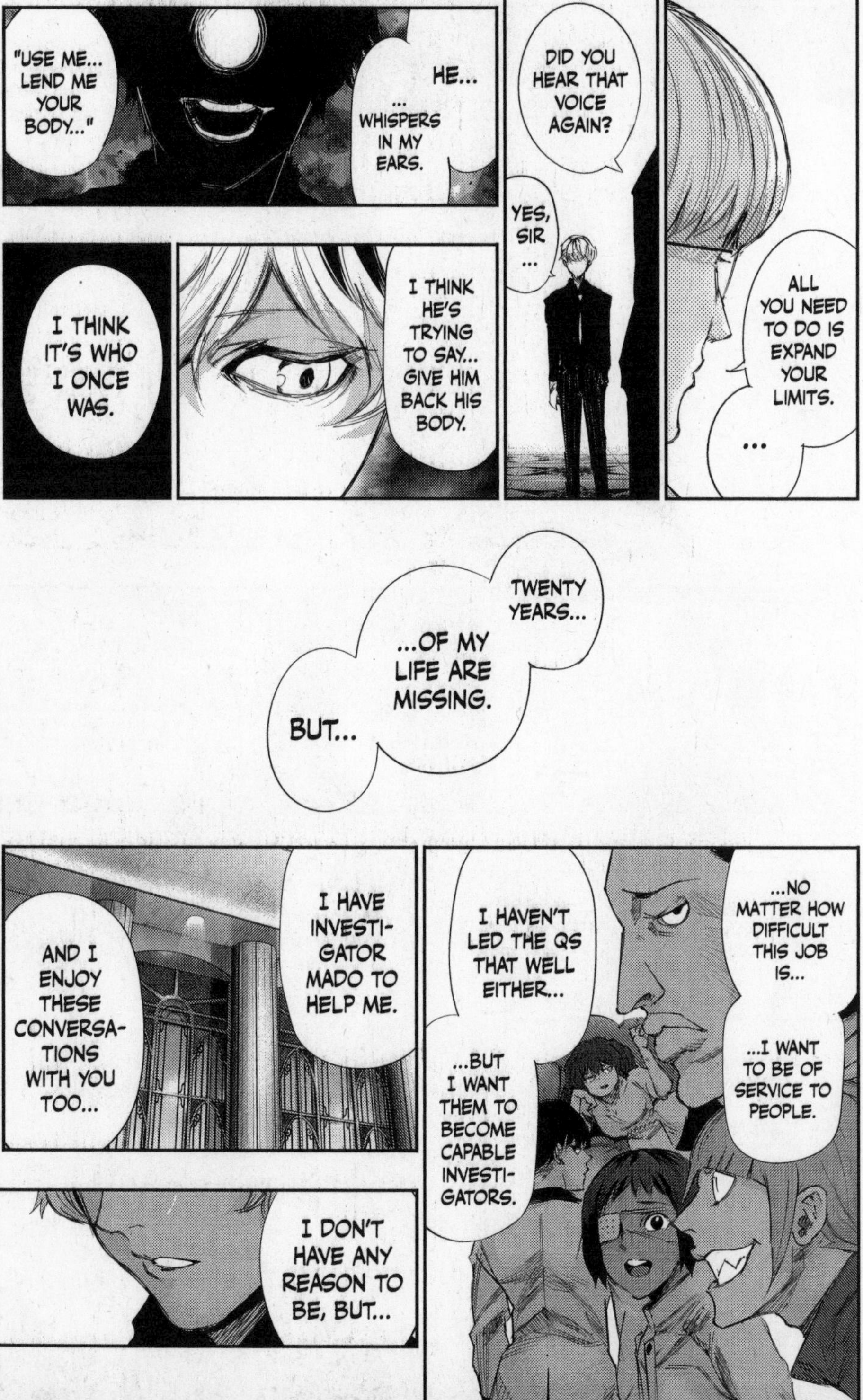
ALL YOU NEED TO DO IS EXPAND YOUR LIMITS.
...
DID YOU HEAR THAT VOICE AGAIN?
YES, SIR ...
HE... ... WHISPERS IN MY EARS.
"USE ME... LEND ME YOUR BODY..."
I THINK HE'S TRYING TO SAY... GIVE HIM BACK HIS BODY.
I THINK IT'S WHO I ONCE WAS.
TWENTY YEARS...
...OF MY LIFE ARE MISSING.
BUT...
...NO MATTER HOW DIFFICULT THIS JOB IS...
...I WANT TO BE OF SERVICE TO PEOPLE.
I HAVEN'T LED THE QS THAT WELL EITHER...
...BUT I WANT THEM TO BECOME CAPABLE INVESTI-GATORS.
I HAVE INVESTI-GATOR MADO TO HELP ME.
AND I ENJOY THESE CONVERSA-TIONS WITH YOU TOO...
I DON'T HAVE ANY REASON TO BE, BUT...

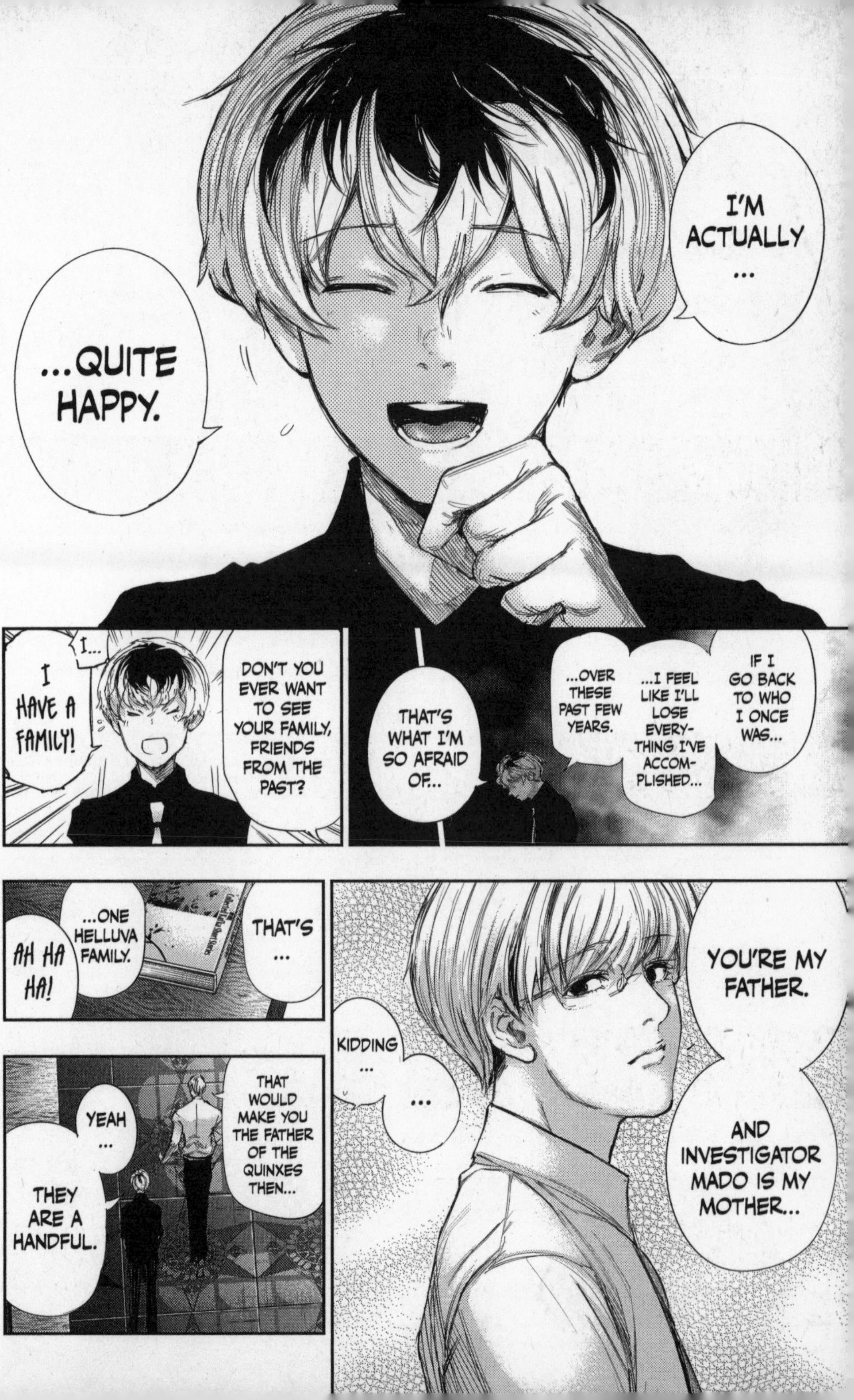
I'M ACTUALLY ...
...QUITE HAPPY.
IF I GO BACK TO WHO I ONCE WAS...
...I FEEL LIKE I'LL LOSE EVERY-THING I'VE ACCOMPLISHED...
...OVER THESE PAST FEW YEARS.
THAT'S WHAT I'M SO AFRAID OF...
DON'T YOU EVER WANT TO SEE YOUR FAMILY, FRIENDS FROM THE PAST?
I...
I HAVE A FAMILY!
YOU'RE MY FATHER.
AND INVESTIGATOR MADO IS MY MOTHER...
...
KIDDING ...
THAT'S ...
...ONE HELLUVA FAMILY.
AH HA HA!
THAT WOULD MAKE YOU THE FATHER OF THE QUINXES THEN...
YEAH ...
THEY ARE A HANDFUL.

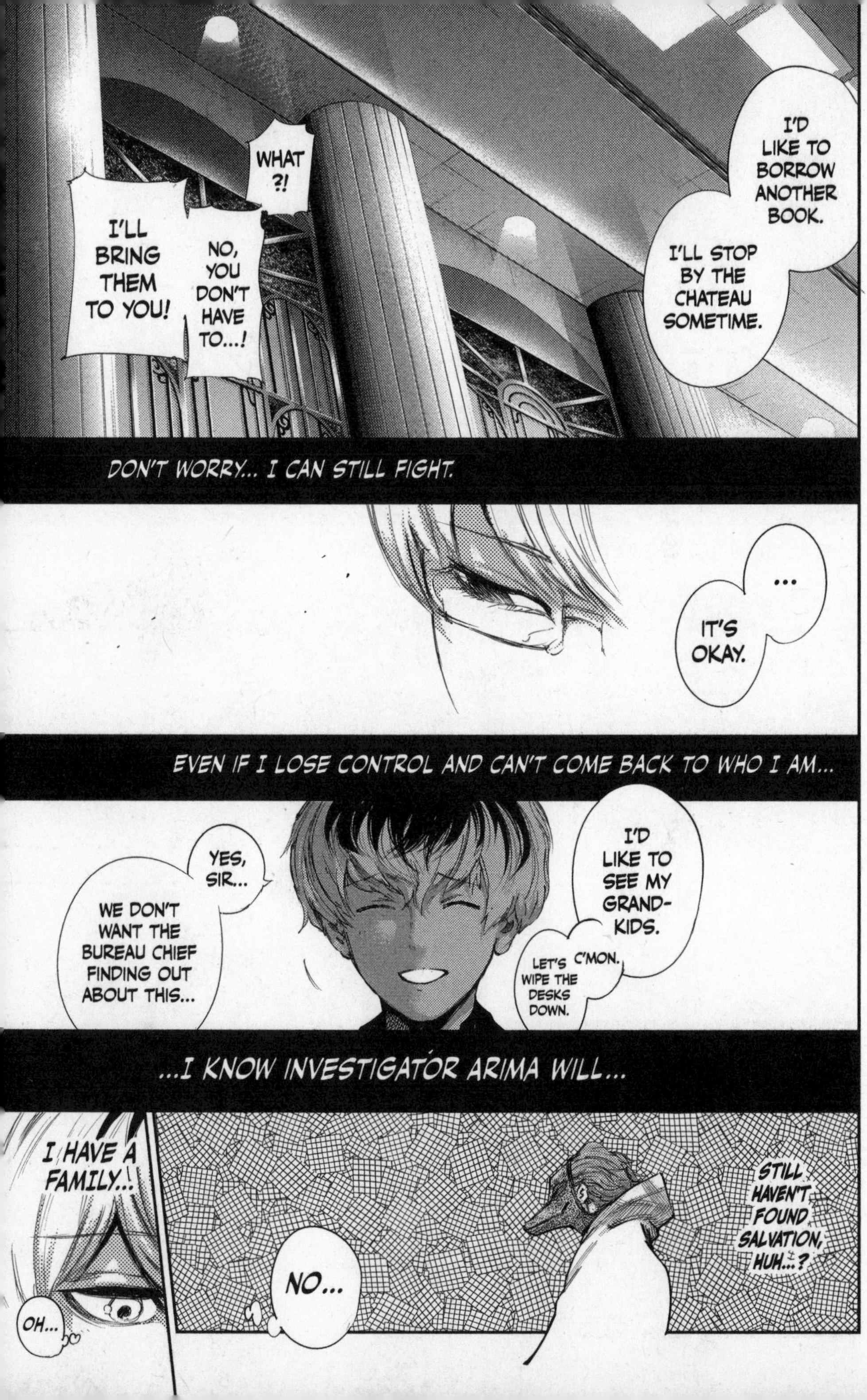
I'D LIKE TO BORROW ANOTHER BOOK.
I'LL STOP BY THE CHATEAU SOMETIME.
WHAT?!
NO, YOU DON'T HAVE TO...!
I'LL BRING THEM TO YOU!
DON'T WORRY... I CAN STILL FIGHT.
...
IT'S OKAY.
EVEN IF I LOSE CONTROL AND CAN'T COME BACK TO WHO I AM...
I'D LIKE TO SEE MY GRAND-KIDS.
C'MON. LET'S WIPE THE DESKS DOWN.
YES, SIR...
WE DON'T WANT THE BUREAU CHIEF FINDING OUT ABOUT THIS...
...I KNOW INVESTIGATOR ARIMA WILL...
STILL HAVEN'T FOUND SALVATION, HUH...?
NO...
I HAVE A FAMILY...!
OH...

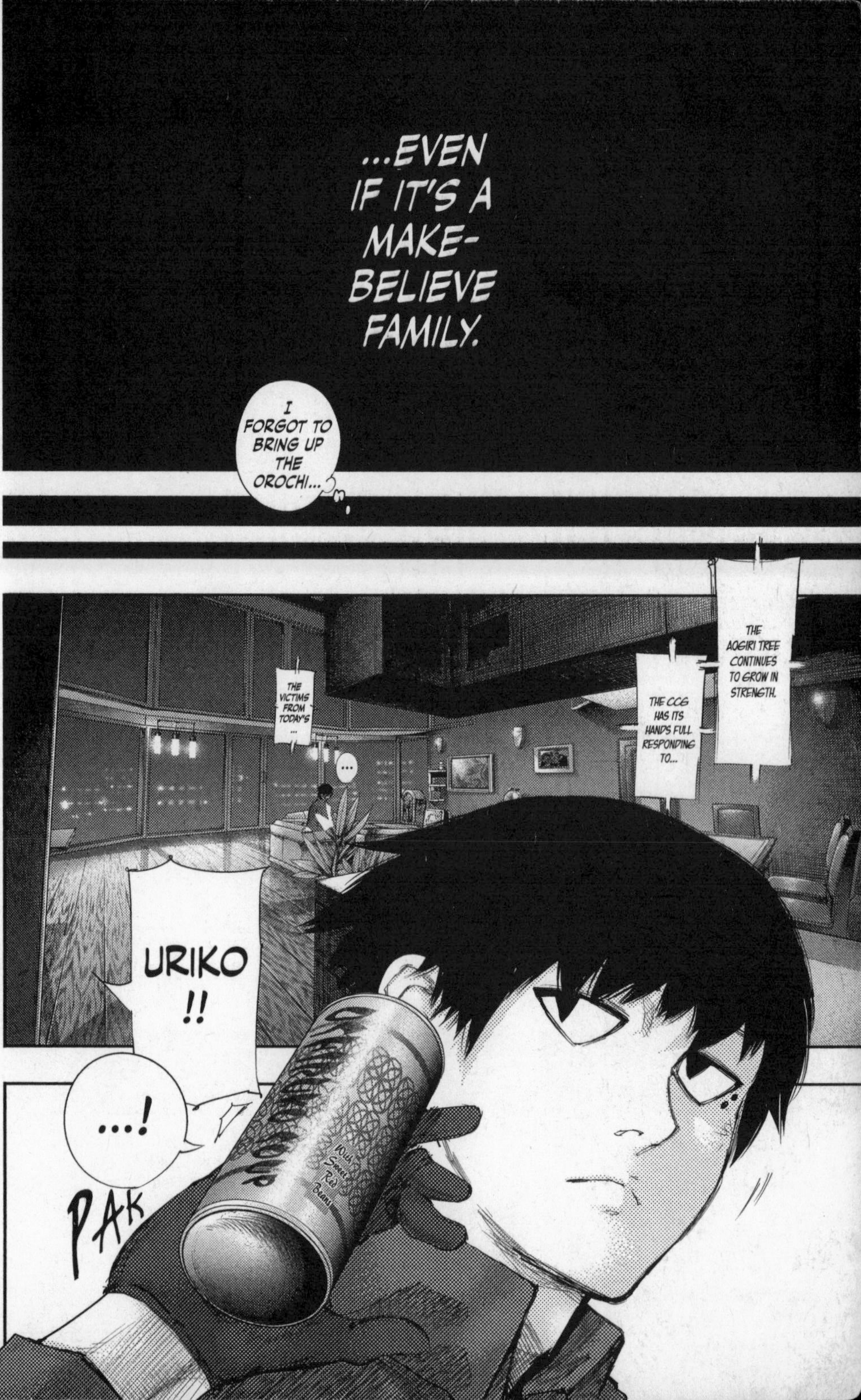
...EVEN IF IT'S A MAKE-BELIEVE FAMILY.
I FORGOT TO BRING UP THE OROCHI...
THE AOGIRI TREE CONTINUES TO GROW IN STRENGTH.
THE CCG HAS ITS HANDS FULL RESPONDING TO...
THE VICTIMS FROM TODAY'S ...
...
URIKO !!
...!
PAK
With Sweet Red Beans

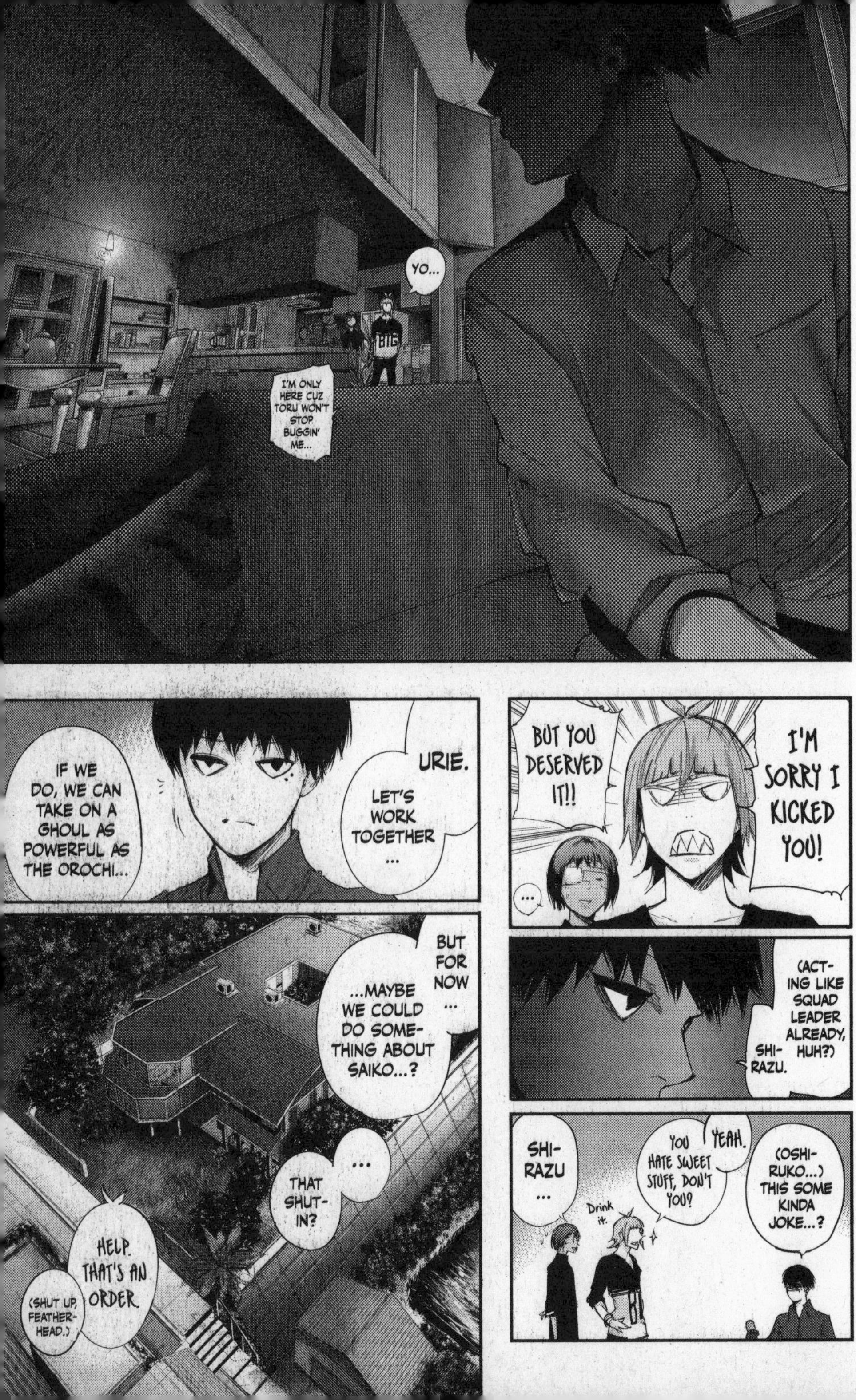
YO...
I'M ONLY HERE CUZ TORU WON'T STOP BUGGIN' ME...
I'M SORRY I KICKED YOU!
BUT YOU DESERVED IT!!
...
URIE.
LET'S WORK TOGETHER ...
IF WE DO, WE CAN TAKE ON A GHOUL AS POWERFUL AS THE OROCHI...
(ACTING LIKE SQUAD LEADER ALREADY, HUH?)
SHIRAZU.
(OSHIRUKO...) THIS SOME KINDA JOKE...?
YEAH.
YOU HATE SWEET STUFF, DON'T YOU?
Drink it.
SHIRAZU ...
BUT FOR NOW ...
...MAYBE WE COULD DO SOMETHING ABOUT SAIKO...?
...
THAT SHUT-IN?
HELP. THAT'S AN ORDER.
(SHUT UP, FEATHERHEAD.)

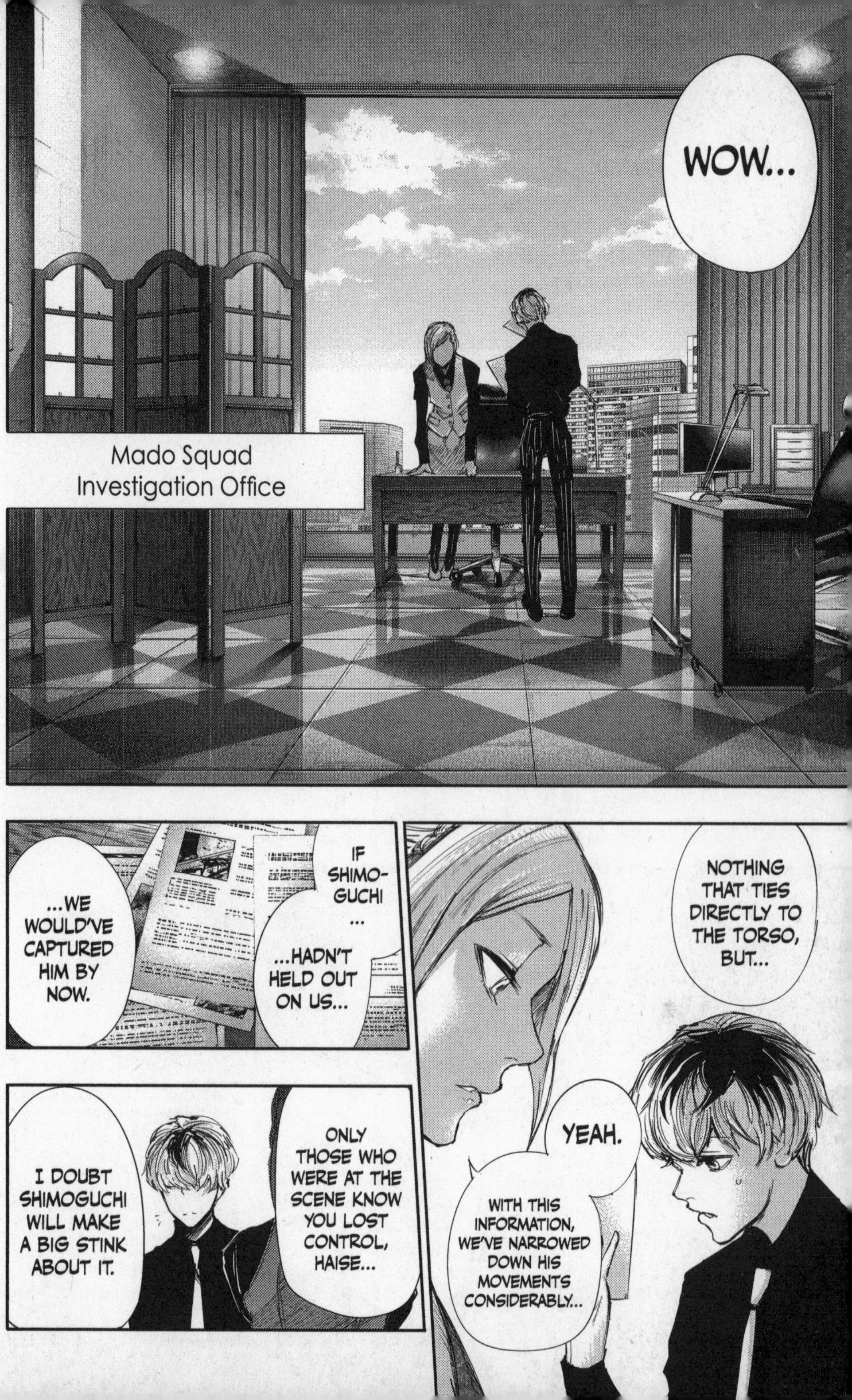
WOW...
Mado Squad Investigation Office
NOTHING THAT TIES DIRECTLY TO THE TORSO, BUT...
YEAH.
WITH THIS INFORMATION, WE'VE NARROWED DOWN HIS MOVEMENTS CONSIDERABLY...
IF SHIMO-GUCHI ...
...HADN'T HELD OUT ON US...
...WE WOULD'VE CAPTURED HIM BY NOW.
ONLY THOSE WHO WERE AT THE SCENE KNOW YOU LOST CONTROL, HAISE...
I DOUBT SHIMOGUCHI WILL MAKE A BIG STINK ABOUT IT.

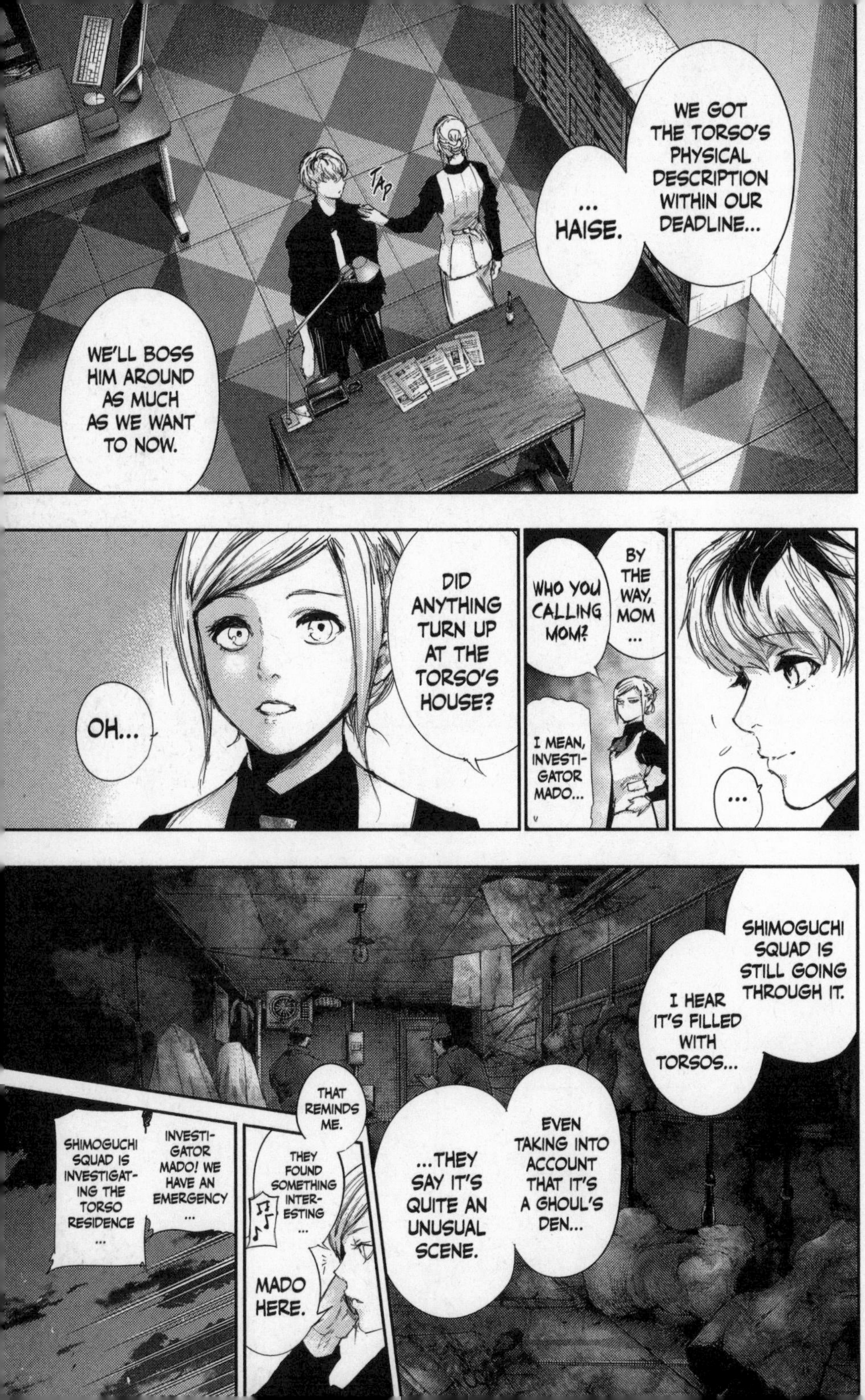
WE GOT THE TORSO'S PHYSICAL DESCRIPTION WITHIN OUR DEADLINE...
... HAISE.
WE'LL BOSS HIM AROUND AS MUCH AS WE WANT TO NOW.
...
BY THE WAY, MOM ...
WHO YOU CALLING MOM?
I MEAN, INVESTIGATOR MADO...
DID ANYTHING TURN UP AT THE TORSO'S HOUSE?
OH...
SHIMOGUCHI SQUAD IS STILL GOING THROUGH IT.
I HEAR IT'S FILLED WITH TORSOS...
EVEN TAKING INTO ACCOUNT THAT IT'S A GHOUL'S DEN...
...THEY SAY IT'S QUITE AN UNUSUAL SCENE.
THAT REMINDS ME.
THEY FOUND SOMETHING INTER-ESTING ...
MADO HERE.
INVESTI-GATOR MADO! WE HAVE AN EMERGENCY ...
SHIMOGUCHI SQUAD IS INVESTIGAT-ING THE TORSO RESIDENCE ...

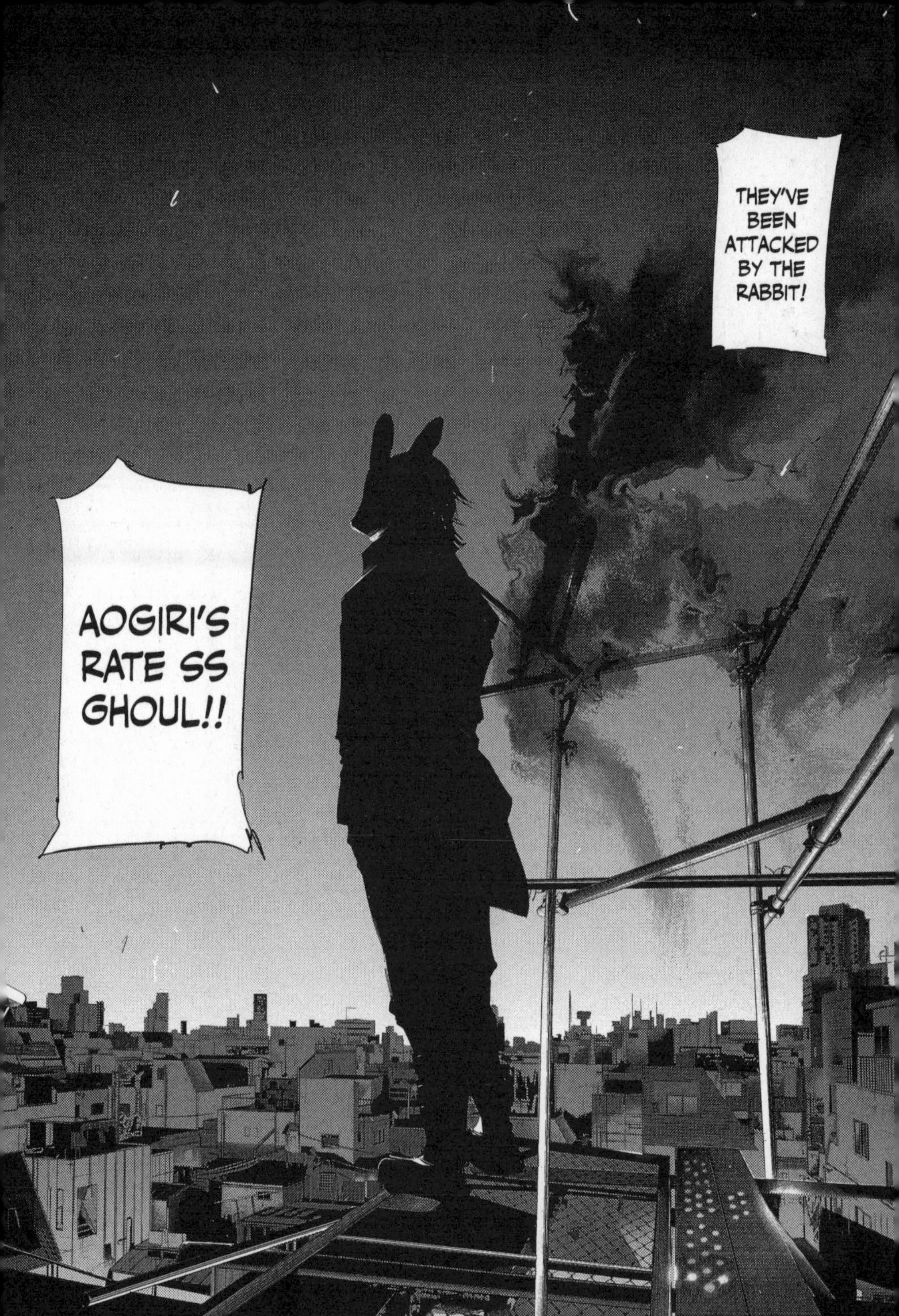
THEY'VE BEEN ATTACKED BY THE RABBIT!
AOGIRI'S RATE SS GHOUL!!

Quinx Squad Daily Report
Date: 10/9   Weather: Cloudy   Responding Investigator: Ginshi
Incident: Ex-Squad Leader Urie

Actions Taken:
The night I became Squad Leader, Toru said it'd be ahkwurd if we keep fighting so I decided to apolojize to Urie. I didn't want to go empty-handed, so I decided to by some drinks. Urie hates sweet stuff. He once didn't even lay a finger on some sweet buns we got as a gift so I bought him some sweet red-bean soup. (The kind with whole beans in them) As expected, he looked discussted.

Alternative Response:

Maybe I coulda bought a better drink.

Notes:
• I think I want a motorcycle
• I don't know how to be Squad Leader
• I'm not sure I spelled ahkwurd right

Comments: So have you guys made up...? Leaders are expected to reprimand, but also offer support. They are both equally important. So I'm glad you took action. (Thank you too, Mutsuki.) I know it's difficult being Squad Leader, but you have my full support!

ahkwurd – awkward • apolojize – apologize • discussted – disgusted

---

Quinx Squad Daily Report
Date: Weather: Responding Investigator: Sasaki
Incident: Rank 3 Investigator Saiko Yonebayashi

Actions Taken:

Alternative Response:

Notes:

Comments:
Please submit your daily report.

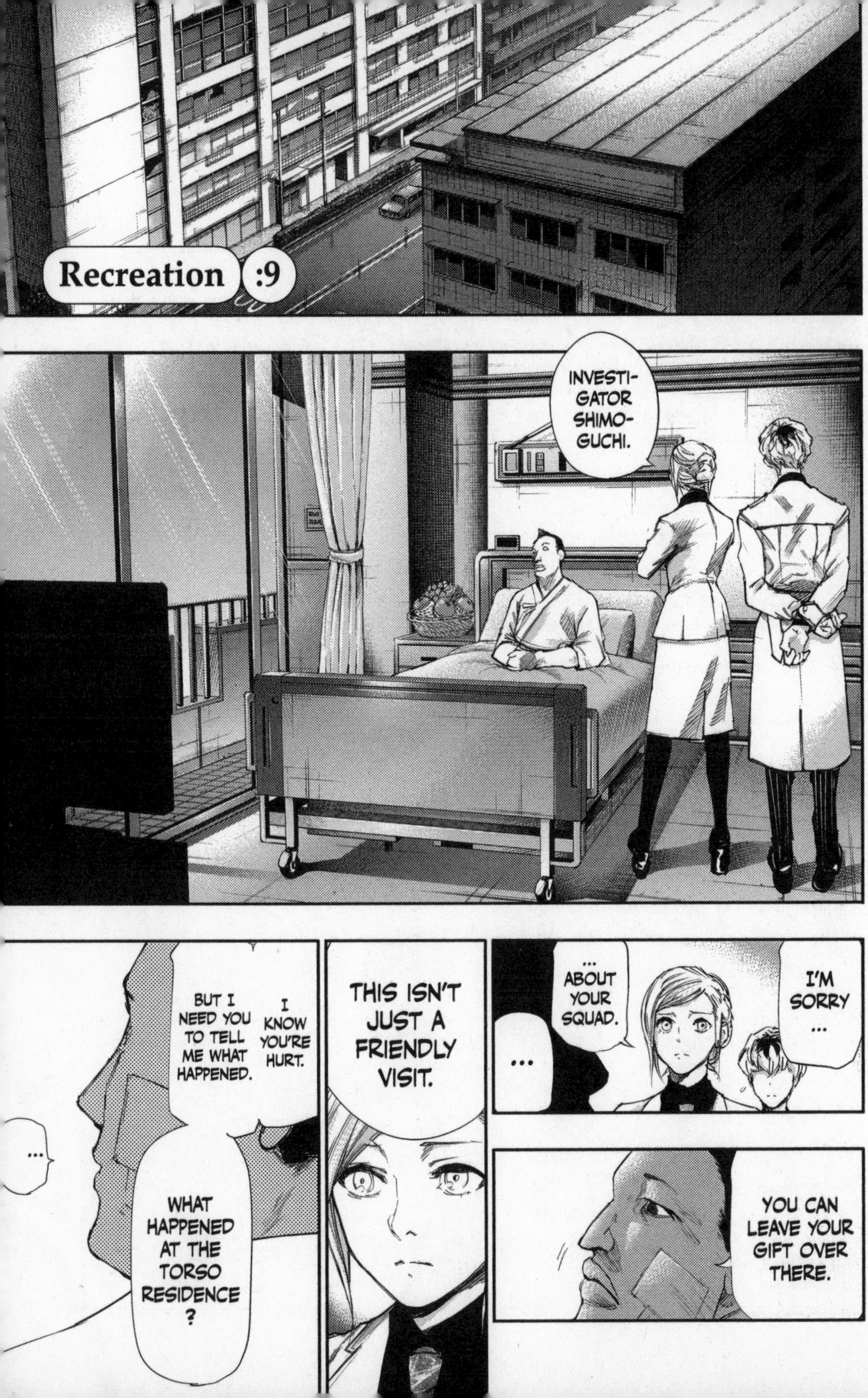
Recreation :9
INVESTIGATOR SHIMOGUCHI.
I'M SORRY ...
... ABOUT YOUR SQUAD.
...
YOU CAN LEAVE YOUR GIFT OVER THERE.
THIS ISN'T JUST A FRIENDLY VISIT.
I KNOW YOU'RE HURT.
BUT I NEED YOU TO TELL ME WHAT HAPPENED.
WHAT HAPPENED AT THE TORSO RESIDENCE?
...

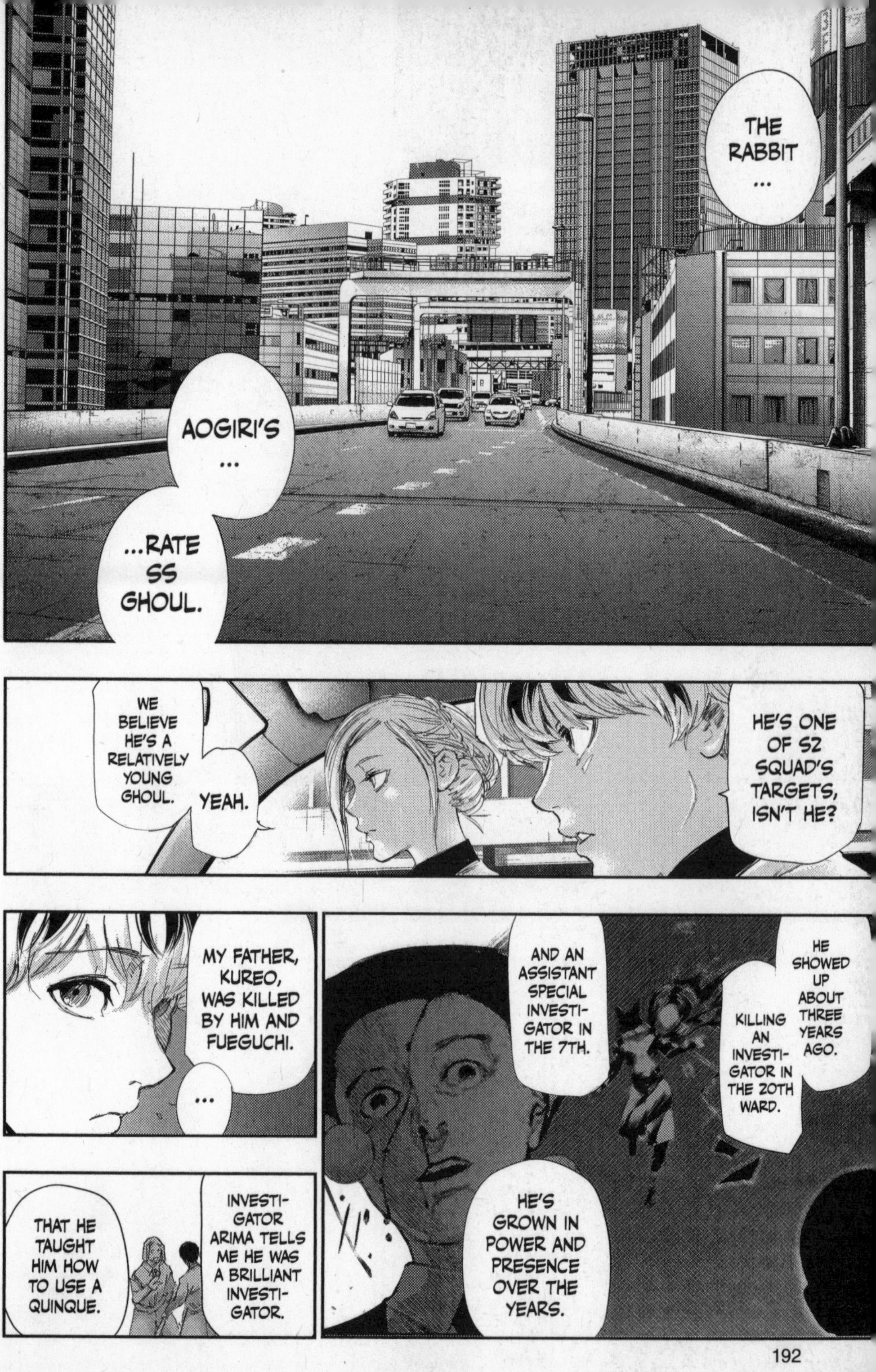
THE RABBIT ...
AOGIRI'S ...
...RATE SS GHOUL.
HE'S ONE OF S2 SQUAD'S TARGETS, ISN'T HE?
YEAH.
WE BELIEVE HE'S A RELATIVELY YOUNG GHOUL.
HE SHOWED UP ABOUT THREE YEARS AGO.
KILLING AN INVESTIGATOR IN THE 20TH WARD.
AND AN ASSISTANT SPECIAL INVESTIGATOR IN THE 7TH.
HE'S GROWN IN POWER AND PRESENCE OVER THE YEARS.
MY FATHER, KUREO, WAS KILLED BY HIM AND FUEGUCHI.
...
INVESTIGATOR ARIMA TELLS ME HE WAS A BRILLIANT INVESTIGATOR.
THAT HE TAUGHT HIM HOW TO USE A QUINQUE.

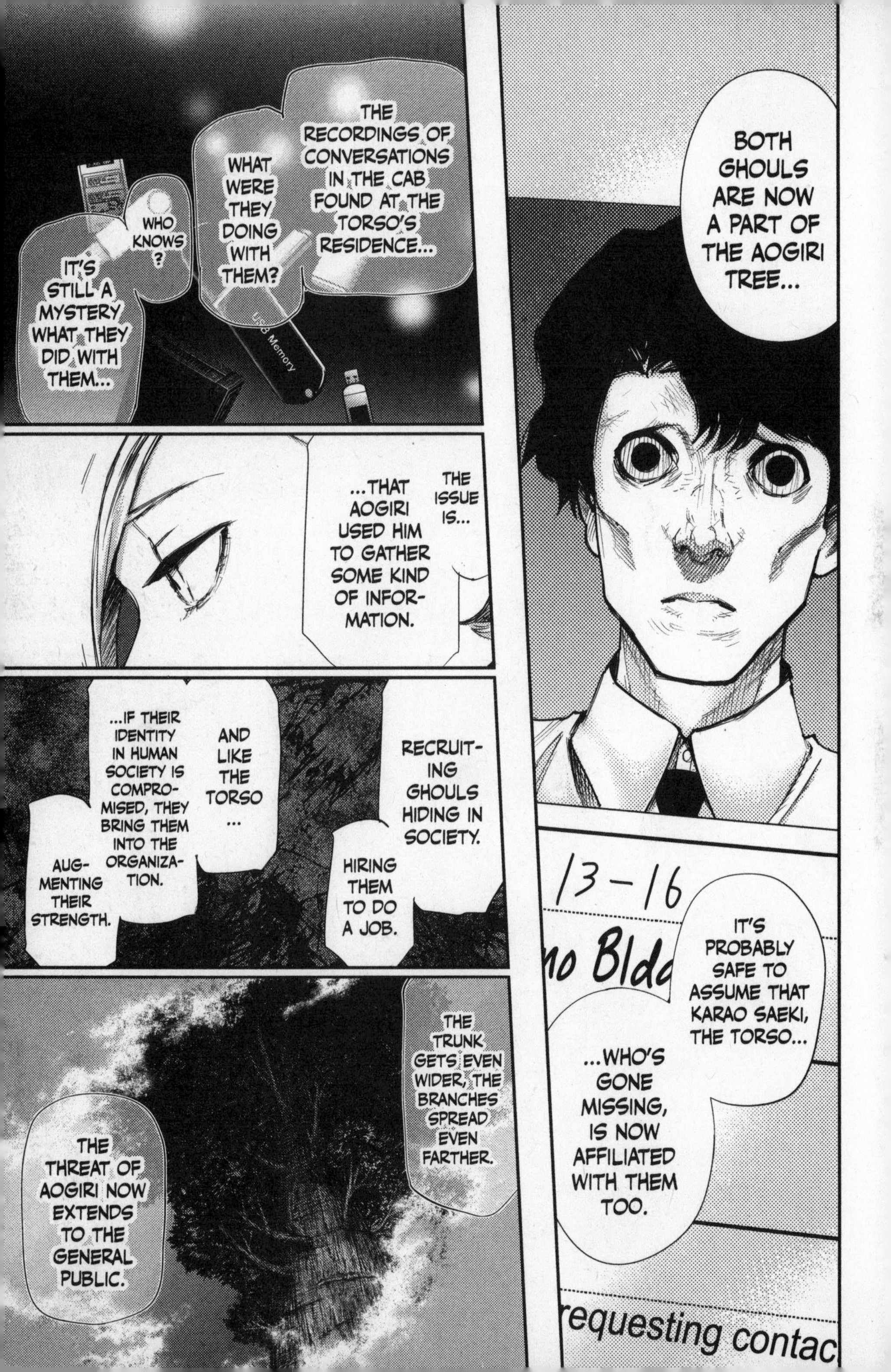
BOTH GHOULS ARE NOW A PART OF THE AOGIRI TREE...
13-16
IT'S PROBABLY SAFE TO ASSUME THAT KARAO SAEKI, THE TORSO...
...WHO'S GONE MISSING, IS NOW AFFILIATED WITH THEM TOO.
requesting contac
THE RECORDINGS OF CONVERSATIONS IN THE CAB FOUND AT THE TORSO'S RESIDENCE...
WHAT WERE THEY DOING WITH THEM?
WHO KNOWS?
IT'S STILL A MYSTERY WHAT THEY DID WITH THEM...
USB Memory
THE ISSUE IS...
...THAT AOGIRI USED HIM TO GATHER SOME KIND OF INFOR-MATION.
RECRUIT-ING GHOULS HIDING IN SOCIETY.
HIRING THEM TO DO A JOB.
AND LIKE THE TORSO...
...IF THEIR IDENTITY IN HUMAN SOCIETY IS COMPRO-MISED, THEY BRING THEM INTO THE ORGANIZA-TION.
AUG-MENTING THEIR STRENGTH.
THE TRUNK GETS EVEN WIDER, THE BRANCHES SPREAD EVEN FARTHER.
THE THREAT OF AOGIRI NOW EXTENDS TO THE GENERAL PUBLIC.

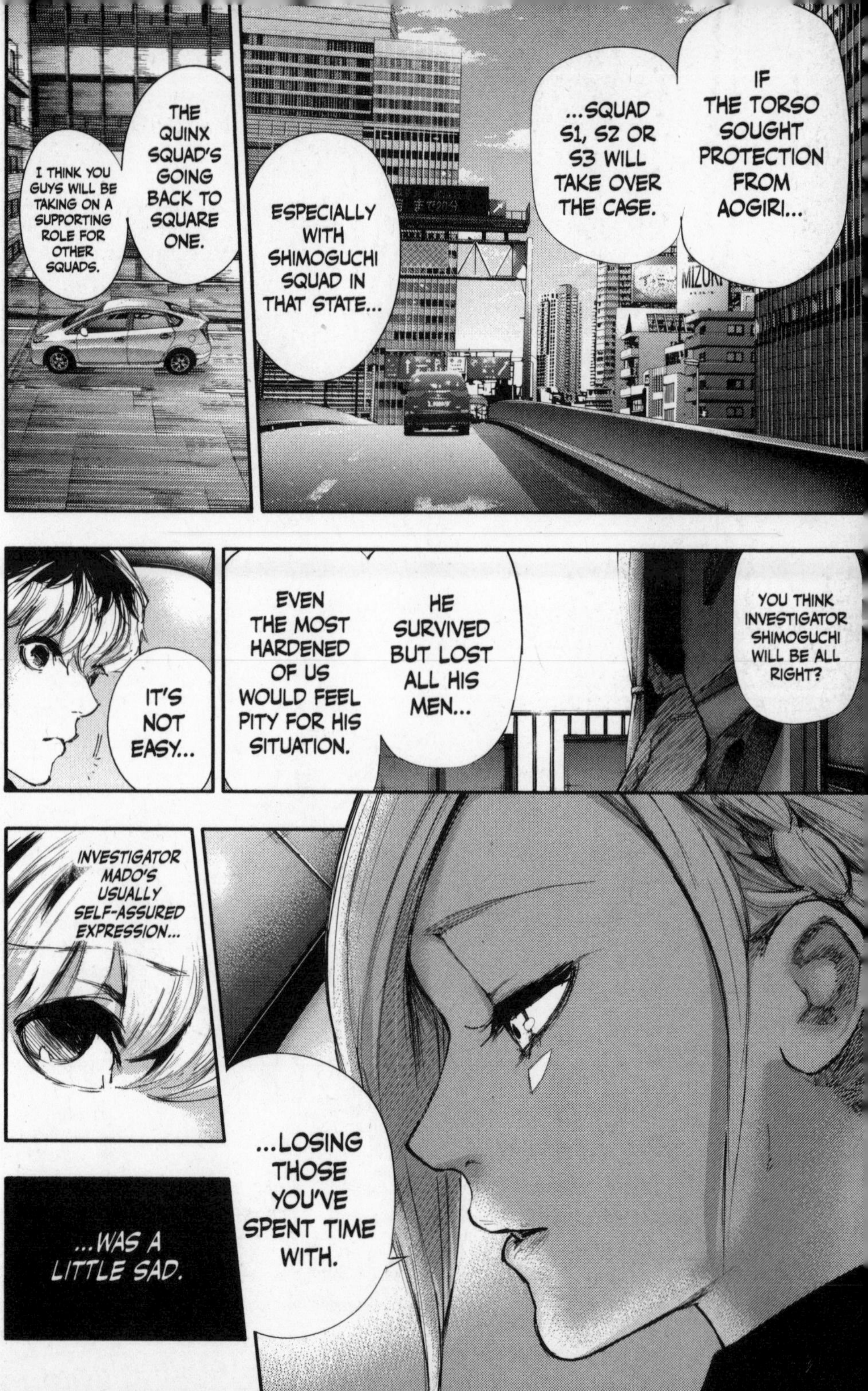
IF THE TORSO SOUGHT PROTECTION FROM AOGIRI...
...SQUAD S1, S2 OR S3 WILL TAKE OVER THE CASE.
ESPECIALLY WITH SHIMOGUCHI SQUAD IN THAT STATE...
THE QUINX SQUAD'S GOING BACK TO SQUARE ONE.
I THINK YOU GUYS WILL BE TAKING ON A SUPPORTING ROLE FOR OTHER SQUADS.
YOU THINK INVESTIGATOR SHIMOGUCHI WILL BE ALL RIGHT?
HE SURVIVED BUT LOST ALL HIS MEN...
EVEN THE MOST HARDENED OF US WOULD FEEL PITY FOR HIS SITUATION.
IT'S NOT EASY...
...LOSING THOSE YOU'VE SPENT TIME WITH.
INVESTIGATOR MADO'S USUALLY SELF-ASSURED EXPRESSION...
...WAS A LITTLE SAD.

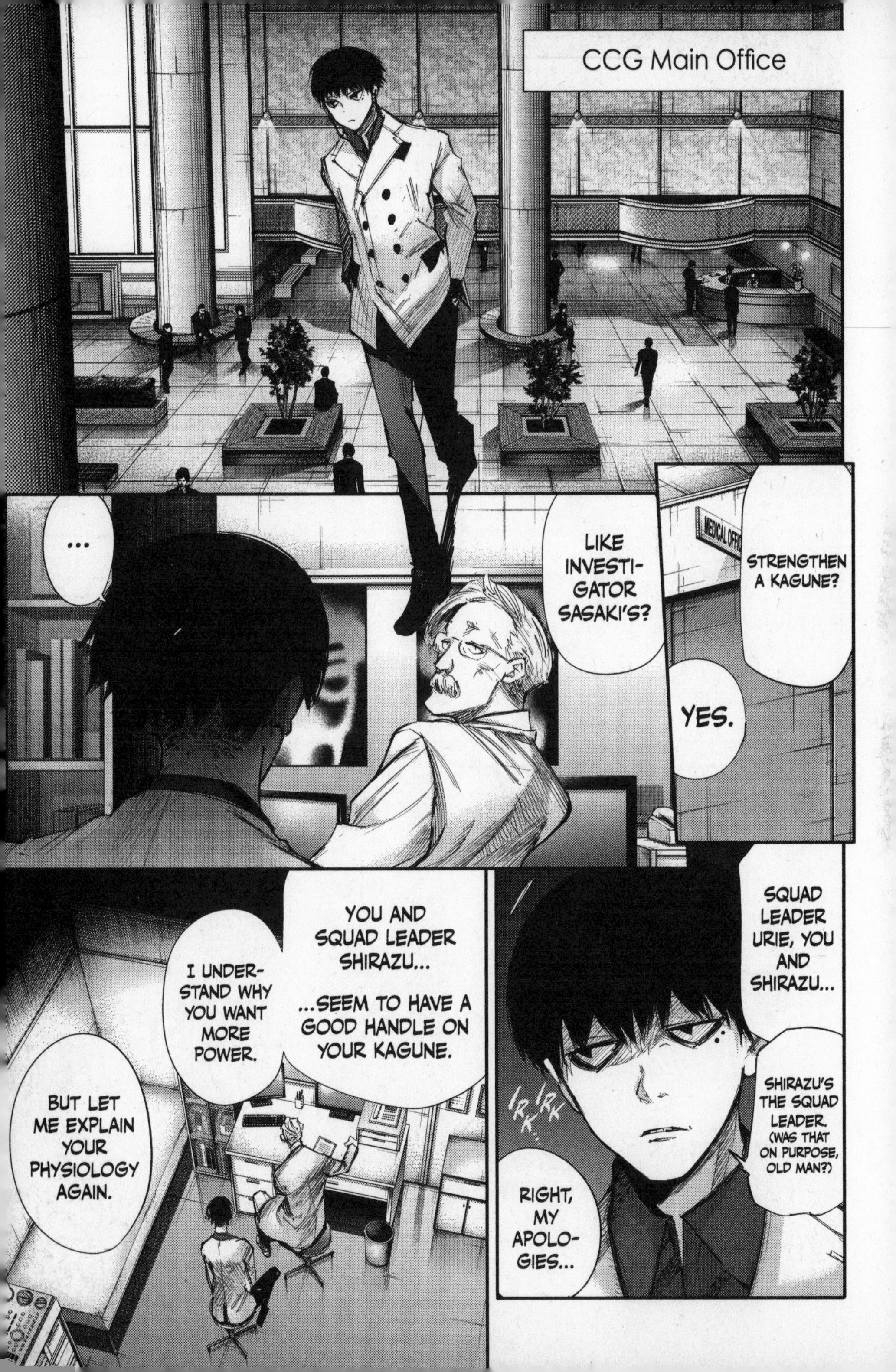
CCG Main Office
STRENGTHEN A KAGUNE?
YES.
LIKE INVESTIGATOR SASAKI'S?
...
SQUAD LEADER URIE, YOU AND SHIRAZU...
SHIRAZU'S THE SQUAD LEADER. (WAS THAT ON PURPOSE, OLD MAN?)
IRK IRK
RIGHT, MY APOLOGIES...
YOU AND SQUAD LEADER SHIRAZU...
...SEEM TO HAVE A GOOD HANDLE ON YOUR KAGUNE.
I UNDERSTAND WHY YOU WANT MORE POWER.
BUT LET ME EXPLAIN YOUR PHYSIOLOGY AGAIN.

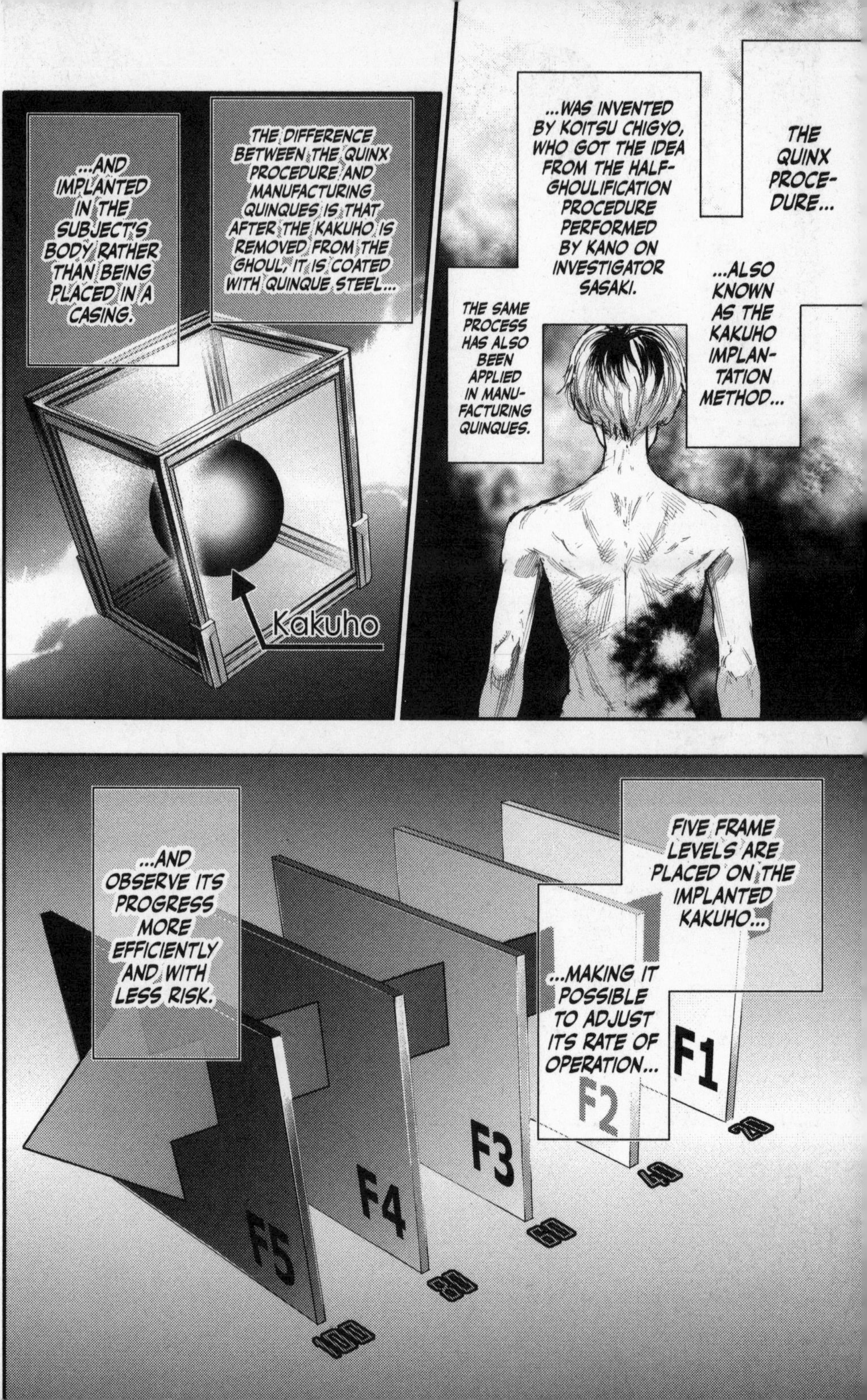
THE QUINX PROCEDURE...
...WAS INVENTED BY KOITSU CHIGYO, WHO GOT THE IDEA FROM THE HALF-GHOULIFICATION PROCEDURE PERFORMED BY KANO ON INVESTIGATOR SASAKI.
...ALSO KNOWN AS THE KAKUHO IMPLANTATION METHOD...
THE SAME PROCESS HAS ALSO BEEN APPLIED IN MANUFACTURING QUINQUES.
THE DIFFERENCE BETWEEN THE QUINX PROCEDURE AND MANUFACTURING QUINQUES IS THAT AFTER THE KAKUHO IS REMOVED FROM THE GHOUL, IT IS COATED WITH QUINQUE STEEL...
...AND IMPLANTED IN THE SUBJECT'S BODY RATHER THAN BEING PLACED IN A CASING.
Kakuho
FIVE FRAME LEVELS ARE PLACED ON THE IMPLANTED KAKUHO...
...MAKING IT POSSIBLE TO ADJUST ITS RATE OF OPERATION...
...AND OBSERVE ITS PROGRESS MORE EFFICIENTLY AND WITH LESS RISK.
F1
20
F2
40
F3
60
F4
80
F5
100

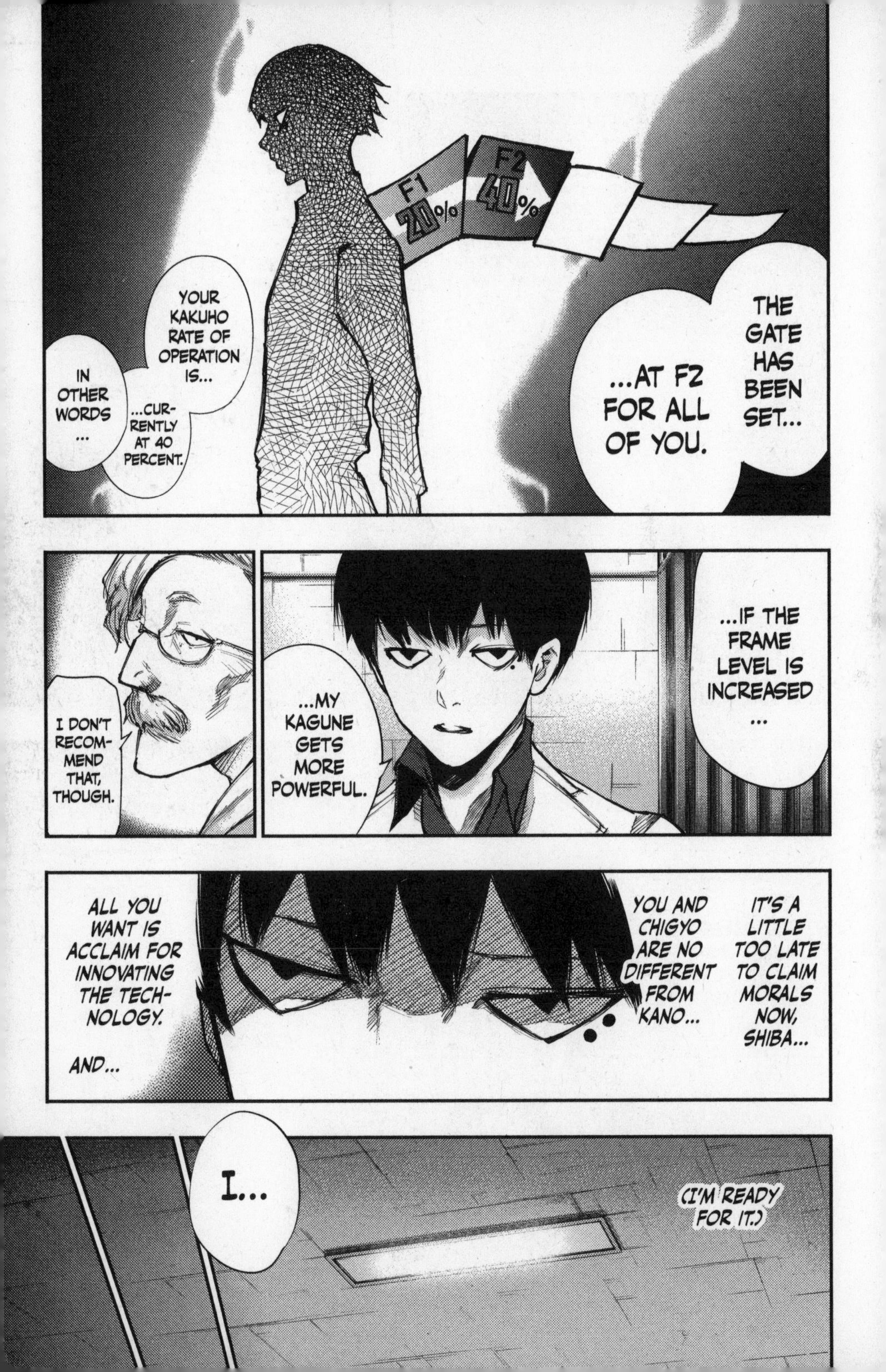
THE GATE HAS BEEN SET...
...AT F2 FOR ALL OF YOU.
F1 20%
F2 40%
YOUR KAKUHO RATE OF OPERATION IS...
...CUR-RENTLY AT 40 PERCENT.
IN OTHER WORDS...
...IF THE FRAME LEVEL IS INCREASED...
...MY KAGUNE GETS MORE POWERFUL.
I DON'T RECOMMEND THAT, THOUGH.
IT'S A LITTLE TOO LATE TO CLAIM MORALS NOW, SHIBA...
YOU AND CHIGYO ARE NO DIFFERENT FROM KANO...
ALL YOU WANT IS ACCLAIM FOR INNOVATING THE TECH-NOLOGY.
AND...
I...
(I'M READY FOR IT.)

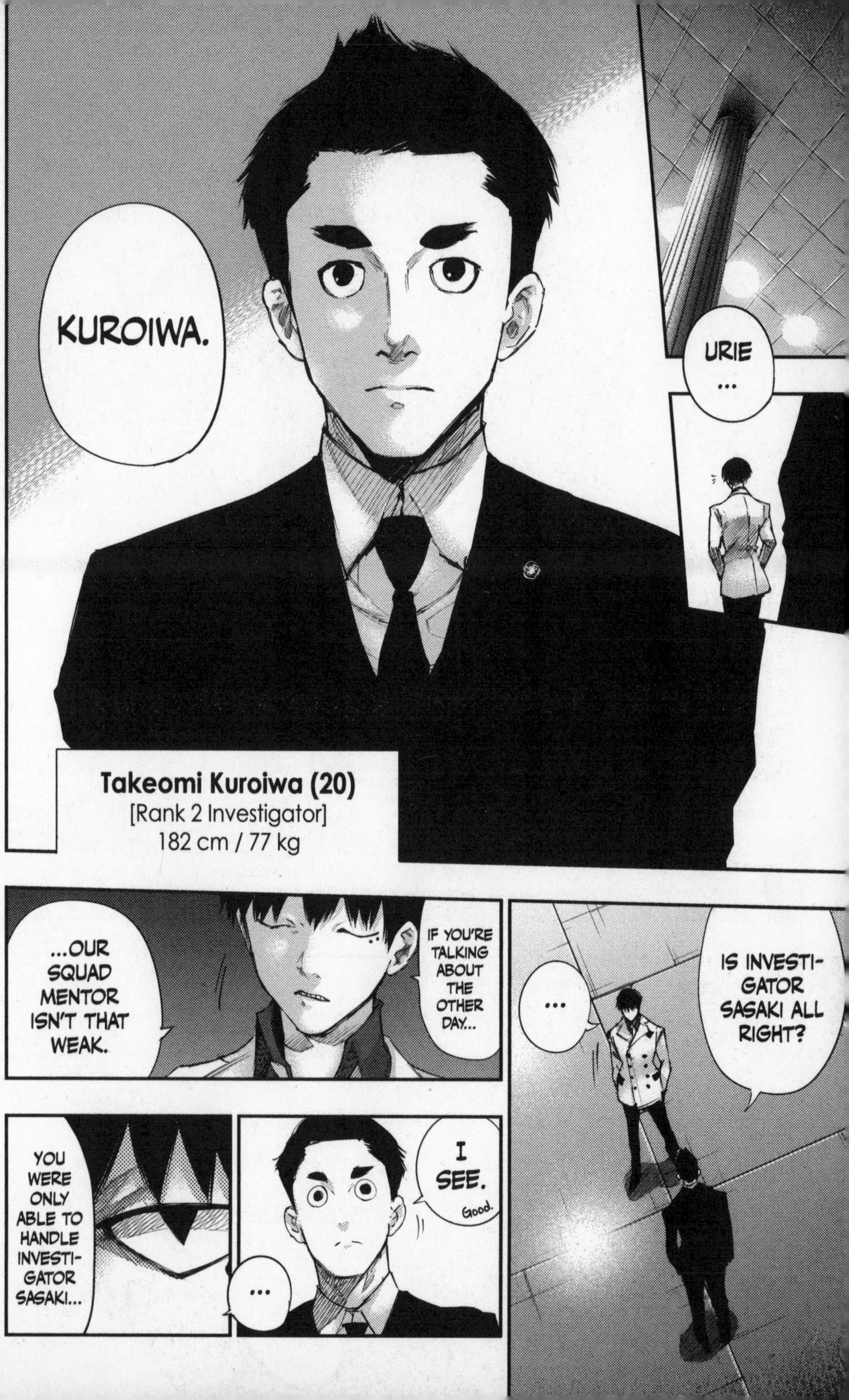
URIE ...
KUROIWA.
Takeomi Kuroiwa (20)
[Rank 2 Investigator]
182 cm / 77 kg
IS INVESTIGATOR SASAKI ALL RIGHT?
...
IF YOU'RE TALKING ABOUT THE OTHER DAY...
...OUR SQUAD MENTOR ISN'T THAT WEAK.
I SEE.
Good.
...
YOU WERE ONLY ABLE TO HANDLE INVESTIGATOR SASAKI...

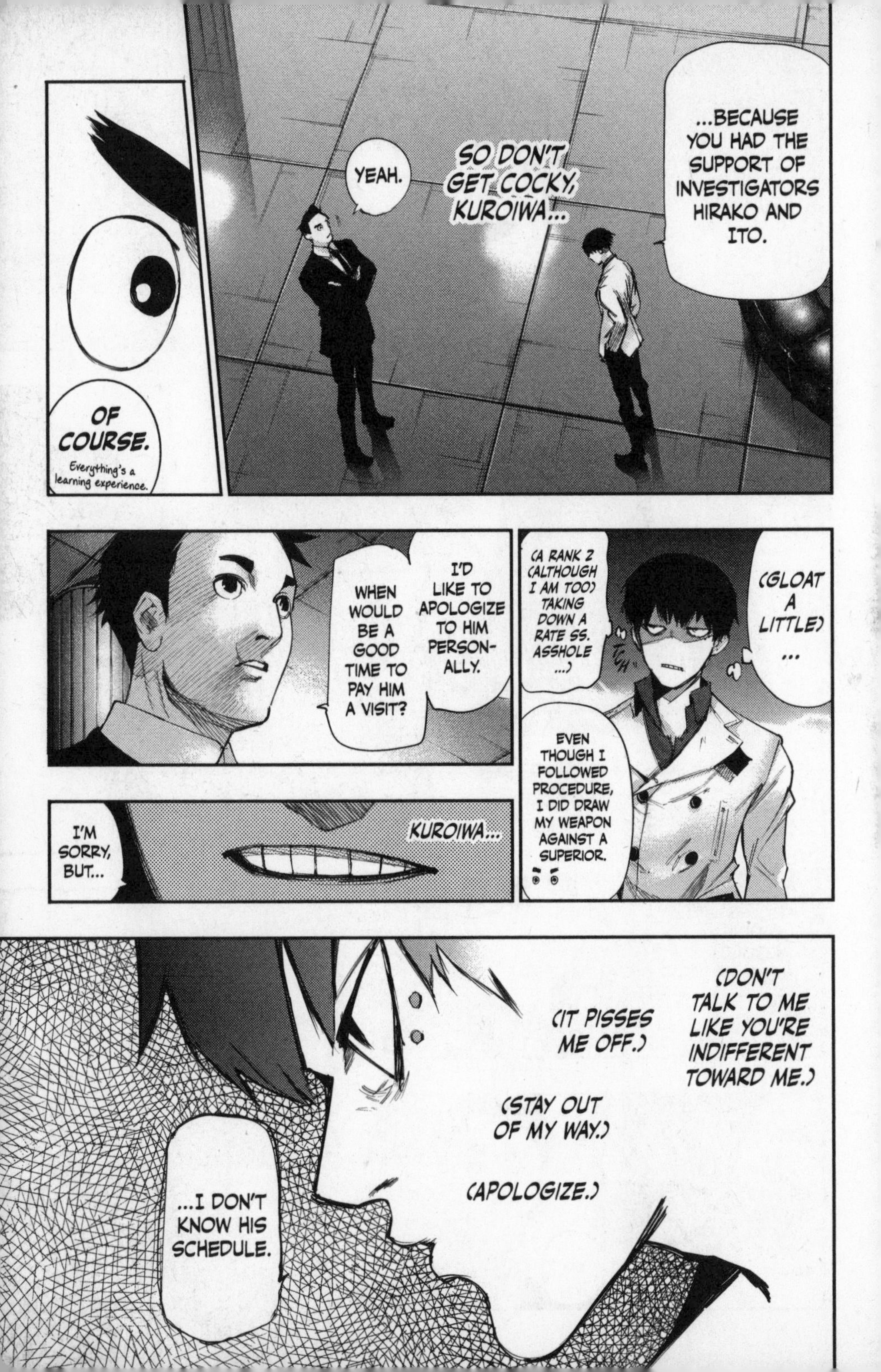
...BECAUSE YOU HAD THE SUPPORT OF INVESTIGATORS HIRAKO AND ITO.
SO DON'T GET COCKY, KUROIWA...
YEAH.
OF COURSE.
Everything's a learning experience.
(GLOAT A LITTLE) ...
(A RANK 2 (ALTHOUGH I AM TOO) TAKING DOWN A RATE SS. ASSHOLE ...)
EVEN THOUGH I FOLLOWED PROCEDURE, I DID DRAW MY WEAPON AGAINST A SUPERIOR.
I'D LIKE TO APOLOGIZE TO HIM PERSONALLY.
WHEN WOULD BE A GOOD TIME TO PAY HIM A VISIT?
KUROIWA...
I'M SORRY, BUT...
(DON'T TALK TO ME LIKE YOU'RE INDIFFERENT TOWARD ME.)
(IT PISSES ME OFF.)
(STAY OUT OF MY WAY.)
(APOLOGIZE.)
...I DON'T KNOW HIS SCHEDULE.

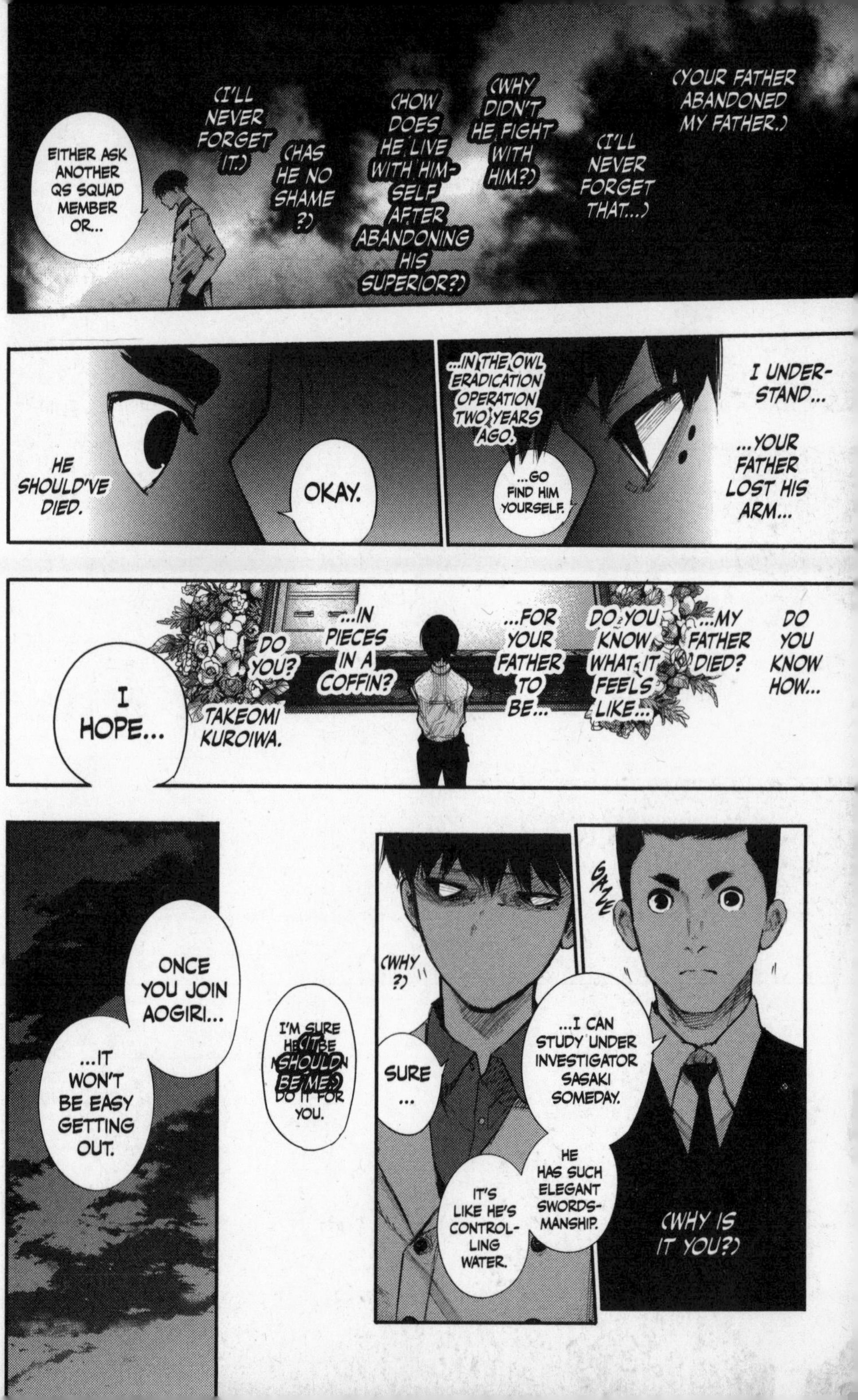

(YOUR FATHER ABANDONED MY FATHER.)
(I'LL NEVER FORGET THAT...)
(WHY DIDN'T HE FIGHT WITH HIM?)
(HOW DOES HE LIVE WITH HIMSELF AFTER ABANDONING HIS SUPERIOR?)
(HAS HE NO SHAME?)
(I'LL NEVER FORGET IT.)
EITHER ASK ANOTHER QS SQUAD MEMBER OR...
I UNDERSTAND...
...YOUR FATHER LOST HIS ARM...
...IN THE OWL ERADICATION OPERATION TWO YEARS AGO.
...GO FIND HIM YOURSELF.
OKAY.
HE SHOULD'VE DIED.
DO YOU KNOW HOW...
...MY FATHER DIED?
DO YOU KNOW WHAT IT FEELS LIKE...
...FOR YOUR FATHER TO BE...
...IN PIECES IN A COFFIN?
DO YOU?
TAKEOMI KUROIWA.
I HOPE...
GAZE
(WHY IS IT YOU?)
...I CAN STUDY UNDER INVESTIGATOR SASAKI SOMEDAY.
HE HAS SUCH ELEGANT SWORDSMANSHIP.
IT'S LIKE HE'S CONTROLLING WATER.
(WHY?)
SURE...
(IT SHOULD BE ME.)
I'M SURE
DO IT FOR YOU.
ONCE YOU JOIN AOGIRI...
...IT WON'T BE EASY GETTING OUT.

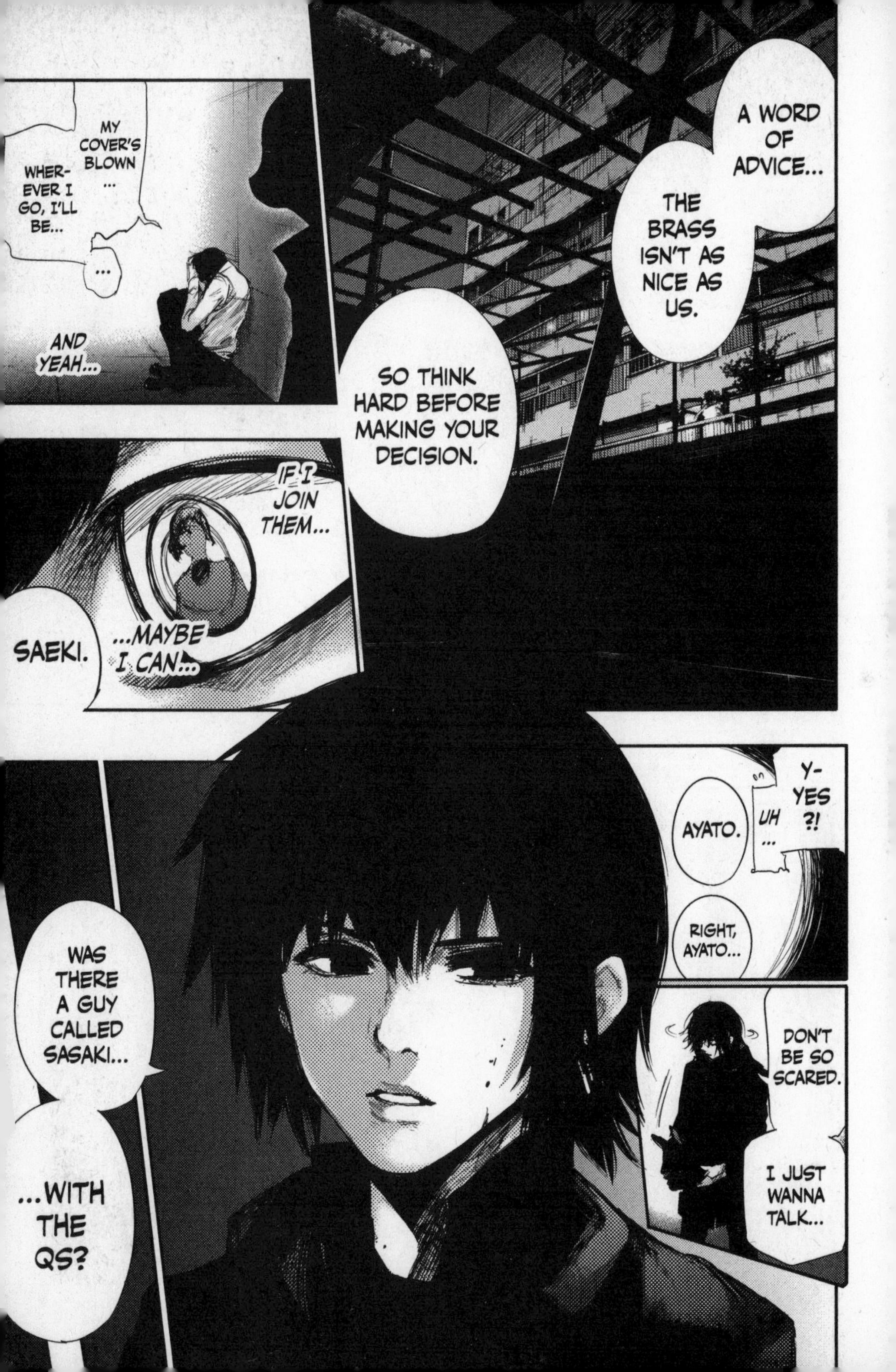
A WORD OF ADVICE...
THE BRASS ISN'T AS NICE AS US.
SO THINK HARD BEFORE MAKING YOUR DECISION.
MY COVER'S BLOWN...
WHER- EVER I GO, I'LL BE...
...
AND YEAH...
IF I JOIN THEM...
...MAYBE I CAN...
SAEKI.
Y- YES?!
UH...
AYATO.
RIGHT, AYATO...
DON'T BE SO SCARED.
I JUST WANNA TALK...
WAS THERE A GUY CALLED SASAKI...
...WITH THE QS?

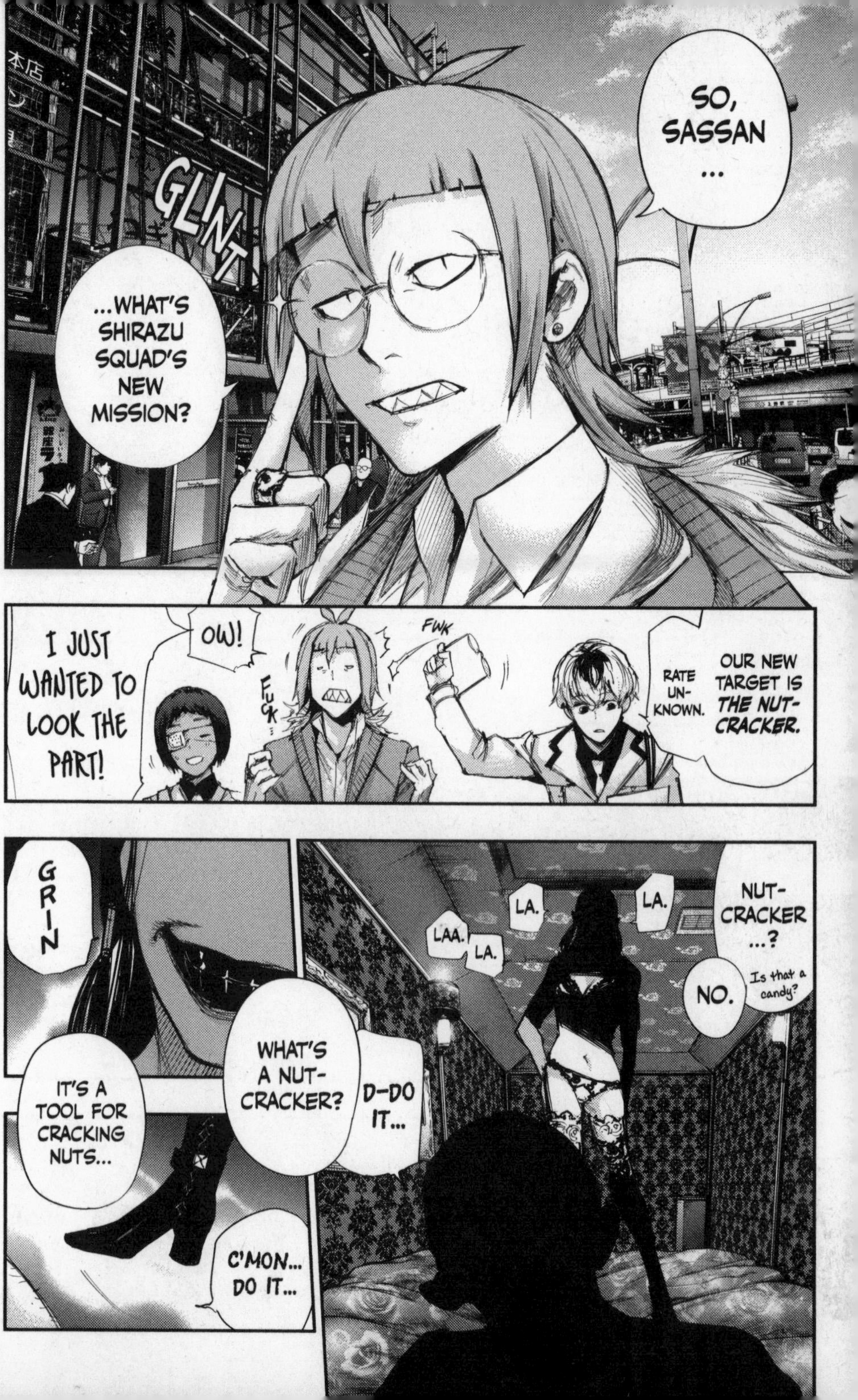
SO, SASSAN ...
GLINT
...WHAT'S SHIRAZU SQUAD'S NEW MISSION?
OUR NEW TARGET IS THE NUT-CRACKER.
RATE UN-KNOWN.
FWK
OW!
FUCK
I JUST WANTED TO LOOK THE PART!
NUT-CRACKER ...?
Is that a candy?
NO.
LA.
LA.
LAA.
LA.
GRIN
WHAT'S A NUT-CRACKER?
D-DO IT...
IT'S A TOOL FOR CRACKING NUTS...
C'MON... DO IT...

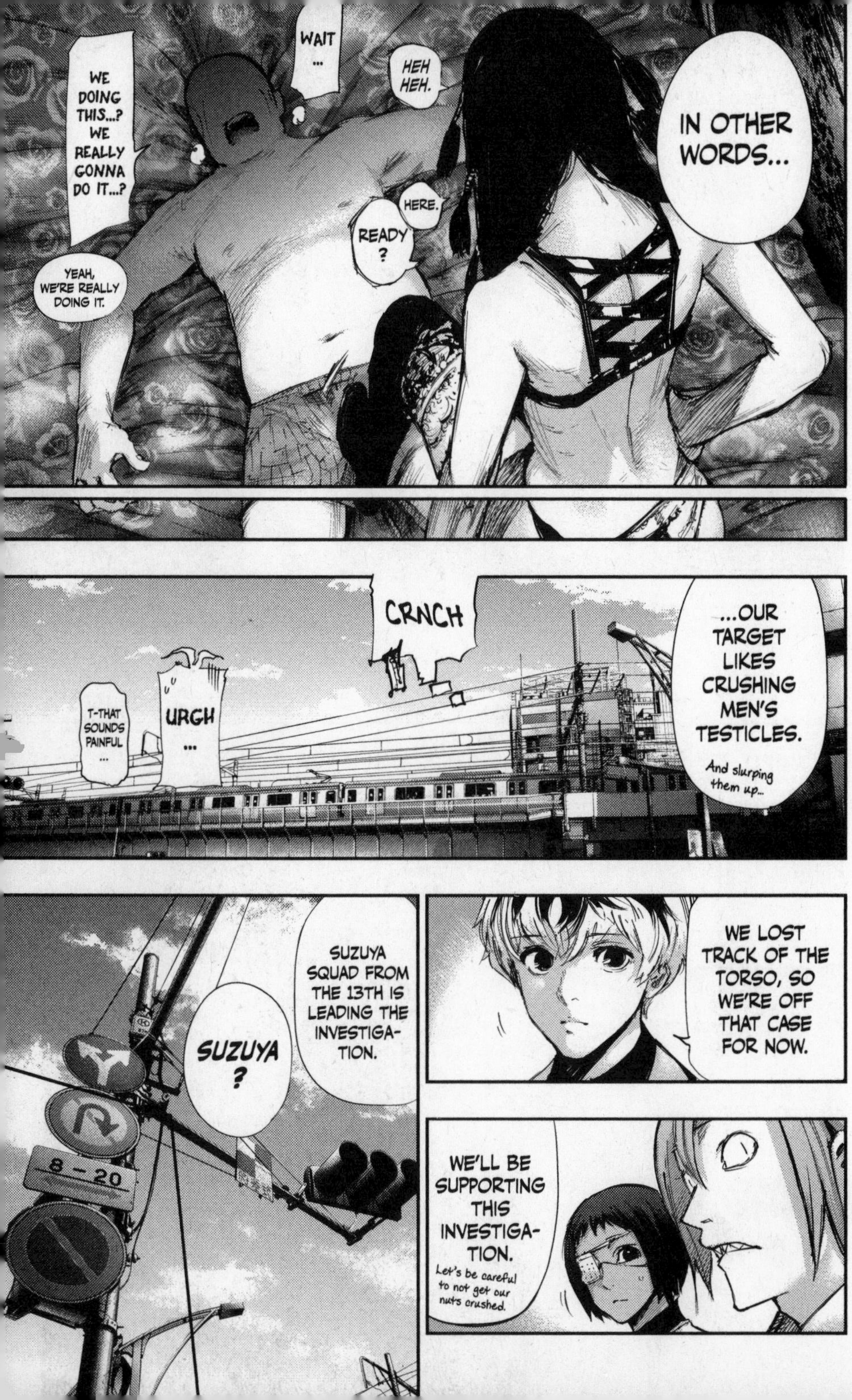
IN OTHER WORDS...
HEH HEH.
WAIT ...
WE DOING THIS...? WE REALLY GONNA DO IT...?
HERE.
READY ?
YEAH, WE'RE REALLY DOING IT.
...OUR TARGET LIKES CRUSHING MEN'S TESTICLES.
And slurping them up...
CRNCH
URGH ...
T-THAT SOUNDS PAINFUL ...
WE LOST TRACK OF THE TORSO, SO WE'RE OFF THAT CASE FOR NOW.
WE'LL BE SUPPORTING THIS INVESTIGA-TION.
Let's be careful to not get our nuts crushed.
SUZUYA SQUAD FROM THE 13TH IS LEADING THE INVESTIGA-TION.
SUZUYA ?
8 - 20

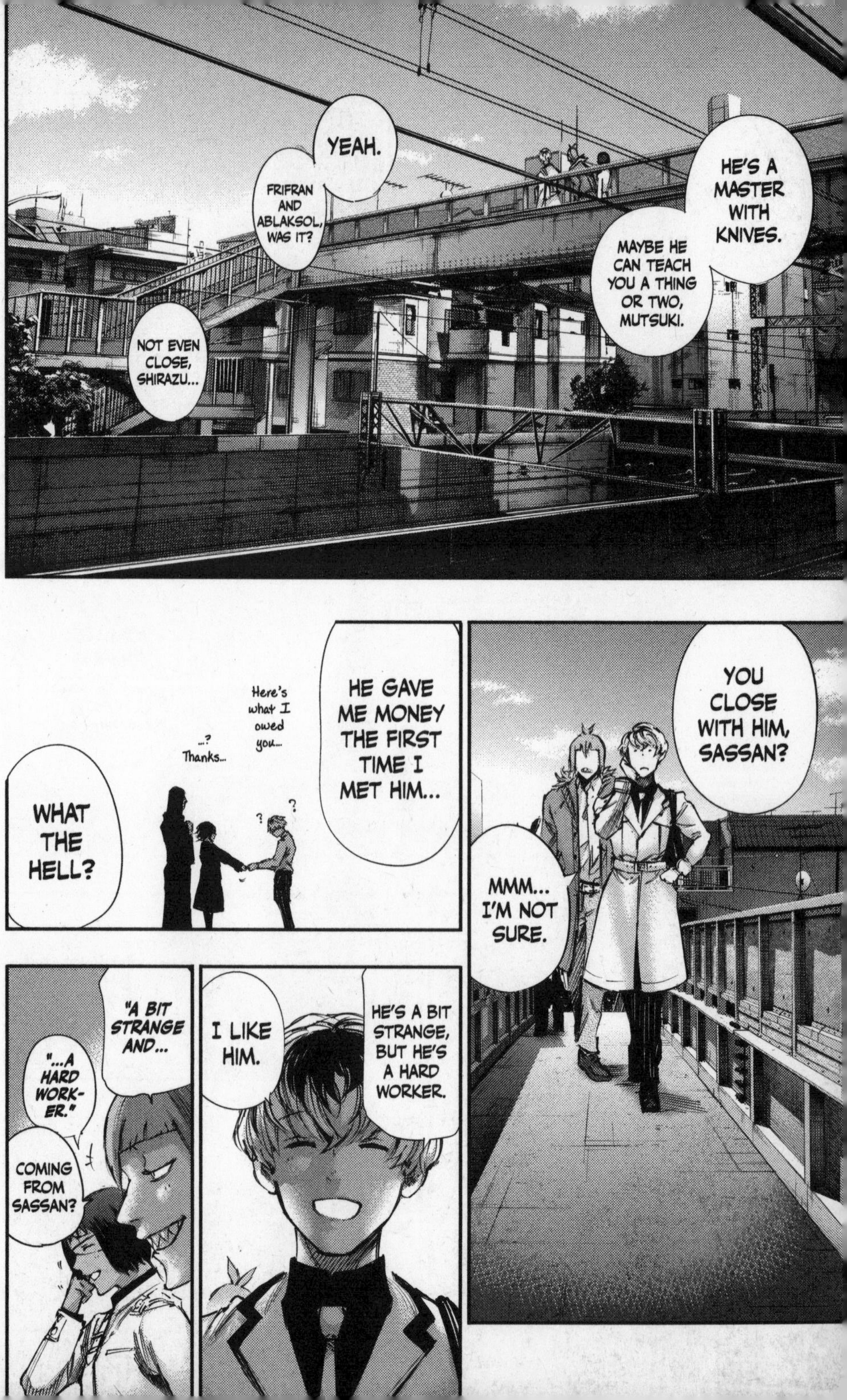
HE'S A MASTER WITH KNIVES.
MAYBE HE CAN TEACH YOU A THING OR TWO, MUTSUKI.
YEAH.
FRIFRAN AND ABLAKSOL, WAS IT?
NOT EVEN CLOSE, SHIRAZU...
YOU CLOSE WITH HIM, SASSAN?
MMM... I'M NOT SURE.
HE GAVE ME MONEY THE FIRST TIME I MET HIM...
Here's what I owed you...
...? Thanks...
WHAT THE HELL?
HE'S A BIT STRANGE, BUT HE'S A HARD WORKER.
I LIKE HIM.
"A BIT STRANGE AND...
"...A HARD WORK-ER."
COMING FROM SASSAN?

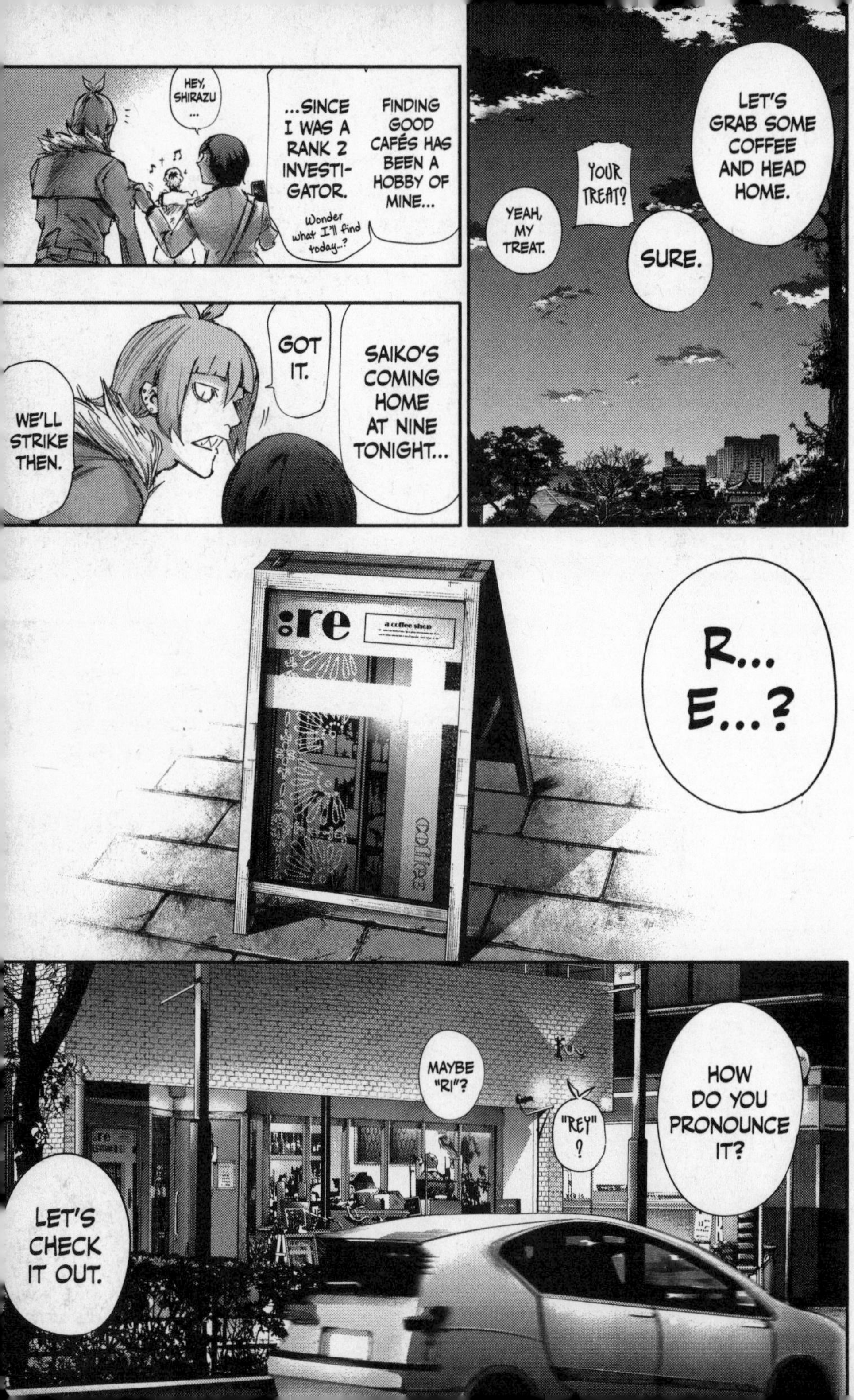
LET'S GRAB SOME COFFEE AND HEAD HOME.
YOUR TREAT?
SURE.
YEAH, MY TREAT.
FINDING GOOD CAFÉS HAS BEEN A HOBBY OF MINE...
...SINCE I WAS A RANK 2 INVESTIGATOR.
Wonder what I'll find today...?
HEY, SHIRAZU...
SAIKO'S COMING HOME AT NINE TONIGHT...
GOT IT.
WE'LL STRIKE THEN.
R... E...?
:re
a coffee shop
coffee
HOW DO YOU PRONOUNCE IT?
"REY"?
MAYBE "RI"?
LET'S CHECK IT OUT.

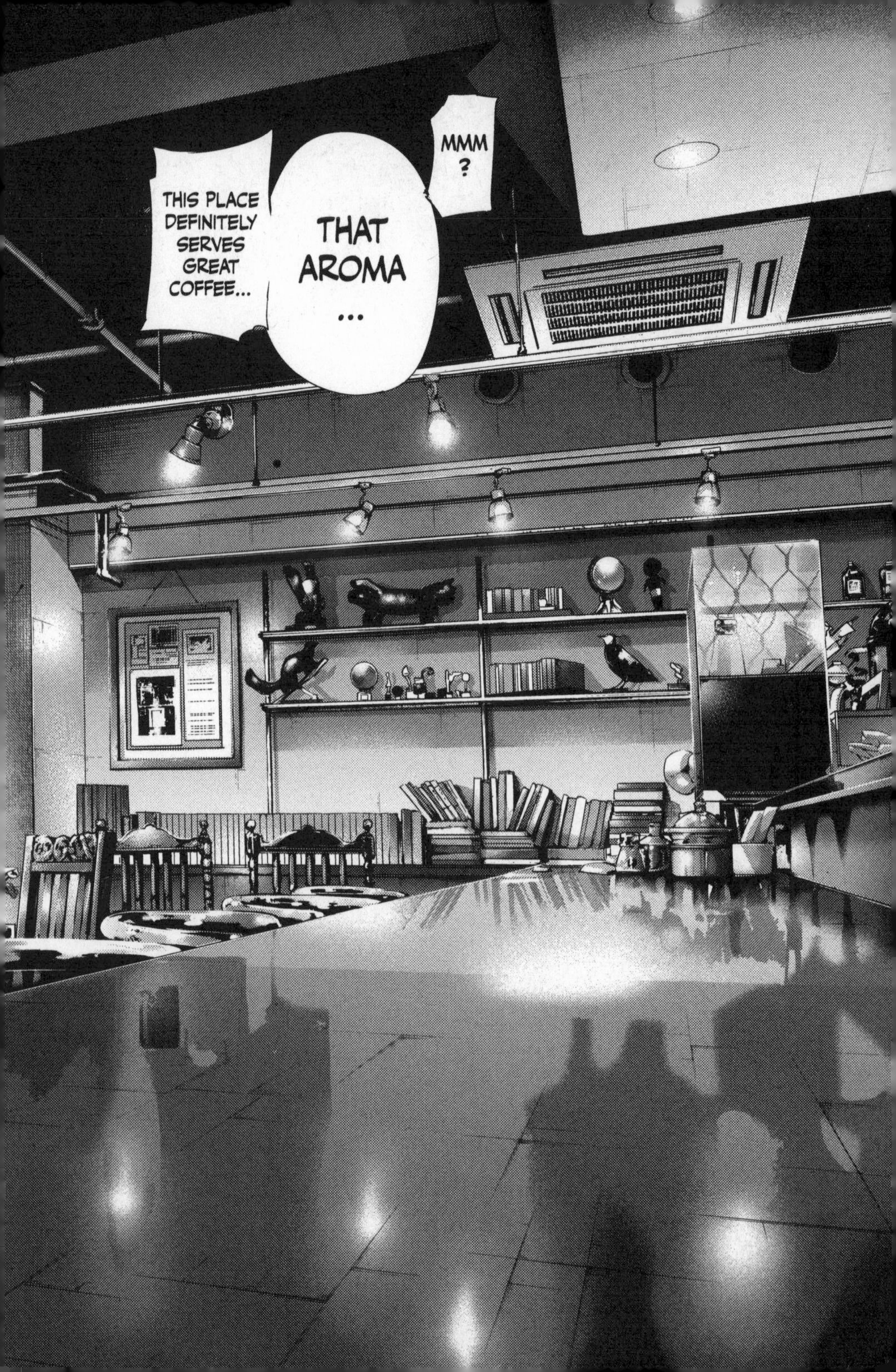
MMM ?
THAT AROMA ...
THIS PLACE DEFINITELY SERVES GREAT COFFEE...

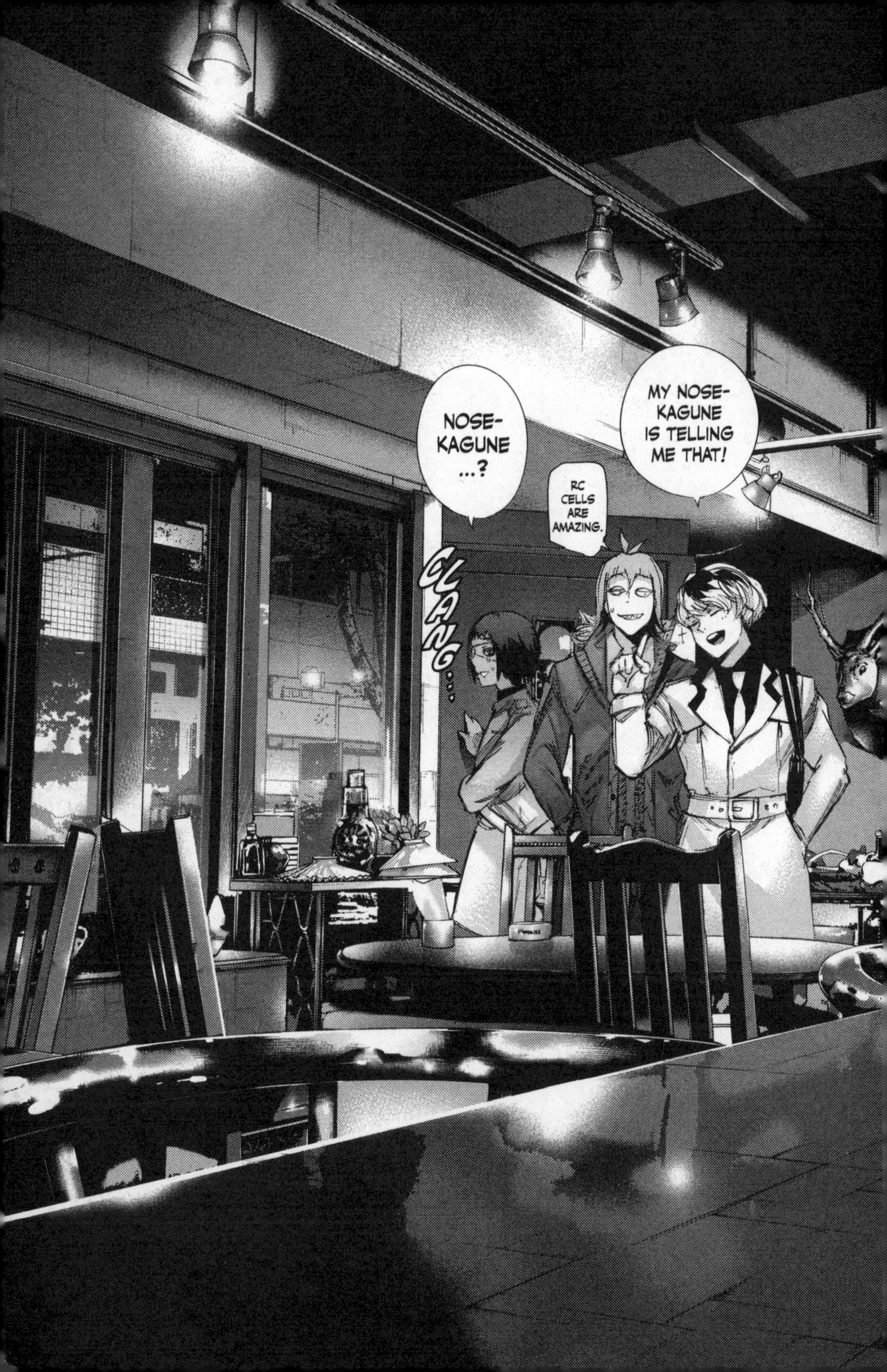
MY NOSE-KAGUNE IS TELLING ME THAT!
RC CELLS ARE AMAZING.
NOSE-KAGUNE ...?
CLANG...

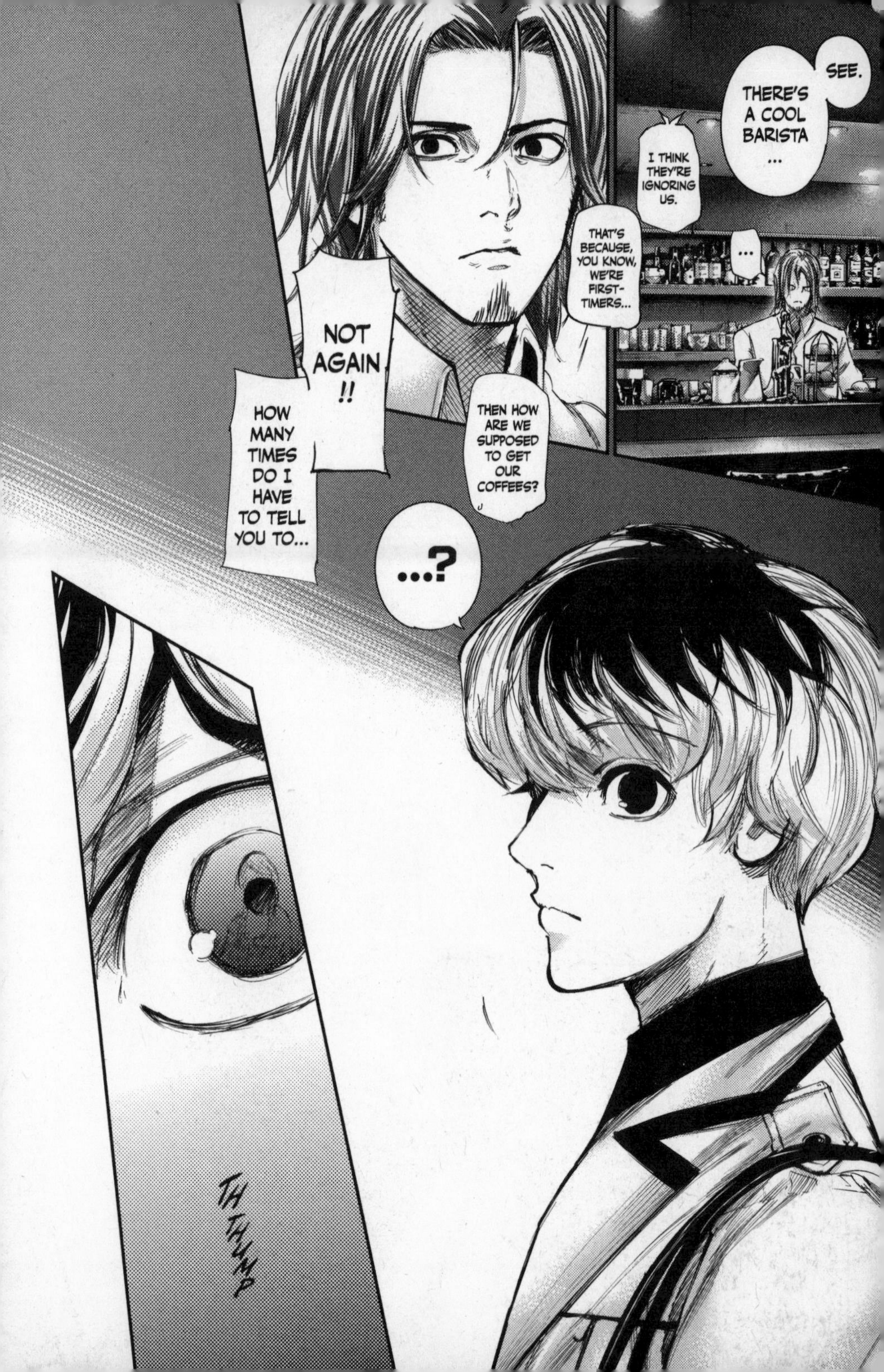
SEE.
THERE'S A COOL BARISTA ...
I THINK THEY'RE IGNORING US.
...
THAT'S BECAUSE, YOU KNOW, WE'RE FIRST-TIMERS...
THEN HOW ARE WE SUPPOSED TO GET OUR COFFEES?
NOT AGAIN!!
HOW MANY TIMES DO I HAVE TO TELL YOU TO...
...?
THTHUMP

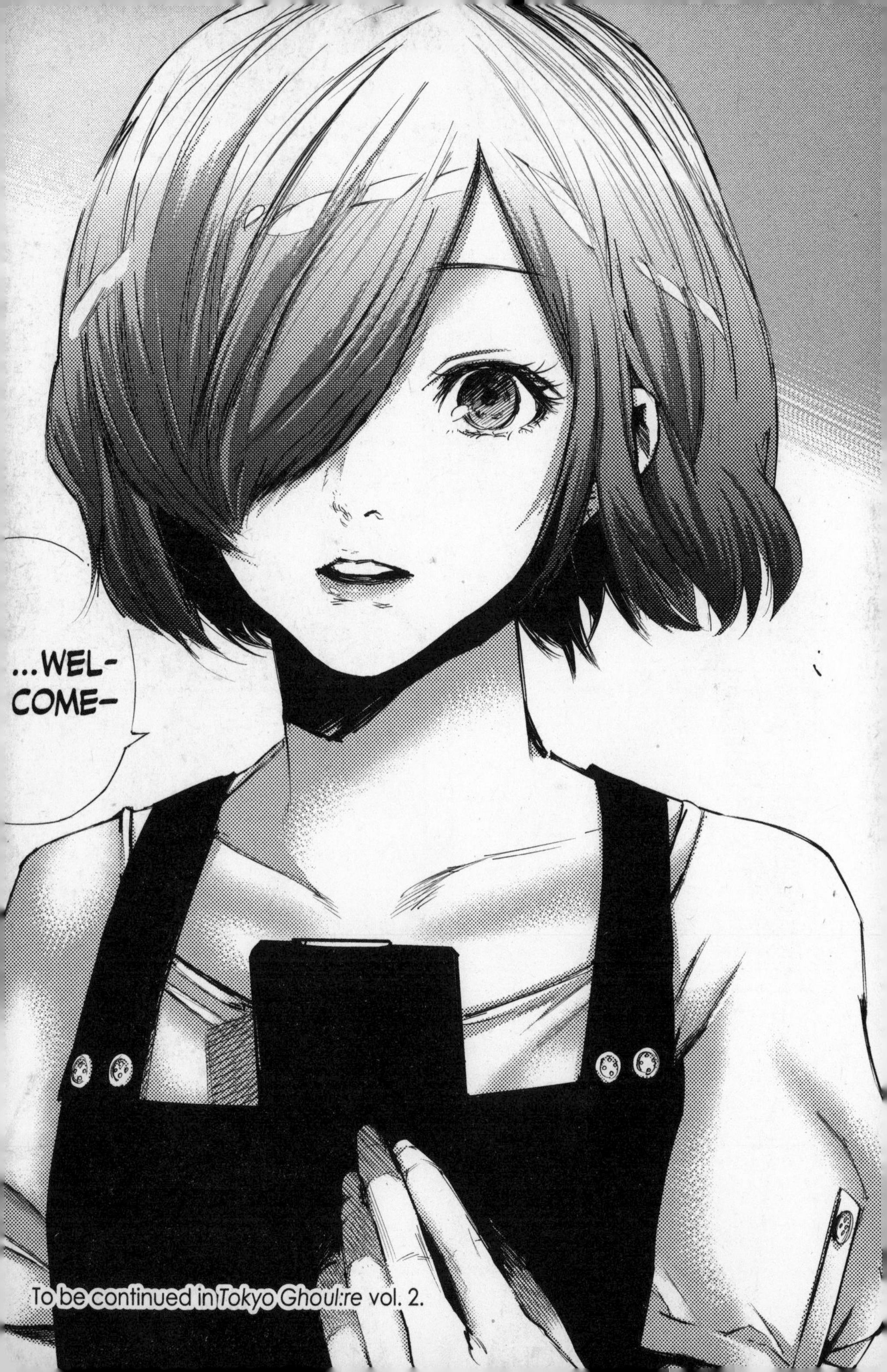
...WEL-
COME-

To be continued in *Tokyo Ghoul:re* vol. 2.

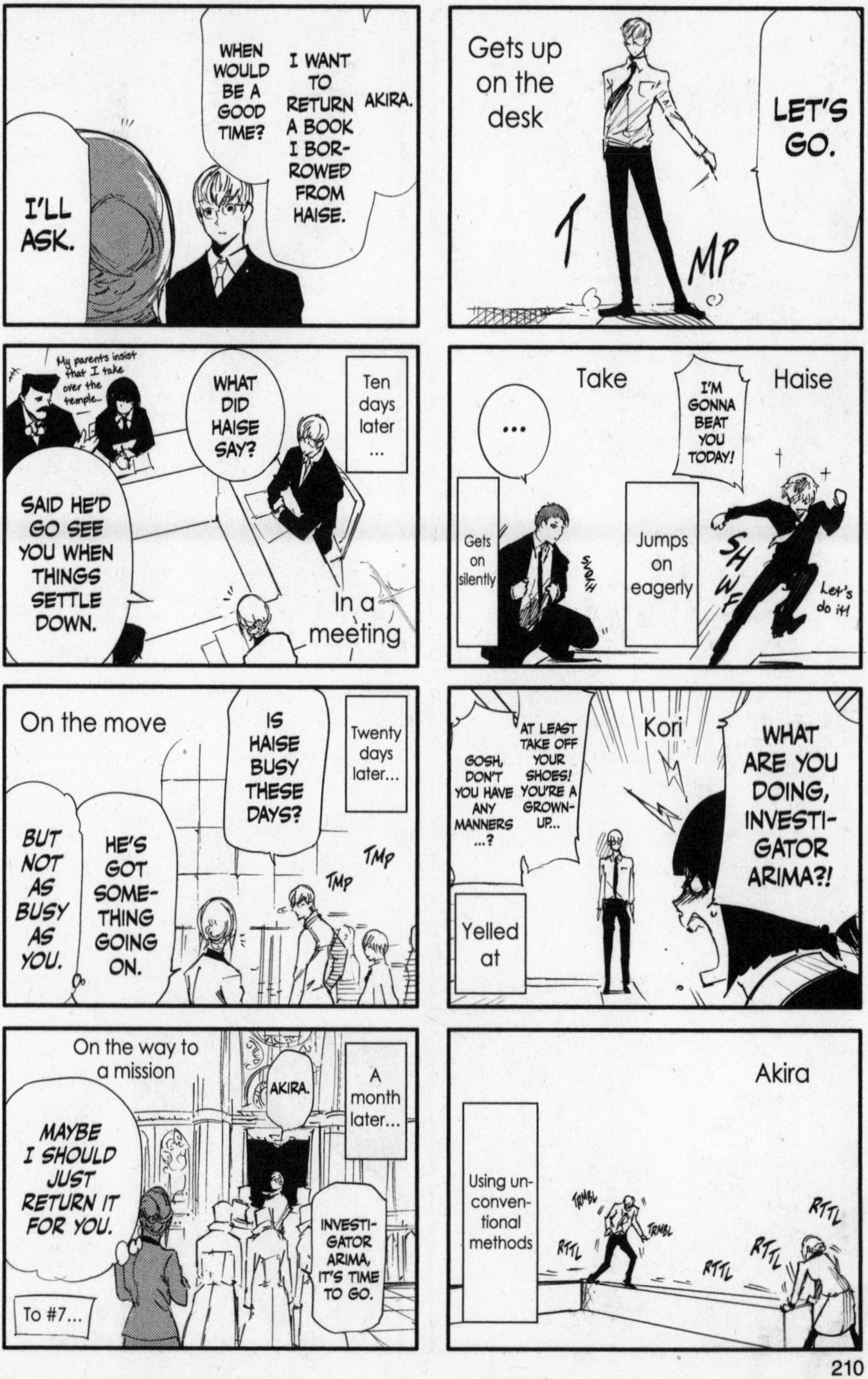
LET'S GO.
Gets up on the desk
TMP
Haise
I'M GONNA BEAT YOU TODAY!
Let's do it!
SHWF
Jumps on eagerly
Take
...
Gets on silently
WHAT ARE YOU DOING, INVESTIGATOR ARIMA?!
Kori
AT LEAST TAKE OFF YOUR SHOES! YOU'RE A GROWN-UP...
GOSH, DON'T YOU HAVE ANY MANNERS...?
Yelled at
Akira
RTTL
RTTL
RTTL
TRMBL
TRMBL
RTTL
Using unconventional methods
AKIRA.
I WANT TO RETURN A BOOK I BORROWED FROM HAISE.
WHEN WOULD BE A GOOD TIME?
I'LL ASK.
Ten days later...
WHAT DID HAISE SAY?
My parents insist that I take over the temple...
In a meeting
SAID HE'D GO SEE YOU WHEN THINGS SETTLE DOWN.
Twenty days later...
IS HAISE BUSY THESE DAYS?
On the move
TMP
TMP
HE'S GOT SOMETHING GOING ON.
BUT NOT AS BUSY AS YOU.
A month later...
AKIRA.
On the way to a mission
INVESTIGATOR ARIMA, IT'S TIME TO GO.
MAYBE I SHOULD JUST RETURN IT FOR YOU.
To #7...

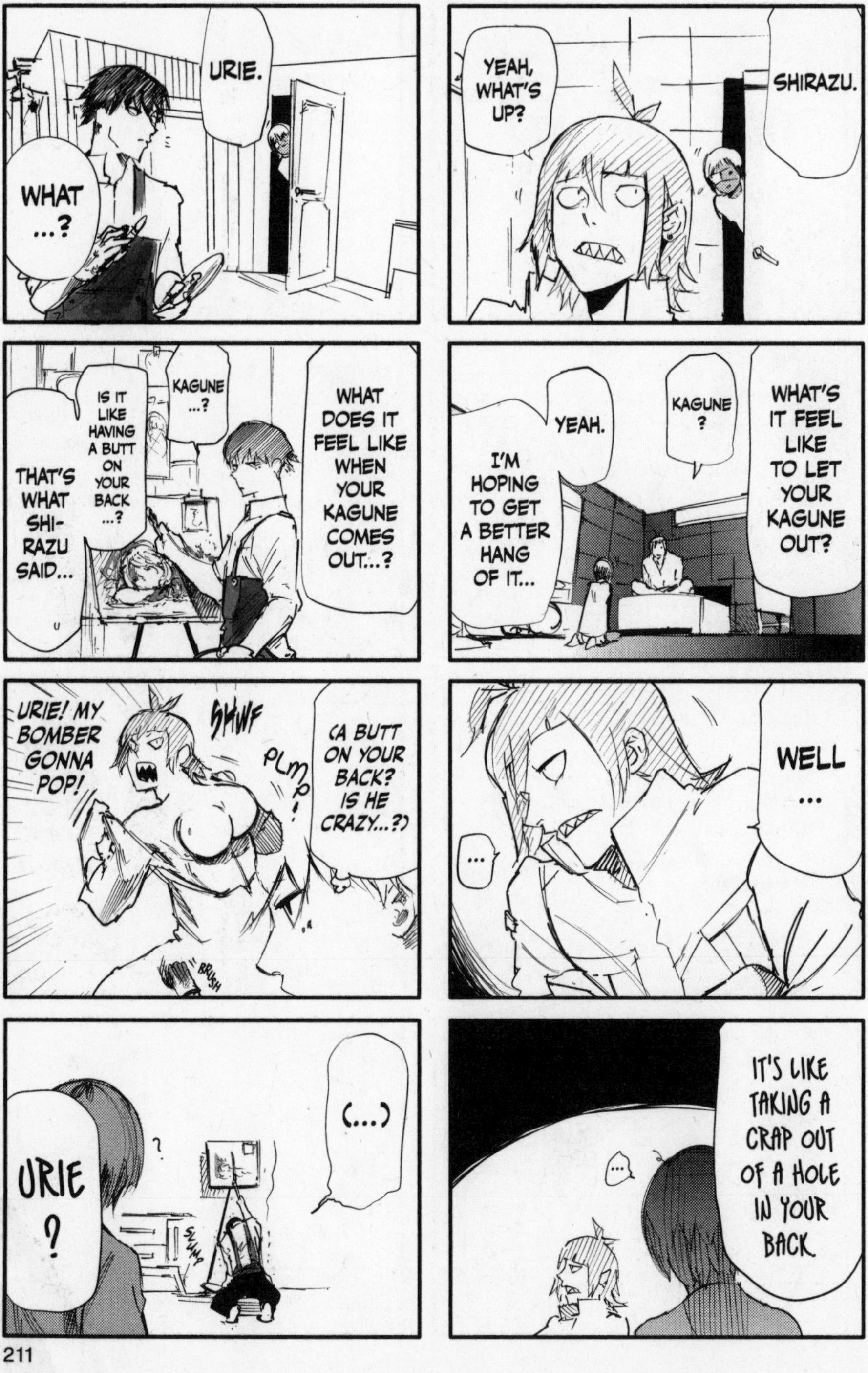
SHIRAZU.
YEAH, WHAT'S UP?
URIE.
WHAT ...?
WHAT'S IT FEEL LIKE TO LET YOUR KAGUNE OUT?
KAGUNE ?
YEAH.
I'M HOPING TO GET A BETTER HANG OF IT...
WHAT DOES IT FEEL LIKE WHEN YOUR KAGUNE COMES OUT...?
KAGUNE ...?
IS IT LIKE HAVING A BUTT ON YOUR BACK ...?
THAT'S WHAT SHI-RAZU SAID...
WELL ...
...
(A BUTT ON YOUR BACK? IS HE CRAZY...?)
PLMP!
SKWF
URIE! MY BOMBER GONNA POP!
BRUSH
IT'S LIKE TAKING A CRAP OUT OF A HOLE IN YOUR BACK.
...
(...)
URIE ?
SLUMP

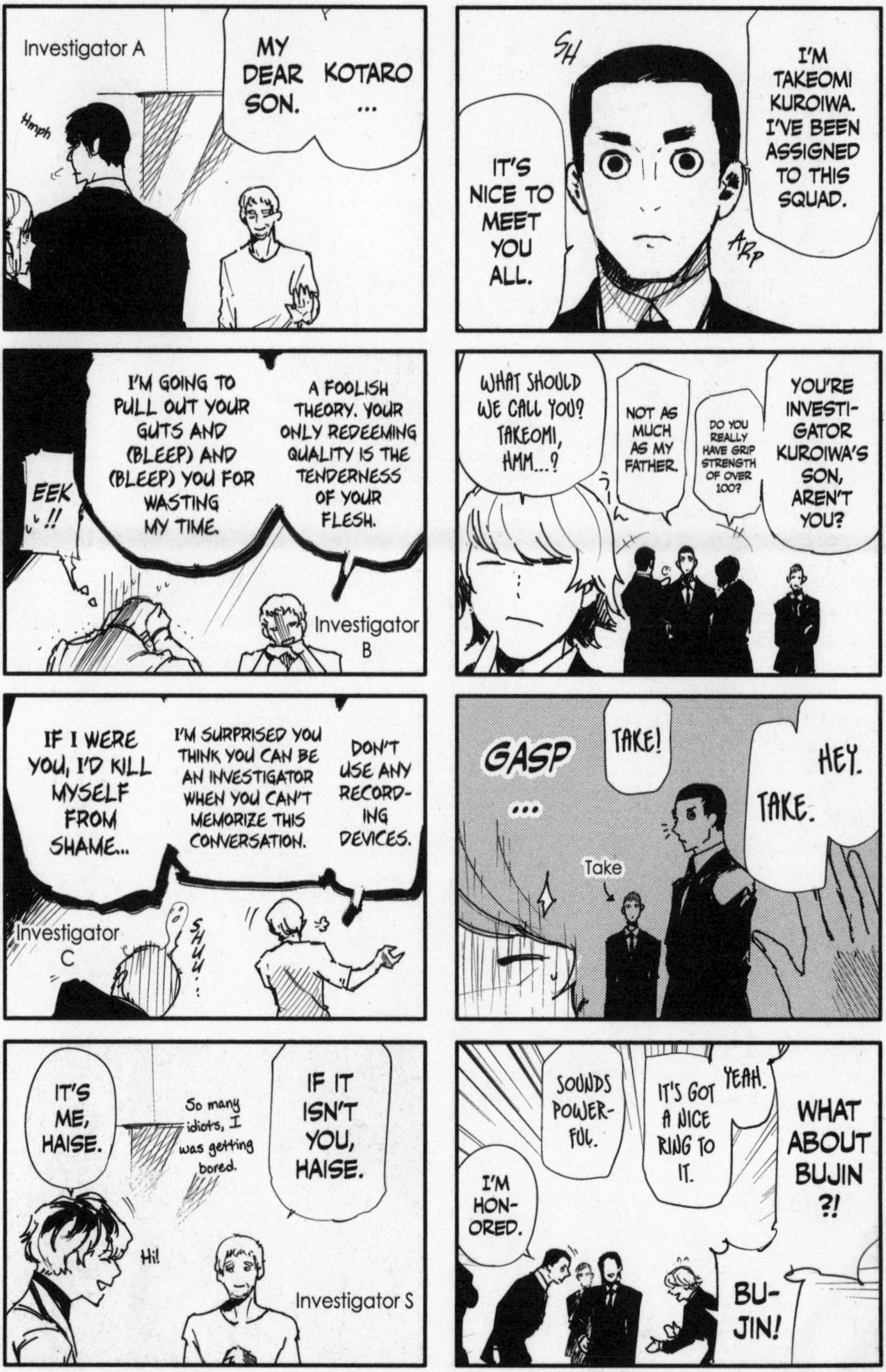

SH
I'M TAKEOMI KUROIWA. I'VE BEEN ASSIGNED TO THIS SQUAD.
IT'S NICE TO MEET YOU ALL.
ARP
KOTARO...
MY DEAR SON.
Investigator A
Hmph
YOU'RE INVESTIGATOR KUROIWA'S SON, AREN'T YOU?
DO YOU REALLY HAVE GRIP STRENGTH OF OVER 100?
NOT AS MUCH AS MY FATHER.
WHAT SHOULD WE CALL YOU? TAKEOMI, HMM...?
A FOOLISH THEORY. YOUR ONLY REDEEMING QUALITY IS THE TENDERNESS OF YOUR FLESH.
I'M GOING TO PULL OUT YOUR GUTS AND (BLEEP) AND (BLEEP) YOU FOR WASTING MY TIME.
EEK!!
Investigator B
HEY. TAKE.
TAKE!
GASP...
Take
DON'T USE ANY RECORDING DEVICES.
I'M SURPRISED YOU THINK YOU CAN BE AN INVESTIGATOR WHEN YOU CAN'T MEMORIZE THIS CONVERSATION.
IF I WERE YOU, I'D KILL MYSELF FROM SHAME...
SHUU...
Investigator C
WHAT ABOUT BUJIN?!
YEAH.
IT'S GOT A NICE RING TO IT.
SOUNDS POWERFUL.
I'M HONORED.
BUJIN!
IF IT ISN'T YOU, HAISE.
So many idiots, I was getting bored.
IT'S ME, HAISE.
Hi!
Investigator S

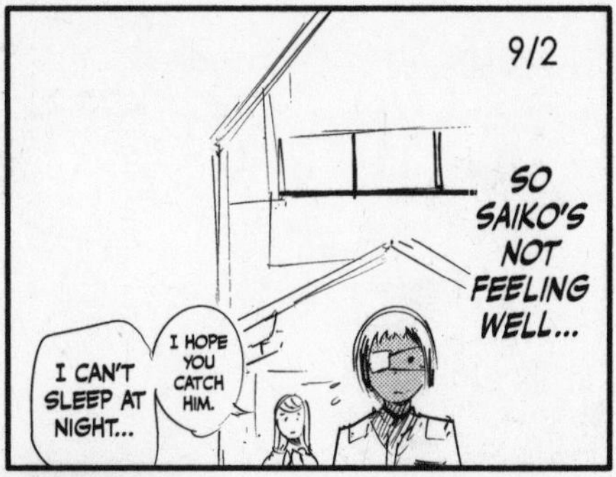
9/2
SO SAIKO'S NOT FEELING WELL...
I HOPE YOU CATCH HIM.
I CAN'T SLEEP AT NIGHT...

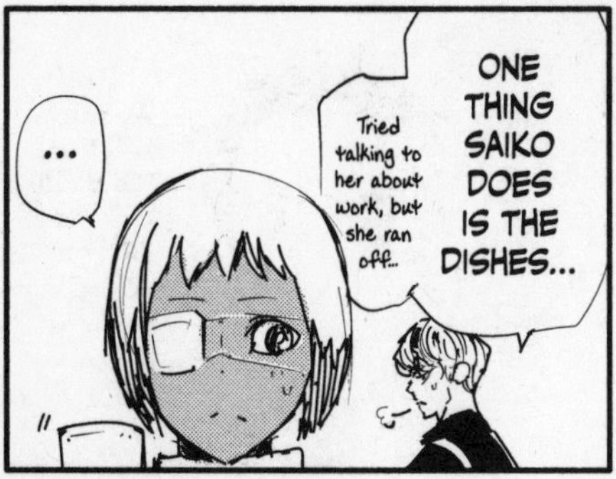
ONE THING SAIKO DOES IS THE DISHES...
Tried talking to her about work, but she ran off...
...

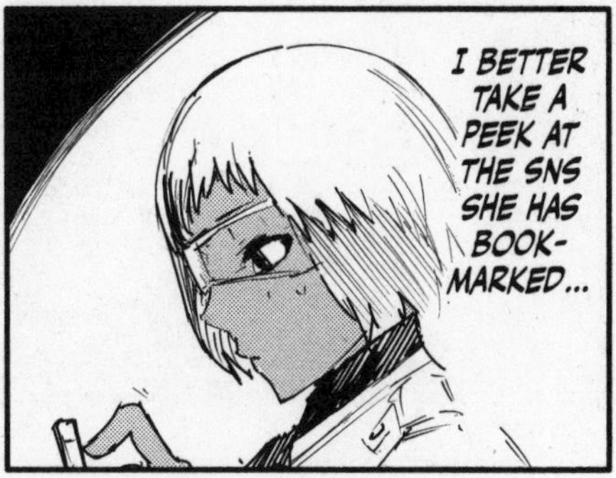
I BETTER TAKE A PEEK AT THE SNS SHE HAS BOOK-MARKED...

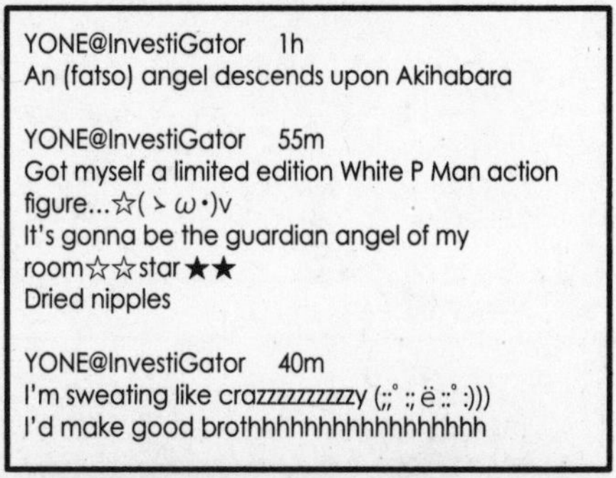
YONE@InvestiGator 1h
An (fatso) angel descends upon Akihabara
YONE@InvestiGator 55m
Got myself a limited edition White P Man action figure...☆(≻ω•)v
It's gonna be the guardian angel of my room☆☆star★★
Dried nipples
YONE@InvestiGator 40m
I'm sweating like crazzzzzzzzzy (;;° ;; ë ;;° ;)))
I'd make good brothhhhhhhhhhhhhhhh

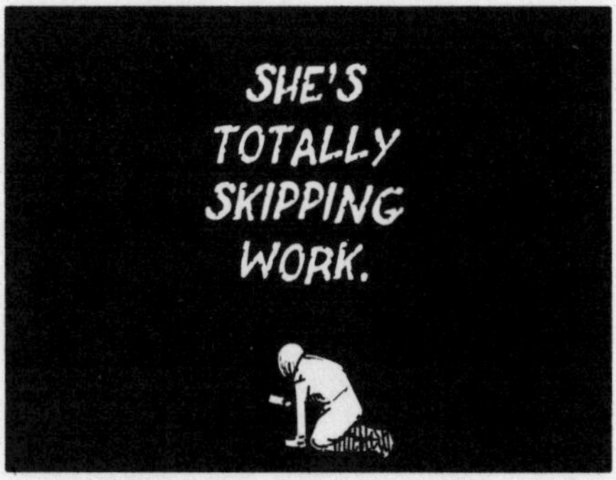
SHE'S TOTALLY SKIPPING WORK.

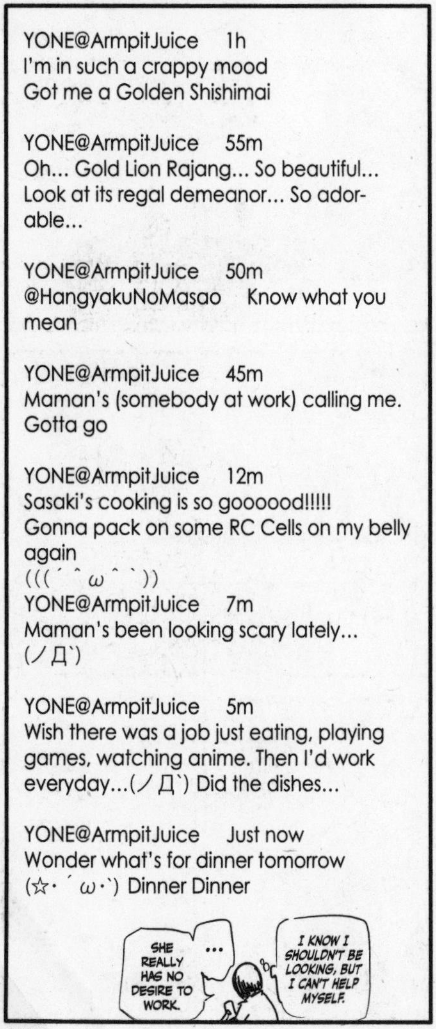
YONE@ArmpitJuice 1h
I'm in such a crappy mood
Got me a Golden Shishimai
YONE@ArmpitJuice 55m
Oh... Gold Lion Rajang... So beautiful... Look at its regal demeanor... So adorable...
YONE@ArmpitJuice 50m
@HangyakuNoMasao Know what you mean
YONE@ArmpitJuice 45m
Maman's (somebody at work) calling me. Gotta go
YONE@ArmpitJuice 12m
Sasaki's cooking is so goooood!!!!!
Gonna pack on some RC Cells on my belly again
(((´^ω^`)))
YONE@ArmpitJuice 7m
Maman's been looking scary lately...
(ノД`)
YONE@ArmpitJuice 5m
Wish there was a job just eating, playing games, watching anime. Then I'd work everyday...(ノД`) Did the dishes...
YONE@ArmpitJuice Just now
Wonder what's for dinner tomorrow
(☆・´ω・`) Dinner Dinner
I KNOW I SHOULDN'T BE LOOKING, BUT I CAN'T HELP MYSELF.
...
SHE REALLY HAS NO DESIRE TO WORK.

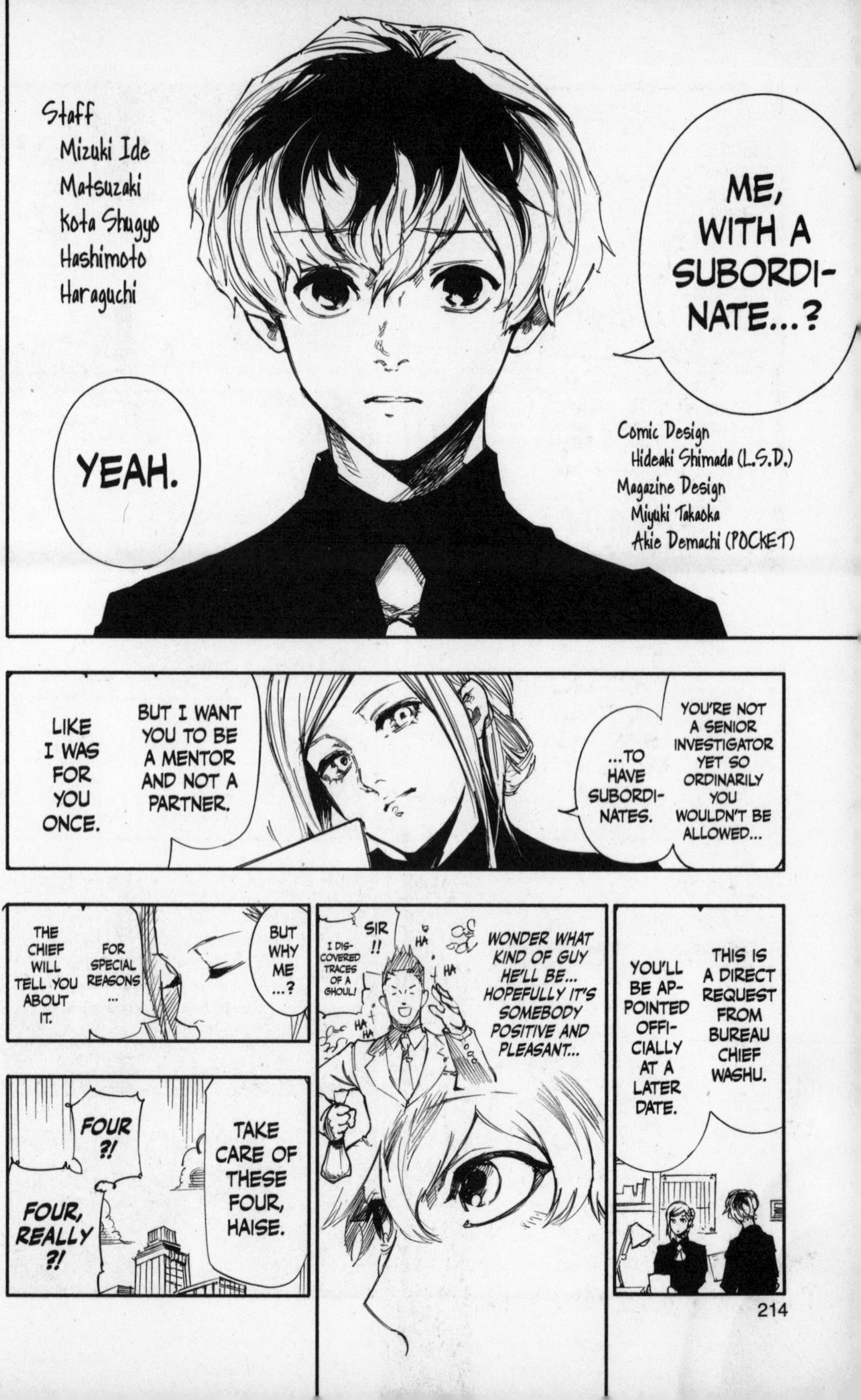
ME, WITH A SUBORDINATE...?
YEAH.
Staff
Mizuki Ide
Matsuzaki
Kota Shugyo
Hashimoto
Haraguchi
Comic Design
Hideaki Shimada (L.S.D.)
Magazine Design
Miyuki Takaoka
Akie Demachi (POCKET)
YOU'RE NOT A SENIOR INVESTIGATOR YET SO ORDINARILY YOU WOULDN'T BE ALLOWED...
...TO HAVE SUBORDINATES.
BUT I WANT YOU TO BE A MENTOR AND NOT A PARTNER.
LIKE I WAS FOR YOU ONCE.
THIS IS A DIRECT REQUEST FROM BUREAU CHIEF WASHU.
YOU'LL BE APPOINTED OFFICIALLY AT A LATER DATE.
WONDER WHAT KIND OF GUY HE'LL BE... HOPEFULLY IT'S SOMEBODY POSITIVE AND PLEASANT...
SIR!!
I DISCOVERED TRACES OF A GHOUL!
HA HA HA HA
BUT WHY ME...?
FOR SPECIAL REASONS...
THE CHIEF WILL TELL YOU ABOUT IT.
TAKE CARE OF THESE FOUR, HAISE.
FOUR?!
FOUR, REALLY?!

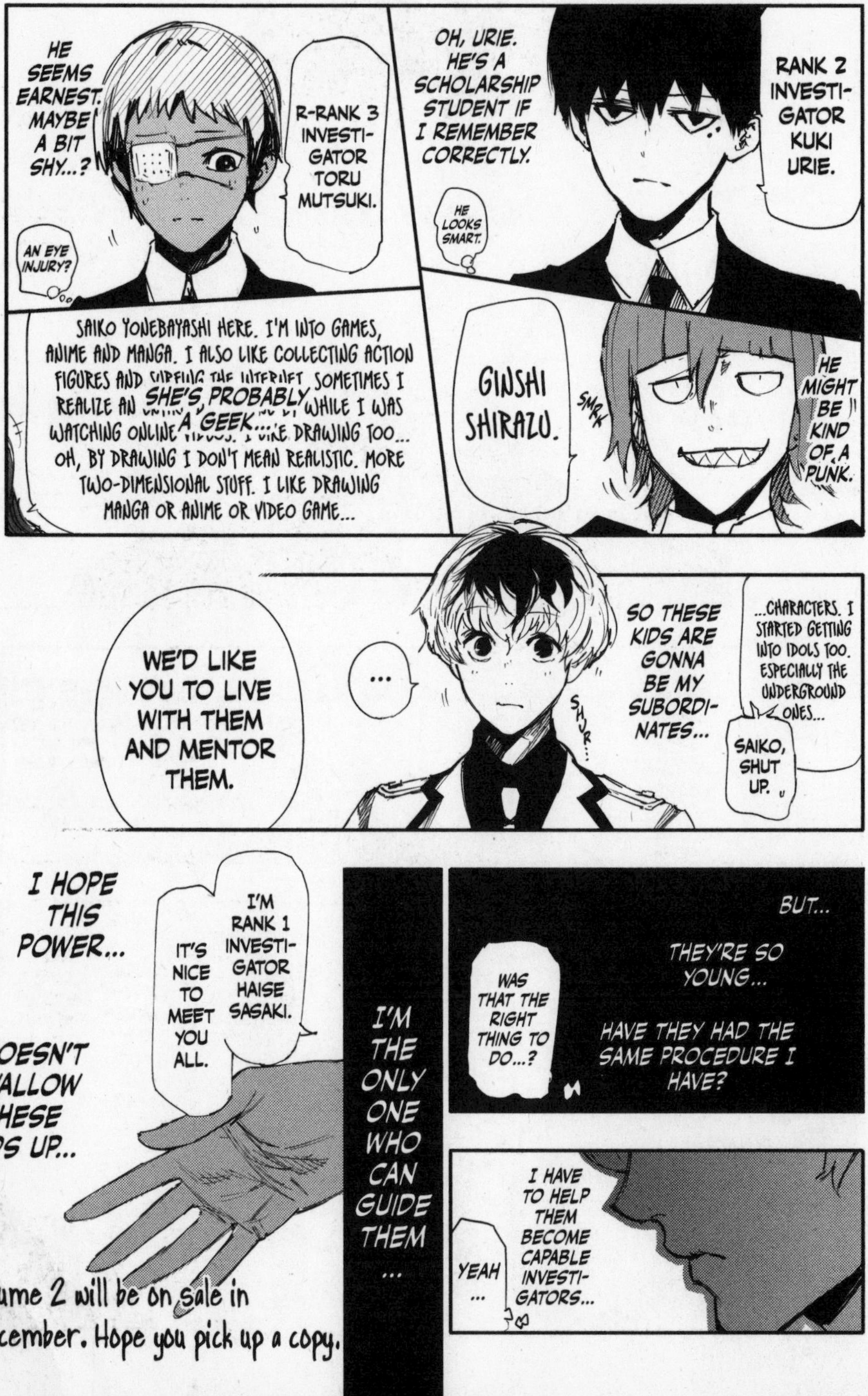
RANK 2 INVESTIGATOR KUKI URIE.
OH, URIE. HE'S A SCHOLARSHIP STUDENT IF I REMEMBER CORRECTLY.
HE LOOKS SMART.
R-RANK 3 INVESTIGATOR TORU MUTSUKI.
HE SEEMS EARNEST. MAYBE A BIT SHY...?
AN EYE INJURY?
GINSHI SHIRAZU.
SMRK
HE MIGHT BE KIND OF A PUNK.
SAIKO YONEBAYASHI HERE. I'M INTO GAMES, ANIME AND MANGA. I ALSO LIKE COLLECTING ACTION FIGURES AND ... SOMETIMES I REALIZE AN ... WHILE I WAS WATCHING ONLINE ... DRAWING TOO... OH, BY DRAWING I DON'T MEAN REALISTIC. MORE TWO-DIMENSIONAL STUFF. I LIKE DRAWING MANGA OR ANIME OR VIDEO GAME...
SHE'S PROBABLY A GEEK...
...CHARACTERS. I STARTED GETTING INTO IDOLS TOO. ESPECIALLY THE UNDERGROUND ONES...
SAIKO, SHUT UP.
SO THESE KIDS ARE GONNA BE MY SUBORDINATES...
SHUR...
...
WE'D LIKE YOU TO LIVE WITH THEM AND MENTOR THEM.
BUT...
THEY'RE SO YOUNG...
HAVE THEY HAD THE SAME PROCEDURE I HAVE?
WAS THAT THE RIGHT THING TO DO...?
I HAVE TO HELP THEM BECOME CAPABLE INVESTIGATORS...
YEAH...
I'M THE ONLY ONE WHO CAN GUIDE THEM...
I'M RANK 1 INVESTIGATOR HAISE SASAKI.
IT'S NICE TO MEET YOU ALL.
I HOPE THIS POWER...
...DOESN'T SWALLOW THESE KIDS UP...
Volume 2 will be on sale in December. Hope you pick up a copy.

White Wing Badge

Awarded to investigators for achieving a certain rank or eradicating Ghouls of a certain rate.

The badges are designed to invoke a dove's wing, which is also the symbol of the CCG.

Single White Wing Badge
Rate S

Double White Wing Badge
Rate SS

White Dragon Wing Badge
Rate SSS

TOKYO

Quinx Squad Organization Chart

● **Kuki Urie** (Squad Leader)   Rank 2 Investigator (Class 77)
瓜江久生 (うりえ くき)   7th Academy Junior

- Age: 19 (DOB 2/12) ♂ • Blood type: O • Height/weight: 173.5cm/60kg
- RC Type: Kokaku • Quinque: Tsunagi <plain> (Bikaku-Rate/C)
- Honors: Awarded scholarship to CCG Academy

● **Ginshi Shirazu**   Rank 3 Investigator (Class 77)
不知吟士 (しらず ぎんし)   7th Academy Junior

- Age: 19 (DOB 3/8) ♂ • Blood type: A • Height/weight: 176cm/55kg
- RC Type: Kokaku • Quinque: Tsunagi <plain> (Bikaku-Rate/C)
- Skills: Driver's license (car and motorcycle)

● **Toru Mutsuki**   Rank 3 Investigator (Class 77)
六月透 (むつき とおる)   2nd Academy Junior

- Age: 19 (DOB 12/14) ♀ • Blood type: AB • Height/weight: 165cm/48kg
- RC Type: Bikaku • Quinque: Abksol, Ifraft (Rinkaku-Rate/B)
- Skills: Ambidextrous, constant Kakugan (right)

● **Saiko Yonebayashi**   Rank 3 Investigator (Class 77)
米林才子 (よねばやし さいこ)   7th Academy Junior

- Age: 19 (DOB 9/4) ♀ • Blood type: B • Height/weight: 143cm/⚥0kg
- RC Type: Rinkaku • Quinque: Bokusatsu No. 2 (Kokaku-Rate/B)
- Skills: Typing certification level 1

● **Haise Sasaki** (mentor)
佐々木琲世 (ささき はいせ)   Rank 1 Investigator (Class 75)

- Age: 22 (DOB 4/22) ♂ • Blood type: AB • Height/weight: 170cm/58kg
- RC Type: Rinkaku • Quinque: Yukimura 1/3 (Kokaku-Rate/B)
- Honors: Silver Osmanthus Badge, Single White Wing Badge

TOKYO G

GHOUL:re

SUI ISHIDA is the author of the immensely popular *Tokyo Ghoul* and several *Tokyo Ghoul* one-shots, including one that won second place in the *Weekly Young Jump* 113th Grand Prix award in 2010. *Tokyo Ghoul:re* is the sequel to *Tokyo Ghoul*.

TOKYO

Story and art by
SUI ISHIDA

TOKYO GHOUL:RE © 2014 by Sui Ishida
All rights reserved.
First published in Japan in 2014 by SHUEISHA Inc., Tokyo.
English translation rights arranged by SHUEISHA Inc.

Translation Joe Yamazaki
Touch-Up Art & Lettering Vanessa Satone
Design Shawn Carrico
Editor Pancha Diaz

Printed in the U.S.A.

Published by VIZ Media, LLC
P.O. Box 77010
San Francisco, CA 94107

10 9 8 7 6 5 4 3 2 1
First printing, October 2017

TOKYO

TOKYO GHOUL:re

This is the last page.
TOKYO GHOUL:re reads right to left.